THIRTY-THREE YEARS
AMONG THE INDIANS

A POPULAR ACCOUNT OF

THEIR SOCIAL LIFE, RELIGION, HABITS, TRAITS, CUSTOMS, EXPLOITS, ETC.

WITH THRILLING ADVENTURES AND EXPERIENCES

ON THE GREAT PLAINS AND IN THE MOUNTAINS OF OUR WIDE FRONTIER.

BY

COLONEL RICHARD IRVING DODGE

UNITED STATES ARMY.

AID-DE-CAMP TO GENERAL SHERMAN

WITH AN INTRODUCTION By GENERAL SHERMAN

1882

COPYRIGHT 2015 BIG BYTE BOOKS

Discover more lost history from BIG BYTE BOOKS

Contents

PUBLISHER'S NOTES 2
AUTHOR'S PREFACE 3
INTRODUCTION...5
ADVENTURES AMONG THE COMANCHES 9
BEYOND THE MISSISSIPPI.. 18
INDIAN CHIEFS AND RULERS 37
SWINDLING AND ROBBING THE INDIANS 50
THE GREAT MYSTERY OF INDIAN "MEDICINE" 57
POWER AND INFLUENCE 71
AN INDIAN MYSTERY 79
THE GREAT MEDICINE DANCE 86
ENDURANCE AND DEFIANCE OF PAIN 93
BURIAL OF THE DEAD 97
HOW INDIAN'S FEEL AND SHOW THEIR GRIEF 106
THE HAPPY HUNTING GROUNDS 112
LIFE AND TRAINING OF INDIAN BOYS AND GIRLS 117
LOVE-MAKING IN AN INDIAN CAMP 124
INDIAN WOMEN—VIRTUES AND VICES 132
INDIAN NAMES, TITLES, AND EPITHETS 146
EVERYDAY INDIAN LIFE 152
OCCUPATIONS OF CAMP AND LODGE 164
TRADE AND BARTER 172
INDIAN COOKS AND COOKING 180
THE BUFFALO AND ITS DESTRUCTION 188
CLOTHING, FINERY AND ADORNMENT 199
THE STRUGGLE FOR EXISTENCE 209
GAMES OF SKILL AND CHANCE 219
WONDERFUL FEATS AND MARVELLOUS EXPLOITS 227
POETRY AND SONGS... 235
INDIAN DANCES—LUDICROUS EXPERIENCES 240
EXPERTNESS OF INDIAN SIGN-TALKERS 256
INDIAN CHRONOLOGY 271

THEIR PICTURES AND INSCRIPTIONS	276
INDIAN WEAPONS—SKILL AND EXPERTNESS	282
SIGNAL FIRES AND SMOKES	289
WARFARE—THRILLING ADVENTURES AND EXPERIENCES	297
ARMY LIFE ON THE PLAINS	320
ARMY EXPERIENCES ON THE FRONTIER	326
MACKENZIE'S FIGHT WITH THE CHEYENNES	335
WINTER ON THE PLAINS	343
TAKING THE SCALP—THRILLING INCIDENTS	350
PRISONERS AMONG INDIANS	357
THE CAPTIVE'S FATE—INDIAN CRUELTY	363
DARING AND SKILL	370
PLAINSCRAFT	376
READING "SIGN"—THE CAREER OF PEDRO ESPINOSA	383
ADVENTURES ON THE PLAINS—EXCITING SCENES	393
ANECDOTES AND INCIDENTS	401
TRAPPERS, SQUAW MEN, POSTS AND INDIAN AGENTS	410
FRONTIERSMEN, TEXAS COWBOYS AND BORDER DESPERADOES	418
THRILLING PERSONAL EXPERIENCES	427
AMOS CHAPMAN—FACING DEATH	431
THE PRESENT AND FUTURE	441
L'ENVOI	451

DEDICATED

(BY PERMISSION)

TO

WILLIAM TECUMSEH SHERMAN

GENERAL

OF

THE ARMY OF THE UNITED STATES

PUBLISHER'S NOTES

It's not a stretch to surmise that most Americans or anyone interested in the period known as the Indian Wars would be surprised at how many soldiers of the period held very sympathetic feelings towards their adversaries. The memoirs of Generals Hugh Scott, Nelson A. Miles, Oliver O. Howard, and others express admiration for some qualities they found in Native-American life and certainly admired the intelligence and courage of many of the individuals with whom they came in contact.

Colonel Richard Dodge's memoir, which you are now reading, is a step apart from the others. In his 33 years in the West, he not only met and befriended many Native-Americans but had a fervent desire and curiosity to understand and record their culture. Native-Americans today would tell us he didn't always get it right but he did an admirable job in presenting to his contemporaries a view of native peoples that was far from the dime-novel image many of them carried. As he states in this volume, he considered himself a friend of the Indian and didn't see much system in the government's policies towards them. This book has long been regarded as source material for history of the period.

Remarkably, his former boss, William Tecumseh Sherman, wrote the introduction for this book. He praises his former aide but takes issue with his condemnation of government policy. Sherman's legacy is intertwined closely with Manifest Destiny after the Civil War and his connection to native peoples was much more tenuous than the soldiers in the field.

Richard Irving Dodge was born on May 19, 1827 in Huntsville, North Carolina to James Richard Dodge and Susan Williams. In 1858 he married Julia Rhinelander Paulding, with whom he had one son. A cadet in 1844, Dodge was commissioned an officer in the regular Army, 8th Infantry Regiment on May 03, 1861 and served throughout the Civil War. He established the first Fort Dodge on the Santa Fe Trail, which was later the site of Dodge City, famous for Boot Hill and Wyatt Earp. Dodge died on June 16, 1895 and is buried in Arlington National Cemetery.

AUTHOR'S PREFACE

THE greater part of the past thirty-four years of my life has been spent on the frontier in more or less direct contact with Indians. It was not, however, until 1872 that I was induced to attempt to excite for them the interest of others. From and after that year I occasionally wrote short articles on Indians and the Indian question, some of which were contributed anonymously to the press.

In 1877 I published a book entitled *The Plains of the Great West*, a work mainly descriptive of the topography, climate, game, etc., of that portion of our country known as the "Plains," to which I added some sketches of Indian life. Determined to be entirely unbiased in my opinions, and with, I hope, a not unpardonable vanity to be original, I carefully abstained from consulting contemporaneous authorities—either books or men.

The extremely flattering reception which that book met at the hands of the critics, and, more especially the unexpected encomiums bestowed upon the brief and imperfect Indian sketches (which I had added to the volume more as a finale than with any hope of attracting particular attention to the subject) encouraged me to continue my studies of Indian life, but in a wider field. In those sketches I had briefly given my opinions; I now determined to know the facts; and this could only be done by comparison of my opinions with those of other men who had written on the Indian. I therefore procured the works of Catlin, Schoolcraft, and many other "lesser lights," and studied them assiduously, comparing their ideas with my own. For many years past I have been most fortunately situated for such study, having been stationed directly among the wild tribes, whose characteristics have always been of most interest to me. Whenever I have found that my ideas differed from those of" an authority," I have taken the case directly to the Indians themselves. My position as commanding officer—"Big Chief"—enabled me always to get a hearing and an answer on any subject; and my well-known friendship for the race caused the Indians to give me more frank confidence than a white man usually obtains. I have thus been enabled to get at facts; to correct the errors of my previous desultory writings, as well as errors of accepted Indian "authorities."

For two years past I have been importuned by friends whose opinions I value most highly, to give to the world the result of my observations and labors. I have consented to do so, not without hesitation, because having previously written on the same subject, I must occasionally repeat myself, or commit the affectation of clothing the same ideas in different words. My friends have overruled this objection, and I present in this volume a detailed account of the characteristics, habits, and—what I particularly desire to invite attention to—a minute and careful study of the social or inner life of the wild Indian of the present day.

INTRODUCTION

BY

GENERAL WILLIAM T. SHERMAN

Col. Richard I. Dodge,
23rd U. S. Infantry, Aide de Camp, &c.

Dear Colonel—I have now completed the first reading of the proof-sheets of your forthcoming book on *Our Wild Indians*, and congratulate you upon having accomplished a work of such general interest so well and so handsomely.

The Indian of America has been for centuries the subject of study and of romance; alternately treated as an unmitigated savage, or as the dashing, bold hero fighting for his native land and his inherited privileges. Yours is the first attempt of which I have knowledge, to treat him as he exists in fact—the creature of ancient habits, of manners and customs imposed on him by former ages, modified by recent and modern changes—and I am sure that your work will be of inestimable value to the army, and to members of Congress, who alone can legislate so as to save what is valuable in his character, and provide against the everlasting conflict necessarily incident to his clinging to old prejudices and habits in the midst of a race so dissimilar as ours.

You have had the experience of a third of a century in absolute contact with the various tribes of the Indians from the British line to Texas, New Mexico and Arizona, living with them, hunting with them, in peace And in war; and therefore your book is the record of your own personal observations, with dates, facts and figures, which constitute the very best testimony possible on the subject-matter treated of. I and nearly every army officer, with less personal experience, can verify much that you describe, and in reading your chapters I have been struck by the skill with which you have grouped the various branches of the subject discussed, making plain and logical deductions from the scattered observations of many army officers, who have had similar experience; I notice with great satisfaction that unlike most authors who have preceded you, you draw the broad distinction between the tribes like the Chippewas of the Lakes; the Seminoles of Florida; the Kiowas, Comanches, etc., of Texas; the Cheyennes, Arapahos and Sioux of the Plains; the Utes and Apaches of the Mountains; the Navajos and Pueblos of New Mexico; the Diggers and the fish-eating tribes of the Pacific Coast. There is as wide a difference in these types of the same race as between the Swedes, French, Spanish, and Italian peoples. The character of each tribe or nation has been formed by long antecedent events, by the nature of the country in which they have resided, and the means necessary to obtain a livelihood.

I do not agree with you and the world generally in accusing our ancestors and the General Government with a deliberate purpose to be unjust to, and to defraud these people. I think a perusal of the statutes and of the many treaties exhibit a purpose to deal with them liberally; but so rapid has been our development that violence was sure to happen. Our wisest and best statesmen did not and could not foresee the future. Mr. Van Buren, in 1838, in urging the Cherokees, Creeks and Choctaws to exchange their possessions in Georgia, Alabama, and Mississippi for lands west of Arkansas, announced, as he believed truthfully, that there they could never again be disturbed by white neighbors, because the land was not suitable for white men, but admirably adapted to Indian life. So in 1868, the Indian Peace Commission, composed of four most humane and honorable citizens, and three army officers (Generals Harney, Terry, and Sherman), had no conception that in ten years the region north of Laramie and east of the Rocky Mountains could become habitable to the white race. Nor do I think it just to accuse all Indian agents of being incompetent, if not dishonest. I have personally met a great number of these, who are generally kind, honest, and well-meaning people, badly paid, and deprived of all the comforts which civilized men desire to enjoy. Some motive higher than a desire to plunder must actuate men who risk so much, and endure such hardships and privations. If our Indian policy has failed, we should seek for the cause elsewhere, in the nature of things, rather than in a systematic desire to do wrong.

In the treatment by the National Government of the Indian, the military and civil officers of Government have generally been diametrically opposed, the former believing the Indians to be as children, needing counsel, advice, and example, coupled with a force which commands respect and obedience from a sense of fear, the latter trusting mostly to moral suasion and religious instruction. The absolute proof produced by you that the Indian has a strong religious bias but is absolutely devoid of a moral sense as connected with religion, more than ever convinces me that the military authorities of the United States are better qualified to guide the steps of the Indian towards that conclusion which we all desire, self-support and peaceful relations with his neighbors, than the civilian agents, most of whom are members of someone of our Christian churches. Congress, however, alone has jurisdiction of the whole matter, and I am sure your volume will .be received by its members with great satisfaction, as it will enable them better to understand a subject which has always been involved in honest doubt.

As you are perfectly aware the treaty system began at an early period of our history when the white settlers and Indian tribes were more nearly equal than now, and my recollection is that this system was first discountenanced on motion of General A. H. Terry, by the Indian Peace Commission of 1868-9. Still, as long as distinct tribes like the Sioux, Cheyennes, Kiowas, Arapahos, Utes and Apaches are assigned to specific reservations, there must always exist something like a treaty or bargain, so that both Indians and whites may understand their true relations.

My recollection also is that the same Peace Commission recommended to Congress to provide for each group of Indian reservations something like a territorial government, with a code of laws applicable to each member of the tribe; with a governor, courts, and executive officers to enforce the law as against individual criminals, instead of as now, resorting to war to punish a whole tribe for the individual acts of a few. The time is now opportune to perfect that system, and your volume will greatly aid Congress in the accomplishment of that end.

The subject-matter of your volume has dramatic interest to a large class of the American people, is fair and just in its reasoning, and liberal in its tone; and I therefore take great pleasure in recommending it to the military student and to the general reading public, as by far the best description extant of the habits, manners, customs, usages, ceremonies, etc., of the American Indian as he now is.

You are hereby authorized to use my name as authority for its publication and circulation; and I invite all persons interested in the subject of the North American Indian to read this book carefully, to the end that public opinion may aid the national authorities to deal justly and liberally with the remnants of that race which preceded us on this continent.

Washington, D. C., January 1, 1882.

ADVENTURES AMONG THE COMANCHES

I WAS born in western North Carolina. My earliest recollections are tinged with stories of Indian atrocities; for the Cherokees yet occupied "the land of their Fathers" and were only a short distance from us. It is true the Cherokees had committed no outrages, but their white neighbors, being in constant dread of what three or four thousand warriors might do, were vociferous in demands for their removal beyond the limits of the State.

This "hue and cry" was led by some men of intelligence and position (who may have had solid pecuniary reasons for wishing to get rid of the Indians), and these so worked upon the fears of the masses of uneducated whites, that there was constant danger of rupture of peaceable relations.

The negroes were especially terror-stricken, and, forgetting for the time, their usual stories of witches and ghosts, often caused my "hairs to stand on end" with their thrilling narratives of the cunning, ferocity, and immunity from danger, of Indians. According to them an Indian could make himself invisible as air, and was much harder to kill than even a witch.

Several times in each year, small parties of Indians would suddenly make their appearance in the little village in which my parents resided; and I can yet feel the thrill of horror and dismay which quivered through my frame when, a small delicate lad of six years, I one day found myself in the midst of a band of thirty or forty stalwart, painted, feather-crowned warriors, bows in hand, and some in the very act of discharging arrows which, my negro nurse had oftentimes assured me, were a thousand times more dangerous than bullets. Instinctively seizing the hand of a venerable friend of my father, who was in the crowd about the Indians, I gazed with wonder and dread; which was hardly dispelled when I comprehended that the Indians were shooting at sixpences held in cleft sticks, stuck in the ground at thirty or forty yards distance.

In spite of the assurances and protective kindness of my old friend, it was some time before I could regain my equanimity, and I had hardly begun to be interested in, and enjoy the sport, when at a loud call from one of the number, the whole party started with rapid strides towards my father's house, which was nearby. Again I was tormented with doubt, suspicion and fear, and I could scarcely be made to comprehend that the Indians had gone to our house to ask my mother to play for them on the only piano that our small village then boasted. Here, their grave and quiet demeanor, their appreciative notice of myself and sisters, and their unalloyed delight at the music, allayed all my fears, and I began to believe the Indians a greatly slandered race.

Next day they were gone, and the favorable impression made was soon almost entirely effaced by continual repetition of stories of their horrible cruelties.

Each succeeding visit of Indians left me with more favorable impressions of them, but each such visit seemed more and more to exasperate the white men. Before I was ten years of age, I had heard all the changes rung on the terrible possibilities of Indian character, and though my personal experience made me something of a doubter, I could not gainsay the evidence of the people about me, backed as it was by the history of the colonies, of which, about this time, I began the study.

My next experience dissipated all my doubts.

A beardless second lieutenant of the army, I was stationed in Texas at a little two-company frontier post, exposed to the wiles and machinations of the most cunning, the most mischievously artful, of all the United States Indians, the Comanches. While not so coldly bloodthirsty as some other tribes—priding themselves upon their silent stealth and cunning, and ranking the expert horse-thief above the dashing warrior—the Comanches are at night the most dangerous of all Indians. Crawling into camp and bivouac, he will, in his efforts at theft, harmlessly pass close by sleeping men, whom one blow of his knife might silence forever. But woe betide the unfortunate who discovers him, or attempts to interfere with his favorite pastime. His weapons are ever ready. A shot, or quick plunge of his knife, and, in the confusion and darkness, he vanishes like a ghost, leaving death and terror behind him.

For months after the establishment of this little post, there was scarce a night when an attempt was not made on our picket line. The sentinels soon learned their lesson, and hiding themselves, watched the ground and fired at every unusual object. On each such occasion the commanding officer required the officer of the day to turn out the whole guard, deploy it as skirmishers, and scour the chaparral around and in the vicinity of the corral. How often, when engaged in such duty, thrusting my sword into every clump and cover, have I inwardly thanked the Indian for his disposition to put as great a distance as possible between himself and danger. Though I hunted faithfully many nights, I never found an Indian. If I had, these papers would probably never have been written.

Exasperated by the constant failure of their efforts to steal, and possibly emboldened by the lack of casualties, resulting from the fire of our poorly armed and badly drilled soldiers, the Indians became more enterprising, no part of the post being safe at night. Finally, the blacksmith—an excellent man—happening to stumble one night over a crawling Indian, was shot dead within a few feet of his tent.

Up to this time, our annoyance had come from little marauding parties of from two to six Indians on foot, who, separating on occasions of alarm, left no trail which could be followed with any hope of overtaking them. Now, however, they began to come in larger parties, and on horseback. Our cavalry was therefore ordered out, and at least twenty men kept continually on the move; watching passes through the mountains, following trails, and making the Indians understand that they could not visit our section of country without danger.

This led to my third scene of Indian experience. A party of Comanches passed near the town of Castroville, Texas, committing various thefts and depredations, finally murdering a whole family of Germans. I was ordered with twenty-five soldiers to pursue and punish them. For more than four weeks I followed the devious windings of the trail, and finally overtook and surprised them in their camp, killing some, dispersing the others, and capturing all their horses, saddles and equipments.

This was so severe a blow that the Comanches almost entirely ceased to frequent that portion of country, and in a very few years after, that military post was abandoned, as no longer necessary.

Before this occurred, however, I had been transferred with my company to another post, near which were located several tribes and bands of Indians, all apparently peacefully disposed, and here I gained another experience of Indian life.

I had been at the post but a few weeks when it was visited by a party of Lipans, who were exceptionally demonstrative in their evidences of friendly feeling. They encamped near the post for some days.

One day I was out with dog and gun after quail, and finding a large covey near the Li pan camp, had got it nicely scattered in good cover and was thoroughly enjoying the sport, when I found that I had a following of at least a dozen Indians. Having no knowledge of the shot-gun, their hunting was confined to large game, and they were filled with astonishment, not only at my hitting so small an object, but that I lolled it flying. At each successful shot, they gave vent to their admiration in loud applause. When my dog could no longer find any birds, I stopped hunting, and with some vanity (for I had shot unusually well) showed the Indians my gun and equipments. They were so delighted, especially with the minute No. 9 shot (which they had never before seen), that the chief invited me to visit his main camp on the head waters of the Perdinales, promising me not only an abundance of those "little birds" (quail, for which they had no special name) but also of Guaealotes (turkeys). The offer was too tempting to be refused. Returning to the post, I stated the case to the commanding officer, and obtained his permission to be absent.

Two days after, mounted on a good horse, accompanied by one soldier, who led a pack-mule, laden with our tents and supplies, I started with the Indians for their main camp. Arriving there, I pitched my tent in a pretty clump of trees near the village, and for nearly a week had a most delightful time, bagging great quantities of small game. The Indians, as a rule, kept aloof from me, which I attributed to the difficulties of intercourse; our only means of communication being a mere smattering of very bad Spanish on both sides. One day the chief came to me and told me I had better go home, as some of his young men had "bad hearts" towards white men. Thanking him for his hospitality and warning, I was soon packed, and returned without molestation to my post.

Within two weeks after my return, information was brought that these very Indians had broken out, and were murdering settlers, right and left. It afterwards transpired that the outbreak had been determined upon sometime before; that the visit of the chief to the post was for the purpose of obtaining information as to the numbers and character of troops that could be put into the field; and that my invitation to visit his camp was to ward off any suspicion of their intent until all their arrangements had been completed.

Not very long after this I had yet another experience, differing from all the others. I was returning with my command from a long scout; our route led through the Guadeloupe mountains, by the Bandera pass. These mountains were at that time infested by hostile Indians, who, secure in their fastnesses, watched the plains below, pouncing upon settlements or unwary travellers, and hurrying with their plunder through the Bandera pass to their secure retreats.

Coming upon a pretty stream, we startled a flock of ducks, which, flying a short distance, settled upon the limpid water. Hurrying off alone, I followed eagerly; for our larder had run to its very dregs. For an hour or more, I was tantalized with "the delusions of hope," the provoking birds flying but a little way, but always flying before I could get within shot. At last they went far away, and I started to rejoin my command; but, though I took the proper direction, and watched most carefully for the trail, night overtook me in the wilderness.

To go twenty-four hours without food, and be thrown entirely on his own resources for shelter, was not, in those days, so uncommon as to be regarded as a special hardship by any soldier or sportsman. So, finding a deep ravine, with plenty of water, wood, and grass, I dismounted, unsaddled, picketed my mule, and went into camp. My tent was modelled after the Indian tepee; straight sticks, stuck in the ground in a circle, and crossing each other four feet above, formed the frame. Over these was fastened my wide india-rubber poncho, and over the slit in the top was secured my hat. My bed was the saddle-blanket, my pillow the saddle. I had hardly completed my arrangements, when a rain-storm, such only as Texas can get up, burst upon me. In spite of it I slept comfortably and dry from above, but the rain soaked in underneath, and I was thoroughly annoyed and not a little alarmed to find, next morning, that my gun, in spite of all precautions, was so wet, that I could not discharge it. I had a revolver, but having no cartridges to reload, did not attempt to fire it off. From appearance, I judged it to be in the same condition as the gun. I was practically disarmed, in a most dangerous country.

Deciding not to waste time nor incur dangerous chances in looking .for my command, I determined to make the best possible speed for my station, then not less than seventy-five miles off. I was mounted on a powerful mule, a most excellent riding and hunting animal, and I did not doubt her ability to make the distance in a day; but in order to do so, I must go through the Bandera pass, at that time the most dangerous locality in Texas. Needs must, and I started at daylight for the pass.

Soon after sunrise, I reached the Guadeloupe River; and was travelling rapidly, but comfortably, along the broad Indian trail which led up that stream. I was on a small open prairie, surrounded by thickets, when my attention was attracted by a thin, scarcely-defined column of smoke rising apparently from the very bed of the river. Naturally thinking of Indians, I turned my mule, darted at once into the thicket, and, keeping out of sight, skirted around until I got above the smoke.

My first impulse was now to put as much distance between myself and it, and in as short a time as possible; but the idea suddenly occurred to me that it might be the camp of my command, and that I never could overcome or outlive the ridicule that would attach to me, were it known that I had run away from my own comrades. Acting on this, I turned my mule and cautiously made my way back towards the smoke. The thicket was very dense; pushing slowly and carefully through it, I suddenly emerged to find myself in a herd of about twenty horses and mules, which were picketed in a small open space, scarcely thirty yards wide, and just on the bluff back of the river.

To make matters worse, my mule no sooner saw the animals, than she lifted up her voice in a bray that woke the echoes for many miles around. There were mules in the herd, or this bray would have sealed my fate; but not thinking of this most fortunate incident, I tumbled off her back, thrust my hand into her mouth, stopped the tell-tale bray, and backed her out of sight in the thicket in much less time than it takes to tell it.

After fastening her, I, from the thicket, carefully reconnoitred the open space. The animals were Indian ponies and stolen stock.

I knew too much not to be obliged to know more. The camp was evidently just under the bluff. Crawling most cautiously to the edge, I peeped over the bank, and my heart felt dead within me, as I saw, not forty yards away, seven Indians squatted around a pot, eating their breakfast. I got back to the thicket as quickly and cautiously as possible. What to do was the question. My mule, though strong and enduring, was slow in a race. I had two alternatives, either to make off at once on the mule, trusting that the Indians might not discover my trail until I had a good start; or to steal a horse and get away on that. Under the circumstances I had no conscientious qualms on the matter of theft, but I doubted my ability to select the best horse; and the selection, and the necessary change of saddle, would take precious moments. Besides, the loss of a horse would be discovered at once; my trail might not be noticed for some time.

I mounted the mule, and proceeded cautiously until sure of being beyond hearing of the Indians, when whip and spur were vigorously applied. The mule responded nobly, and, as if comprehending the necessity for extra effort, fairly flew over the ground for the next five or six miles. The Guadeloupe was crossed, then the Verde, and yet no sign or sound of pursuit.

The race so far had been on a broad Indian trail, through woods and thickets, but from the timbered fringe along the Verde to the summit of the pass, was a three-mile slope of bare prairie. Until I could get through the pass I was obliged to keep the trail, the mountains being elsewhere almost impassable; but once through it I was safe, for then, leaving the trail, and plunging into the ravines and thickets of the Medina River, I could elude pursuit until night should give me the opportunity to reach my post. When about half way over this bare ground, to my inexpressible delight, I ran into the trail of my command, but had hardly time to congratulate myself when several Indians emerged, in full pursuit, from the thickets of the Verde. Under whip and spur, my good mule soon brought me to the summit of the pass, and looking back I found the Indians had stopped, on striking the trail of the troops, and were carefully examining it. Feeling very easy, I also stopped to watch them, and to give my mule time to recover her wind. After some consultation, the Indians turned about, and went off as fast as their horses could carry them, evidently expecting that the pursuers might in turn become the pursued. In an hour or two I overtook my command, none the worse for my adventure.

These experiences, with numbers of others of similar character though less marked, had come to me by the time I was twenty-three years of age, and had been scarcely two years an officer of the army.

For more than thirty years (with the interlude of the war of the rebellion), I have been more or less among Indians, having in that time had intercourse with thirty-four tribes, speaking different languages, having somewhat different manners and customs, and occupying various and widely sundered portions of country—from the coasts of Texas to the waters of the Yellowstone; from the banks of the Mississippi to the Pacific Ocean. At one time hunting Indians, at another time being hunted by them; now, associated together, but at daggers' points, holding them in check only by the fear engendered by military power, and the stern enforcement of military rule; again living together in free and unrestrained friendly intercourse, hunting, fishing, chatting, dancing, visiting, I have had exceptional opportunities for a comprehensive knowledge of Indian character.

In 1872 I attended a grand Medicine-Dance of the Cheyennes and Arapahos (corresponding to the Sun-Dance of the Sioux), which lasted for several days. I was greatly impressed with the earnestness of their religious beliefs, and the spirit of martyrdom which this earnestness develops. I determined to make a close study of this (to me) unexpected phase of savage life. My first writings on Indians was on the subject of their religion, and made from notes and sketches taken during this great meeting. These were necessarily unsatisfactory. One peculiarity of a people grows out of, or is involved in, other peculiarities, and I soon found that I could give no explanation of the Indian religion which would be satisfactory even to myself, without a thorough knowledge of all his other characteristics and peculiarities. From the study of his religion I began to study the man. In this I have been greatly favored, much of the last nine years of my life having been passed directly among the wild Indians, and with peculiarly exceptional advantages of association and friendly intercourse.

The result of my studies under these favorable circumstances will be found in the following pages.

My desire is to delineate the Indian exactly as he is (judging him, however, necessarily from the civilized stand-point), to note his peculiarities of thought and action, and to give a minutely correct picture of his daily life, as connected with his government, his religion, his social and family relations. I bring to this task a mind which I believe to be unbiased by enthusiastic admiration for the "noble Red Man," or prejudice against the ignoble savage. My desire is to state "the truth, the whole truth, and nothing but the truth." If I err, the fault is in my perceptive faculties, not in the intention of the expression of them.

BEYOND THE MISSISSIPPI

ANY discussion of the origin of the American Indians is out of place and unnecessary, until scientific men have finally agreed as to the origin of the human race. Suffice to say here that the Indian is, to my mind, an evidence of the unity of races. Wherever we find them, savages have something in common each with the other, and the most civilized races have not so far outgrown their ancestry as to have entirely gotten rid of every savage trait.

Supposing the Western continent to have been originally uninhabited by man, there is no physical or geographical reason why it should not have been peopled from Asia or elsewhere. Even before the days of David, people "went down to the sea in ships;" the winds blew then as now, and a succession of adverse storms might have peopled America, from anyone of the earlier maritime nations of the Eastern world.

Whether the very many customs which the Indians have in common with the ancient Jews are evidences that the "Lost Tribes" have been found, or whether the fair complexion, blue eyes, similarity of language and "coracle" of the Mandans, prove that the Welsh expedition under Madoc really settled on the banks of the Ohio, it is not my purpose to inquire.

My object is to give a minute and accurate account of the manners, customs, habits, social life, and modes of thought of the wild Indians of the present day.

Many admirable writers have preceded me on this subject. Chief of all, and, illustrating and ennobling his theme with both pen and brush, is Catlin.* But the supreme defect of Catlin, and, indeed, of almost all writers on the Indian, is, that they have contented themselves with externals; giving page after page, illustration after illustration, to portraiture of dress, dances, ceremonies; but scarcely a word to government, religion, character, social life, etc.

*George Catlin (1796–1872) was an American painter, author and traveler who specialized in portraits of Native Americans. On five journeys to the American West during the 1830s, Catlin was the first *white man to visually record Plains Indians in their native lands.—Ed. 2015*

Catlin, who, of all other writers, has had the most perfect opportunities, is, of all others, most remiss in this particular, and, however much the reader may enjoy his vivid descriptions and graphic illustrations of scenes and incidents, it is impossible to finish his book without a feeling of dissatisfaction.

We see the Indian in a thousand curious and picturesque scenes, but we see him as we see the actor on the stage. However beautiful the dress and faultless the delineation, we do not know him. Our natural curiosity is not gratified by even a glimpse of his every-day character, or peep into the scenes of his every-day life.

In my own reading I have found this to be the one great lack of all writers on the Indian, and to supply this lack, to the extent of my ability, is the purpose and intent of these pages.

Whether the Indian languages have been derived from one, or from several roots, must, and probably will, be determined by the eminent philologists who are now making this subject their special study.

Their great number and infinite dissimilarity have always excited the marvel of all who have had cause to look into the matter, either by contact with Indians, or through books.

At the present moment, there is, for about every thousand of the North American Indians, a language, more or less imperfect, but amply sufficient for all the needs of an illiterate people, and differing in every essential particular from every other language. This wonderful diversity can only be accounted for by a knowledge of the Indian character and habits.

War is, and so far as we can know from history and tradition, has always been, the pleasure and passion of the Indian. With or without cause, tribes occupying lands adjacent to each other were almost constantly on the war-path.

Each tribe, with vanity not entirely aboriginal, believed in its own infinite superiority, and disdained to learn even a few words of its enemy's language, though this might easily have been done through prisoners. This warlike disposition and the necessity for widely extended domains (entailed on all people who live solely by the chase) kept the tribes far apart. There were no intermarriages, no social intercourse, no intermingling of any kind, except that of mortal strife. There was no disposition and little opportunity to learn anything of the language of their neighbors, and thus to adopt words and phrases not properly belonging to their own language.

So long as a tribe was surrounded closely by powerful and warlike neighbors, it remained intact, keeping in large villages and under control of one chief. "When those neighbors were driven off, or, through their own successes elsewhere, moved away, and the tribal territory became greatly extended, the tribe broke up into bands for the more easy and convenient supply of food. This was the opportunity of the ambitious sub-chiefs, leaders of bands, who, preferring to be chiefs of small bands rather than sub-chiefs of large ones, took every care to prevent any subsequent concentration except when forced to it by war, or by the imperative demand of the "Medicine Chief," the supreme expounder of religious doctrine and dogma.

At this moment, there are no less than sixty-six bands of Utes, separated widely in localities, and speaking languages undoubtedly referable to one root, but $9 various as to dialect, that, any but the closest observer might with reason insist that they are different languages.

So, also, there are thirty-four different bands of Sioux, which were rapidly undergoing the same process of disintegration of language, until the government unwittingly stopped it, by concentrating these Indians on reservations.

There are nineteen bands of Shoshones or Snakes, two bands of which, wandering eastward over the Rocky Mountains, became entirely estranged from the parent tribe, and are now known as Bannocks, having lost even their tribal name. They cannot speak or understand a word of their mother tongue.

There are twenty-eight bands of Apaches, speaking-dialects of the same language, and undoubtedly offshoots from the same parent stock; yet, before they were conquered and placed on reservations, they waged incessant war with each other, and no tribes on this continent were more bitterly and uncompromisingly hostile, than were these bands of the same tribe, one to the other.

The Apaches were strong in numbers, warlike in spirit, crafty and energetic in action, and occupied a country almost inaccessible to whites. But for this internecine strife, it would have cost the United States Government many years of bloody and expensive war to have subdued them.

It will thus be seen that his own warlike temperament and disposition to roam have been to the Indian the cause—fruitful as Babel—of the confusion of tongues. There are other causes which may not have been without effect, to add to this confusion. The indisposition or inability of the Plains Indians to learn a spoken language other than their own, undoubtedly led to the adoption of the sign-language as a medium of communication, and the knowledge of this, reacting, forever precluded the necessity of learning any oral language.

For sixty years the Cheyennes and Arapahos have been the firmest friends, occupying the same country, living in the same camps, making peace or war with the same enemies at the same time, and conducting themselves in everything (except intermarriages) as if they were one and the same tribe.

The children play, fight, hunt, and constantly associate together, yet not one in ten of the men, women, or children of either tribe can hold even the most ordinary conversation in the language of the other.

What makes this fact yet more remarkable is, that while one language is comparatively easy, the other is so exceedingly difficult, that even the best interpreters are forced to resort to sign-language.

Under these most exceptional circumstances, it would seem inevitable that the easy language would in time become the common means of communication of the two tribes. Such, however, is not the case; each tribe uses its own language to communicate with its own people, and the sign-language to communicate with the people of the other tribe.

When the white trader invaded the solitudes of the Indian, he took with him, or soon picked up, a small stock of words which, by his constant use among the tribes, have become, as it were, common property; thus "squaw," the Narragansett name for woman, the Algonquin "papoose" for child, "chuck," food, and many other words, have become universal among all the North American Indians east of the Rocky Mountains, when speaking to a white man, or Indian not of their own tribe.

The multitude of languages is a peculiarity of savage life. Let the student remember the condition, in this respect, of Northern and Western Europe, even as late as the time of Julius Caesar; of Africa and South America at the present day, and (without intending to be facetious, and with the desire simply to call attention to the tenacity with which barbarous peculiarities of language hold their grip on human nature,) of England, Scotland, and Wales, through which, even in this enlightened age, an American can scarcely travel, satisfactorily to himself, without an interpreter.

As in all other matters where mere guess-work forms the basis of argument, authorities differ extremely as to the probable Indian population of the country now known as the United States at the time of its first settlement by whites, these estimates varying from three hundred thousand to three millions. Basing my guess on my knowledge of the warlike disposition of the Indians; of their natural tendency constantly to split into bands, which possibly soon became fiercely hostile to each other; of the wide extent of territory required by each tribe, not only for its food-supply, but for its safety; and of the almost universal lack of fecundity of their women, I am of opinion that the number of the aboriginal inhabitants of the territory mentioned has never at anyone time much exceeded half a million of souls.

The number of Indians has always been, and is now, very greatly overrated. This comes from the vanity of the individual Indian, who, if asked about his tribe, will tell you that they are as "the leaves on the trees" for numbers; and from the interested reports of agents, who dearly like to feed, on paper, a tribe of a thousand Indians, but which has actually only five hundred (or less) mouths.

Catlin, on the authority of Major Pilcher, an Indian Agent, estimates the Blackfeet at sixty thousand (about 1835). There were really, probably, not more than a fourth of that number.

All Indians have a strong superstitious repugnance to being counted, and this of late years, (that is since the government has been issuing rations to Indians), is liable to a suspicion of self-interest,. the Indians themselves entirely appreciating the advantage of getting from the agent five hundred rations for three hundred or less mouths.

The number of Indians in the United States (exclusive of Alaska), as stated in the last official report of the Commissioner of Indian Affairs, is, in round numbers, two hundred and fifty-three thousand. This is probably at least one-fifth too great, but it will be impossible to arrive at the exact population so long as the government makes it to the interest both of the agent and of the Indian to exaggerate their numbers.

The Indians have, undoubtedly, greatly diminished in numbers within the last fifty years. This is not due to unusual wars, nor even to the white man's firewater (as is commonly believed), but principally to those great Indian exterminators, small pox, measles, and cholera, and to that "humane" policy of the government, which takes Indians from salubrious mountainous regions, and settles them on reservations in malarious districts, where they are soon decimated by fever and nostalgia.

Probably because they live in tents, which are easily and frequently removed, we generally think and speak of Indians as "nomads." They are nomadic, but this peculiar life does not prevent their having the strongest possible "home" attachment, and the most ardent love of country. I have already spoken of the wide extent of territory necessary to the comfortable existence of even a small tribe. During the spring, summer, and autumn, the tribe roams at will throughout the whole length and breadth of this territory, wherever it is led by abundance of grass for their ponies, or food for themselves, the camp being changed as frequently as necessity or caprice indicates. Within the limits of their territory, and during the seasons mentioned, Indians are veritable" nomads."

The winter encampment is regarded by them as permanent, its location not being changed during the whole three, four, or five months of cold and bad weather. The spot selected for the winter encampment one year may be many miles away from that selected the year before or the year after; but the memory of each is affectionately cherished; a specially good and happy encampment not unfrequently giving the name to the year.

Outside the limits of their territory Indians never go, except on war or hunting parties; on rare occasions to pay a visit of ceremony to a neighboring friendly tribe; or on long solitary journeys, as will be described.

Within the limits of their territory they are nomads," but the territory itself is their home. Their attachment to it is one of the strongest traits of their character. No people are more truly "lovers of their country," no people suffer more from "homesickness," when forced to leave it.

The mental capacity of the Indian is of superior order. His perceptive faculties are remarkably developed, and his reasoning powers are not to be despised, however crude. He is thoroughly master of all branches of education necessary to the comfort and safety of his savage life, thus giving evidence of capacity for a higher order of education.

That he has shown little aptitude for, or devotion to, the rudiments of our civilized education, is due partly to his excitability of temperament and impatience of restraint, and partly to the simple fact that those who had charge of his education cared more for their compensation than for the progress of their pupils, or were impressed with the idea that the necessities of his soul were paramount to those of his intellect. Until very recently the efforts at Indian education were so ill-directed, so entirely unadapted to the real necessities of the problem, as to be absurd.

No important question can be decided among Indians without a vast amount of verbiage; and the faculty of speech-making seems to be even more universal among Red, than White Americans.

Every male Indian is his own reporter, his own newspaper. He is expected and required to sound his own praises, and to be modest about it would only redound to his discredit.

Knowing that he is obliged to speak in public, he spends no little time, not only in the preparation and elaboration of the matter of his speech, but by frequent rehearsal satisfies himself in the manner.

Almost every warrior speaks well, some few of them eloquently; but his best efforts are those addressed to his own people, when seeking to establish his reputation as a warrior and orator, or when endeavoring to sway his audience to his own views on some contested point of Indian policy. As a rule, his speeches to white people are trite and commonplace, a parade of the Indian poverty, as compared to the white man's wealth; and his peroration is almost invariably a whining and abject appeal to the charity of his hearers.

WILD LIFE ON THE PLAINS

THE term "Indian" is applied to all the aboriginal inhabitants of the Western Hemisphere; comprising hundreds, possibly thousands of tribes, occupying every diversity of climate from Arctic snows to Equatorial heats. As climate exerts a marked influence not only on the habits, but on the character of a people, it is not possible, nor to be expected, that these tribes can be grouped in any truthful common description.

Ulloa has said: "See one Indian and you have seen all," a remark neither witty nor wise. With equal truth he might have said: "See one savage and you have seen all," or "See one European and you have seen all."

Even within the comparatively narrow limits of the United States, the Indian tribes, though presenting a general similarity of character, vary in habits, manners, customs and beliefs, in so remarkable a degree, that no general description is applicable to all, except, that all are savage, all are swindled, starved, and imposed upon.

Though I have served in almost every portion of our wide frontier, my largest experience has been with the" Plains Indians," those inhabiting the country between the Mississippi River and the Rocky Mountains. Among these Indians I have spent many years, much of the time in peaceful, every day intercourse.

Within the limits specified, reside at the present time hot less than sixty distinct tribes, cut up into bands innumerable, comprising more than half of the whole Indian population of the United States.

Extending from the British line almost to the Gulf of Mexico, they would appear to be subjected to such climatic variation as might greatly influence their character. That this is not the case is due to the peculiarity of those great elevated plains, or steppes, high, dry, and generally destitute of trees, except along the margin of streams. All these tribes are mounted, and all, until recently, depended upon the buffalo for all the necessaries and comforts of life.

Though distinct in language, differing somewhat in character, and each tribe, as a rule, hostile to all others, their common necessities have so assimilated their habits arid modes of thought as to enable the student to group them, for description, into one general class.

These Indians I know best, and from them I have drawn most of my illustrations. In the following pages, when I speak of Indians, I mean the "Plains Indians," except when the context shows that I mean the whole race. When I wish to draw attention to the peculiarities of other Indians, as Utes, Apaches, etc., I will speak of them by name.

The ideal Indian of [novelist James Fenimore] Cooper is a creation of his own prolific brain. No such savage as Uncas ever existed, or could exist, and no one knew this better than Cooper himself. All hostile Indians—Mingoes, Iroquois, etc.—are painted as fiends, in whom the furies themselves would have delighted.

His stories are striking and artistic, but they will not hear the test of consistent criticism. He assumed his ideal, clothed him in moral and Christian virtues, and placed him prominently in contrast with his surroundings. How he could possibly have arrived at those good qualities, when born and reared among savages without a moral code, is a question that admits of but one answer—"no such individual could possibly have existed."

The wild Indian of to-day is the Mingo painted by Cooper, modified somewhat by time and his surroundings; a human being, in the earliest stage of development; a natural man.

Of all writers on the North American Indians, Catlin deservedly stands first. In an intercourse with Indians extending over half an ordinary lifetime, I have frequently been struck by his quickness of apprehension, and the vividness of his colorings of Indian life. But Catlin, as he himself admits, was an enthusiast. Though a poor painter, he was wrapped up in his art of painting. Give him a model suited to his taste—a wild, free savage, adorned with all the tinsel-trappings of barbarous life—and he immediately clothed him with all Christian virtues and knightly honors.

His pen-portraits of Indians are admirable in one sense, in another faulty beyond measure. Indians of whom he wrote are still living, their tribes maintaining to this day the same manners and customs which he so vividly describes. To see them now is to have seen them then, yet how different the pictures from those he drew. He could see only the natural noble qualities. To the natural ignoble qualities (inseparable from the savage state) he evinced a blindness inexplicable in a man of such perceptive faculties, except on the hypothesis of excessive enthusiasm.

Of the miserably low condition of the Crows and Blackfeet, he has not a word to say, but gives pages of eloquent writing to the beauties of their dresses and the magnificent length of their hair.

He descants on the modesty of some tribes, but tells us, in almost the same breath, that several families, consisting of men with two, three, or more wives, and children of all ages and sexes, occupy, for all purposes, one single lodge of twelve or fifteen feet in diameter.

His whole attention is occupied with externals—dress, dances, religious and other ceremonies. Nowhere does he give us a close insight into their inner life, their religion, social and domestic habits and customs. Had he written of these things, his characters must have assumed other shadings than those his "fancy painted."

Here and there throughout his works are evidences that he does see these things, but is determined to say nothing about them. He evidently regarded the Indian as doomed to speedy extinction, and in so far, already dead. He constitutes himself his biographer, and closely adheres to the charitable Homan maxim, "*nil de mortuis nisi bonum*" (say nothing but good of the dead).

Writing of the Indian of forty years ago, Catlin says, "In his native state, he is an honest, hospitable, brave, warlike, cruel, revengeful, relentless, yet honorable, contemplative, and religious being." To these epithets, which are yet true in a certain sense, as I shall show hereafter, I add, that he is vain, crafty, deceitful, ungrateful, treacherous, grasping, and utterly selfish. He is lecherous, without honor or mercy; filthy in his ideas and speech, and inconceivably dirty in person and manners. He is affectionate, patient, self-reliant, and enduring. He has a marvellous instinct in travelling, and a memory of apparently unimportant landmarks simply wonderful. In short, he has the ordinary good and bad qualities of the mere animal, modified to some extent by reason.

Primitive man is an animal differing from other animals in but one single quality, the greater development of the reasoning faculties. The condition of the races of mankind is simply the greater or less progression of each from that starting-point. The Indian, though so far behind in this race of progress as to be still a savage, is yet far ahead of many tribes and people. The grand difference between the North American Indian and the civilized people of the same continent comes not from degrees of intelligence, or forms of religion, but from what we call morality. The intellect of an Indian may be as acute as that of a congressman, and his religion as austere as that of a bishop, yet he remains a savage simply from lack of a code of morals.

People of enlightened countries, particularly moral and Christian people of our own land, will have difficulty in understanding this lack.

Religion is the disposition of man to recognize some power superior to, and hidden from, himself. It is innate, a part of the constitution of man, common alike to "savage and to sage." It is doubtful if there be a race of mankind so low as to be without a religion.

Morality recognizes and inculcates the rights and duties of individuals in their relation to their social life. It is above religion, and its possession by a people is indicative of great strides in advance of the primitive condition.

The Jewish code, the ten commandments, mingled the two in one common law, and the embodiment of these into two simple commandments by Christ (himself a Jew) nearly nineteen hundred years ago, have forever, to all Christian people, so welded together religion and morality that the one cannot exist without the other.

We are taught in childhood, at our mother's knee, that certain things are right, others wrong. The morality is inculcated with the religion, and we with difficulty separate the one from the other.

As will be seen further on, the Indian has a religion, as firmly seated in his belief as Christianity in the faith of the Christian; but that religion has no added moral code. It teaches no duty or obligation either to God or man.

Right and wrong, as abstract terms, have no meaning whatever to the Indian. All is right that he wishes to do, all is wrong that opposes him. It is simply impossible for him to grasp the abstract idea that anything is wrong in itself. He has no word, or set of words, by which the ideas of moral right and wrong can be conveyed to him; his nearest synonyms are the words good and bad.

He will tell you that it is wrong (bad) to steal from a man of his own band, not that theft is wrong, but because he will be beaten and kicked out of the band if detected. There is no abstract wrong in the murder of a white man, or Indian of another tribe; it is wrong (bad) simply because punishment may follow.

The Indian is absolutely without what we call conscience, that inward monitor which comes of education, but which our religious teachers would persuade us is the voice of God.

He is already as religious as the most devout Christian, and if our good missionaries would let him alone in his religion, cease their efforts to proselyte him to their particular sect, and simply strive to supply him with a code of morals, his subsequent conversion might be easy and his future improvement assured.

In his manner and bearing, the Indian is habitually grave and dignified, and in the presence of strangers he is reserved and silent. These peculiarities have been ascribed by writers on Indian character to stoicism, and the general impression seems to be that the Indian wrapped in his blanket and impenetrable mystery, and with a face of gloom, stalks through life unmindful of pleasure or pain. Nothing can be farther from the truth. The dignity, the reserve, the silence, are put on just as a New York swell puts on his swallow-tailed coat and white choker for a dinner party, because it is his custom. In his own camp, away from strangers, the Indian is a noisy, jolly, rollicking, mischief-loving braggadocio, brimful of practical jokes and rough fun of any kind, making the welkin ring with his laughter, and rousing the midnight echoes by song and dance, whoops and yells.

He is really as excitable as a Frenchman, and as fond of pleasure as a Sybarite. He will talk himself wild with excitement, vaunting his exploits in love, war, or the chase, and will commit all sorts of extravagances while telling or listening to an exciting story. In their every-day life Indians are vivacious, chatty, fond of telling and hearing stories. Their nights are spent in song and dance, and for the number of persons engaged, a permanent Indian camp (safe from all danger of enemies) is at night the noisiest place that can be found.

One of the strongest traits of Indian character is curiosity, a positive craving to know all that is going on about him. He must know the meaning of every mark on the ground; he must know all the camp tattle. A stranger arrives in the village and goes into a lodge. In a few moments half the inhabitants of the village are in or about that lodge standing on tiptoe, straining eyes and ears, and crowding each other and the stranger, with as little compunction as if the whole thing were a ward primary meeting.

Whether or not he evinces surprise at anything depends on his surroundings, and somewhat on the nature of the thing itself. In a formal assemblage, or when in the presence of strangers, it would be the height of bad manners to show surprise, however much might be felt. Uneducated people of our own race feel no surprise at the rising and setting of the sun, the changes of season, the flash of lightning or the roll of thunder. They accept them as facts without explanation, and though beyond their comprehension, without surprise. One shows surprise at something out of the ordinary range of his experience. It is an act of comparison.

The Indian has actual and common experience of many articles of civilized manufacture, the simplest of which is as entirely beyond his comprehension as the most complicated. He would be a simple exclamation point, did he show surprise at everything new to him, or which he does not understand. He goes to the other extreme, and rarely shows, because he does not feel, surprise at anything.

He visits the States, looks unmoved at the steamboat and locomotive. People call it stoicism. They forget that to his ignorance the production of the commonest glass bottle is as inscrutable as the sound of the thunder. The whirl and clatter of innumerable spindles are as far beyond his power of comprehension as that the summer's heat should be succeeded by the winter's snows; and a common mirror is as perfect a miracle as the birth of a child in his lodge. He knows nothing of the comparative difficulties of invention and manufacture, and to him, the mechanism of a locomotive is not in any way more a cause for surprise than that .of a wheel-barrow.

When things, in their own daily experience, are performed in what to them is a remarkable way, they feel and express the most profound astonishment. I have seen several hundred Indians—men, women, and children—eager and excited, following from one telegraph pole to another, a repairer whose legs were encased in climbing-boots. When he walked easily, foot over foot, up the pole, their surprise and delight found vent in the most vociferous expression of applause and admiration.

I once rode into a large Indian village, accompanied by a beautiful lady, an accomplished horsewoman. The horse, not liking his surroundings, brought out, by his plunges and curvetings, all her grace and skill. Had she been astride, as is customary with Indian women, no notice whatever would have been taken of her, but, being perched on a side-saddle, in what to the Indian was an almost impossible position, she was soon surrounded by a crowd of all ages and sexes, evincing in every possible way their extremity of surprise and delight.

Surprise in an Indian sometimes takes very comical forms. An officer, now on the retired list, who having lost a leg in service, had had it skilfully replaced by one of light hollow wood, with open slits, was one day visiting the lodge of a distinguished Sioux chief (now dead). After some rather abortive attempts at conversation, the officer took a knitting-needle from the hand of the old wife of the chief, and passed it through his leg. This at once attracted the notice of all. The chief made signs asking to see the leg. Stripping up his pantaloons the officer managed to show the artificial limb, but concealing its connection with the leg proper. After a long and minute examination the chief asked if the other leg was the same. The amused officer could not resist a little lie, and nodded yes, whereupon the chief took him by the shoulders and thrust him out of the lodge as "bad medicine."

The excitability of the Indian results in another peculiarity, generally overlooked by his historians. Though undoubtedly brave, and performing feats and taking chances almost incredible, he is, when surprised, more easily and thoroughly stampeded than any other race of people of which I have any knowledge.

The Indian's endurance of pain and suffering of any and every kind is his "patent of manhood." Custom and Indian public opinion have made endurance the exponent of every manly virtue; and he who can subject himself, without a look or expression of pain, to the greatest amount of excruciating torture, is the best man, whatever may be his other qualities.

Another most admirable quality he possesses in an eminent degree. This is patience. Endurance and patience would seem to be naturally allied, and to a close observer they appear to be the warp and woof of Indian character. Every manly quality possessed by the Indian is the outgrowth of one or the other of these traits. His skill and success as warrior, or thief, or hunter; his avoidance of quarrels or conflicts with his associates; his submission to wrongs, outrages and starvation, all come from his endurance and his patience. Even his disposition to torture his enemies is, to some extent, but the reflex of the conscious pride which would enable him to bear those tortures without flinching.

Modesty, as we understand the term, is totally lacking in the Indian character. The chief or warrior who put a low estimate on his qualities or achievements would be taken at his word and nothing thought of. There are no reporters, no newspapers, to herald the praises of a skilful warrior. He must blow his own trumpet, and he does it with magnificent success. Self-praise is no disgrace to him, and half the talk of warriors to each other is made up of exaggerated boasts of what they have done, and most extraordinary assertions as to what they intend to do.

The ordinary conversations, at home or in company, are broad even to indecency. In some of the tribes the women are retiring and modest in manners, because custom requires it, but they listen with delight to the story-teller's most filthy recitals, and receive with great applause indecent jests and proposals in the sign-dance.

Clothing is for ornament, not for decency. Ordinarily, even among the wildest tribes, men and women wear some covering (very frequently the men only the breech-clout), but I have seen entirely naked men stalking about a village, or joining in a dance, without exciting surprise, comment, or objection from others. Although most gayly bedecked on occasions of ceremony, the ordinary covering of the male Indian is not what would be regarded as decent among civilized people. The women are more decently clothed habitually, but men and women, even young girls, think nothing of bathing together in *puris naturalibus*, and it is not at all unusual to see boys and girls, even up to ten years of age, running around the camp in the same condition.

There is a curious difference of opinion among writers as to the honesty of the Indian, some asserting that he is an errant thief, others insisting that he is exceptionally honest. Catlin says that the Indian is "honest and honorable," and that he "never stole a shilling's worthy of property" from him. The fact is that all these authors are both right and wrong.

In their own bands, Indians are perfectly honest. In all my intercourse with them, I have heard of not over half a dozen cases of such theft. It is the sole unpardonable crime among Indians. There being no bolts nor bars, no locks nor safes, and each Indian having by common custom the right to enter into any lodge of the band, at any and at all hours, the property of no one would be safe for a moment but for the most rigid infliction of the severest punishments on the perpetrator of this solitary Indian crime.

The value of the article stolen is not considered. The crime is the theft. A man found guilty of stealing even the most trifling article from a member of his own band, is whipped almost to death (every individual of the band having the disposition, as well as the right, to take part in the amusement, and there being no limit, except his own will, to the amount of punishment inflicted by each), his horses are confiscated, his lodge, robes, blankets, and other property destroyed or divided among the band, and, naked and disgraced, he is, with his wives and children, unceremoniously kicked out of the band, to starve, or live as best they can. A woman caught stealing is beaten and kicked out of the band, but her husband and children are not included in the punishment.

Children detected in thefts are thrashed most unmercifully, not only by the person from whom they stole, but by the father, who is also obliged to pay damages.

But this wonderfully exceptional honesty extends no further than to the members of his immediate band. To all outside of it, the Indian is not only one of the most arrant thieves in the world,* but this quality or faculty is held in the highest estimation, the expert thief standing in honor, and in the estimation of the tribe almost, if not quite, on the same plane as the brave and skilful warrior.

These judgments are made from the perspective of a different culture.

The earliest lessons of the youthful brave are in stealing. The love-sick youngster can only be sure of winning his mistress by stealing enough horses to pay for her. Indians are not very successful breeders of horses, and every man of the tribe expects to keep himself in stock by stealing.

Even different bands of the same tribe (when not in one general encampment) do not hesitate to steal from each other. A most flagrant case came under my personal observation. In the winter of 1867-8, I was stationed at North Platte, Nebraska, in charge of Spotted Tail's band of Brule Sioux. A party of six Minneconjou Sioux came into Spotted Tail's camp on a visit. They were stalwart, good-looking youngsters, beautifully dressed, well-armed and mounted, and claimed to have been in the Phil. Kearny massacre of the year before. They were received as most distinguished guests, with all hospitality and honor. Feasted and honored by day, danced with, ogled and made love to at night, the happy visitors, fascinated with their surroundings, apparently thought only of pleasure; but early on the morning of the fourth or fifth day after their arrival, I was waked up by an Indian who informed me that the Minneconjous had gotten away in the night with over one hundred of their entertainers' ponies. A war party was promptly organized for pursuit, but returned unsuccessful, after running the fugitives for over a hundred miles.

The Indian, as a rule, is honorable after a fashion of his own. Hide anything from him and he will find and steal it. Place it formally in his possession, or under his charge for safe keeping, and it will in all probability be returned intact, with, however, a demand for a present as reward for his honesty.

I apply the term "wild" to a class of Indians to distinguish it from another class inhabiting the Indian Territory, or living within the boundaries of some of the States, and which has made some progress in civilization and moral knowledge. With these exceptions, the vast numbers of Indians in the territory of the United States are "wild." Sioux, Cheyennes, Arapahos, Comanches, Apaches, Utes, Shoshones, Chippewas, and the almost numberless small tribes and fragments scattered through the vast region west of the Mississippi, or collected at agencies, or on reservations, all furnish material and shading for the picture I give of them. Here and there a small tribe—as the Nez Perces—show a slight advance in morality, due to the efforts of Roman Catholic priests so many years ago that their traditions but vaguely fix the time. Here and there, also, even among the wild tribes, are found men who give some evidence of moral perception, probably due to the influence of missionaries and teachers. These cases are, however, individual. The mass of the wild tribes are as depicted.

A large class of most excellent people conscientiously believe that the Indian is a supernatural hero, with a thousand excellent qualities, so admirably woven and dove-tailed into his nature that even civilization and Christianity could not improve him. To such persons I have nothing to say. Their opinions are simply sentimental prejudice, without foundation in knowledge or reason, and could not be changed, "though one rose from the dead."

There is another class of excellent people who firmly believe that it is impossible to civilize the Indian, and who argue that humanity and policy alike point to his extermination as the most prompt and effectual way of solving our Indian problem. These are also wrong. The Indian has never had a fair chance, and he is entitled to a full and fair trial. That, with his miserable opportunities, he has been at least partially civilized, as shown by the exceptions before noted, and by the condition of the more advanced of the Cherokees, is ample evidence of capacity for a further improvement.

INDIAN CHIEFS AND RULERS

THE government of the Indian tribes in their natural condition was a compound of absolutism, oligarchy, and democracy.

The absolutism natural and usual among them may be designated a patriarchal despotism.

Fifty years ago, the head chief of each tribe was a despot, with absolute and unquestioned power over the life and property of each and every individual of his tribe. Each petty chief was in like manner the despot of his band, and each head of a family of the members of that family.

This absolutism was subject to some curious modifications, all growing out of the universal recognition of the law of retaliation, and of the right of property in women. Any man, chief or commoner, of the tribe might kill his own wife with impunity; she belonged to him. He might kill the wife of another man, and get off by paying her value in ponies. If he killed the man himself, he was subject to no punishment, or danger of it from his superiors in authority, but he at once incurred the penalty of death by the hands of the relatives of the dead man, anyone of whom was justified in waylaying and shooting him like a dog. In the same band this blood-feud might or might not end with the death of the first slayer, but in different tribes, and frequently in different bands of the same tribe, each death involved the necessity of another. This accounts, in a great measure, for the deadly hostility of Indian tribes to each other.

A chief, or sub-chief, might with impunity beat or destroy the property of anyone under his authority, but if he killed him with his own hand he incurred the inevitable *lex talionis*, which, however, he might evade by paying a number of ponies to the relatives of the dead man.

This is the almost universal custom even at the present day, and though the last few years have witnessed extraordinary changes in the character of the internal government of the tribes, these have been principally in the influence and control of the chiefs, and in the power of the "dog-soldiers."

Fifty years ago the office of chief was hereditary, a son, though not necessarily the eldest, succeeding. Indian tradition says that, as the father grew old, he took more and more into his councils and plans that son who, in intellect and manly qualities, was best fitted to succeed him; gradually yielding, until the

6 active exercise of power was almost entirely in the hands of the son, but liable to be withdrawn at any moment. This, in most of the tribes, has been changed entirely.

It was fitting that the United States government, which had freed itself from hereditary monarchy, should strike the first blow to free the Indian from hereditary despotism. In many instances unruly chiefs have been deposed by the United States authorities, and others exalted to their places; the subjects themselves having no voice in the matter. This could only have been done, at first, by taking advantage of the ambition of the sub-chiefs, each probably an aspiring man, envious of his superior, and jealous of his equals.

It must have been a great shock to the Indian nature, for the despotic idea runs through all their tribal and family relations; but they very soon caught at the advantages suggested by this new and improved process of making a ruler.

Each chief of a band, or subdivision of the tribe, no longer overawed by the "Divine Eight" of a hereditary ruler, immediately set up for himself. Previous to this the head chief was always the first man of the tribe; after this it was a mere matter of accident, or good management, whether he was so or not.

The preference of the Indians for a dynastic ruler led to the necessity for a war chief, a rank common to all tribes.

The hereditary chief was always recognized, reverenced, and obeyed, as sovereign ruler (even though his age or temperament unfitted him for duties in the field.) If the acknowledged first warrior of the tribe, the hereditary chief was also the war chief, but if not, a war chief was elected by the council. As his function was only to lead in war, the man of the tribe (chief or warrior) most renowned for his skill and ferocity was generally selected.

In times of peace he might be little thought of; indeed was oftentimes only hated and feared, and his influence in the council might be of the smallest; but in times of war he became a power, and his word was law, to which even the hereditary chief might have to submit. In some of the tribes the war chief and the medicine chief are one and the same person.

There are no gradations of rank among the subchiefs who have charge of bands. All are equal as chiefs, and the greater or less power of each comes from his own standing in the tribe, the amount of influence he can bring to bear, either through his eloquence or his reputation as a warrior.

The sons of chiefs and sub-chiefs have a certain subordinate rank, and are regarded as chiefs, even though they have no following.

For some years there has been a struggle between the head chief, on one hand, and the insubordinate sub-chiefs on the other, resulting in many dramatic situations.

The actual condition, at the present moment, of each tribe, with respect to its rulers, is a pretty fair criterion, not indeed of advance towards civilization, but of departure from customary and long-established ideas. It is more difficult to unlearn than to learn, and for this reason, if for no other, this departure is something gained for the Indian.

Sitting Bull and the indomitable bands which, with him, preferred to exile themselves to an inhospitable and starving land, rather than tamely submit to be starved on a reservation, yet enjoy to the full all the unmixed blessings of despotism; and there may be a few small bands, or fragments of tribes, in the United States, who are similarly situated.

Next come a class of tribes as the Utes, who, while yet acknowledging a head chief, are not disposed to yield obedience to his every command.

This, as Ouray found, is not a pleasant condition of affairs, for while the government demands of him as head chief, certain things, he finds his prestige as head chief so far gone that he has little power, even had he the will, to comply with the demands.

In the very large majority of tribes, at the present time, the head chief is but a name, the tribes being broken into small bands, each owing allegiance only to the chief it follows.

Little Kobe, head chief of the Cheyennes, and Little Raven, head chief of the Arapahos, were a few years ago all powerful, each in his own tribe. How, each is leader and chief of a small band, and neither has much standing or influence.

The destruction of the power of the head chiefs has resulted wonderfully well for the private subjects of the tribes. Formerly each sub-chief kept his band as much as possible away from others, and ruled with absolute sway. A change of allegiance from one sub-chief to another was always attended with great danger of loss of property or life, possibly of both. The rule was that if detected in an attempt to change his allegiance, he might be stripped of his property, whipped, or even put to death; but if he succeeded in making the change he was thereafter absolved from blame and secure from punishment.

In 1867, the Cheyennes were waging bitter war against the United States. This tribe and the Sioux are very warm friends, and a portion of the Brule band of Sioux were anxious to join them. Spotted Tail, at that time, head chief of the Brules, did all in his power to prevent this. In spite, however, of his influence, his power, and his most peremptory orders, it was one morning discovered that twenty or more lodges of the malcontents had decamped during the night. Assembling his "dog-soldiers," Spotted Tail pursued the fugitives, overtook and captured them.

Every deserting warrior and many of the women were terribly whipped, their horses were killed, their arms broken or confiscated, all the lodges, robes, clothing and property of every kind ruthlessly destroyed, and the miserable band driven back to camp, naked beggars, powerless for evil.

While, under Indian ruling, this was a perfectly just and proper thing to do, the deserters would have been free from blame, and in no present or future danger from Spotted Tail, had they succeeded in reaching the Cheyenne camp.

This is an exceptional instance, and the severity of the punishment was justified by the magnitude of the interests involved. The attempted desertion was to a different tribe, and with the intention of taking part in a war against the United States. Such action was likely to compromise the whole Brule band, and possibly involve it in the war.

The collection of Indians on reservations and in the vicinity of agencies, so very greatly facilitated the opportunities for change of allegiance, that the chiefs soon found they must depend on some persuasive other than force, if they wished to retain their power.

Thereupon resulted an "era of good feeling." The chief, heretofore so stern and relentless, became as suave as a cross-roads politician, and sought to keep up his power and strength by very similar means. The result is, that individual Indians and families do just as they please. If they dislike one chief they go to another. Indians are born lovers of aristocracy and stick to their chiefs as long as possible, but a specially shrewd and popular man, or brave and successful warrior, may now secure to himself a following even though he were born "one of the common herd."

The Council was and is a prominent feature, the oligarchical element in tribal government.

The chief has control in matters of discipline, or what might be regarded as the details of administration, but everything of importance, every proposition or measure bearing on the general good or ill, must be discussed in council.

Spouting must be a purely American characteristic. As among our highly civilized American citizens nothing, however trivial, can be done without a preliminary letting off a vast amount of verbiage; so the Indian can never do anything without speechmaking.

When a camp is to be moved, a hunt made, a medicine-dance proposed; when youths are to be initiated as warriors, or peace or war discussed; whether in the spring, laying their plans for summer before leaving the agency, or in the fall, returning to it to loaf, dance and gamble the winter away, there must always first be a council more dignified, and almost as loquacious as our supreme council in the year of a presidential election.

A council lodge is provided for every band, and the council is summoned to meet on any and every occasion. All warriors are ex officio members of the council. Each may speak, but, as in civilized councils, a comparatively few individuals do most of the talking. The conclusion is arrived at by acclamation. The old men are swayed by reason and eloquence, the younger by passion and the personal popularity of the speaker or his subject, but though these latter are usually in the numerical ascendancy and might have their own way, they generally acquiesce in the decision of the chiefs, sages, and medicine men.

Besides the chiefs and council there is in the government of each Indian band a "third estate," to which in all matters pertaining to its rights and duties all have to submit. This power consists of the men of the band who have passed the ordeal as warriors, and are yet not old enough to be exempt from active service. It is the mobilized militia of the band. It is a sort of "guild," has its secret meetings, its councils, and decides many questions without consulting chiefs or council. They are the soldiers of the band, and are generally called "dog-soldiers," from the fact, I presume, that among the Cheyennes or Dog Indians, they are at their greatest perfection. All chiefs in their youth are obliged to serve in the ranks of the dog-soldiers, not necessarily in command, for these redoubtable warriors will not permit even the chief to name their leader. They elect him themselves from among the most sagacious and popular hunters. In "old times" the powers and duties of the dog-soldiers were far greater than now. Then the women and children, horses, lodges, and property of every kind were under their protection. They regulated the marches in all movements of the village, selected the camping-places, furnished guards for the camp and animals. They planned all hunts, directed all surrounds, and distributed the game. The widows and orphans of the tribe were under their special charge, and were by them provided with food and other necessaries of life. They were at once the police force and commissariat of the tribe. Then they were constantly occupied, now they have little to do.

Singular as it may seem, the diminution of the power of the chiefs, instead of increasing, as might naturally have been expected, the power of the dog-soldiers, has very greatly diminished it. This I attribute to the greatly reduced number of lodges in the bands. Formerly a sub-chief of influence controlled fifty to one hundred lodges; now it is difficult to find a chief who can control more than ten or twenty, sometimes only half a dozen.

Instead of a hundred or more young and energetic dog-soldiers, a band will have sometimes but six or eight. Their loss in numbers has resulted in more than proportionate loss of power, and instead of electing a leader, they are now, in what I regard as the most advanced tribes, directly under the control of the chief, to whom they are a body-guard and little standing army.

The present tendency is towards a complete breaking down of the central despotic power in each tribe, under which large bands were kept together, and the result is to the advantage of the individual Indian as well as to the United States Government. It is the very first step towards civilization.

Tribal government, heretofore a sort of democratic despotism, is daily becoming more and more simple and patriarchal. A very small expenditure of wisdom on the part of the United States authorities and lawmakers, would soon settle quietly and happily the whole question; but unfortunately it is not to the interests of many influential people that it should be settled.

Of course, having no writing, there is no written law among Indians, nor indeed is there anything like an oral code. There is no crime worthy, in their opinion, of very severe punishment. In the "olden days," change of allegiance was regarded as the gravest of crimes, and punished as treason. Now there is no crime against the "body politic." Violations of the orders of the chief are punished severely, by whipping and destruction of property. Crimes against individuals, as assaults, or stealing his neighbor's wife, are compounded by the payment of damages, the amount of which is assessed by the chief, assisted by two or more prominent men. A theft from an individual of another band is no crime. A theft from one of the same band is the greatest of all crimes. Assaults and injuries to one member of a family by another are religious wrongs to be repented of.

Not long ago a Cheyenne woman in a fit of passion stabbed her grown daughter. No notice whatever was taken of the act by chief or council, but the mother immediately retired to the top of a hill some distance off, and remained there for four or five days, without shelter, bedding, food or drink, when the other members of the family, thinking she had sufficiently atoned, brought her back to the lodge and to life.

In 1879, when seeking for building material, I went to examine a high, rocky hill. On reaching the summit, I saw a short distance from me, a small mound or cairn of stones. At its foot was spread a blanket on which was lying, face downward, an Indian, entirely naked. He did not move or notice me until I had almost made the circuit of the flat top of the hill, when he arose and rushed towards my party, with extravagant gestures and vociferous exclamation, ordering us off. We of course paid no attention to him. When we had completed the circuit of the hill, he wrapped himself in his blanket and sat down on a rock, looking moody and disconsolate enough. When we had finished our examination we returned to our wagon at the bottom of the hill, spread our lunch on the rocks and prepared to enjoy ourselves. The sight was too much for the Indian, who slowly came down and sat near us. He was evidently very unhappy. Two or three pounds of corned beef, half a loaf of bread, and a canteen of cold coffee quickly disappeared, and under its influence he thawed out sufficiently to inform us that he was expiating a sin, that at sundown on that afternoon he would have completed his third day without food or drink, and his penance would have been over; that, in going around him, we had destroyed the whole effect of his medicine, rendered all his sufferings nugatory, and all would have to be gone through with again. He would not tell me what crime he had committed, but from subsequent inquiry, I suspect it was striking his father.

About three years ago a Cheyenne woman, having become for some reason greatly exasperated with her husband, murdered him with an axe while asleep. About a month after, she gave birth to a child, which, as soon as it was born, she threw as far as possible into a thicket, saying she would "have nothing to do with anything belonging to that dead man." No notice whatever was taken of either of these crimes, and the woman is still a member in "good standing" of the band.

Her acts did not, to her, seem to require even a religious penance, and her only punishment has been her inability to get another husband, the bucks wisely steering clear of a woman of such vigorous action.

The child was picked up by one of the old women, and being nursed in turn by the mothers of the band, is now a healthy, sprightly, good-looking little lassie, petted and spoiled by all the band except the mother, who cannot be induced to notice it.

Had the Indians of years ago had a written language, their literature would probably have abounded with personal histories as interesting and dramatic as those of Greece and Home.

They seem, however, to be lacking both in memory and in inventive faculty, and, though great storytellers, to be unable to weave fact and fancy into tradition.

A warrior of the present day is scarcely able to recount the deeds of prowess of his own father, though of his own remarkable achievements he is never weary of talking. I have, therefore, no choice, but am forced to select from among the living or recently dead, for personal histories illustrative of the past and present power of chiefs, and of the changes taking place in tribal government.

When Texas was annexed to the United States, the Comanches, by far the most powerful Texan tribe of Indians, were governed by San-ta-na, a chief distinguished above all others by his eloquence and wisdom in council, and his daring, skill, and success in the field. His word was law, and such his popularity with his tribe, that sub-chiefs and warriors vied with each other in anticipating his wishes. When the United States troops were sent to occupy and defend Texas, it was found that scarcely a place in all the length and breadth of this immense new state was safe from the incursions of this tribe of daring warriors. Whites were killed and scalped on the very outskirts of San Antonio, then the most populous town in the state; and a very considerable village, New Braunfels, was sacked, the men massacred, and the women and children carried into captivity.

The scanty force of regular troops, though well-nigh ubiquitous (as it is always expected to be), failed necessarily to protect so immense an extent of territory from the inroads of the most dashing and venturesome of all Indian raiders.

At this juncture a successful effort was made to bring San-ta-na into council with the whites. He was loaded with presents, and induced to make a visit to Washington city.

The effect of such a journey on this utterly "untutored savage" may be imagined. The immense distances traversed, through a country entirely occupied by white men, the number of people, the great cities, the quantities of arms and warlike appliances of all kinds, convinced him of the utter futility and certainly disastrous consequences of further warfare with the whites.

On his return to his tribe he explained, as far as he was able, what he had seen, and attempted to impress on his people the necessity of keeping the peace.

They at once attributed his change of mind to bribery, and his account of his journeyings and the wonders of the white man's country were set down as fabulous tales "got up" for a purpose. He was looked upon with suspicion, as a traitor to the interests of his people, and regarded as a remorseless and criminal liar. His influence declined, his people fell away from him, and ambitious sub-chiefs seized the opportunity of increasing their own power and influence.

A few years, and this once-powerful leader, heartbroken, deserted by all except two faithful wives, paid the last debt to nature. In a little cañon , near the Bandera Pass, was, twenty years ago, a small mound of stones. It marked the final resting-place of the greatest

Indian warrior of his time. Such was the fate of an hereditary chief who dared to go against the prejudices of his tribe.

The history of Red Cloud, the head chief of the Ogallala Sioux, now living, almost reverses the picture. Not an hereditary chief, he owes his prominence to his persistent hostility to the whites.

The United States government determined to open a road to Montana by way of Powder River. It must necessarily pass through a favorite hunting-ground of the Sioux. Treaties were made with prominent hereditary chiefs of the Sioux bands, by whom the right of way was granted. So great was the dissatisfaction among the Indians that Red Cloud saw his opportunity, and, denouncing the treaties and their makers, he declared war to the knife against every white man who came over that road, or ventured into that country. Clouds of warriors, the ambitious and the disaffected of all the tribes and bands of that country, flocked to his standard. The hereditary chiefs found themselves deserted and powerless, and in some instances were only too glad to preserve their control over their bands by acknowledging Red Cloud as master. A long and tedious war ensued, in which Red Cloud made a great reputation, and constantly received accessions to his power, at the expense of the hereditary chiefs.

Avoiding any general or even serious engagement, he so harassed all trains and expeditions that the few troops then in his country could scarcely be said to hold even the ground they actually stood upon. Several forts were established, but they protected only what was inside the palisades. A load of wood for fuel could not be cut outside without a conflict. This at last culminated in the terrible massacre of Fort Phil Kearney, in which half the garrison (gallantly, though unwisely, meeting the enemy outside) perished to a man.

Instead of sending more troops, and promptly and terribly punishing the Indians, a "humane" commission was appointed to treat with them. The garrisons were withdrawn, the road abandoned, and in their own opinions the Indians were unconquerable, and Red Cloud the greatest warrior in the world.

Spotted Tail, another Sioux chief (already mentioned), also rose from the ranks. When a boy of nineteen or twenty years, he incurred the implacable enmity of a sub-chief, already noted for his daring and ferocity, by aspiring to a girl on whom the chief had set his eye. One day, meeting accidentally a short distance from the camp, the chief peremptorily demanded of Spotted Tail a renunciation of the girl under penalty of instant death. Drawing his knife, Spotted Tail defied him to do his worst. A long and bloody conflict ensued. Some hours after, a straggler from camp found the two bodies locked in a death grip, and each gaping with innumerable wounds. The chief was dead. Spotted Tail recovered to step at once into prominence) custom, among all the Plains tribes, investing the victor in such a duel with all the honors previously borne or won by the vanquished. "When, a few years after, the hereditary chief died, he was almost unanimously selected as principal chief, in spite of the most determined opposition of the sub-chief, who by regular succession should have obtained the position.

Spotted Tail proved an able and judicious ruler, and well justified the choice of his tribe.

In 1876, General [George] Crook, the commander of the Military Department of the Platte, wearied with the constant dissensions of the Sioux, each band of which was ruled by a selfish, ambitious and independent chief, determined to settle the difficulty by a coup d'état, which would bring all the bands under one controlling influence.

Crook commanded the southern force of U.S. troops during the 1876 Yellowstone Campaign. He was attacked by warriors under Crazy Horse at the Battle of Rosebud Creek on June 17, 1876. Though considered a draw, Crook had to withdraw for supplies and to attend to wounded. Eight days later, George A. Custer, commanding the eastern forces of the campaign (the U.S. 7th Cavalry) led his troops over the divide between the Rosebud and the Little Bighorn. Custer and over 200 of his command died that day.

Spotted Tail, who had proved himself not only a man of intelligence and ability, but a firm friend of both Indian and white, was selected to be the supreme ruler, and, with much ceremony, was crowned" King of the Sioux."

One instance of what may be termed a political execution, and I have done with the subject of Indian government.

Big Mouth, another chief of the Brule Sioux, was the peer of Spotted Tail in most manly and warlike qualities. In the constant complications arising of late years from the more direct contact of Indian and white, Big Mouth steadily gained in power and influence. A few years ago Spotted Tail made a visit to Washington, New York, and other eastern cities, and was much feted. On his return, with changed views and" new-fangled" notions as to the policy of the Indians, Big Mouth eagerly seized the opportunity of increasing his power by disparaging the honesty and good sense of his superior in position. Finding matters inclined to go against him, Spotted Tail one day called at the door of Big Mouth's lodge and asked to speak with him. On Big Mouth's appearance, he was seized by two warriors, who held him fast, while Spotted Tail drew a pistol, placed it against his body, and shot him dead.

The death of Spotted Tail was a curious and tragic coincidence. A feud existed between him and a chief named Crow Dog. On the 6th August, 1881, these enemies met near the Rosebud Agency. Their quarrel was terminated by Crow Dog, who, suddenly drawing a pistol, shot Spotted Tail dead.

In addition to its duties as supreme arbiter of all important internal affairs of the tribe, the council is vested with the right and power to regulate its intercourse with other tribes and with whites,

What may be termed international questions are carefully and gravely discussed in a tribal council. The line of policy or action being agreed upon, the most prominent and sagacious chiefs and warriors are selected to present and argue it in the international council. Such a council of eminent United States officials and prominent chiefs of Sioux, Cheyennes, and Arapahos is represented on page seventy-one, from a photograph.

SWINDLING AND ROBBING THE INDIANS

IT would be out of place here to enter into an analysis of the steps by and through which the absurd "treaty system" was foisted upon, and, until very recently, acted upon as the basis of all governmental intercourse with the hundreds of petty Indian tribes which inhabit our wide country. I say absurd, for if we admit that they are so far independent states that their relations towards us must be regulated by treaty, we necessarily concede their sovereign right to make treaties with other nations.

The mere statement of the case is sufficient demonstration of its absurdity, but the iniquities of the "system" warrant a much stronger adjective.

Solemnly to "covenant and agree" to do that which we have no intention of doing, or which, with the best intent, we know is impossible to do, is criminal. In consideration of certain concessions of land, we "covenant and agree" to pay certain fixed annuities to the Indians, yet by negligence we connive at the sequestration of a large percentage of the money or goods. We "covenant and agree" to keep white men out of the limits of the new reservation, though we well know that a government constituted as ours, resting on a popular basis, and with a tide of immigration unparalleled in modern times, can by no possibility keep the faith of any such treaty.

From the earliest years of our independence as a nation, and before any effort had been made to confine the western tribes within restricted areas, each tribe or tribes has had with or near it an agent appointed by the government. What were his functions in those earlier days it is almost impossible to determine, but after the passage of the "trade and intercourse" laws in 1834, he represented the machinery by which those laws were supposed to be carried out. Those laws were enacted for the control of white men, and had no binding force on the Indians. The agent had no power or control over the tribes, which were left free and independent sovereign peoples, untrammelled by any obligation of law, either of God or man.

Loaded with this incubus, "the treaty system," the United States Government, in all its hundred years of "control and management" of the Indians, has never awakened to the facts that these wild and savage natures might be improved by the discipline of law, and that no steps in civilization are possible, until the savage has some fixed principle of action by which to guide himself.

It is common to talk of the crimes of the Indians. However horrible the atrocities committed by them, and recorded in almost every page of our history since the landing of the Pilgrims, there are no crimes. A crime is a willful violation of law or moral obligation. The Indian knows no law either human or divine, nor does he understand any moral obligation. His deeds of rapine and cruelty are simply his mode of making war, and are a part of his savage condition. The grandest of exploits, the noblest of virtues to him, are comprehended in the English words theft, pillage, arson, rapine, murder. He is a savage, noxious animal, and his actions are those of a ferocious beast of prey, unsoftened by any touch of pity or mercy. For them he is to be blamed exactly as the wolf and tiger are blamed.

Leaving out of consideration the half-civilized tribes of the Indian territory, there are yet within the limits of the United States near two hundred thousand savages—"wards of the nation," for whom the government in its wisdom thinks no law is necessary. Indians may murder Indians; Indians may ravage the settlements, committing all the acts known in our statutes as capital crimes, and there is no court of justice, either civil or military, which can legally punish them. Such atrocities have been punished. Modoc Jack and his associates, for the murder of General Canby and the commissioners; the ringleaders of the Sioux massacres in Iowa, and many others have expiated their deeds on the gallows, but the punishment was not by virtue of any law of the land. They suffered under the operation of the old, old law, the foundation of all law, "the law of retaliation."

One of the first and most necessary steps towards the civilization of any savage people is to establish and enforce a code of laws, but to do this we must necessarily give up the pet idea of many humanitarians. We cannot make laws for other "independent nations," and we must elect either to let the "independent nations" die out in ignorance and squalor, or to throw overboard the whole system, treaties and all.

Since the confinement of the Indians to comparatively restricted areas (reservations) the government has found it absolutely necessary to exercise more control of them than is consistent with their independence as nations, or warranted by treaty stipulations. As in many other cases, it carries water on both shoulders, appeasing the humanitarians by a pretence of conformity to treaties, while actually by means of the agent and the army, controlling the Indians almost as effectually as if they were recognized prisoners of war. This control is, however, restricted to the confinement of the Indians to the reservation, no interference with their social or moral habits being permitted. The consequence is that the Indians have not and cannot advance beyond their original barbarism.

For all purposes of restraint the power of the chiefs has greatly diminished, and tribal government is practically extinct. While destroying the slight safeguard with which Indian custom had surrounded individual rights, the government has furnished no substitute. There is absolutely no protection for life, property, or individual rights, except that which each head of a family can give to his belongings, and the condition of affairs is becoming worse every year. The only punishment ever inflicted by the agent is a short confinement in the guard-house, and even this is illegal and purely arbitrary. This punishment has little terror for the vicious, and every day outrages are committed with impunity.

The class of men selected as agents, and the mode of their selection, have always been one of the scandals of the government, but the last device, the leaving of that selection to the Christian churches of the country, is a fitting climax to the preposterous acts which for a century have stultified the governmental "control and management" of Indians. The Indian agent is actually the governor of one or more tribes of wild men. He is the representative of the power and will of the United States. His duties are the "control and management" of the whole political and financial affairs of the tribes, as connected with the government. These tribes are a warlike race, whose pastime is pillage and bloodshed, whose idea of right is simply might, whose respect for, and appreciation of their ruler, is exactly in proportion to his character as a soldier, and the power of will which enables him to control masses of men. To place a poor old man like Mr. Meeker, however faithful, honest, and earnest he may be, in charge of a set of wild brigands like the Utes, is simply to invite massacre.

There are very few voters in this country, even Christians, who would be willing to submit to a law requiring that every governor of a state or territory must be a member of someone of the numerous Christian denominations. Ignoring religious qualifications, they require for their own governor a man of standing and well-tried administrative ability. Yet the governor of a state composed of intelligent and law-abiding citizens, is a very easy matter compared to the government of a tribe of savages.

While requiring high character and marked capacity for the easy office, we are inconsistent enough to give the difficult and dangerous offices to men whose only merit consists in supposed earnestness of Christian feeling and sentiment. I doubt if there be among civilized nations any but our own which could so completely have submerged itself in the slough of ridiculous and criminal absurdity.

The condition of Indians and Indian affairs on the different sides of the British line has been the subject of contrasts by many eloquent speakers and writers. That difference is due, in my opinion, almost wholly to the iniquitous "treaty system," and the innumerable ills growing out of it.

We have spent one hundred millions of money in Indian wars, the British nothing. We have lost thousands of soldiers in battle with Indians, the British few.

We have lost tens of thousands of settlers and emigrants ruthlessly slain, the women carried into revolting captivity, their homes and property destroyed; the British have lost almost none.

We call the Indians dependent nations, the British call them the Indian subjects of her Majesty.

We make solemn treaties with them, the British make laws for them.

We attempt to control them by an almost irresponsible agent, backed by bayonets; the British control them as they do their other citizens, by magistrates and police.

It is true that the problems are not the same on the two sides of the line. The pressure of our resistless tide of immigration has a constantly exasperating effect on the Indians, but that very pressure should warn the government that its treaties cannot be carried out, and for that reason, if for no other, should be abrogated.

In a previous chapter I have given some illustrations of the moral condition of the Indians. Inadequate as were their own rules for the punishment of social wrongs, there was yet that natural law of retaliation, which, under the tribal government, somewhat deterred even the most reckless from the grossest acts of selfishness and passion. Now that the agent has some control, even these poor safeguards are torn away, and license stalks rampant.

A case occurred in November, 1880, under my own observation, near the cantonment in the Indian Territory, which for cold-blooded scoundrelism and utter disregard of social rights and duties, surpassed anything in even my widely extended experience of Indian atrocity.

Stone Calf is a prominent chief of the Southern Cheyennes. He is about sixty years of age, and though in his earlier days was a ruthless and most uncompromising enemy to the white race, has within the last few years accepted the inevitable, and is one of the foremost of the Cheyennes in his eagerness for instruction and enlightenment, and in his desire to "travel the white man's road."*
He is brave, truthful, and manly, an exceptionally good specimen of barbaric life. The child of his old age, his pet and jewel, was a pretty little maiden of thirteen years. One day he wished to communicate with a sub-chief whose camp was some seven miles from his down the river. Without a thought or suspicion of danger to her, he directed his daughter to go to the camp of the sub-chief and convey his message. Starting out, accompanied (as is imperatively

demanded by Indian custom) by another girl, she executed the commission and started on her return to her father's camp.

*The Indian idiomatic mode of expressing "the adoption of all the manners, customs, habits, and laws of the whites."

About half way between the two camps was located the tepee of a member of Stone Calf's band, a stalwart, reckless ruffian, impatient of restraint and generally living away from other people of his tribe. He noted the southward journey of the two girls, and laid his plans. Hiding in a small ravine which it was necessary for them to cross on their return, he suddenly sprung from his covert, seized the bridle of the horse ridden by Stone Calf's daughter, and presenting a pistol at the head of her companion ordered her to leave on pain of death; a hint which was immediately acted upon.

Leading the horse of the unhappy girl he conducted her to his lodge, and there in the presence of his two or three wives, brutally outraged her, keeping her a prisoner all that night and the following day until afternoon, when, fearing some action of Stone Calf, he carried her off into a thicket where both remained hid until dark. Anxious to discover what Stone Calf was doing or intended to do, and yet afraid to leave the girl, he forced her to accompany him to the military post. Threatening her with sure death if she moved, he left her behind a dark corner of the trader's store, while he cautiously peered into the uncurtained windows in search of Stone Calf. The poor girl, watching her opportunity, disappeared in the darkness, and made her way to the tepee of one of the Indians employed at the post as scouts. Here she was recognized, and on telling her story, was protected until morning, and then delivered to her father. That day Stone Calf came to me almost heart-broken, related all the horrible details, and begged for vengeance.

"Have you among yourselves no remedy for such outrages?" I asked.

"Yes," he replied, "I can kill him, and I ought to kill him, but the agent is not my friend, and if I do kill this scoundrel, the agent will put me in the guardhouse, and when I get out not only my daughter, but my wives and family will all be gone or outraged."

"I am truly sorry for you, my friend," I said, "but I can do absolutely nothing. If this were a white villain I would put him in my guard-house, and turn him over to the civil authorities for trial, but he is an Indian, and there is no law to punish such acts when committed by Indians."

Covering his face with his hands, the old man was bent and racked with emotion. Recovering himself he placed his hand on my arm, and in a quivering voice, said:

"I am sick of the Indian road, it is not good;" then raising his eyes to Heaven, he added: "I hope the Good God will give us the white man's road before we are all destroyed."

THE GREAT MYSTERY OF INDIAN "MEDICINE"

I HAVE elsewhere remarked that it is difficult for a Christian to draw the line between religion and morality, but unless he can do so, it will be impossible for him to understand the Indian. He must even go further; he must tone his mind to the consideration of a people not only without a code of morals, but without a God in our sense of the term. Religion is by us understood to be the love and reverence borne towards the Supreme Creator of all things, and a performance of all those duties which are presumed to be in accordance with his will. In this sense the Indian has no religion.

Abstractly, religion is the disposition implanted in the inner constitution of man to bow down before the "Unknowable." In this sense, man is so universally a religious being that travellers' tales of finding a people in Africa, so low in the scale of humanity as to have no religious belief or superstition of any kind, have met with doubt, if not absolute discredit.

Polytheism would seem to be the first and most natural form in which religious belief would manifest itself, and this first idea would naturally, after a time, be modified according to circumstances of locality, or the peculiar idiosyncrasies of the people.

This is eminently the case among the Indian tribes. Some believe in a great many gods, some in but few. There is not to my knowledge a single Indian tribe that believes in but one. Some believe in gods of mountains, of rivers, of plains, etc., others believe that these are not gods but subordinate spirits. It would be a life-time labor for many men to collect all the shades and gradations of belief among Indians. I will give here the religion of the Southern Cheyennes, premising that, for every individual Indian of this or any other wild tribes who has mounted above the plane of religious belief here set forth, a hundred are still below it.

In a letter to Schoolcraft, Major Neighbors asserts that the Comanches believe in "one Supreme Being, the author of both good and bad, who lives beyond the sun, and rules the world."

I knew Major Neighbors well, while he was agent of the Comanches, and had frequent conversations with him as to the habits and beliefs of those Indians. The ideas expressed to Schoolcraft were those entertained by both of us while we were comparatively unacquainted with the Indians.

Subsequent study and better opportunities for forming a correct opinion, convinced me that the Comanches believe, as do most of other Plains tribes, in two gods, but are more than ordinarily indisposed to speak of the Bad God.

Robert Simpson Neighbors (1815–1859) was an Indian agent and Texas state legislator. Known as a fair and determined advocate of Indian interests, he was murdered for his beliefs by a Texan.—Ed. 2015

The Indian is as religions as the most devout Christian, and lays as much stress on form as a Ritualist. He believes in two gods, equals in wisdom and power.

One is the Good God. His function is to aid the Indian in all his undertakings, to heap benefits upon him, to deliver his enemy into his hand, to protect him from danger, pain, and privation. He directs the successful bullet, whether against an enemy, or against the "beasts of the field." He provides all the good and pleasurable things of life. Warmth, food, joy, success in love, distinction in war, all come from him.

The other is the Bad God. He is always the enemy of each individual red man, and exerts to the utmost all his powers of harm against him. From him proceed all the disasters, misfortunes, privations, and discomforts of life. He causes all the pain and suffering, he brings the cold, he drives away the game, he deflects the otherwise unerring bullet; from him come defeat and wounds and death.

The action of these two gods is not in any way influenced by questions of abstract right or morality, as we understand them.

The Good God is always the Indian's friend and assistant in everything that he wishes or proposes to do. If the Indian desires to steal a horse, or the wife of a friend, to kill another Indian, or to raid a settlement of whites, it is the Good God to whom he turns for countenance, and it is by his assistance that he hopes to accomplish his purpose.

The Bad God always thwarts; and from the lameness of a horse to final death, every annoyance, mortification, or disaster is attributed to the direct influence of the Bad God.

Having no sense of right or wrong (as we understand those terms), no innate consciousness, no idea of moral accountability, either present or future, the Indian ascribes to the direct action of one power all the good, and to that of the other power all the bad, that may happen to him.

Why, or wherefore, the Indian knows not, but he is firmly convinced that not an hour, not a moment passes, without a struggle between the two gods, of which he is the immediate cause and subject.

The Good God is not an exacting or jealous god. For his unremitting labors, his devoted services, his constant watchfulness in behalf of the Indian, he demands nothing in return. No prayers are necessary, for he does the very best he can without being asked. No thanks are necessary, for he does these things because he chooses to do them. He is the Indian's friend as the Bad God is his enemy, for some reason of his own, impenetrable, inscrutable.

These two gods are the gods and rulers of the life only in this world, for while the Indian firmly believes in the immortality of the soul, and life after death, the power of these gods does not extend to it. Their function is restricted entirely to benefits or injuries in this life, and the Indian's condition after death does not in any way depend either on his own conduct while living, or on the will of either of the gods.

All peccadilloes and crimes bring, or do not bring, their punishment in this world, and whatever their character in life, whatever the actual "deeds done in the flesh," the souls of all Indians reach, after some days' journey, a paradise called by them "The Happy Hunting Grounds," unless debarred by accident.

There are two ways in which the Indian soul can be prevented from reaching this paradise. The first is by scalping the head of the dead body. Scalping is annihilation; the soul ceases to exist. This accounts for the eagerness of Indians to scalp all their enemies, and the care they take to avoid being themselves scalped. Not unfrequently Indians do not scalp slain enemies. This comes from their belief that each person killed by them (and not annihilated by scalping) will be their servant in the next world. It will be found invariably that the slain enemies were either very pusillanimous or remarkably brave. The Indian reserves the first to be his servant, because he expects to have no trouble in managing him, and the last, to gratify his vanity in the future state by having a servant so well-known as a stalwart and renowned warrior in this world.

This superstition is the occasion for the display of the most heroic traits of Indian character. Reckless charges are made and desperate chances taken to carry off unscalped the body of a chief or friend. Numerous instances have occurred when many were killed in vain efforts to recover and carry off unscalped the bodies of slain warriors. A Homer might find many an Indian hero as worthy of immortal fame as Achilles for his efforts to save the body of his friend, and no Christian missionary ever evinced a more noble indifference to danger, than the savage Indian displays in his efforts to save (as he thinks) his friend's soul. Let the scalp be torn off, and the body becomes mere carrion, not even worthy of burial.

The other method by which an Indian can be cut off from the Happy Hunting Grounds is by strangulation.

The Indian believes that the soul escapes from the body by the mouth, which opens of itself at the moment of dissolution to allow a free passage. Should death ensue by strangulation, the soul can never escape, but must always remain with, or hovering near the remains, even after complete decomposition.

As the soul is always conscious of its isolation, and its exclusion from participation in the joys of paradise, this death has peculiar terrors for the Indian, who would infinitely prefer to suffer at the stake, with all the tortures that ingenuity can devise, than die by hanging.

This is the only hell that Indian religion or philosophy has arrived at, and it will be noticed that this terrible and endless disaster may be a mere matter of accident. The unfortunate sufferer might be a man of probity and wisdom (from the Indian standpoint), a woman of virtue, or an innocent child, but should one or the other chance to become entangled in the lariat of a grazing horse and strangled, the soul would surely suffer the Indian hell.

Believing that no line of conduct of his own can avail him for good or evil; feeling his helplessness and entire dependence on the relative powers of the two Great Beings who fight continually for or against him; the Indian's first and most important concern is to find some sure means by which he can discover which of the gods has the ascendancy for him at any particular time. For this he resorts to divination.

Every Indian language has a word expressive of the attitude of the gods towards the Indian. For lack of a better term, this is translated into the English word "medicine."

Catlin, writing from among the Crows and Black-feet, says, Medicine' is a great word in this country. ... In its common acceptation here it means mystery and nothing else.. .. The fur traders in this country are nearly all French, and in their language a doctor or physician is called "médecin." The Indian country is full of doctors, and as they are all magicians, and skilled, or profess to be skilled, in many mysteries, the word "medicine" has become habitually applied to everything mysterious or unaccountable."

There is probably no room to doubt this to be the true origin of the term, but Catlin's explanation of its meaning is not correct, or rather not complete.

The Indian thinks that he perfectly understands his religion, and believes himself to be as intimately acquainted with his gods as many of our ministers assume to be with theirs.

"Medicine" not only means "mystery," but religious mystery. The word differing in each Indian language, but universally mistranslated "medicine 55 expresses the relation of the gods to each other, with reference to a tribe or particular individual.

The gods are always hostile to each other. One is always the Indian's friend, the other always his enemy. This much is known with absolute certainty.

Certain things in nature are pleasing and helpful to the Good God; other things to the Bad God. Common use and habit have decided the religious status of all things to which the Indians are accustomed, but of anything new and therefore mysterious they are always in doubt. It may be "good medicine," that is, pleasing to the Good God, but it may be the reverse. As the Indian stands in no fear of the Good God, but in most abject and dreadful awe of the Bad God, it is but natural in him to receive all innovations with the utmost caution and dread.

The term "medicine" is applied to every condition of the Indian life, to almost every object of its surroundings. A man gets up all right in the morning, feels splendidly, everything goes well with him. His "medicine" is good, that is, the Good God is in the ascendant for him that day. Another man don't feel very well, things go wrong, he misses a good shot at a deer, or his sweetheart shows him the cold shoulder. His "medicine" is bad, that is, the Bad God has him in his power for the time.

Everything supposed lucky or healthful, or indicative in any way of the presence and supremacy of the Good God is "good medicine," everything the reverse is "bad medicine."

Being, like all primitive people, extremely superstitious, there is scarcely anything that does not indicate the presence and pleasure of one or the other of the gods. The flight of a bird through the air, the course of a snake in the grass, the yelping of a fox, or the manner in which his pony carries his tail or cocks his ears, each and all have to the Indian a spiritual significance and meaning. Differing in this from the early Romans and some other primitive nations, he requires no augur, but can himself interpret all signs, at least to his own satisfaction. A party starting out on a dangerous foray will watch carefully every sign, and should something occur unusually ominous, it will return to camp to repeat the attempt under more favorable auspices.

For a more intimate knowledge of the immediate future, the Indian depends upon a process of making "medicine," general in its entirety, but varying in its details, according to the peculiar ideas and superstition, of each individual.

Earth or sands of different colors, ashes of certain plants, or of particular bones or portions of birds, animals, or reptiles, and other ingredients, varying with the special superstition of each individual Indian, are mixed together in a shallow dish or pan kept for that sole purpose, and gently stirred with a stick. From the combination of colors, or some other peculiarity developed by the process, the Indian believes he can infallibly divine which god is to him in the ascendant at the time.

Should the "medicine" be good, a small quantity is put up in tiny bags of dressed deer-skin and tied in the hair of the warrior, in the tail of his war-horse, and on the necks of his women and children. Should any be left over it is carefully burned in the lodge fire. Should the process develope "bad medicine," the mixture is carried outside the camp and carefully buried in the ground, no one touching it.

There is no necessary similarity either in the results attained by different individuals, or in the conclusions deduced from them. Each Indian has been taught by his father, or nearest old warrior relative, the general principles involved in making "medicine," and the general rules for determining its good and bad qualities.

At least one ingredient in the "medicine" of each Indian must be special to himself and a secret from all the world beside. On his initiation as warrior he has gone off alone to some solitary mountain or secluded thicket, spending many long and anxious hours in deep religious meditation of the question, the most momentous of his life, "What shall that ingredient be?" When hunger and thirst have exhausted his vital powers, he falls into a trance, during which the important secret is revealed to him. Thenceforward he is not only man and warrior, but priest for himself and family (if he has one), makes his own "medicine," and by oft-repeated experiment becomes as expert in reading the secret involved in the combination as were the augurs of Rome.

According to the best authorities and to tradition, it was the custom thirty or forty years ago for an Indian to select the special ingredient of his "medicine" but once in his life, sticking to and believing in it through all subsequent years of good or ill fortune. This is changed at the, present time, and an Indian who has an unusually Jong or severe turn of bad luck, attributes his misfortune to the failure of his "medicine," and going off alone will starve himself into a trance in the hope of having a new and more efficacious ingredient revealed to him.

The special and secret ingredient used by each Indian in his "medicine" is kept in a little pouch always on his person, and always carefully concealed even from his wives or most intimate friends.

This secret ingredient of each warrior's "medicine" must not be confounded with his "totem." The "medicine" is a purely religious matter, a secret between himself and his gods. The totem is not in any sense religious. It is the "coat-of-arms" of the individual, carried about with him on all occasions of ceremony or display, to be shown, examined, admired, handled. The two are frequently confounded even by persons who ought to know better.

No Indian will commence anything, or undertake a hunt or trivial journey of a few days, without first making "medicine." If "good," he goes away happy and sure of success, unless bad omens should subsequently disconcert and turn him back. If "bad," he remains at home. In spring, summer, and autumn, when the Indian life is active, every head of a lodge will make pp medicine" probably at least once a week.

The power of earnestness is well exemplified in the influence that the Indian religion obtains over the white trappers and "squaw-men" who live with them. Nine-tenths are sooner or later converted to the Indian idea, and many of them have firm faith in their power of making pp medicine."

The Indians believe in the existence of spirits, invisible beings, in no way connected with either of the gods. These spirits are neither good nor bad, and can do no serious injury to man, but delight in mischief. They live in rocks, mountains, woods, and deserts. It is the elf of our forefathers.

Whatever of love or reverence may be in the Indian nature is bestowed on the Good God; and in speaking of the Great Spirit, it is to this god that they allude. Of his friendship and assistance to the extent of his ability they are always assured.

Of the Bad God they stand in most abject fear, and are constantly devising expedients by which they hope to evade or turn aside some portion of his wrathful power. They rarely speak of him; never, if it be possible to avoid it, mention his name.

Those most pious, or timid, put severe and oft-times ridiculous penances on themselves. One man will never allow some certain meat or game to be cooked for food, another will allow no loaded gun in his lodge, nor permit any man to enter it with a pistol on his person. One will always sit down in a certain way, or facing in a certain direction; another will always spit over his left shoulder, or take things given to him with his left hand. There is scarcely a warrior above the middle age who has not some peculiarity special and self-imposed by way of propitiation of the Evil One.

They believe that the Bad God may be sometimes bribed into an act of favor; and in the extremity of danger will vow, if permitted to escape, to consecrate a pony to his service.

These vows are faithfully and publicly carried out, and the pony consecrated becomes thenceforward a sacred animal, no extremity of need ever inducing any Indian of the band either to mount or strike him with a whip. I have seen several of these sacred ponies, and can aver that the Indian drives a shrewd bargain with the devil, the pony consecrated being invariably the most worthless old bag of bones in the whole herd.

Voudouism and Fetichism, being simply forms of belief in magic or idolatry, are discarded as forms of religion; and accepting Polytheism as the starting point of religious belief, the Indians, for so utterly savage a race, have made very remarkable progress in their religious tenets.

I do not think that they are dependent on contact with Christianity for any portion of their belief. They have worked out for themselves a theology, which, if supplemented by a code of morals, might have produced good results.

There is a curious point of resemblance between the beliefs of the wild Indian and the Christian. Both believe in two great beings. The former believes' in a God and a Devil, equals in power and wisdom. Christians believe in an Omnipotent and All-merciful God, but are so inconsistent as to believe in a Devil, who, over human conduct and human souls, has ten times as much power as the Good God.

It is this one point of similarity that makes the conversion of the Indian to Christianity so extremely difficult. He cannot possibly be made to understand how the All-good God, if also all-powerful, can permit the All-bad God to do so much evil, and win so many souls. Might being always right with the Indian, he takes immediate issue on this paradox, and cannot be made to believe what is so entirely inconsistent with his established ideas.

Indians are great sticklers for form and lovers of ceremony, consequently the only Christian denomination that has made any perceptible progress in their nominal conversion is the Homan Catholic. I say nominal advisedly; for while I have known many Indians who professed Christianity, I have never yet met one who in his conversion had really quitted his ancient faith. He is a Christian just so far as it is expedient or useful to him.

Three years ago, when Spotted Tail was using all his fine intellect, his tact, his social and official influence, to prevent his people from joining Sitting Bull, a conference was one day held, at which were assembled a few whites and a large number of Indians—Sioux.

The principal white man present was an officer of the army, only a captain (for higher rank presumes either special good fortune or a life-time of service), but who, in knowledge of Indians and success in their management, is second to no man on the frontier. His Indian name is Black Beard.

Captain George Morton Randall, (1841–1918) 23d United States Infantry and Civil War veteran.—Ed. 2015

After satisfactorily settling the questions of policy which had arisen, the conference closed, and its members engaged in familiar conversation.

Spotted Tail turned to the captain and said:

"Black Beard, I have a serious question to ask you about religion. Can you answer it?"

"I am not very good authority on religious matters," replied Black Beard, "and I don't know whether I can answer it or not. But put your question, and I will give you my honest opinion."

"Well," said Spotted Tail, "I am bothered what to believe. Some years ago a good man, as I think, came to us. He talked me out of all my old faith; and after a while, thinking that he must know more of these matters than an ignorant Indian, I joined his church, and became a Methodist. After a while he went away; another man came and talked, and I became a Baptist; then another came and talked, and I became a Presbyterian. Now another one has come, and wants me to be an Episcopalian. What do you think of it?"

"I was brought up an Episcopalian," said Black Beard, "but I can't give you any advice in the matter. I think that religion must be a matter of conscience, and that sect has little to do with it."

"That," said Spotted Tail, "is just what I am beginning to think. All these people tell different stories, and each wants me to believe that his special way is the only way to be good and save my soul. I have about made up my mind that either they all lie, or that they don't know any more about it than I did at first. I have always believed in the Great Spirit, and worshipped him in my own way. These people don't seem to want to change my belief in the Great Spirit, but to change my way of talking to him. White men have education and books, and ought to know exactly what to do, but hardly any two of them agree on what should be done."

The Plains tribes are extremely poor in tradition of any kind, and have no general belief as to the origin of Creation. To the inquiry, "Who made the world?" the reply is usually a fixed stare and a doubtful shake of the head, as if the question were a new one.

Occasionally I have been answered: "The white man says his God made it, and I guess it is so. I don't know who else could have done it."

I once talked with a grave and dignified Indian of such great age that he was no longer able to number his years. My questions were answered in a way which quite delighted me, and I began to believe I had found a treasure of Indian theological erudition. I finally asked him—

"Who made the world?"

"The Great Spirit," answered he, promptly. "Which Great Spirit," I continued, "the Good God or the Bad God?"

"Oh, neither of them" answered he; "the Great Spirit that made the world is dead long ago. He could not possibly have lived as long as this."

The Indian loves and venerates the Good God, not only as the direct author of all the good that comes to his life, but as his sole refuge and defence against the malevolent power of the Bad God. He speaks of him reverently as the Great Spirit, and feels and acts towards him as an affectionate son towards a tender father, whose devotion and loving kindness are assured, and who requires neither prayers nor thanks.

His feelings and actions towards the Bad God are just the reverse. Him, he hates and fears, bribes and coaxes, prays and entreats. He subjects himself to horrible tortures, and imposes on himself the most rigid and unheard of penances, all for the placation of the Bad God, whose name he never voluntarily mentions.

The Christian prayer, "Good Lord, deliver me," is paraphrased by the Indian—"Please, Bad God, let me escape." He knows that the Good God would "deliver" him if he could, without the asking; he knows that the Bad God is in the ascendancy, or he would not be in extremity; so his appeal and prayer is to that power in whose hands he finds himself, and whose intent must be quickly changed, or he is surely lost.

However crude, the Indian religion is not illogical.

As, in making medicine, each man follows a general rule, with variations and modifications supposed to be suited to his particular case, so the ideas of religion herein expressed must be regarded as those general to all persons of the tribes.

Each individual Indian (priest and interpreter between himself and his God), while believing the general principles, adds his own peculiar shades and modifications, so that no two Indians, even of the same tribe, can be found whose religious beliefs are exactly the same. To get at these modulated shades of belief would require the personal interviewing of each individual warrior, and even that process would be attended with little success, as they are chary of conversation on the subject, except among intimate friends or familiar acquaintances in whom they have confidence.

Unlike their civilized sisters, the women have little to do with religious matters. They believe in the Good and Bad Gods, and have firm faith in the medicine men, but all minor details are left to the warrior-head of the lodge. What he tells them to believe, they believe; what he directs them to do, is done.

The beliefs set forth in this chapter constitute the highest form of religion worked out #for themselves by the aboriginal inhabitants of America.

Through the influence of missionaries a few individuals may have come to believe in a God ruling both this and the future life, and occasionally a man may be found who claims to have so far overcome the great stumbling-block to Indian proselytism, as to believe that the Good God is more powerful than the Bad.

These cases are, however, not only exceedingly rare, but a few pertinent questions will show that the "faith in them" is assumed, and without any foundation in conviction. I have never yet seen a so-called Christian Indian who did not, in times of real trouble or affliction, go back to his ancient faith.

From this spiritual and comparatively exalted form of religious belief there are infinite shades of downward gradation through all the forms of necromancy, divination, conjuration—through the man-tearing wretches of the Pacific coast, down to the hazy, undefined superstition of the lowest Digger.

It is a curious fact, difficult to account for, that no tribe of North American Indians is addicted to "Fetichism" in any of its forms. Though each tribe of Plains Indians has its "tribal medicine," and each individual Indian his special and secret medicine, these material objects are not worshipped. They are merely the "outward and visible signs," embodying a spiritual or superstitious significance, or symbolizing, in some mysterious way, the objects of their reverence and fear.

The term "Digger" was applied by the early settlers of California to a miserable class of Indians of the lowest type, who subsist on snakes, lizards, grasshoppers, and such edible roots as they can "dig" from the ground with short pointed sticks, always carried in the hand ready for use. They are of several different tribes, Utes, Shoshones, etc.

POWER AND INFLUENCE

FROM the lowest form of Fetichism to the Church of Christ, there has been no religion without its priests.

The faint glimmer of a spark of religious sentiment is no sooner awakened in the breast of the savage, than there immediately appears one "clothed with authority" to tell him all about it. Priestcraft has been in all ages the strongest of earthly powers, and man is so constituted that it will probably remain so until "time shall be no more."

In the preceding chapter I have described the religious belief of the Indian, and gone with him through the ordinary routine of his private devotions. But though each warrior head of a lodge is the priest for himself and family, there is in each tribe a "Medicine Chief," whose word, in spiritual affairs, is all-powerful. He is necessarily a man of strongly marked character, with brains, dignity, and knowledge of men. He is not necessarily a chief by birth, nor even the head of a band, though his position as Medicine Chief always gives him a following.

His sacerdotal dignity brings no immunity from the dangers of war. On the contrary, the fighting force of the tribe never takes the field without his presence. In battle, his are the most reckless dashes on the enemy, for, to prove to his flock the efficacy of his medicine, he must show the perfect safety it affords him even in the midst of the greatest dangers. He claims to have power to overcome the devices of the Bad God, and his standing amongst his people depends on the ease and certainty with which he makes his claim good r

The reduction of the power of the head chief and the subsequent breaking up of the tribe into small bands has reduced the temporal standing of the medicine chief, and may have had some little effect towards diminishing his priestly authority; but the religious sentiment is so strongly implanted in the Indian nature, that he must always be the man of his tribe most worthy of consideration.

Formerly he relied upon his influence with the head chief for prompt punishment of any contempt or violation of his orders. Now their respect and obedience depend on the estimation in which he is held by his people, and on their religious training and enthusiasm.

The Indian has no Sabbath or Sunday; no regular time is set apart for the ordinary duties of religion. The Nez Perces, and one or two other small fragments of tribes, observe Sunday as a church day, and have a form of worship, corrupted from that taught them by Roman Catholic priests long years ago; but among the Plains Indians the priest is not expected at ordinary times to hold any meeting for worship, or to perform any ceremonies.

He has one or more wives, a fine herd of ponies, for he is always rich, and lives as do the other Indians. He has no social intercourse with the commons of the tribe, never entering (unless in sickness) any lodge except that of the chief or head men, and permitting no inferior warrior to enter his lodge, except on business. He maintains a grave and dignified demeanor, suited to his sacerdotal office and functions. He is a great favorite with the women of the tribe, all of whom have free access to his lodge, and to them he owes something of his power over the husbands. He is the recipient of constant offerings, nothing specially nice being cooked in any lodge that the women do not bring him a share of it.

Besides being the chief priest, he is also the physician of the tribe. This requires no special knowledge of the healing art, for as all disease is only a manifestation of the presence of the Bad God, if "He" can be exorcised by the spiritual power of the priest, the patient will get well at once.

Almost all Indians have some rude knowledge of herbs and simples in the treatment of wounds, so that the medicine chief is only called in sickness, and in extreme cases. He is paid only in case the patient recovers, a rule which it might be well to adopt in civilized life.

The exorcism of the evil one is accomplished by incantation.

In each tribe and band there are more or less old women who do the howling in all cases of sickness, and who stand only a little lower than the priest in power over the Bad God. These are immediately sent for in any alarming illness, and whether the patient is dying of consumption, or suffering from an acute attack of cholera morbus, the treatment is the same. Howls, only howls, most doleful and lugubrious. As the patient gets worse, the women of the lodge "lift up their voices" and howl in chorus; then the women of other lodges come around and join the howl, until the whole camp is a pandemonium of howls. If all this does no good, the medicine chief is sent for. He mutters incantations, performs some mysterious ceremonies, and finally putting a tom-tom into the hands of a lusty young acolyte, has it beaten with all force immediately over the head of the patient. This treatment generally very promptly .finishes the matter one way or the other.

The Indians have an idea that strangers, particularly white strangers, are ofttimes accompanied by evil spirits. Of these they have great dread, as creating and delighting in mischief. One of the duties of the medicine chief is to exorcise these spirits. I have sometimes ridden into or through a camp where I was unknown or unexpected, to be confronted by a tall, half-naked savage, standing in the middle of the circle of lodges, and yelling in a sing-song, nasal tone, a string of unintelligible words.

At the first sound of his cry, the women and children huddle into their lodges, and in a moment no evidence of life can be seen, except the lank figure of the priest, the black, beady eyes of the occupants of the lodges, as they watch the new-comers through the partially closed doors, and the half-famished curs that sniff and yelp around.

The position or office of medicine chief is not hereditary (though there are a few instances where a father and son have held it), and is not conferred by chief or council. A man gains it by general, and not unfrequently, tacit consent of the people of the tribe.

The constant thought of every Indian man or woman is, "How shall I evade or counteract the power of the Bad God?"

The medicine chief is dead; the tribe in mourning. A warrior comes forward who says, "I have found the proper 'medicine.' I set at naught the power of the Bad God."

In time of war every opportunity is given him to prove his assertion. Every risk that a man can run he has to take. Time and again he must put himself in the "imminent deadly breach," and his "hair-breadth 'scapes" must be so numerous and so marvellous as to be accounted for in no other way than that his medicine is perfect. That point once conceded beyond doubt or cavil, and his character and standing being satisfactory, he glides into the coveted position by general acquiescence.

When the native honors and dignity of hereditary chief are united with the acquired honor, military renown and spiritual power of the medicine chief, the result is an individual most dangerous, most potent for good or bad. Such an one was Black Hawk, and such an one is Sitting Bull. Other than the last named (of whose personal history little is known) the medicine chief most renowned of late years for his power over the Bad God was the Cheyenne, Medicine Arrow (Min-vitz-in-nan-epivomanist).

His father was medicine chief before him. Early in life the young man had gained such renown for his wonderful daring and marvellous escapes from apparently certain death, that when the father died he had no competitor for the vacant place.

He ascribed his wonderful immunity from wounds and sickness to his discovery of the secret of making an arrow so potent in its charm against the "evil one," that no warrior who carried one could ever be hurt in any way.

Fortune favored him, and in the later years of his life, he found a ready sale in the spring, at a pony each, for all the arrows he could make during the winter. The fame of his arrows extended to all the tribes of the Plains; Sioux, Northern Cheyennes, Pawnees, all became his customers, and contended for the privilege of buying one of the life-preserving arrows.

More than any Indian on this continent since Black Hawk, he had the power to have united tribes, hostile to each other, in one grand crusade against the whites.

Fortunately for them, and for the Indians, he was a confirmed drunkard. The ponies gained so easily in spring and summer, were drunk up in autumn and winter. He would give a pony for a gallon, or if specially thirsty, even for a bottle of whiskey. On those terms he, of course, always got what he wanted.

He died on Tongue River in 1874, retaining to the end (in spite of his drunkenness) more repute for spiritual power, and more influence over the Plains tribes, than any Indian before or since.

A vacancy in the office of medicine chief is not necessarily or even usually filled at once.

The Indian sets much store by his life, and a position reached and retained only by most reckless exposure to an endless series of dangers, has attractions for few except the most ambitious, or those who really believe in themselves or their powers.

I have already spoken of the earnest effort made by each individual warrior to discover the proper secret ingredient of his medicine. Should the Indian have a "run of bad luck," he accounts for it at once; his special ingredient is not good. He therefore tries some other, and keeps trying until his luck changes, when he has, of course, found the proper thing at last. The Indian is in solid earnest, and childish as all this appears to us, he has firm faith in himself and his medicine. The medicine that has enabled a warrior to pass unscathed through all the dangers of the road to the position of medicine chief must be perfect, and the faith in it of its fortunate possessor is supreme.

The medicine chief is not an impostor or hypocrite. In 1868 when Forsyth's little band,* buried in their rifle pits, were holding at bay an overwhelming force of red-skins, a Cheyenne medicine man, ambitious to be medicine chief, and firmly believing in the efficacy of his medicine, dashed alone almost into the lines of the whites. His medicine failed him at the critical moment, for he was shot and killed.

*The Battle of Beecher Island, also known as the Battle of Arikaree Fork, was in September 1868. A force led by Major George Alexander Forsyth of the 9th Cavalry, a Civil War veteran, moved out of Fort Wallace and engaged Cheyennes led by Roman Nose. The soldiers were forced to defend themselves on a small sandbar in the Arickaree River for *nearly a week. Four were killed and many more wounded, including Forsyth. Roman Nose was killed.*

Any specially remarkable and long continued run of good luck is attributed at once to the medicine of the fortunate warrior. Others begin to look upon him as a medicine man, and not to be outdone in faith, he firmly believes it himself. These men drop into the practice of medicine, and become healers of the sick by the same gradual process, already described, and under the influence of the same belief in the efficiency of their medicine.

Recollect," good medicine" does not argue any special preference of the Good God (who is already as good and kind to all Indians as he can be); it shows power over the Bad God—or devil.

All disease is simply the manifestation of the presence and power of the devil.

An unfortunate Indian is stretched upon a bed of sickness, tortured with fever, or racked with rheumatism. The devil has him in his power. What more natural than to send for the warrior of the tribe, whose medicine is known to be the most efficacious charm against the power of the evil one?

And just here is where the hypocrisy and deceit come in. While he may really believe in the power of his medicine, he has sufficient knowledge of human nature to be aware that its effect on the patient depends somewhat on the mental condition of the latter. Like the civilized doctor who gives a bread pill when medicine is not really necessary, or like the French surgeon, who cut off the leg of a dying man "to amuse him," the ordinary Indian doctor resorts to every humbuggery that he can invent.

Socially and pecuniarily the office of medicine man is a good one, and when from lack of success with his patients, he has lost faith in the power of his own medicine, he carefully hides the knowledge in his own heart, and keeps up appearances by increase of noise and mystery, and redoubled activity in "blowing" about his powers, advertising himself.

The power of faith can be no more strongly exemplified in any race or sect than is manifested among these ignorant people.

The Nez Perces are a superior race of Indians, and their Chief, Joseph, a man of courage, intelligence, quick perception, and other qualities sufficient to make him much above the average man, either white or red.

When Joseph and his band were held as prisoners of war at Fort Leavenworth, his favorite child, about a year old, was seriously ill. Though he and his band claimed to be Roman Catholics, and though they had the attendance of white physicians, as able as the country affords, when the latter pronounced the case critical, their services were dispensed with, and the medicine chief (who is also priest of the tribe) was called in. All night long a tom-tom was beaten immediately over the head of the poor baby; this music accompanied by the sing-song incantations of the priest and the mournful howls of half a dozen old women. Joseph's good judgment was demonstrated, whatever we may think of his humanity. The child got well.

The medicine chief of the Plains tribes is an essentially different person from the medicine men of the Pacific coast, or those most commonly described by writers on the North American Indian. He does not descend to the tearing and eating of human flesh, or other horrible practices designed to strike terror into the beholders. He ignores posturing dances, or conjuring tricks, and rarely has recourse even to excess of absurdity in dress. His influence is a moral one, founded on belief in himself and knowledge of human nature, and his means are (with a difference) very similar to those practised by civilized doctors and ministers. He gives no drugs, but he beats his tomtom; he makes no prayers, but sings his incantation.

He is the outgrowth, the expounder and interpreter of that higher order of religion of which I have given account.

But by far the largest portion of the Indians are not on that higher plane of religious belief. Just as our ignorant communities select or accept the spiritual ministrations of some self-sufficient donkey, as ignorant, but more brazen than themselves, so most of the Indians put their faith in someone of the number of pretenders who eagerly thrust themselves forward.

From the highest to the lowest, human nature is the same. Be he civilized or be he savage, man delights in being humbugged, and any pretender to mysteries, either medical or spiritual, is sure to find someone to believe him.

In the Indian tribes can be found all grades of medicine men, from the chief, with the firmest faith in himself and his medicine, to the lowest conjuror, without character or standing as a warrior, and who relies, like the fortune-teller of civilized life, on hocus-pocus, and his skilful execution of a few stale tricks of legerdemain. All these quacks, both white and red, make a living, or they would not follow the trade.

AN INDIAN MYSTERY

THOUGH, with all his love and reverence for the Good God, the Indian gives Him no prayers, praise or thanks, he yet worships Him after a manner of his own.

There are no days or stated times set apart for this duty as with us. It is a purely voluntary act, and so far as I can understand, very much like the witty definition of gratitude, "a lively sense of favors to come;" and a sort of cozenage to procure information. At intervals more or less prolonged, once a month, or once in six months, the chief will call such a meeting. It is a conclave, no person being permitted to be present except the chief, the medicine man, and the old or most trusted warriors of the band.

A short time ago a young officer of my post went to call on a chief of the Cheyennes, encamped near us, and, as is customary and proper, entered the tepee without knock or signal. To his astonishment he found a ceremony in progress. Somewhat disconcerted he asked the chief if he must withdraw, and received permission to "stay a little while." In that "little while" he made the best possible use of his eyes, and reports as follows:

Everything of furniture, bedding, cooking-utensils, &c., had been removed from the lodge, which had evidently also undergone a thorough cleaning. Around the circumference of the lodge, in a solemn circle, sat the old men and warriors. In the centre two forked sticks had been planted in the ground, about six feet apart, and from a pole, laid across, was suspended an iron pot, filled with meat, rice, &c., &c. Under the pot was a fire, and at the base of each of the forks was another smaller fire. From one fork to the other, on the side furthest from the door of the lodge, was a wide semi-circle of buffalo chips, which had been plentifully sprinkled with powdered charcoal. Inside this semi-circle was a rectangle of about twenty by thirty inches of fine white sand, divided into two equal rectangles by a strip of black charcoal, two inches wide. In one of these rectangles was the figure of a horse in black, in the other a similar figure in red. Between the outer side of the rectangles and the inner side of the semi-circle of buffalo chips, was another small fire.

The ceremonies, which had been suspended on the entrance of the lieutenant, were now continued. The medicine man took from a pouch a small quantity of dried leaves and sprinkled a pinch on each fire, causing a pungent, aromatic odor, stronger than incense.

The medicine pipe was then filled and lighted by the medicine man, who, holding it in both hands, and pointing it now up, now down, ejected puff after puff upward, downward, laterally, over the fires, over the pot, over the images of horses, and in every direction, as if to envelop everything within its potent influence.

The chief then took the pipe and went through a similar performance. He then informed the lieutenant that they were worshipping the Good God, and trying to find out from him whether they were going to have plenty of ponies this year—and so dismissed him. This is the only instance within my knowledge of a white man's being permitted to have even a peep at these sacred mysteries.

The interpreter of this post (Cantonment, Indian Territory), a white man married to a Cheyenne woman, tells me that they hold these meetings ax irregular intervals. He has never attended one, only a special few even of the Indians themselves being permitted to be present.

The points of resemblance between this and some ceremonies of the Jews, Greeks, Romans, indeed, of almost all comparatively primitive nations, are worthy of note. The burnt-offering in the cooked food, the fires, the images of the things wished for, the incense, all indicate a common and curious instinct of man.

How the divine intention is expressed to the Indian I am unable to ascertain. In my description of individual medicine-making I have indicated the mode of divination, and the method in this case is presumably much the same.

Smoking is always a ceremony.

The pipe among the Indians seems to be a somewhat universal symbol, nothing of importance being done without it. Every council, conference, religious ceremony, gambling bout, dance, or ordinary talk, is opened with a smoke, but though excessively, even passionately, fond of smoking, I have never yet seen an Indian smoke a pipe alone, as a white man does.

If presented with a cigar, he will, if possible, hide it away until he retires to his own tepee, when it will be crumbled up, and mixed with the tobacco in his pouch. When forced by etiquette to smoke it at once, his efforts in that direction must remind every smoker of his own first boyish attempts. The strong and rapid pulls customary to the Indian when smoking a pipe, soon gets the cigar almost ablaze, and then ensues a conflict, satiety and nausea on the one side, avarice on the other. Avarice always wins, the Indian, though it may be with tears in his eyes, smoking as long as possible, then hiding the short stump for future use.

Possibly habituated to it by the circular form of the lodge, or more probably for greater convenience for general conversation, Indians, even out of doors, habitually arrange themselves in a circle when disposed to have a talk. One will then take out a pipe, fill and light it, take a few strong puffs, pass it to the man on his left, who, after his few puffs, passes it to the man on his left, and so around the whole circle. When the last man has had his smoke the pipe is returned to the starter, not as is natural, by handing it direct to him (for the last man and the first are, probably, sitting side by side), but it must be passed from hand to hand from the left to the right, around the whole circle, before it can again be started on its course of usefulness. No Indian would think of putting his mouth to a pipe that came to him from the left.

Nor does the Indian smoke like an American. After a few strong pulls, to get the pipe well started, and of which the smoke is naturally ejected, he takes several long sucks, carrying the smoke into his lungs. When his whole system seems saturated with smoke, he passes the pipe, and for a minute or more lets the smoke issue lazily from his mouth and nose.

This form is always observed, and when hunting, or even on the war-path, when one wants to smoke, all will dismount, seat themselves in a circle, and go through the regular form.

For different occasions or ceremonies they have different pipes. Thus they have a peace pipe, a council pipe, a medicine pipe, and a pipe for common use. Each is sacred to its own purpose, and while no Indian would regale himself with an ordinary smoke out of a peace or council pipe, no power on earth would force him to such sacrilege with the medicine pipe.

In former times it was regarded as a great breach of decorum, so near an insult as to require explanation, for any man in the circle to fail to take his turn at the pipe. Within the last few years, however, they have met so many white men who either did not smoke, or who declined to put his mouth to a stem common to so many and such filthy mouths, that they now take no notice of it, though they do not like it.

Some of these tribes use the pipe for the selection of a man for a special or dangerous service, "casting lots." The pipe is filled, lighted, and passed from hand to hand with a certain regularity. The man in whose hands it goes out is the person indicated by the medicine for the service.

In all my large experience with numbers of tribes of Indians I have never yet seen a squaw smoke. She is never permitted to take active part in any religious ceremony, and the most ordinary smoke is so intimately connected with the mysteries of medicine that she cannot indulge in it.

It is asserted by squaw men, and others in position to know, that almost every tribe of Indians has its secret societies, which have pass-words, grips, and signs as the Masons, Odd-Fellows, etc. I have never been able positively to ascertain the truth or falsity of this statement. Most of the Indians deny it, but from the grim silence that falls upon an occasional old head-man, when asked about it, I suspect it may be true.

Several of the wild tribes have a mysterious material something, which they regard as the Jews did the "Ark of the Covenant."

The Plains Indians are in no sense idol worshippers, and this "something," is not worshipped, but loved, venerated, and held in sacred awe.

The "thing" is not God, but it is the means by which God manifests himself to his people. It is the seat and abiding-place of the Good God. It is the centre around which all important religious ceremonies are enacted. Over it or through it, the Bad God can have no power. From it radiate streams of beneficent influence. In camp it is always held in the careful charge of the head chief. It is carried in war, on all important expeditions, by the medicine chief.

In camp on good days, it is suspended, wrapped in its covering of par-fleche, and carefully concealed from inquisitive eyes, before the door of the chief, where all devout Indians can see the complicated wrappings, and adore the mystery it represents.

The "thing" itself varies in each tribe, and there is no general or comprehensive term by which it is known to all. I have heretofore stated that each individual warrior has for use in his private devotions, or in making his medicine, one or more ingredients unknown to any but himself. The efficacy of his medicine depends on his keeping inviolate his own secret. These unknown ingredients, the special and particular medicine of the individual, are always carried in a little bag on his person, and are buried with him.

The "tribal medicine is only an extension of the idea. As far as possible each tribe does all in its power to keep to itself the secret of its medicine. With some of the tribes, as the Arapahos, the "thing" itself is a secret, and as the obligation of an oath (administered according to their forms) is absolutely sacred with Indians, it is likely to remain a secret until accident or its capture in war shall disclose it. With other tribes, as the Cheyennes, the "thing" is known. The secret in this case is in the forms and ceremonies with which the "thing" is constructed. The secret is still a secret for all purposes of efficacious medicine.

What the tribal medicine of the Cheyennes was fifty years ago, I have no positive knowledge, though I have reason to believe that it was a simple bundle of sage-brush; but after "Medicine Arrow" had electrified the tribe by his wonderful daring and immunity from danger, the "thing" was changed, and thenceforward was, and is at the present time, a bundle of "medicine arrows," made after a style invented, and with ceremonies inaugurated by that great chief. A few of the old men most noted for wisdom and piety were initiated by "Medicine Arrow" into a secret society of which he was founder and chief. This society met in a lodge erected outside of the camp. It was surrounded at a considerable distance by a chain of trusty sentinels. During these meetings the women and children of the camp were required to keep within their lodges, and maintain the most profound silence. The horses were sent far out of hearing, even the dogs were tied up and kept quiet. Not a sound must disturb the awful solemnities. With ceremonies which all were solemnly sworn never to divulge, the arrows were made. They were then tied tightly in a bundle, wrapped in skins, and deposited in a "par-fleche,"—a small trunk made of stiff raw-hide everyone knows what is in the "par-fleche," but no man, other than those present at their making, must ever look upon them.

This bundle of arrows is the medicine of the tribe. It is the visible manifestation of the invisible God. Through and by means of it the favors and protection of God are bestowed upon the people. After some great disaster of war or sickness, another meeting is called, and the arrows renewed with the same ceremonies, but no amount of suffering or terrible disaster could convince a Cheyenne that that bundle is not the source from which emanates to him all Divine beneficence.

Some years ago a band of Pawnees pounced upon a camp of Cheyennes, in which was the precious bundle. In the "*sauve qui peut*" which followed, the "medicine arrows" were abandoned and captured. The tribe was in consternation and mourning. "Medicine Arrow" was then alive and at the summit of his power and influence. , He could easily have made another bundle, but he persuaded his people that unless that special bundle was recovered, all the favor of God would thenceforward be transferred to their enemies. Runners were dispatched to the Pawnees, and, after long haggling, the Holy Bundle was redeemed, at the price of three hundred ponies. These were furnished by voluntary contribution, some families almost impoverishing themselves, again to secure to their tribe the favor of God.

The arrows sold by "Medicine Arrow" in the latter years of his life, to secure the means for a continual drunk, were not, of course, those made and consecrated with the ceremonies spoken of. They were made by himself in his half sober moments, and his sale of them as "medicine arrows" was a pious fraud.

What constitutes the medicine of the Arapahos is known to no man except the initiated few. The "par-fleche" in which it is kept is paraded on all occasions of ceremony. It is hung up, where all may see the elaborately painted outside, but to touch or look into it would be a sacrilege worthy of immediate death.

The medicine of the Utes was a little squat stone figure, of Aztec or Toltec origin, and which the Utes probably obtained from the Navahos or Apaches. There is a story among the Arapahos that a few years ago a small war party of that tribe penetrated some distance into the Ute country, and surprised and plundered a camp, capturing this stone figure. They retreated with all possible expedition, but were so closely pursued by an overwhelming force of Utes, that they had to disperse to hide their trail. Most of them escaped, but some were killed, among them the warrior who had the medicine, but the Utes did not recover it. The presumption is that when so closely pressed in the mountains that he had to abandon his horse, he hid or buried his treasure, for no one has ever heard of it since. The Utes are said to attribute all their troubles of late years to the loss of their medicine, and the finder of it now would be quite as fortunate as the average finder of a gold mine, for the Utes would impoverish themselves to get it back. The Osage medicine is said to be a similar stone figure, smaller than that of the Utes, and showing no marks of chisel. Indian rumor says that Sitting Bull has recently given a new medicine to the Sioux, but no one knows what it is.

THE GREAT MEDICINE DANCE

THE Cheyenne word, Hôch-é-a-yum, is a generic term, applying exactly as the word church in English. It means, not only the structure itself, but the ceremonies performed in it, and the meeting of the bands or people. The literal meaning of the word, in the Cheyenne language, is the "lodge made of cotton-wood poles." This distinguishes it from the ordinary habitation of the Indian, made of skins or cloth. Every Indian of a tribe may attend the "Hôch-é-a-yum," but the special actors who take part in the ceremonies are "Hôch-é-a-tan"—that is," the people who make the medicine in the lodge of cotton-wood poles."

The lodge itself is a large structure, constructed, as the name indicates, of cotton-wood forks and poles, and capable of holding several hundred people. The sides are more or less open, and the top is covered with skins, or boughs of trees, sufficient to keep out the rays of the sun, but scarcely affording any protection against rain. The meeting itself is exactly analogous to the great camp-meetings, so common in various parts of our country.

Of late years, many and remarkable changes have taken place in the Hôch-é-a-yum; in the power which calls it together; in the character of the actors; in the nature of the ceremonies; in the amount of suffering involved and in the results expected to be attained.

As the simplest method of explaining these changes, I give a description of the medicine dance, as practised to within a very few years, by all the Plains tribes, but now carried out, strictly and in its entirety, by only a very few of those wilder tribes, scarcely yet brought fully under the power of the United States. A circular space of some twenty feet in diameter is roped off for the dancers. A concentric space of a few feet is for the guard; all the outer portion of the lodge is for the spectators.

In accordance with his right and duty, the medicine chief now announces his selection of the warriors who are to make the dance.

The number varies, but is, on an average, one for every hundred persons in the bands represented.

The head chief also announces his selection of the guard, whose duty is to see that the dancers are in no way interfered with, and that they perform their duty in accordance with the instructions of the medicine chief. The number of guards is about equal to that of the dancers. The announcement of the names of dancers and guards, and of the hour when the dance is to commence, is made in a loud voice from the door of the medicine lodge. Each and all named are warned that disgrace and death will be the portion of any warrior who fails to appear at the time appointed.

A few moments before the specified time, the guard, fully armed and under its appointed captain, files into the lodge and takes its place just outside the ropes of the inner circle. At the appointed instant, the dancers are escorted by the medicine chief to the inner circle. Each is stripped to the breech clout (sometimes entirely naked), and holds in his mouth a small whistle of wood or bone, in the lower end of which is fastened a single tail feather of the medicine bird.

The medicine chief arranges the dancers in a circle facing to the centre, whilst he himself, having got out of the way, gives the signal to commence. At once every dancer fixes his eye on the suspended image, blows shrilly and continuously on his whistle, and begins the monotonous and graceless Indian dance, the whole line of dancers moving slowly round the circle. Some of the young ones, carried away by religious enthusiasm, bound vigorously into the air; but the older and more experienced expend only a bare sufficiency of force, for this is a dance of endurance. The will of the gods is to be known by the effect of the dance on the dancers, and, until the high priest shall announce himself satisfied, the dancers must continue their weary round, without sleep, food, drink, or obedience to any demand of nature.

For the first eight or ten hours the dance is uninteresting enough, but by that time fatigue, the slow rotary motion, the constant keeping the eyes on one spot, and the expenditure of breath in unceasing whistling, begin to tell. By this time every foot of space inside the lodge is crowded with eager and intensely interested spectators. Relatives and friends watch every movement of the dancers, rouse up the flagging by yells and shouts, by words of encouragement or terms of endearment. The lodge is a frightful babble of sounds, which culminate in shrieks and a rush of women, as some dancer totters, reels, and falls to the ground. The rush is sternly met, and the body dragged by the guard out of the circle of the dancers, and into that of the guards. There it is laid on its back, and the high priest proceeds to paint symbols and hieroglyphics on the face and person, with "medicine paint" of varied colors. If consciousness is not restored by this treatment, the body is taken into the open air and buckets of water thrown over it. This, as a rule, soon revives the inanimate form, at sight of which, the women set up yells of delight, and surround the priest with prayers and entreaties that this dancer may be spared further effort.

Throughout all the ceremony the word of the medicine chief is law, which no power may question. He may now order the revived dancer back to the circle, to dance until he again falls, or he may excuse him. Influenced by the women, or by the promise of one, two, or half a dozen ponies (according to the wealth of the dancer), the priest generally accedes to the request, and the overcome dancer is carried off to his lodge by his women, to be petted and condoled with until fully recovered.

In the meantime the dance goes on. One by one, the dancers fall, to be revived by the same process, and excused by the same persuasion, or sternly ordered back to their work. As the death of a dancer is indicative of "bad medicine," this forcing one back, after falling, is only done in rare and important cases, or when the priest has an object to gain.

If the dance progresses to the end of the appointed time without a resulting death, the priest proclaims "good medicine." The dance ceases, the dancers are feted and caressed, and the medicine lodge is taken down. Happiness and congratulation are expressed in every face. The chiefs and warriors, assured of the power and protection of the Good God, meet in council to decide upon the programme for the year, which after "good medicine," is generally war.

But it may happen that one or more bodies are brought from the dance which neither paint nor water will revive. There is no need to announce "bad medicine," for no sooner is death assured than the whole camp becomes a pandemonium. The howls of the men mingle with the shrieks and wails of the women. The dance is broken up. Horses are killed for the use of the dead in the Happy Hunting Grounds. Their widows inflict ghastly wounds on their arms and breasts. The whole camp is a turmoil of consternation and mourning. As soon as the last rites for the dead are completed, the bands separate, and each in its own way seeks to escape or avert the wrath of the Bad God.

Such was the medicine dance in its rigor. The peculiarities of the dance itself are yet the same, but the power has departed from the medicine chief, until he is scarcely more than master of ceremonies. He can still call the people together, but he has no longer the selection of the dancers. No more can he kill off one or more men when he wants "bad medicine," nor secure ponies and peltries for being lenient when he wants "good medicine."

Any warrior can now hold a "medicine lodge," either as an extra effort of piety, or in fulfilment of a vow. The last held by the Cheyennes was given by one of the warriors, Hog, who was so long confined in jail at Dodge City, under charges of murder and rapine committed on citizens of Kansas in 1878, and who, while in prison, made a vow to give a Hôch-é-a-yum, if aided to extricate himself from his then impending danger.

This grand ceremony involves considerable expense, and is therefore not often given by a private individual. It is generally the result of a call of the medicine chief, or of a combination of warriors who wish to signalize their endurance and piety, to expiate an offence, or perform an act of propitiation. It is sometimes gotten up by the young bucks (both married and single) as a means of bringing the bands together, and thus increasing and widening their opportunities for love-making.

We will suppose the call determined upon. Runners are sent to the bands and families scattered far and wide. As there is now no compulsion of dancers, the summons is a welcome one to all, a frolic on which all expect amusement, excitement, and religious enthusiasm.

A good spot has been selected, with plenty of "wood, water and grass," and at the appointed time crowds pour in from every direction. All is hustle and excitement, camps are pitched, friends long separated met and rejoiced over. The women go to work on the medicine lodge.

When it is completed, a solemn council of all the elders is called to deliberate on the forms to be observed. This is a most serious question, and generally occupies about three days. No women or uninitiated warriors are permitted to enter the lodge during the council. When all has been decided upon, the time of the opening of the dance is officially announced by criers, and all warriors invited to enlist as dancers.

It will be noticed that what but a few years ago was compulsory, and performed under the supervision of the medicine chief and a regularly detailed guard, is now a purely voluntary act. The dancers are actuated to volunteer by every conceivable human motive; some by vanity, to display their vigor and endurance; some by religious enthusiasm; some by love, hoping to render themselves more pleasing in the eyes of their loved ones; some in despair, clinging to this as the last sole chance of melting some obdurate female heart. One dances because he has sickness in his family, which he hopes to eradicate by an act pleasing to God; another because his wife has no children; another as a propitiation or an atonement for some crime. The large majority of the young men enter the dance because it is the "thing to do," in other words, fashionable. If they did not, they would be regarded as lacking either in the manly qualities necessary in a warrior, or in piety, possibly in both. The consequence is that nearly all the unmarried men of the tribe, and numbers of the younger married men, say at least half of the fighting force there present, will go into the dance.

At the appointed hour the dancers appear. Each has his whistle ornamented with the tail-feather of the "medicine bird," for which, as the bird is now rare, extravagant prices are sometimes paid. The dress of the dancers varies with the tribe. The Arapahos and Sioux have only the breech-clout, and are sometimes absolutely "*in puris naturalibus.*" The Cheyennes, more modest, wear during the day time a shawl or kirtle, extending from the waist to below the knee, at night the breech-clout alone.

Under the supervision of the medicine chief the dance commences. Religious observances fix its duration at four days, but general custom warrants a suspension at any hour of the fourth day. Even with this indulgence the wonderful powers of endurance of the Indians are fully displayed. Think of even seventy-five hours without sleep, food, drink, or obedience to any demand of nature; of seventy-five hours of unremitting motion; of seventy-five hours' expenditure of breath in a constant, monotonous whistle.

I have already stated that in this present age of Indian enlightenment the dance is purely a voluntary act. There is, therefore, no absolute obligation for any warrior to "stick it out" to the bitter end. This is fully realized by the dancers, and after about twenty-four hours they begin to fall out.

As, however, the estimation in which a man is held in his tribe depends to some extent on the endurance and pluck displayed by him, each is stimulated to do his best, and those that hold out longest are the best men.

This, however, depends somewhat on the motive of the man in making the dance. If that motive is personal to himself, he can cease dancing whenever he thinks he has done enough, either as propitiation or atonement. If he goes into the dance from purely religious impulses, he is expected to stick to the end. Of a hundred men who start together in the dance, fifty will have given up on the expiration of the first thirty hours, another twenty or twenty-five will collapse before forty-eight hours have expired, and thus they gradually fall out, until the expiration of the dance will find present and at work but ten or fifteen of the original starters.

Usually, however, there are many more at the outcome. There is a spiritual recognition and reward to those who are on duty at the moment when the medicine chief declares the dance at an end, even though they began at the "eleventh hour." Some of the shrewder and more calculating manage to come in for these special benefits, by being "moved by the Spirit" to join the dance, on the second, or even the third day.

In the old times, when the dancers were selected by the medicine chief, and the dance conducted "en rigueur," to the limit of life, no warrior was required to make the dance a second time. Now the same men make it year after year, and though all may come out of the trial more or less exhausted, it is extremely rare that any fatal result attends these marvellous exertions.

The whole character of the medicine dance has changed. "Good medicine," the indication of the ascendancy of the Good God, or "bad medicine," of the Bad God, does not now depend on the accident of life or death to one or more of the dancers, but is indicated by the general condition of the dancers when the ceremony is 'over, by the greater or less harmony of the bands or cliques, by the amount of religious fervor and enthusiasm displayed, and even by the state of the weather. If everything works smoothly and well, and it be fair and calm, the Good God is present and pleased. If there be jars and dissensions, if the rain deluges the dancers, or the wind knocks the "Hôch-é-a-yum" about their ears, the Bad God is around, and not in a good humor.

Note.—The medicine dance is not a worship or devotion; it is an act of divination; a means of ascertaining the relative position of the two Gods towards the tribe. An image representing both Gods (one side being painted white, the other black), is hung up in the centre of the lodge above the dancers.

ENDURANCE AND DEFIANCE OF PAIN

AFTER the dance has ended, and many times when it is yet in progress, the tortures take place.

A few years ago, every aspirant for the position and honor of warrior in the Plains tribes, was obliged to go through an ordeal as brutal and bloody as can well be imagined. That too has gone in the rapid progress of change. The boy of sixteen to twenty years, panting for his promotion to the position of warrior, is no longer obliged to bare his breast to the knife, to be tied up by broad bands of his own flesh, and to fight out alone his battle of pain and suffering. In not one single Plains tribe is the ordeal at present a condition of manhood, or entrance to the brotherhood of warriors.

But though no longer necessary, it by no means follows that the torture is discontinued. The history of mankind shows that the "spirit that makes martyrs" is in inverse proportion to the civilization of a people. Religious faith (or what we call superstition when applied to any religion but the one we happen to believe in) is strongest in the uneducated. The faith of the savage is perfect, for it is unbiased and untrammelled by any doubt that reason might interpose.

The very loftiest virtue of the American Indian is endurance. When religious superstition and the highest social virtue of a people combine in a given direction, or towards anyone action, it may be regarded as sure that that act will be performed.

The Indian believes, with many Christians, that self-torture is an act most acceptable to God, and the extent of pleasure that he can give his God is exactly measured by the amount of suffering that he can bear without flinching. There are, therefore, always some warriors who are actuated to the self-torture of the "Hôch-é-a-yum," by motives as pure and sentiments as holy as ever led a Christian martyr to the stake. Others are actuated by pride or ambition; they wish to signalize to the whole tribe their possession in an eminent degree of the chief of manly virtues, or to lay a foundation for future preferment by an act at once holy and popular.

At every medicine dance there are more or less volunteers for the torture. Occasionally there is a man of middle age, but they are generally from the younger men of the tribe, youth being the season when passion of every kind has most energy. These men do not as a rule join the dance, but spend a few days immediately preceding the ordeal in fasting and silent meditation.

When the medicine chief and old men decide that the time has come for this part of the ceremony, the volunteers are sent for one by one. Each comes into the lodge in breech-clout alone. His person and condition are examined by the managers, who coolly discuss in his presence the particular kind and amount of torture he can bear without fatal consequences.

After some religious ceremonies, the medicine chief passes a broad-bladed knife through the pectoral muscles so as to make two vertical incisions about two inches from each other, and from three to four inches long, in each breast. The portion of the flesh between the incisions is then lifted from the bone, and the ends of horsehair ropes of some three-fourths of an inch in diameter passed through the opening, and tied to wooden toggles. The free ends of the ropes are then fastened to the top of one of the supports of the lodge, so as to give the sufferer some ten feet play. Here he remains without food or water, until his own vigorous efforts, or the softening of the tissues, enable him to tear out the incised muscles and escape from his bondage.

Sometimes the incisions are made in the muscles of the shoulder-blade or of the back, and to the ropes are attached movable objects, preferably the skulls of buffaloes. Sometimes the devotee is dragged up by the ropes until six or eight feet from the ground, and left suspended until his weight and struggles tear out the flesh.

A broad-bladed knife is passed through the muscles of the breast and the flesh is lifted from the bone. Horsehair ropes are then passed through the openings and tied to the lodge-pole. Here the candidates remain without food or water, until by their own efforts they free themselves by tearing out the flesh. It is "good medicine" to tear loose at once: "bad medicine" to be several days about it,

Each devotee makes the most strenuous efforts to free himself. He understands that it is best to tear loose as soon as possible, not only physically as a quicker ending of his torture, but also from a religious point of view. It is "good medicine" to tear loose at once, "bad medicine" to be several days about it.

As soon as freed, he is examined by the medicine chief and old men. If all is right, he is congratulated, other religious ceremonies gone through with; his wounds are washed and dressed with herbs, rudely, but with such skill that in a few weeks they are entirely healed. Singular as it may appear, an instance of fatal result, even in the hottest weather, has never come to my knowledge. Should the devotee flinch under the knife or cry out, or show other evidence of weakness during his subsequent sufferings, he is released at once, and sent off a disgraced man. Formerly he was condemned as a woman, and made to do women's work. He could neither marry nor hold property. These consequences are no longer entailed, his only punishment now being the contempt of the warriors of the tribe.

From mortification, as would seem to be the natural, almost inevitable result of such laceration of the tissues. Immediately on being released from the tortures, the devotees, hot and exhausted as they are, frequently plunge into the river. The shock is often fatal. In March, of 1879, two Cheyenne warriors, who had just undergone the torture, died from this cause.

In former times no white man, except those allied to the tribe by marriage with squaws, was permitted to be present at this ceremony. Now, all is open everyone is welcome, and a white man of rank or distinction is received among the managers and given the best place to see everything.

The ceremonies here described are common, under different names, to most of the Plains tribes. Among the Sioux it is called "the Sun Dance," and celebrated with exceptional pomp and circumstance.

But it is not alone at the Hôch-é-a-yum that these terrible self-tortures are inflicted. Sometimes a warrior who has committed some deed which he thinks requires expiation, will give notice that on such a day, at such a place, he will go through the torture. A stout but pliant pole is planted in the ground. The incisions are made, the ropes inserted, and the toggles secured. The top of the pole is then bent and the rope fastened to it. This is .probably the most exasperating form of the torture. In the Hôch-é-a-yum, the rope being fastened to rigid uprights, the victim can exert all his force to tear loose. In this case, the pole, yielding to his every effort, still retains its ghastly hold, and it sometimes happens that the victim is several days freeing himself.

BURIAL OF THE DEAD

THERE is nothing in which the Plains Indian varies so much as in the respect paid to the dead, in the care and management of the body, and in the greater or less elaboration of the funeral services. This variation is not in the customs of the different tribes, but is due almost entirely to circumstances. During the long enforced inaction of the winter camp, which the Indian must get through, as best he can, in gambling and sleep, the death of some prominent person is almost a matter of rejoicing. It breaks in upon the monotony of the daily routine of life in a delightful way, bringing both excitement and occupation, which from the commencement of the elaborate preparations to the final ceremony, may last for quite a month. All may indulge in the luxury of grief. All may assist in preparing the corpse, and in arranging its last resting-place. The cold weather preserves the body from decomposition, thus enabling relatives and friends to devote what time they wish to celebrate the character and exploits of the warrior while living, and to mourn for his departure.

The death of the same person in summer would cause some general excitement, and possibly a few days might be given to the obsequies; but should he unfortunately die during the fall hunt, or while on some important expedition, the body would most likely be thrust into the first convenient hole in rock or prairie, not only without ceremony, but without feeling or mourning except from his immediate relatives.

Those of the northern Plains tribes, who live in somewhat permanent villages, usually place their dead on scaffolds. A site for a cemetery is selected convenient to the village, yet sufficiently removed to escape the effluvia constantly arising from the dead bodies. Some of these sites are very picturesque.

While the women of all the Plains tribes are specially given to excessive demonstrations of grief in mourning, and frequently visit the graves to give free vent to their sorrow, these tribes yet differ in their beliefs as to the length of the journey to the Happy Hunting Grounds, and as to what is proper and necessary to the dead during its performance. Some believe that the soul is fully two months on the road, through a space devoid of every necessity to its comfort or even to its existence. Every day, therefore, during all that time, food and water are brought and placed upon, or hung around, the scaffold. Other tribes believe that the final journey is made in one, two, or more days, and the necessary provision is deposited with the body at the time of burial.

It is curious to note the influence of the habits of a tribe on these beliefs, the dead of the more permanent tribes making a much longer journey than those of the more nomadic.

The favorite burial-place of the more wandering of the Plains Indians is a tree. From the care taken in its selection, and the more or less elaborate construction of what may be termed the burial case, a very fair estimate may be formed of the rank and standing of the dead.

We will suppose the Indians in their winter encampment. A chief, or promising son of a chief, is to be buried. The country for miles around the camp will be scouted over, and several eligible burial sites selected, the relative merits of which form a subject of discussion, worthy the consideration and determination of the general council. The position is finally determined upon. It must be a sound, strong tree, well sheltered, and apparently safe from any chance of being uprooted by the terrific windstorms of the Plains. The branches must be so situated that the final resting-place will be nearly horizontal. It must not be so near any favorite Indian camping-place that the inhabitants might be annoyed by disagreeable effluvia from the decomposing remains. It must not be near any military post, or any road or line of travel of white men. This last is an important condition, for of late years the

Indians have had ample cause to complain of the desecration of the last homes of their dead, by the bone-picking proclivities of white doctors, or the more ruthless and less excusable plunder by white hunters, travellers, or cattle men.

Poles are cut for the construction of a platform, and the whole is firmly bound together and to the branches by thongs of raw hide. It is from six to ten feet long, and from three to five feet wide. Upon it are spread rushes, grass, or the leaves and small boughs of trees, and over these is laid one or more buffalo robes. On this bed the corpse is disposed, sometimes in a sitting posture, but generally lying on the back in a natural position.

The body is dressed in the most gorgeous apparel obtainable; for the spirit will appear so dressed in the Happy Hunting Grounds, and as good a first impression as possible is greatly desirable.

Such articles of civilized manufacture owned by the dead in life, or furnished by the generosity or piety of friends, as are considered necessary to his comfort or his appearance in the future world, are buried with him.

Around his neck is suspended the medicine bag, containing the bones, ashes, earths, etc., used in his private devotions, and by his side, or fastened to his lance or rifle, is his "totem" skin. At his girdle (or on his lance, or shield among the more southern Plains Indians), are hung all the scalps he has taken in life. His face is painted in the most splendid style of Indian art.

All being completed, light but strong branches are attached to the sides of the platform, and bent over the body like the bows of a wagon. The enclosure for a body buried in a horizontal position is not over two feet high; over these are stretched buffalo hides (green if they can be obtained), with the hair out, and securely fastened to the platform and to the boughs with thongs of raw hide. Every aperture is closed as tightly as possible. Such necessary articles as pots, kettles, etc., as might be in the way inside, are securely fastened to the platform or the neighboring branches; and over all are hung streamers of red and white cloth to frighten away any animals or birds which might venture to disturb the remains. Such a tomb in the dry climate of the Plains will last for several years.

The bodies of common warriors, or sons of warriors—and occasionally of the favorite wife of a chief—who die while the tribe is in its winter encampment are deposited in 'trees, but with less elaborate care and ceremony.

Ten years ago, I saw on the Purgatory River in Southeastern Colorado, seven graves in one tree. Every vestige has long since disappeared, and the tree now shades a comfortable farmhouse.

The body of a chief who dies in other than the winter season is generally deposited in a cave; that of a common warrior in any convenient hole or ravine, a few handfuls of earth, or sometimes only grass or leaves, being thrown over them. "Women and female children of the common people are thrust out of sight in the most convenient way, without ceremony or special manifestation of grief. Scalped warriors are never buried.

The country in the vicinity of the Cimarron River, south of Fort Dodge, is almost exclusively a gypsum formation. Instead of wearing channels on the surface of the ground and forming ravines, the rains have penetrated the soil, dissolved the gypsum and formed for watercourses long, intricate tunnels and caverns innumerable. These are favorite burying-places. During a visit to this locality with a party of soldiers, a cave, elaborately walled up, was discovered and broken into by some of the men of my command, and a great quantity of useful and curious articles, trinkets, and Indian finery taken from it. I was little disposed to scold them for the desecration when they brought me a string of at least a dozen white scalps, some of infants, and one of long, fair, and most beautiful silky hair, which had undoubtedly adorned the head of some woman sufficiently cultured to appreciate and take excellent care of the lovely ornament.

Even chiefs are not always buried with religious care and attention. Once, on a scout, I came upon an Indian encampment very recently abandoned, and which, from the dead horses, broken arms, cut-up lodges and signs of blood, I at first supposed had been harried by a hostile band. A more critical examination soon convinced me that these were only evidences of the death of some prominent man. I found where a heavy body had been dragged over the ground. Following this trail for about two hundred yards, I came to a small mound of dry leaves. Pushing them aside, I was astonished to recognize the body of the war chief of the Comanches, a man greatly loved and feared by his tribe. He was dressed in a uniform coat, his head was adorned with a hat and feather, his face was painted; his gun and equipment, complete, were beside him, and in his hand he held a box of matches. A closer examination disclosed the fact that one end of a rope had been tied around his ankles, the other evidently attached to the pommel of a saddle, and the body, thus dragged naked from camp, was afterwards dressed for the grave. All the skin was torn from the back, sides and loins, and the body otherwise greatly mutilated by this rough treatment. It was not until some months after that I learned that this chief had died of delirium tremens. The tribe had gone into all the usual mourning ecstasies and had given him a good outfit for the Happy Hunting Grounds, but had shown its appreciation of the mode of his death by treating his body with indignity.

In many portions of the Plains—even where sufficient wood may be found to tempt the Indian to make his winter encampment—the trees are too small to serve the purpose of a burying-place. Four light poles are set in the ground and the platform constructed on their tops, sometimes but six or eight feet from the ground, scarcely beyond the reach of the hungry wolves which soon collect about it. The Indians near the agencies now frequently use the boxes in which stores are sent to them, and the inscription, which at a little distance looks like an elaborate epitaph, may turn out, on closer inspection, to be "Best Soap or "Star Crackers."

The platform on poles, though frequently used, has never been a favorite way of burying with the southern Plains Indians. It is too easily overthrown. The buffalo in the old, and the cattle in the present time, equally disregarding the feelings of the surviving friends, make short work of such a grave by rubbing against it.

Since the collection on reservations and near agencies of large bodies of Indians of different tribes, burial in trees is becoming less common. His religious superstition will prevent an Indian from desecrating the grave of one of his own tribe, but he has no such scruple in regard to the graves of another tribe. The exposed grave of a chief, or warrior of means, presumably containing many valuable articles, is so great a temptation to Indians of other tribes, and to the worthless whites who surround the agencies, that almost all tribes have recently taken to regular burial in the ground.

Apropos to this, a story is told (for which I do not vouch) of a recent occurrence at the Cheyenne and Arapahoe Agency. An Indian died of some disease, or in some way, professionally interesting to the doctors. An autopsy was determined upon. As in their belief, the cut and mutilated body would transmit to the Happy Hunting Grounds a spectre cut and mutilated in the same way, it would have been the height of absurdity to ask the friends of the body for permission to open it. It was determined to steal it from the grave at night. Unfortunately for the "body-snatchers," they had forgotten that the female mourners have a habit of going to the grave at any hour of the day or night, for a consolatory howl. The body had been uncovered, and two persons were in the grave in the act of lifting it out, when they were astounded by the wail of half a dozen women who had silently surrounded them. Dropping the body, they leaped from the grave, and scurried away in the darkness. The women, terrified at this supernatural apparition, set up a truly feminine scream, and darting back to camp, soon brought the whole body of Indians to the scene of action, when the mystery was explained. The "snatchers" were never discovered, and as the Indians are said now to keep watch over their new-made graves, no further attempts in that direction are reported.

The Sioux seem to attach some special importance to green as a funeral color. I have never seen a Sioux Indian use in life a green blanket, but in all the Sioux graves examined by me, the remains were found wrapped in blankets of that color. The Cheyennes and Arapahos seem to have no special color.

Among the Ute Indians, the death-bed scenes, the preparatory and funeral services, and the place and mode of burial, are even to this day profound secrets to all but themselves. It would be extremely dangerous for a white man to be in a Ute camp when any resident of it died, for the death would at once be attributed to the malign influence of the white, and his life would probably be the penalty.

Within two miles of my camp, on the Uncompagre River, in June, 1880, I discovered a Ute camp in which a death had undoubtedly occurred.

The lodge covering was cut to useless shreds, the poles broken, the bedding (buffalo robes, now exceedingly valuable to the Indian) cut up and thrown away, and the ground all round littered with clothing, bridles, blankets, cooking utensils, tin-ware, every article so torn to pieces, or cut with knife or hatchet as to be entirely worthless. They had even cut down trees across the ground, to prevent its again being used for a camp, and from these trees, which were bare of leaves but with the buds considerably swollen, judged the death to have occurred in April.

Mr. Berry, the Indian Agent at Los Piños, informs me that he has never himself witnessed, nor has he ever seen a white man who had witnessed, the funeral ceremonies of the Utes, nor has he ever seen a Ute grave, or any white man who had seen one.

A very acute and observing officer of the army tells me that he has seen a Ute grave which was discovered by accident. When on a scout, someone of the command noticed human bones, scattered at the foot and along the face of a declivity so abrupt as to be almost inaccessible. Following upwards with great difficulty, they came to where a small excavation had been made horizontally into the almost perpendicular face of the hill. This excavation had been carefully lined with a wall of stones cemented together with adobe mud, and the whole inside had been thickly plastered with the same material. The body had been placed within, the opening walled up, plastered thickly on the outside with mud, and dry earth thrown over the whole so as completely to conceal it. It was only when the face of the hill was washed away by heavy rains that the burial-place was disclosed.

The Utes will not talk about their dead or their graves, differing in this from all other Indians of whom I know anything. The whites in the best position to learn of these things tell me that, after the body is dressed for burial, it is taken away from camp by a party, and buried in such a place and mode as I have described. After the burial is completed the footprints of the party are carefully erased, the place and everything connected with the burial remaining a profound secret from all but the immediate actors in the scene. There are said to be two graves of Ute Indians in the cemetery at the Los Piños Agency, but they are of Indians connected with the agency, and were buried under white auspices.

I have in my possession the skull of a young Ute Indian which was found at the base of a steep, sharp hill. I doubt not that the grave is somewhere in the face of that hill, but it is safe from mortal eyes, the hill being now utterly inaccessible on that side.

A few days after the above was written, Ouray, the head chief of the Utes, started from his house, near which I was encamped, across the country, to meet the Indian Commissioners at the Southern Ute Agency. Soon after a runner came for the agency doctor; Ouray was very sick. In a week we heard he was dead. He was chief of the ten or twelve bands of Colorado Utes, commonly known as the confederated Utes; a man of great strength of character, power, and influence.

Having been several times to Washington, he had adopted, as far as was possible with his surroundings, the habits of white men. He lived in a house comfortably furnished, used a large easy-chair, took his meals at a table supplied with proper table furniture, and when visited by a guest whom he wished to honor, he brought out wine and cigars.

For some years he had been in receipt of a salary of one thousand dollars a year from the United States Government, and he died probably the richest Indian in America. He died away from home at the agency of the Southern Utes, and they took charge of the body, and buried it after the Ute custom.

An officer who was present writes me the following account: "The Indians took sole charge of him during his sickness, not permitting the whites to have anything to do with him. There were three white doctors present, but the Indian medicine man held his pow-wows so continuously that his white rivals could only occasionally get into the tent. All they were able to do was to diagnose the case (it was Bright's disease), and satisfy themselves that they could have done no good even had they been permitted to act. The funeral was conducted as that of any other (Ute) Indian, no ceremony, no pomp. When life was extinct, they wrapped the body in a blanket, threw it across a horse, and accompanied by a few Uncompagre Utes, it was in that way conveyed to the place of burial. The agent, some of the commissioners, officers, other whites, and Mariano, a Mexican, who for four years past has lived in the most intimate relationship to Ouray (his private secretary), wanted to show their respect by going to the funeral, but they were ordered back by the Indians. No one whatever was permitted to accompany the burial party, and no one knew, nor could find out, the place of burial, until the question of the removal of the remains to the Uncompagre was agitated. The Uncompagre Indians were very anxious that this should be done, and the Southern Utes making no objection, some of the burial party, two weeks after the burial, took some of the commissioners and officers to the spot. They found the body deposited in a natural cave, the entrance to which had been walled up with rocks. The body was found to be in such a state that the effort at removal was abandoned. There was no stone or mark to indicate the grave, nothing, except at a little distance the putrefying carcasses of five horses that had been killed near the grave, for his service in the Happy Hunting Grounds.

HOW INDIAN'S FEEL AND SHOW THEIR GRIEF

THE mourning of the Indian is an active passion. It is not displayed in—

> "inky cloaks,
> Nor customary suits of solemn black,
> Nor windy suspiration of forced breath,
> No, nor the fruitful river in the eye."

"These indeed, seem;" but the mourning of the Indian "is."

The mourning of a chief over a beloved son is sublime in its severe simplicity. Literally in "sackcloth and ashes" he prostrates himself before his gods. He has not the verbosity of Job, nor the sounding phrases of the Jews in their lamentations. It is not "Rachel weeping for her children," but a man on whom God has set a mark of heavy displeasure. He mourns not only the taking off the being dearest to his heart, and more to him than life itself, but that in some way he has fallen under the direct displeasure of God.

If the son was killed in battle and not scalped, there is nothing to mourn for on his account. He has gone direct, in all his youth and vigor, to enjoy an eternity of youthful pleasure. The blow of the All-Powerful which killed the son was really aimed at the father.

To his parental and personal anguish is added the haunting superstitious dread of still further persecution by the Bad God, and laxity of intervention on the part of the Good God.

His medicine is wrong!

The tortures that rack his heart and torment his brain are not displayed in words. Stripped of all clothing save his breech-clout, he lies for days prone on the dirt of his lodge floor, or squatted alone in a corner. His hair, of which ordinarily he is so careful and proud, has been hacked off with a knife, and stands about his head, neglected, disordered, and filled with earth. His eyes are tearless, his visage firm and solemn, as if about to be led to the tortures of the stake. His person is neglected. He is a mass of filth and dirt.

After from three weeks to three months, according to the character of the mourner, he is induced by the importunities of his friends to wash and dress himself, after which he approaches gradually to his normal condition.

His mourning for a favorite daughter may be attended with similar self-abnegation and personal neglect, but its duration is more limited.

His mourning for his wife, the mother of the son or daughter so bewailed, is entirely a different matter. It is weakness to display anything like sentiment in the marital relation.

Passion is manly, sentiment is puerile. The dead wife may receive the honor and distinction of a tree-burial, but the bereaved husband recognizes in his loss no special displeasure of God, and, therefore, mourns with a "mitigated grief."

Even though very savage the Indian is very human. He may deeply feel his loss, but fashion debars him from evincing that feeling. Besides this there are other wives in the lodge, and too excessive mourning for the dead might foster unpleasant jealousies among the living.

Mourning is regulated somewhat with reference to rank. The common warrior may have as ardent sympathies and as devoted affection as the chief, but it would be an unwarranted assumption, almost an impertinence, to permit his grief to manifest itself to the same extent. Consequently his mourning, though of the same kind and quality, is less abject, and much more limited in duration.

The mourning of the women is something fearful. In all ages and climes the blessed sex have arrogated to themselves the right of exaggeration in all matters of sentiment or affection. In savage life the woman's opportunities for display in all these feelings of which she claims to be the richest possessor and best judge, are very greatly restricted. She makes up for it, to the best of her ability, by a supernatural extravagance on every occasion when custom gives her the right of action.

A chief has three, four, or more wives. They are really only slaves. He treats them in public as servants, and gives his orders with a considerate deference, such as any civilized gentleman might bestow on a favorite servant, to whom forgetfulness and disobedience are impossible. Whatever may be their private feelings, whatever of sentiment or dalliance may exist in their personal relations, their external bearing and conduct are such as only evidence the relation of master and maid.

The chief dies. The quiet rivalry of attention to his wants heretofore only displayed by them, gives place to a furious rivalry in demonstrations of grief All howl continuously and in unison; but lest the more strongly-lunged should obtain advantage in this exercise, they continue the rivalry in such acts of self-abasement and self-torture as are almost incredible. The hair is hacked off; the clothing torn from the person; ghastly, horrible, and even dangerous wounds are inflicted; their breasts are slashed open; their arms and legs slit and cut with knives; their faces and persons disfigured; and covered with blood, and dirt, and filth, they croon, and wail, and howl until nature is exhausted. It is only wonderful that death does not more frequently ensue from these self-inflicted tortures, for the women appear to be perfect maniacs for the time, and cut and slash themselves without regard to consequences.

The mutilations and disfigurements are performed over and in presence of the dead body. Its burial puts an end to these, but the mourning continues for any unlimited time thereafter. When the civilized woman would relieve her feelings by a "good cry," her savage sister enjoys a good howl. At any time of the day or night some of the bereaved widows may feel in the humor for a special wail. Its first sound calls up the others, who are not to be outdone, and all proceeding to the grave howl in chorus until tired of the recreation. Women are sympathetic. The friends of the widows show their sympathy, by joining in the howl. All are supposed to mourn the demise of a chief, and any woman of the band or tribe who may feel somewhat lugubrious, or disposed to have a little private enjoyment, may proceed to the grave and let off her superfluous unhappiness in any amount of howling.

I have elsewhere spoken of the "luxury of grief." The term is strictly correct when applied to the grief of an Indian woman. She has always in store a large amount of lamentation; and, however long the person lamented may have been dead, whether a relative, or only a friend, she rarely comes within reach of a grave without raising a howl, which is sure to start the howl of others equally sympathetic.

The death of a son is mourned by the mother with similar, but less extensive, manifestations of grief. She may cut her breasts or arms, but they are far from being the reckless, half-crazy slashes of the bereaved widow. Once in a while, one or more of the other wives may feel a grief sufficiently poignant to require a little personal blood-letting. This, however, is only in the case of a son of a chief, which may be regarded as a national calamity. The right of every woman to bewail the death of any member of the tribe is conceded, but the prerogatives of relationship are held very sacred. Cutting one's self is a manifestation of grief only permitted to the closest relationship, or where the calamity is tribal.

The death of a daughter is the hardest blow to an Indian woman. As will be seen further on, the daughter is the only person in the tribe to whom she can look for full sympathy and companionship, yet she cannot signalize her sorrow in accordance with her savage ideas of fitness. Though her mother-heart may be broken with the loss, she cannot manifest her grief by personal injury and disfigurement. She can only mourn.

Whatever may be the private feelings of the parents, there is no special manifestation of grief for the death of a very young child; indeed it is generally believed that the father sometimes kills those that are sickly or idiotic. I have known but few deformed or idiotic Indians, and they are almost invariably the children of widows.

Some writers have stated that warriors mourning for sons or for a chief frequently mutilate themselves by cutting off one or more fingers. The number of men who have lost fingers is extremely small for a people so prone to war. In every case where I have noticed such loss and asked the cause, I have found that it was either a bullet, or some accident common to those who manage wild and vicious horses.

The Cheyennes and Arapahos laugh at the idea of self-inflicted mutilation by a warrior. He may cut his hair, or kill a horse, but cutting their own flesh is the prerogative of women. Whatever it may have been in the past, no such custom exists among the Plains tribes at present.

The Utes carry their mourning ecstasies to great length. Not content with killing one or more horses to bear the shade on its journey to the Happy Hunting Grounds, they destroy everything of which the dead dies possessed. When, therefore, a Ute feels that he is about to die, the relatives and friends are sent for and formal distribution made of all his property. The tepee is given to one wife, bedding to another, horses to wives, children, or friends, in short a formal will is made, and the property handed over then and there. Women also make their wills, dividing out their dresses, trinkets, etc. Everything, no matter how valuable or how worthless, not given away before death, is ruthlessly destroyed.

Ouray died away from home and without making a will. Ouray was "wise in his generation," and very rich. When it was positively known in the tribe that Ouray was dead, nearly every Indian of the Uncompagre band collected at his house and made preparations for the destruction of all his property. In great alarm Chipita, his widow, sent for Mr. Berry, the Indian Agent. He arrived just in time. Using all his influence and eloquence, and working with them all day, he succeeded in obtaining a promise from a large majority that no harm should be done to Chipita or the property. Leaving some seventy Indians on guard about the premises he returned to the agency.

But the malcontents had very strong grounds to work on, and when Mr. Berry had gone they renewed their arguments, protesting against this violation of their ancient and honored customs, and predicting the dire punishment of God. Custom and superstition so far prevailed that after wrangling half the night, the followers of the "white man's road" were glad to effect a compromise, turning over to the others seventeen horses for sacrifice.

Ouray's house is built on a bluff bank, some thirty feet high, overlooking the bed of the Uncompagre River. Directly under a perpendicular part of this bank the Indians piled an immense quantity of dry driftwood. The seventeen horses were led one by one to the edge of this bank, killed, and their bodies tumbled on to the pile of wood. "When all had been killed the pyre was fired, and the spirits of the horses sent to join their master. These, with the five killed at the grave, will give him a comfortable start in his new life.

THE HAPPY HUNTING GROUNDS

NO religion has been able to give a satisfactory idea of heaven. It is not, therefore, a matter of wonder that the Indian's idea of the future life in the Happy Hunting Grounds is as vague, confused, indefinite, and inconsistent as is possible to conceive. He believes he will be happy, perfectly happy, but of the how, why or wherefore, he not only knows nothing, but evidently doubts his belief to such extent that a few pertinent questions will throw him off his balance, and send him all agog.

He accepts what the medicine chief and old men tell him as a faith, something to be taken without inquiry or discussion; pin him down to his belief and his reasons for it, and he becomes "dumb as an oyster."

The medicine chief flouts discussion. The thing is so because he says it is so. To doubt is sacrilege, and the doubter little better than one of the wicked." If beaten out of his reasons for belief, he takes refuge in the belief itself. Faith is the foundation of every religious edifice. Believe open-eyed or blindly, with reason or without reason, but believe.

The Indian creed is a wide one, for all persons, of all ages, sexes, colors, or beliefs, who die unscalped or unstrangled, will meet in that final "haven of bliss." He goes there just as he was here, with the same passions, feelings, wishes and needs. His favorite pony is killed at his burying-place, to enjoy an eternity of beautiful pasture and to bear his master in war or in the chase.

He will need arms to defend himself against enemies (man or beast); his rifle, pistol, bow and quiver are buried with him. He will need fire; so flint and steel, or a box of matches, go towards the outfit for his final journey.

There is no death in that life; but wounds and pain, hunger and thirst, love, revenge, ambition, all the passions, or incentives to action, are there. The Indian knows no happiness in this life, except in the gratification of his natural appetites. His future life will develop greater capacity and wider opportunity for the enjoyment of those appetites.

How an unhappy disposition here can be happy there, he does not try to explain. He has no conception of, or belief in, any special divinity presiding over the future state; consequently he cannot conceive of a special miracle in each case fitted to the necessity of the beneficiary.

He will meet enemies, whom, however, he strives to make few in that world, by scalping as many as possible in this. He will encounter dangerous beasts; for the spirits or phantoms of all animals, reptiles, birds, insects, and fishes, go also to the Happy Hunting Grounds. In short, the next world is to be an intensified continuation of this, death alone overcome.

The conception of the abolition of death in the future state seems to be attended with a doubt or modification. He expects to kill and eat all the game he wishes; to clothe himself with the skins of animals; to fight with, and even take the scalps of, his enemies; but what becomes of the phantoms of animals, or the spirits of scalped ghosts of men, is a problem which he wisely leaves for future solution.

Prom what has been said it will be truly inferred that not only animals, but inanimate nature is represented in the future state. All things which the Indian can make for himself in this life he can make in the next; consequently there is no need to take that class of things along with him. He can there procure skins for his clothing and for his lodge, robes for his bed, etc. But articles beyond his skill in manufacture, gun, powder, lead, caps, knife, blankets, and an iron pot for cooking, must all be carried into the next world by the dead man, who is, moreover, buried in shirt, pants, and coat of civilized manufacture, or as many of these articles as the owner possessed during life.

The Indian understands perfectly well that the dead does not actually take with him into the next world the material articles buried with him in this, for some of them' are hung around the burial place exposed to view. He believes, however, that if the articles are allowed to remain with or near the body until the soul reaches its paradise, the spirit of the dead man will have in the next world the use of the phantasms of those articles.

The most touching trait of Indian character is the universal desire that the dead shall enter the Happy Hunting Grounds with as complete an outfit as possible. Any article supposed necessary in the future state, which the dead man did not possess in life, is at once supplied by relatives or friends, often at considerable sacrifice.

Whatever the absolute needs of an Indian life, there is no known instance of his despoiling, to satisfy them, the grave or burial-place of another Indian of his own tribe. He will go hungry from lack of means to kill game, though he knows a dozen trees containing graves, in each of which are gun, powder and lead.

The personal misfortunes and peculiarities which an Indian has in life stick to him beyond the grave. A one-legged man in life is one-legged to all eternity. One who loses his sight here gropes blind through the Happy Hunting Grounds. Time is no more. There is no growing older there, consequently everyone remains forever at exactly the age at which he entered the new life. The puling infant, the decrepit hag, the young virgin, the stalwart warrior, as each dies, so shall he or she remain to all eternity. Those who are so fortunate as to die by quick disease take with them to the Happy Hunting Grounds no reminders of pain; but a body emaciated and distorted by chronic disease sends on the long journey a soul which must suffer always in the same way.

A warrior killed in battle and not mutilated, shows, in the future life, no sign of wound; but if the soul be not annihilated by scalping, every mutilation inflicted on the body after death also mutilates the soul. If the head, or hands, or feet are cut off, or the body ripped open after death, the soul will so appear and exist in the Happy Hunting Grounds. Some believe that if the dead body is transfixed with arrows and left to decay, the soul must always wear and suffer from the phantasms of those arrows. This accounts for this habit, quite common, especially with the Sioux, and for the great apparent waste of arrows. If a body so found, pierced with many arrows, is unscalped, it was the vindictive purpose of the murderers forever to torment the soul. If the head was scalped, the shooting was in mere bravado and cruel wantonness.

I have taken great interest in patiently studying out the varied and ingenious developments of thought by which the Indian seeks to reconcile these beliefs with the idea of happiness in the future state. He does this to his own entire satisfaction by his abundance of faith. His belief as to the effect on the soul of certain previous conditions of life and death are, according to his ideas, solidly founded on reason. His belief in the perfect happiness of his Paradise is purely a matter of faith.

Another well-known superstition of the Plains Indians is, that a man killed in the dark will dwell in darkness throughout eternity. This, for the white man, is a most fortunate belief, and materially lessens the dangers and labors of the troops. With their stealth, craft, patience and knowledge of the country, the Indians would be truly terrible in night attacks. As it is, such an attack is very rare, and, when decided upon, is invariably made by moonlight. They will crawl into a camp and steal horses, and may sometimes fire a few shots into it from a distance; but on a dark night there is little danger, even though surrounded by the most hostile Indians.

In common with the ancients of our history, the Indians believe that the manes or shades of the departed slain in battle require to be appeased by the death of the slayer, if possible; or, failing his, by that of someone of the slayer's nation or tribe.

In the spring of 1873 a band of Cheyennes on a marauding expedition to New Mexico were surprised by troops, and some six or eight killed. When the survivors reached home with the news, the most fearful excitement prevailed throughout the Indian camp, and a party was at once made up to go to the settlements to obtain white victims in retaliation. Fortunately for the unprepared settlers, but most unfortunately for themselves, a small party of surveyors were at work on the route of the Indian march. They were set upon by the Indians, who, when they had killed a number sufficient to appease the shades of their slain friends, returned satisfied to their encampment without molesting the settlers.

Two or more warriors of contiguous tribes have a collision in which one is killed. His relations and friends seek every opportunity to retaliate by killing one or more of the relatives of the slayer. Their shades appeal in turn to their friends for appeasement, and in course of time what may have arisen in a mere broil between two half-drunken bucks, has widened and deepened until almost every family of each tribe has a blood feud with one or more families of the other.

LIFE AND TRAINING OF INDIAN BOYS AND GIRLS

AS soon as the Indian baby is born it is placed in a coffin-shaped receptacle, where it passes nearly the whole of the first year of its existence, being taken out only once or twice a day for washing or change of clothing. This clothing is of the most primitive character, the baby being simply swaddled in a dressed deer-skin or piece of cotton cloth, which envelopes the whole body the neck. The outside of the cradle varies with the wealth or taste of the mother, scarcely two being exactly alike. Some are elaborately ornamented with furs, feathers, and bead work, others are perfectly plain. Whatever the outside, the cases themselves are nearly the same.

A piece of dried buffalo hide is cut into proper shape, then turned on itself and the front fastened with strings. The face is always exposed. The whole is then tightly fastened to a board, or in the most approved cradles, to two narrow pieces of board joined together in the form of an X. It forms a real "nest of comfort," and as the Indian is not a stickler on the score of cleanliness, it is the very best cradle that they could adopt. To the board or boards is attached a strap, which, passed over the head, rests on the mother's chest and shoulders, leaving the arms free. When about the lodge the mother stands the cradle in some out of the way corner, or in fine weather against a tree; or if the wind is blowing fresh it is hung to a branch, where it fulfils all the promise of the nursery rhyme.

When the baby is ten months to a year old it is released from its confinement, and for a year or two more of its life takes its short journeys on its mother's back in a simple way. It is placed well up on her back between the shoulders; the blanket is then thrown over both, and being drawn tightly at the front of her neck by the mother, leaves a fold behind, in which the little one rides securely, and apparently without the slightest inconvenience to either rider or ridden. I have seen a Nez Perce woman play a vigorous game of ball with a baby on her back.

On long journeys, or when changing camp, the children too heavy to carry on the mother's backs, but too young to ride on horseback, are confined in a wicker cage, which is fastened on the lodge-poles which trail alongside of some reliable, steady-going old horse, an arrangement called a "travois" by the French trappers.

For a little while thereafter they may be mounted before or behind the mother, but by the time they are four years old they are considered quite large enough to ride by themselves.

At first, to prevent any possibility of their falling off, they are tied by a complicated set of straps to the saddle of a steady horse, which is then turned loose, and in the movement of a camp the little urchins of that unpleasant age will be seen seated on the tops of packs, in apparently the most uncomfortable positions, but happy, or at least resigned. This rough schooling soon tells, and at an incredibly early age, the children of both sexes are worthy scions of the parent stock of riders, unsurpassed by any in the world.

Children are highly prized by every Indian man. The wife who brings him most sons is the most honored, though not always most favored.

"While the child, either boy or girl, is very young, the mother has entire charge, control, and management of it. It is soon taught not to cry by a very summary process. When it attempts to "set up a yell," the mother covers its mouth with the palm of her hand, grasps its nose between her thumb and forefinger, and holds on until the little one is nearly suffocated. It is then let go, to be seized and smothered again at the first attempt to cry. The baby very soon comprehends that silence is the best policy.

Almost as soon as the male child is weaned, its control is taken from the mother, and it becomes practically its own master. The mother is never permitted to strike a boy, no matter what his fault. She may, however, punish him by refusing food or pulling his hair. Among those Indians who live habitually about the agencies, this exemption from whipping, though still the rule, has frequent exceptions, and a mother, worried out of all patience by a troublesome urchin, will give him a vigorous box on the ear and send him sprawling to the ground. The discretion of the father generally blinds him to such little exhibitions of feminine temper.

The mother retains her control over her girls until they are young women, and whatever comfort she derives from her children is from them.

Though almost all Indian women are anxious to have children, and evince great fondness for them, the maternal instinct does not appear to be very strongly developed. All are what we call "motherly," having the disposition to love children, whether their own, or those of other people. An infant which has lost its mother is assiduously and tenderly cared for by the nursing mothers of the band, and a very young captive child is sure to be adopted, and not unfrequently in a family where there are other children. The affection seems to be a general one, and somewhat dependent on the beauty and sprightliness of the child. I was stationed at a post in Texas much visited by the Comanches. A brother officer had a beautiful healthy boy baby. When it was eight or ten months old, yet unable to walk, it was habitually, during the day, placed in a baby-jumper on the back piazza of his house. It was soon discovered by the squaws, who, crowding around, spent hours each day in admiration of its beauty, and its (to them) wonderful jumps and capers. Scarce one of them but made propositions, either to swap their own babies for, or to buy it, and the officer's young wife was kept in a constant state of watchfulness and anxiety lest they should steal it.

Though the mother has all the trouble and worry of the children, the father seems to have the strongest love for them, and this is especially the case with sons. His pride in and affection for them knows no bounds. They keep alive his ambition, and in their brave deeds he renews his youthful fire and vigor. I have heard many instances of the strength of this affection, but that most touching is the one given by Schoolcraft.

In a war between the Chippewas and allied Foxes and Sioux, the Foxes captured the son of an old and celebrated chief, Bi-ans-wah. The old man hearing the terrible news, and knowing the sure destiny of his son, followed alone the trail of the enemy, and "reached the Fox village while they were in the act of kindling the fire to roast him alive. He stepped boldly into the arena and offered to take his son's place.

"'My son,' said he, 'has seen but a few winters, his feet have never trod the war-path, but the hairs of my head are white, I have hung many scalps over the graves of my relatives, which I have taken from the heads of your warriors; kindle the fire about me and send my son home to my lodge.' The offer was accepted, and the old man, without deigning to utter a groan, was burnt at the stake."

The Indian father's affection for his daughters is open to the suspicion of interest. They are, if tolerably good-looking, a sure source of revenue when marriageable, and his affection for them does not blind him to the superior argument of the highest bidder.

The little children are much petted and spoiled; tumbling and climbing, unreproved, over the father and his visitors in the lodge, and never seem to be an annoyance or in the way.

The boys grow up as it happens, without moral restraint of any kind, and subjected only to the mild, paternal control of the father, in such duties as are necessary to supply the family with food, and to watch and care for its stock.

The girls are early taught the lessons of subordination, and begin to labor almost as soon as they can walk.

It is very rare to see Indian boys and girls of over five or six years playing together; all the boys of and above that age have bows and arrows, and, collected in squads, they roam about the country in the vicinity of their camp, shooting at every animal or bird that shows itself, and thus early beginning the lessons of their life. The little girls are very fond of dolls which their mothers make and dress with considerable skill and taste. Their baby houses are miniature tepees, and they spend as much time and take as much pleasure in such play as white girls.

After they get out of their cradles, Indian children are never "put to bed" until they go to sleep of their own accord, but are "au courant" of everything that goes on in the lodge, or in all out-door amusements and ceremonies. They are debarred only from the council lodge. As "little pitchers have big ears" they are very precocious, and an Indian boy or girl of six years knows more of the possibilities of the future than an American child of fifteen or sixteen.

He is a natural animal. He knows nothing of right and wrong, as we understand those terms. No dread of punishment restrains him from any act that boyish fun or fury may prompt. No softening stories of good little boys are poured into his attentive ears at a mother's knee. No lessons inculcating the beauty and sure reward of goodness, or the hideousness and certain punishment of vice, are ever wasted on him; wasted, for virtue and vice are abstract terms, utterly incomprehensible to him.

The men by whom he is surrounded, and to whom he looks as models, are great and renowned just in proportion to their ferocity, to the scalps they have taken or the horses they have stolen. His earliest boyish memory is probably a dance of rejoicing over the scalps of strangers, all of whom he is taught to regard as enemies. The acclamations which rewarded each warrior as he bounded into the circle, and in glowing words described the conflict and the death of the enemy, have influenced his imagination, and he yearns for the time when he can take his part in fight and foray, and for opportunity to signalize his craft and courage.

At twelve or thirteen these yearnings can no longer be repressed; and banded together, the youths of from twelve to sixteen years roam over the country; and some of the most cold-blooded atrocities, daring attacks, and desperate combats, have been made by these children in pursuit of fame.

From each of these excursions return, with crest erect and backbone stiffened, one or more youngsters, whose airs and style proclaim that each has made his coup, and is henceforth candidate for the distinction of warrior.

The chiefs and warriors assemble in general council and with the utmost gravity listen to the claims of the candidates. Each in turn, frenzied with excitement, with bounds and yells and frantic gestures, pours forth, in almost incoherent language, a recital of the special deeds on which he bases his claim. When conflicting claims are made by the candidates, as is almost sure to be the case, their companions on the excursion are called on for their statements; and when all the testimony is in, the candidates, their friends, comrades, and spectators, are turned out of the council, which then proceeds to deliberate.

After some time, the names of the happy few are proclaimed formally and loudly from the door of the council lodge.

Until within a very few years, the initiation was a religious as well as a military ceremony, and varied with each tribe. The process in the most warlike tribes was identical with that described as the torture of the "Hôch-é-a-yum." At the present time I know of no tribe that demands the ordeal, as the process of initiation as a warrior.

The simple announcement by the council is all now necessary to the military standing of the candidate, and the religious rites are consummated by his going off alone to some high hill, or other secluded place, and there starving himself into a condition of trance, during which he decides upon his medicine. When he returns to his camp, it is to step into his position as warrior. He becomes at once a "dog-soldier," is no longer under the control of his father (unless he still chooses to live in the paternal lodge), and whatever his age, may marry and hold property.

The girls are very precocious and begin to "go into society," to attend dances and social gatherings, when but eight or ten years of age.

At the very last Indian dance I witnessed, the belles of the evening, and the most forward in "keeping up the hilarity," were two little girls of about ten years old.

At this age they are frequently pretty, and show by their actions not only that they are as well aware of that fact, as are their white sisters under similar circumstances, but that they already begin to feel matrimonial hankerings, and are determined to make the most of their chances in their season of freshest bloom.

Their hard life and constant work tell upon them very soon, and by the time they are sixteen, very little of their early freshness is left. Indeed, it is almost impossible, after that age, to make from appearances even an approximate guess at the age of any Indian woman. I know a married woman of eighteen who looks as old as her mother, who must be thirty-five, and this is not at all unusual.

LOVE-MAKING IN AN INDIAN CAMP

THERE is a vast amount of love-making in an Indian camp, for aside from that common and natural to unmarried youth of both sexes, the custom of most Plains tribes makes every man a possible suitor for the hand of every woman, though either or both may be already married.

No sooner has the boy been proclaimed a warrior than he begins to look for a wife. Although the only real essential in the affair is that he have ponies," or other property, to pay for her, yet, for reasons which will hereafter appear, it is always better to win, if possible, the love of the girl.

So far as my observation and experience go, Indians of neither sex are afflicted with bashfulness, but while the male Indian prides himself on the violence of his passions, custom has denounced sentiment as unmanly, and love a weakness.

The first approaches of the lover are therefore shy and constrained. Wrapped in his buffalo robe, or in summer in his wide cotton mantle, with his face painted in the highest style of Indian art, his locks combed, greased and adorned with silver or plaited buckles, he frequents the lodge of his inamorata, standing for hours without a word, showing only by looks the feelings that agitate his bosom.

After such number of visits as make his intentions entirely plain, the old folks send for their relatives and intimates, and hold a family council, at which the eligibility of the *"parti"* is discussed; his standing in the tribe, his wealth, present and prospective, and the number of ponies and other things he is likely to give for the girl. After all these matters have been satisfactorily settled, the girl gives her lover such looks of encouragement as induce him to hope.

Up to this time the two persons most interested may have never exchanged a word in private. Now, however, as soon as it is dark he lies in wait near the door of her lodge, watching for the appearance of his beloved, but carefully concealing himself from the observation of any other person. Every member of the lodge, indeed, possibly, every individual of the band, knows he is there, but it is one of the strongest social fictions of Indian life that the lover is supposed to be entirely unseen by any but his mistress.

After keeping the impatient lover waiting as long as her feminine nature thinks proper, the girl having properly "roped" herself, slips out of the lodge, and is immediately pounced upon by her lover. If she resists or cries out, he is obliged immediately to quit her. If she yields without noise, he carries her to a little distance, just out of hearing of the lodge. During the earlier interviews they stand facing each other, each wrapped in his or her own garment. If the affair progresses favorably, they still remain standing, but find one blanket or robe sufficient for both. When they may be considered as engaged, they seat themselves on the ground, and throwing a blanket over the heads or around the forms of both, make love to their hearts' content. Couples so engaged are never disturbed. Though dozens may be watching with true Indian curiosity, etiquette requires that they not only keep aloof, but act as if they had seen nothing.

It not unfrequently happens that two or more lovers are paying their addresses to the same girl at the same time. All are lying flat on the ground, each possibly in plain view of the others, but each presumed, by the fiction of custom, to be entirely concealed from all the world.

The girl appears. A rush is made. A lover seizes her; if the one she wishes to flirt with on that occasion, she yields passively, and is borne off, the others disappearing at once. If a wrong one, a slight resistance or exclamation, and she is at once released, to be seized again by another, and to repeat the process until satisfied with her captor.

Where there are several lovers the opportunity and incentives to coquetry are immense.

I once met a beautiful half-breed Sioux girl, who was said to have kept at least a dozen lovers lying about her lodge door for a year or more, flirting with each in turn, and managing so adroitly that each felt he would be the happy man in the end.

In each tribe there are more or less desperate flirts, and their conduct is not specially objected to by the fathers, who, realizing that "competition is the life of trade," mentally raise their price on the accession of each new lover.

When the parties come to an understanding the lover lays the case before his mother, or if she be dead, some old female relative or friend is selected.

Dressed in her best she proceeds to the lodge of the mistress, and interviews the old people.

The question of price is discussed in all its bearings, and the old lady finally returns with the ultimatum of the other side. This forms a subject of discussion among the relatives and friends of the family.

Sometimes more is asked than the lover can give, or his father is willing to give for him. In that case the suit may either be abandoned at once, or an effort made to effect a compromise.

In the afternoon all the ponies, buffalo robes, saddles, etc., etc., the lover can afford, are taken over to the lodge of his mistress, the ponies tied near the door, the other things distributed around. When morning comes, if the ponies and other things are where they were left, the suit has been rejected. If the ponies have been sent to the herd and the other things taken into the lodge, the lover's offer is accepted.

In former times among all, but at present only among the poorer Indians, the young husband conducts his new purchase to the lodge of his father, there to remain until the increase in his family, or his wealth and consequence in the tribe, force or enable him to set up a lodge for himself.

In later years, and among the better class of Indians, the mother and female friends of the bride set up a tepee a little way from the parental lodge and furnish it for the use of the new-married couple, who immediately take possession.

There is no marriage ceremony or formality of any kind. The price being paid and accepted, the man becomes the absolute owner of the woman. He may make her his wife, or his slave; he may sell her or kill her, with no one to gainsay or "make him afraid."

The daughter being led by her heart or her fancy, and the father by careful consideration of what he can get for her from some other man, it not unfrequently happens that they differ as to which lover should be accepted.

All fiction teaches that among whites the poor lover is almost invariably more handsome and fascinating than the rich one, and the rule holds good among red men. But the white sister can get up on her dignity and say "I won't," words which would bring to the red sister a sound thrashing, if not worse.

There is but one possible method of escape from the will of the terrible red father, and that is by an elopement.

Custom makes it not only improper, but very dangerous, for an Indian woman to be found alone away from her lodge; and as the family live all together in one room, the elopement of an Indian girl is a most difficult undertaking, especially when, having cause to suspect such intention, the father and all his family are on constant watch. She never goes out at night to meet her lovers but many eyes are upon her, and escape then would be impossible.

As among whites, "love laughs at locksmiths," so among reds, love laughs at watchful eyes; and creeping out of the lodge when the family are buried in sleep, the girl joins her lover, and, mounted on one horse (if they are unable to steal another), they, by morning, have put many miles between themselves and the wrathful pursuers. Should they be overtaken the lover would probably pay the penalty of his love-venture with his life, while the girl would come in for a terrible beating; but it is Indian against Indian now, and the fugitives move so rapidly and constantly that the pursuing party, having to follow the trail, concealed by every device, generally after one or two days abandon the pursuit and return to camp to demand damages of the father of the successful lover.

These are awarded by the chief and old men, not in accordance with the demand of the father of the girl, but with reference to her actual market value and the wealth of the father of the lover.

After a few weeks the fugitive lovers, knowing that all has by that time been settled, return to the camp and set up housekeeping as if nothing had happened.

Being by their confinement on reservations debarred from the exercise of their favorite accomplishment, horse-stealing, the tribes are now comparatively poor, and it is by no means easy for the ardent swain to procure enough ponies to satisfy the avarice of the obdurate father, consequently elopements are becoming more and more frequent, and property in marriageable daughters exceedingly precarious.

In November, 1880, a citizen employed at the military post of Fort Reno, being on a journey on horseback, overtook a family of Cheyenne Indians moving their camp. The bucks were in front, some distance ahead of the squaws, who had charge of the pack animals and loose stock. Among the women was one of about twenty years of age, a very handsome girl, for an Indian. Riding alongside of her, the American, who was a perfect master of the Cheyenne language, opened a conversation. To pass away the time and have some "fun" he soon commenced to make furious love to her, a proceeding so common as almost to be etiquette among Indians.

This was received so pleasantly that after a while he proposed an elopement. Greatly to his consternation the proposition was not only accepted, but the lady at once elaborated a plan for the accomplishment of their purpose, fixing time, place and all details with the utmost minuteness.

"Now don't make any mistake," said she, "for my father watches me very closely, and you will have to be careful.

"I am so glad you asked me," continued she gushingly. "My father asks five ponies for me, though he knows I am not worth them. Nobody will pay that price, and here I am almost an old woman, without a husband, while all the girls of my age have husbands and babies. When we come back from our 'runaway? the chief will not make you pay more than one pony for me."

The luckless love-maker, utterly overwhelmed by his own success, soon made excuse to leave, and to the discredit of my sex, I am obliged to admit, willfully failed to make his appearance at the rendezvous.

Polygamy seems to be the natural condition of mankind, lit least, it is a custom among almost all primitive or natural people. Each red man has as many wives as his inclination prompts, or his wealth allows.

Of the lovers which any Indian maiden may have, it is safe to say that at least half have already one, two, or more wives.

These are generally the men of means, consequently the favorites of her father.

These may be, and ofttimes are, successful in their suit with her, but they are not the men to elope. They leave too much at stake behind them.

Jealousy would seem to have no place in the composition of an Indian woman, and many prefer to be, even for a time, the favorite of a man who already has a wife or wives, and who is known to be a good husband and provider, rather than tempt the precarious chances of an untried man.

Until, therefore, he is so old as to care no longer for the gentle sex, every man of the tribe, whether married or single, is a possible suitor for the hand of any unmarried girl in it. I have known several Indians of middle age with already numerous wives and children, who were such favorites with the sex that they might have increased their number of wives to an unlimited extent, had they been so disposed, and this too, from among the very nicest girls of the tribe.

Among the Cheyennes, Arapahos, and other southern tribes, there is a very curious custom. I have heard that it extends to the Sioux and other northern Indians, but have no positive warrant of the fact.

The mail who marries the oldest daughter of a family, by fair and open purchase from her father, has a lien upon, and is entitled to the refusal of all the other daughters, full sisters to his wife.

As they arrive at marriageable age, he has a right to take them as wives if he sees fit, without paying anything for them. If he declines them their ownership reverts to the father again, who can sell them to whom he pleases.

If a man married to the oldest daughter signifies his intention of taking her sister to wife when she is old enough, and she should in the mean-time elope with another man, the damages would be paid to the brother-in-law, and not to the father.

An Arapahoe chief, Yellow Bear, is married to three sisters. Having married the oldest, the others fell to him naturally by custom, as they became of marriageable age, and without further payment.

In March, 1880, a Cheyenne woman appealed to me against this custom. She was a widow with four daughters. Eight years before a Cheyenne Indian had married her oldest daughter. A few years after he took the second, the third was taken when marriageable, and now he demanded the fourth, a girl of fourteen years.

The widow's appeal was pathetic.

"I have no son. This man has had three of my daughters to wife. He has no children by any of them. Now he wants my last daughter. He will have no children by her, and I will go to my grave knowing that I leave no posterity behind me."

I could do nothing, of course, army officers not being permitted to have any say in Indian affairs, but I suggested flight. This was shown to be impracticable, and I gave up the case when I found that the man intended to take the girl by force, and that the girl herself, having no other lover, was ready and willing to be taken.

The concentration of large numbers of Indians of different bands and tribes on comparatively restricted areas (reservations), while greatly increasing the opportunities for love-making, has made no material change in any of these customs. But the diminution of the power of the chiefs, and the failure of the United States Government to furnish any adequate substitute, work greatly to the injury and demoralization of the women. Under the tribal government a man who outraged a girl was obliged to pay for and take her to wife, under penalty of death. Now there is no punishment. The only protection that any woman has, is that derived from the custom of "roping" herself, and the fear lest the father or husband might execute his right of revenge on the perpetrator of an outrage on the woman so "roped."

INDIAN WOMEN—VIRTUES AND VICES

THE life of an Indian woman is a round of wearisome labor. Her marriage is only an exchange of masters, and an exchange for the worse, for the duties devolved upon a girl in the parental lodge are generally of the lightest kind. She may be required to assist in the cooking, in making or repairing the lodge, to make and mend clothing, and most of the elaborate ornamental bead and feather work comes from her hand. All her labors, however, are in or near the family lodge, and where she is immediately under the eyes of her parents. For an unmarried girl to be found away from her lodge alone, is to invite outrage, consequently she is never sent out to cut and bring wood, nor to take care of the stock.

She may sometimes be required to go with her mother on these errands and duties, or to work with her in the fields, but as a rule all the hard out-door work devolves on the married women.

The pride of the good wife is in permitting her husband to do nothing for himself. She cooks his food, makes and mends his lodge and his clothing, dresses skins, butchers the game, dries the meat, goes after and saddles his horse.

"When making a journey she strikes the lodge, packs the animals, cares for all the babies, and superintends the march, her lord and master, who left camp long before her, being far off in front or flank looking after game.

On arriving at the camping-place, she unpacks the animals, pitches the lodge, makes the beds, brings wood and water, and does everything that is to be done, and when her husband returns from his hunt, is ready to take and unsaddle his horse.

What she gets in exchange for all this devotion it is impossible to say, but whether from ignorance of any better fate, or from constant occupation, it is absolutely certain that a happier, more light-hearted, more contented woman cannot be found.

The husband owns his wife entirely. He may abuse her, beat her, even kill her without question. She is more absolutely a slave than any negro before the war of the rebellion, for not only may herself, but her person be sold or given away by her husband at his pleasure and without her consent.

In spite of all this the women are not without their weight and influence, not only in their own household, but in all the affairs of the tribe, and though not permitted even to enter the council lodge, they are very frequently "the power behind the throne," directing and guiding almost without knowing it themselves.

The custom in the Plains tribes which makes every man in the tribe a possible suitor for the hand of every woman, though either or both may be already married, is so at variance with all established ideas of what savages regard as "the rights of woman;" is so entirely unparalleled among other savage races of mankind, that I have devoted unusual time and care to its study, more especially from the fact that the custom is not mentioned, so far as I know, by any writer on the North American Indians.

This custom gives to every married woman of the tribes the absolute right to leave her husband and become the wife of any other man, the sole condition being that the new husband must have the means to pay for her.

How the savage Indian with his utter lack of any sense of justice to woman, his mere slave, could have permitted such an act to grow into a custom, is one of the curiosities of mental progression.

We may naturally suppose that it arose at first from the tendency of the chiefs to take to their bosoms the handsome wives of the commoners of the tribes. They probably paid for them liberally, and the bereaved husband was obliged to be satisfied. The new wives did not lose, but gained standing and position.

The example of chiefs was followed, and thus, what at first were mere acts of rapine, became firmly engrafted on the tribes by custom.

However it may have originated, it is certain that this custom exerts a most beneficial influence in ameliorating the condition of the women. Abject slave as the wife is, she has, if moderately good-looking or having a fair reputation as a worker, a sure remedy against all conjugal ills, in being able to leave her husband for any other man who will take her and pay for her.

The transfer of devotion and allegiance of women to other men than their rightful owners, is not an unusual occurrence among the Plains Indians. It may come from ill treatment on the part of the husband, or from what our civilization would term "an affinity," an ordinary love affair.

A woman is ill-treated by, or lives unhappily with her husband. She secures the services of some friendly and cautious old woman of the tribe, secrecy being most essential, the husband having a perfect right to kill the wife should he suspect what is going on. The old woman sounds the warriors, and finding one willing to take and pay for the woman, the affair is accomplished.

Or a man has taken a fancy to another man's wife. He makes his advances, is met by encouragement, and, after a siege more or less protracted, wins her.

In either case, the husband wakes up some morning to find his wife gone. He searches for her through the encampment and finds her in another man's lodge, doing the ordinary work as if she belonged there, and he is informed that she has become the wife of that man.

Etiquette and custom prevent his saying a word to the new husband, or to upbraid or injure the woman. He has but one recourse. He immediately proceeds to the chief and states his grievance. One or two prominent old warriors are summoned. They and the chief examine into the case and assess the damages, somewhat in accordance with the actual market value of the woman, but more usually by simply considering the relative wealth of the two men. If a rich man takes a poor man's wife he would probably be heavily assessed; while the poor man who took the rich man's wife would get off with a comparatively small bill of costs.

There is no appeal from the decision, and whatever forfeit is declared must be paid at once. This done, the affair is over. There is no wrangling or fighting, and in every case, forfeit or none, the woman has the right to remain with the man of her choice.

Should the wife of a chief change her allegiance, nothing, as a rule, is said or done about it. The chief is too great a man, too high and mighty, too far removed from the common feelings of humanity, to waste a moment's time or thought on so insignificant a thing as a woman.

His runaway wife may be in the same camp, in the very next lodge; he may pass her every day, or even chat with her when she comes to his lodge to see her children, but no look or word from him will ever show that he is aware that she has changed her allegiance.

"With a custom giving her the absolute right to change her husband at will, and with the temptation arising from the constant approaches of all other Indian men—who, animal like, approach a female only to make love to her—it is very remarkable that so many are chaste, and that these exchanges of husbands are the exception and not the rule. The concession of the right to change takes from most of them the temptation to avail themselves of it.

The new husband must be prepared to pay at once for the runaway woman whatever price is assessed by the chief and old men. This rule is imperative, and a failure to comply with this sole condition may, lead to most disastrous consequences, the abandoned husband having the right to inflict death on the absconding wife.

A young girl had become the third or fourth wife of a man at least fifty years old. As was perhaps natural, she became enamoured of a young warrior who, not having the means to pay for her, persuaded her to run away with him.

The elopement was successfully accomplished and the young couple arrived at the encampment of another band of the same tribe, where they set up housekeeping as man and wife.

Some five or six months after the whole tribe was called together for the "Medicine Dance." The old man found his runaway wife and demanded either that he be paid for her or that she be turned over to him for punishment. The young man could pay nothing and the girl was, by order of the chief, delivered to her first husband. Seating her on the ground he crossed her feet so that the instep of one was directly over that of the other, and deliberately fired a rifle ball through the two. He then formally presented her to the young man, grimly remarking—

"You need not fear that she will run away with any other man."

Custom has given to the unmarried girls of the tribes a somewhat similar right of self-protection against arbitrary sale by their fathers. The girl is sold. If, after two or three days, the husband's entreaties have failed to make her his, she may return to her father's lodge, who in this' case, however, is obliged to return to the purchaser the price he paid for her.

I have known but few such cases, the reward given the girl by her father in the shape of a most outrageous whipping having the effect to discourage such perverseness. Besides this, she knows that after marriage she can leave her husband almost at will, and it ministers to her vanity to know that her father got an exceptionally good price for her.

I have been at pains to show that the Indian has not only no moral code, but that he has not the faintest conception of an idea of moral obligation. This is exemplified not only in their general customs, but in their individual every-day life.

For the man there is no such word, no such idea, as continence. He has as little control over his passions as any wild beast, and is held to as little accountability for their indiscriminate gratification. Of all the tribes that I know of, Indian men are the same.

No tribe visits any punishment on the lover. Every man's right is to importune, to win, if possible; and the attempt of one on the virtue of another's wife is not at all incompatible with the closest and most intimate friendship between the men. And what is more singular, the friend may make the most violent love to the wife, with every protestation of passion, and every promise of love, devotion, constancy, and kind treatment, in the immediate presence and hearing of the husband, who, whatever he may feel, is debarred by custom from noticing it in any way.

There is no single point in which tribes differ so greatly as in the average chastity of their women.

The Cheyenne and Arapahoe tribes occupy the same territory, live together in the same camps, and are constantly and intimately associated. The men of the two tribes are identical in their habits of personal incontinence, but differ entirely in their ideas of family government, and in the management of their women.

Among the Arapahos infidelities are not specially reprobated, even by the husband. Among the Cheyennes a discovery of such conduct would entail most serious consequences, possibly death to the woman.

The result is remarkable. The Cheyenne women are retiring and modest, and for chastity will compare favorably with the women of any nation or people. The Arapahoe women, on the contrary, are loose almost without exception.

Under tribal government the Plains tribes differed very greatly in the punishment meted out to unfaithful wives, that is those who entered into a "liaison" while yet living with the husband, or those who by neglect of some rule become culpable. In all tribes the husband absolutely owns the wife, and may put her to death, which, as before stated, was sometimes, though rarely, done by the Cheyennes. The Comanches split their noses, while the Apaches and Navahos frequently cut that organ off entirely.

Since the almost utter impoverishment of the tribes by the benignant action of the government, punishment of the woman for infidelity is extremely rare. The bereaved husband, whatever may be his feelings, cannot afford the loss of so much valuable property. He, therefore, sends the wife back to her father, and gathers in from the lover whatever spoil he can lay his hands on, the interference of the chief to assess damages not in this case being necessary. The woman, though living in her father's lodge, is now the property of the lover, and though he may not take her to wife, she is obliged by custom to remain faithful to him. He, therefore, keeps a close watch on her, and should he discover her in a liaison with another man, he proceeds to levy damages from that man equal to those taken from himself by the rightful husband. The ownership of the woman and duty of watching her now devolve on the latest lover. I have known several instances where a loose but good-looking woman has thus passed through half a dozen different ownerships, though all the time living in the lodge of her father.

It must be understood that the women here spoken of are those who enter into liaisons while yet living with and presumably faithful to their husbands. It is rare that the successful lover takes such an one to wife, he naturally fearing that one lapse from fidelity may be followed by another.

The exchange of husbands, as heretofore described, is in no sense a violation of the rules of the strictest chastity. It is customary, legitimate, and proper. It is the woman's protection against tyranny. The Cheyenne woman, being of a spirited, high-strung race, is quick to resent the ill treatment or neglect of one husband by taking another.

The Cheyennes and Arapahos have a curious custom which also obtains, though to a limited extent, among other of the Plains tribes. No unmarried woman considers herself dressed to meet her beau at night, to go to a dance, or other gathering, unless she has tied her lower limbs with a rope, in such a way, however, as not to interfere with her powers of locomotion; and every married woman does the same before going to bed when her husband is absent. Custom has made this an almost perfect protection against the brutality of the men. Without it, she would not be safe an instant, and even with it, an unmarried girl is not safe if found alone, away from the immediate protection of her lodge.

A Cheyenne woman, either married or single, is never seen alone. Though any man has the right to assault her, she is required to protect herself, and this can only be done by always having someone with her.

The sale of a wife is not unusual, though becoming less so every year. The Indians are very fond of children, and anxious to have as many as possible. Should the wife not bear a child in a reasonable time, she is liable to be sold, and very likely with her own full consent.

Should a husband sell a wife, by whom he has children, which is now extremely rare, he generally keeps the children, though I have heard of cases where wife and children were sold together. The possibility of separation from her children helps to keep the wife in proper subjection, though neither her sale, nor her voluntary abandonment of her husband for another, as already described, prevents her visiting or receiving visits from her children at pleasure.

It is regarded as effeminate in a man to show any special affection for his wife in public. A very notable exception to their habit in this particular is "Powder Face," a prominent chief of the Arapahos, a desperate and dangerous man, covered with scars, and celebrated for the number of scalps he has taken, and the risks he has run. His wife is a woman of average good looks, and of some thirty years of age. They have been married about fifteen years, and have no children. In spite of this, no two people could be more devoted and apparently happy. Contrary to custom he has but one wife, and she goes with him everywhere, his most devoted and willing slave. He will sit for hours before his lodge door combing her hair, painting her face, petting and fondling her; conduct which would disgrace a less determined or well-known warrior.

"Powder Face" has some other peculiarities somewhat inconsistent with Indian custom. When talking to him one day about the Indian habit of making love to each other's wives, I asked, "What would you do if another Indian made love to your wife?" He made no answer in words, but putting his hands to his belt he seized the sheath of his knife, and turned the handle towards me, putting on at the same time a scowl of malignant determination that completed the pantomime, and assured me that it would be very unhealthy for any Indian to devote himself to that woman.

Indians are gregarious, even the chief preferring to have one or more families, besides his own, in his lodge. These are generally relatives, or poor dependents.

The ordinary estimate of the inhabitants of an Indian village is three fighting men, or from twelve to fifteen individuals to the lodge. When it is recollected' that even the very largest lodge is scarcely over more than eighteen feet in diameter, and contains but one room, some idea may be formed, not only of its crowded condition, but of the utter lack of privacy of the inmates, and consequently their entire lack of modesty and delicacy, either in word or act.

The husband of one wife brings home another and another. Each wife has a bed, in which she sleeps with her smaller children, the husband generally keeping the latest favorite to himself. I have never heard of any serious difficulty or trouble between the wives on that account, and the sentiment of jealousy seems to be nearly wanting in the woman. The devotion of a man to a new wife, or his infidelity to them all, seems not to awaken the slightest feeling or idea of resistance to so universal a custom. In their sexual and marital relations, the Indians are scarcely above the beasts of the field. They marry very young; the youth as soon as he is fortunate enough to steal horses enough to pay for a wife, or can persuade his father to buy one for him.

About a year previous to this writing, the seventeen year old son of a prominent and wealthy chief having been initiated as warrior, informed his father that he wished to marry.

The fond and proud father immediately presented him with quite a number of ponies, and told him to look around and choose his wife. He went directly to the father of a pretty girl, to whom he had already been paying his addresses, after Indian fashion.

After some haggling, the price of the girl was agreed upon, the youngster, however, making the unusual condition that the affair must be kept a profound secret until a certain day, when he would bring the ponies, and take away the girl. He then went to the father of another girl and closed a bargain with him. A third bargain was also consummated, all on the same terms.

The parents of the youth were informed that he would be married on a certain day, but were kept in profound ignorance as to the intended wife. However, a new and large tepee was provided by his loving mother, and all arrangements made for a grand marriage feast.

The day arrived. The precocious young rascal drove up his herd of ponies, and proceeding to the tepee of one of the fathers with whom he had bargained, paid over a number of them and carried off the girl. Then going to the tepee of the second and the third he paid their prices, and returned to his bridal tepee, minus ponies, but bringing with him the three prettiest girls in the village.

The affair caused the greatest sensation, all applauding his ingenuity and cunning. He became the hero of the hour, and the old father was so tickled that he gave him another supply of ponies, to enable him to begin his married life in style suitable to his birth and talents.

Girls generally marry very soon after the age of puberty, the father as a rule being anxious to realize her value, and the girl, with true feminine instinct in these matters, wishing to be a woman and have a husband as soon as possible.

Sometimes a father gets "hard up" and has to sell his girls while they are yet mere children. These are bought up cheap by well-to-do bucks, who give them, even while mere children, all the rights and privileges as wives.

San-a-co, a Comanche chief, and the best Indian from our standpoint I have ever known, had as wife a pretty little maid of ten years, of whom he was very fond.

In March, 1880, "Red Pipe," a Cheyenne, sold his little unformed daughter of eleven years, to be the wife of a man old enough to be her grandfather; and I have known several other warriors who have mere children as their third or fourth wives.

Either from lack of suitable food, or the constant drudgery of her hard life, the Indian woman, though perfectly healthy, is not prolific. The mother of even four children is very rare and many women are barren. The average in most bands is scarcely more than two children to each woman; while some lodges, even where there are several wives, are childless.

The widows and orphans of a tribe are cared for after a fashion by the "dog-soldiers," who, in the general division of meat and skins, set aside a portion for their maintenance. This, when buffalo were plenty, was sufficient for their wants; but the present scarcity of game and scanty issues of the Indian Department cause no little suffering among this class.'

Among the Plains tribes a woman, on the death of her husband, becomes not only herself free, but the owner of her female children as property, provided that no man has gained a lien on them by marrying the oldest daughter. The sons are independent, but are obliged to support the mother and sisters, if old enough, or if they have no families of their own.

The widows are like their white sisters in their aversion to the sweets of single blessedness, and, if at all young and good-looking, are soon married again. The old and ugly, who have no sons to support them, not unfrequently purchase for themselves a husband by giving over to him the ownership of their daughters, not as wives, but as so much saleable property. The life of an Indian woman, who has a husband to provide for and take care of her, is so much more secure from insult and outrage, so much freer from the chance of hunger and want, that every woman greatly prefers even the annoyance of a bad husband to the precarious hazards of widowhood.

A grave trouble to the Indians, and one of which I have heard many complaints, is the number of widows and orphans left on their hands by white men. The Indians have this whole matter in their own hands, having but to prohibit their women from marrying white men. But this is not at all to their taste. A father can get for his daughter possibly twice as much from a white man as an Indian would pay, and he sells at the highest price. To prohibit his selling his own property would be regarded as an invasion of his most sacred and vested rights. Having sold and got his price, he feels himself relieved of all responsibility regarding her. She should henceforth be supported by the husband; and the father regards it as a hardship, an outrage, a real cause of complaint, to be obliged, even partially, to assist in the support of a woman, his own daughter, sacrificed by his cupidity to a man whom he knew would abandon her sooner or later.

At the very important council at North Platte in 1867, one of the chiefs spoke feelingly on this subject. He said that his tribe was poor and could not support the widows and orphans left on their hands by white men, and begged that special provision might be made by the Government for them.

One old childless widow was earnestly recommended to particular consideration. Subsequent examination of her claims disclosed the following facts, remarkable even among the many curious and wonderful Plains histories.

The spring and summer of 1867 had seen a succession of raids, plunderings and murders. All the Plains tribes were "on the war path," making a last desperate effort for the preservation of their favorite hunting grounds, the country between the South Platte and Arkansas Rivers, commonly known as the Republican Country. Custer with a considerable force was operating between the Kansas Pacific Railroad and the Platte River. It was necessary to communicate with him. Lieutenant Kidder and thirteen men of the 2nd Cavalry, with "Red Bead," a friendly Sioux chief, as guide, were sent from Port Sedgwick to intercept him. The Lieutenant was very wary and used every precaution against surprise, making no camps, but halting at uncertain intervals to rest and refresh his men and animals. He had, however, to deal with" Pawnee Killer," the most redoubtable of all the hostile chiefs, and from whom this account comes.

One night Lieutenant Kidder marched until nearly morning, then halted, and, without making fires or unsaddling,-allowed his exhausted men to lie down and sleep. Pawnee Killer, who was attending him like a fate, crawled with a large force on to the sleeping men, and just at dawn, one volley sent every sleeper, save two, to his long account. These two men were a corporal and" Red Bead." The corporal sprung to his feet, pistol in hand, and as the enemy rushed upon him, fired two shots, killing the two Indians in advance. Before he could do more he was riddled with bullets "Red Bead" ran, was pursued, and, in spite of his Indian cunning and endurance, was overtaken and killed.

The two men killed by the corporal in his last gallant effort, were the half-breed sons of the old widow by a trapper who had abandoned her twenty years before. By their courage, ferocity and cunning, these two half-breeds had gained great influence among the tribe, and their companions vented their rage on the lifeless bodies of their white victims, by unusual mutilation and barbarity; and hoping forever to torment their souls, left the head unscalped, but transfixed the bodies with arrows innumerable.

Sometime afterwards the remains were found by troops, and properly buried.

In looking for a wife the man is careful to select one who has no blood relationship to himself. A man who would marry a whole lodge full of sisters will not think for an instant of marrying his own cousin, even though twice removed. The relationship of first cousin is regarded as almost the same as brother and sister, and the affection of these close relationships is very warm and tender.

It is a very remarkable fact, as showing the utter want of chivalrous feeling among Indians, that though the brother may love his sister most tenderly, he never, under any circumstances, interferes to protect her from insult, or to avenge her outrage by other bucks.

There are very few madmen or idiots among the Indians. They are never confined or maltreated, but, being looked upon as directly under the malevolent influence of the Bad God, are rather avoided.

Some years ago a gentleman, now a prominent scientist, was in pursuit of knowledge on the Upper Missouri. In spite of the remonstrances of his friends and the captain, he insisted on being put off the steamboat, that he might walk across a great bend which it would take the boat some days to go around.

In a country full of hostile Sioux, without a blanket or mouthful to eat, he started alone, armed only with his butterfly net and loaded only with his pack for carrying specimens. One day, when busily occupied, he suddenly found himself surrounded by Indians. He showed no fear, and was carried to the village. His pack was found loaded with insects, bugs, and loathsome reptiles. The Indians decided that a white man who would come alone into that country unarmed, without food or bedding, for the accumulation of such things, must be crazy; so, the pack having been destroyed as "bad medicine," the doctor was carefully led out of camp and turned loose.

Note.—The story of the "Kidder Massacre," was told me by the Cheyenne Chief Turkey Leg in the fall of 1867. It is now known that the details are utterly untrue. I give this version as an evidence how cunningly the Indian can lie, when he has a purpose to serve, and because the truth can now do no good, and would needlessly harrow the feelings of the friends of the victims. The facts in the case are detailed in Custer's *Life on the Plains*.

INDIAN NAMES, TITLES, AND EPITHETS

THE recognition of relationships may be regarded as the first broad step between the lower reason of the animal and the higher reason of the man. An animal brings its offspring into existence, cares for it until maturity, then dismisses it, to become in time the possible mate of parents, brothers or sisters. Man alone recognizes relationships, and this distinctive feature is discovered even among the most debased of the race.

Very few tribes of North American Indians have any tradition as to the origin of creation; almost all have traditions as to the origin of families. Some of the tribes on our extreme northern frontier are said to believe that the whole tribe is the miraculous result of the intercourse of some god or spirit with some animal, bird, fish, or reptile, but this belief is not at all general. As a rule, they recognize the fact that the tribe is a mere aggregation of families, each one of which, however, firmly believes that it thus descended from someone of the lower order of creation. Even in the most barbarous of these tribes each family has such a tradition of origin, and evinces more or less pride of blood.

The representation of that animal, bird, or reptile becomes the "coat of arms" of the whole family. Its skin, carefully stuffed, bedecked with ornaments and feathers, is tied to a staff and carried about in the hand on grand full-dress occasions. In good weather, it is frequently stuck up in front of the door of the lodge, and when the head of the family dies it is suspended to the top of a strong, high pole, which is firmly planted beside his grave. It is the family crest, the title of honor, the symbol of its ancestry and descent, and whatever may be the name of the individual of that family, his signature is a rude representation of the creature to which he believes he owes his origin.

This is the Totem. It is not a mystery, and has no religious meaning or significance. It must not be confounded with the "Medicine-bag," which is purely religious, and the contents of which are a secret between the Indian and his gods.

Like the Jews of the Old Testament, Indians have no surnames. Among the Jews, individuals were identified by being members of one or other of twelve tribes among Indians, they are identified as belonging to one or other of the comparatively few families into which the tribes are divided. Were it not for this arrangement it would be, in the absence of surnames, an almost impossibility for them to keep track of their relationships. The splitting of tribes into two or more bands results also in splits in families; and at the present time, in tribes which have no tradition of former relationships, there will be found families having the same totem, indicating a common descent, and these recognize relationships to each other.

In the matter of names, Indians are a very peculiar people. A man may have a dozen names, or no name at all. He may name himself, or be named by his companions.

The male child is called by some diminutive or pet name, sometimes expressive of the pride and affection of the father, but more commonly something equivalent to the" Toodelums" and "Tweetlebugs" of fond white fathers and mothers. This is his name in his own family. By others he is spoken of' as "the son of so-and-so," or he may be given a name by his boy companions, either in admiration or derision.

All the world knows the fondness of boys for bestowing nicknames, and the Indian boy is no exception. But, a nickname, to stick, must be palpably applicable or appropriate to the character or some peculiarity of the person named. At a school or college a fourth or possibly half of each class will have nicknames, the others not.

So the nicknames given by Indian boys do not always stick, and I have met several full-grown warriors who have no names, and are known only as their father's sons.

On his initiation as warrior, which to him is a ceremony equivalent to baptism among Christians, he has the right to name himself, and from this time he has the right, and it is his custom, to change his name after every successful raid or expedition, each change of name being expressive of the fullest appreciation of his own importance and exploits.

These names are intended to be expressive of some particular action or situation, and are generally adapted to a real or fancied resemblance of the actor to the known habits of animals or birds with which they are familiar. Thus a warrior who, brought to bay, has beaten off his enemies, names himself the "Standing Bull;" another who makes a dash on a camp or village, and carries off a woman or child, calls himself the "Eagle;" yet another, who goes off alone, and prowling about the enemy's camp, returns with stories or evidence of successful rapine, names himself "Lone Wolf." The paint used on all these expeditions has more or less potent influence on the "medicine," and he does not forget its efficacy, consequently many names indicate not only the action, but the color of his paint. The most common names, therefore, among Indians, are those indicating some animals or material object as a sort of surname, while the color with which he has bedecked himself furnishes the first, or what we would call the Christian name; as "Yellow Bear," "White Eagle," "Black Beaver," "Red Dog," etc., etc.

But these changes of name, though gratifying to his own vanity, are not always accepted by his companions or the tribe generally. Even the most renowned warriors cannot always control the disposition to ridicule or nickname, which the Indians possess in a remarkable degree, and however he may name himself, he is likely to be addressed, known, and spoken of by the people of the tribe by an entirely different name.

Any personal defect, deformity of character, or casual incident furnishing ground for a good story, is eagerly seized upon as a fit name. "Powder Face," the war chief of the Arapahos, has won, in well fought combats and desperate ventures, the right to adopt a dozen names, yet he is known to all Plains tribes, and to the whites, by the title which was given him from having his face badly burned by an explosion of powder when he was a young man "Man-afraid-of-his-horses," received, it is said, his name from having, on the occasion of an attack on his camp by hostile Indians, saved his horses but left his family in the hands of the enemy.

Some of these names are expressive of early indiscretions, as "Pa-ha-yu-ka;" others of utter contempt, as "Mu-la-que-top;" but it is a curious fact that, however unworthy, vulgar, or opprobrious the title by which a warrior is commonly known in his tribe, he is sure in his maturer years to acquiesce in and accept it.

Girls are named by their mothers, and frequently have fanciful titles indicating something that the mother may think worthy of commemoration, as the Hebrew women of the Old Testament named then children. This name in the family is liable to be lengthened by affectionate diminutives, or contracted into a nickname, but it is not changed as the names of boys.

Married women do not take the names of their husbands, or change their names in any way. There are no equivalents for Mr. or Mrs., and in her name, title or designation, there is nothing to show whether a woman is single or married.

When on reservations, or thrown into close contact with whites, the Indian is prone to adopt some "white" name, and at every military post near a reservation there is always a lazy lot of "Jims," "Bills," "Franks" or "Tonys" loafing as an occupation, and living by the most unblushing beggary.

Almost every river, creek, spring, permanent water-hole, mountain or prominent landmark, has a name given to it, not only by the tribe in whose country it is, but by those who raid into that country. In most cases, they are named from some peculiarity, incident, or adventure. These names in the soft language of the Dacotas are oftentimes very beautiful. "Minni" in this language means water; "Minni-ha-ha" is "laughing or frolicsome water," given to all falls and cascades; "Minni-cot-ta" is "warm water," and one of the bands takes its name from the fact that it was once nearly destroyed by a waterspout, "Minni-con-jou," "drowned with water."

In some cases, the striking and beautiful Indian names are retained, but in the large majority of instances the names on the map, and by which they are known to the whites, are either crude translations of the Indian names or such others as happen to suggest themselves to the army officer who first makes the survey of the country. The consequence is, that the maps are crowded with "Sand Creeks," "Deer Creeks," "Walnut Creeks," etc., etc.

A curious and interesting story was told me by an old Mexican, apropos to the name of what is known on our map as the "Purgatory River."

When Spain owned all Mexico and Florida, the Commanding Officer at Santa Fe received an order to open communication with Florida. An Infantry Regiment was selected for this duty. It started rather late in the season, and wintered at a place which has been a town ever since, and is now known as Trinidad. In the spring, the colonel, leaving behind all camp followers—both men and women—marched down the stream which flows for many miles through a magnificent cañon . Not one of the regiment returned or was ever heard of after, their fate being shrouded in mystery.

When all hope had departed from the wives, children and friends, left behind in Trinidad, information was sent to Santa Fe, and a wail went up through the land. The priests and people called this stream, "El rio de las animas perdidas," "The River of the lost Souls."

Years after, when the Spanish power was weakened and Canadian French trappers permeated the country, they adopted a more concise name. The place of lost souls being purgatory, they called the river "Le Purgatoire." Then came the "Great American Bull-whacker," he whose persistent efforts opened and maintained the enormous trade between Santa Fe and St. Louis. Utterly unable to twist his tongue into any such Frenchified expression, he called the river the "Picketwire," and by this name it is known to all frontiersmen and to the settlers on its banks.

As a rule each tribe has its own name for the larger rivers of the plains, though some are said to have names common to all those tribes who live near or occasionally visit them.

Every white man of consequence, with whom the Indian comes in contact, secures a name suggested by his occupation or some personal peculiarity. The commanding officer of a post is always "the big chief," the Quartermaster the "mule chief," and the Commissary "the chuck-chief," but the other officers come in for a full share of ridiculous names, as "long beard," "gray beard," "bald head," "crooked leg," etc.

On his campaigns with, and against Indians, General Crook always wears a full suit of gray. This taken in connection with his wiliness, has suggested his name, and he is known to all Indians as the "Gray Fox."

EVERYDAY INDIAN LIFE

THE habitations of the Indians are constructed in many different ways, varying with the necessities or the state of advancement of the tribe. Each particular style of structure has a name of its own, in Indian language, but all are comprehended in the English word "lodge."

The ordinary home of most of the Plains Indians is called by them a "tepee." It is a conical tent, made of dressed buffalo skins, or of late years of cotton cloth, supported on a framework of light peeled poles, spread out at the bottom in a circle, and crossed near the top. It is from twelve to eighteen feet in diameter, and from twelve to fifteen feet high. The covering, of whatever material, is cut into the form of a cone, and sewed tightly, except one straight seam from top to bottom, which is fastened by a lacing from the top to within four or five feet of the ground. The opening thus left is the doorway, the door itself being a buffalo robe or piece of cloth, fastened above, and left to hang loose, except in bad weather, when it can be tightly stretched by thongs attached to the lower corners.

From its size and weight the tepee would seem to be an unwieldy arrangement, little adapted to convenience of moving; but it is really remarkable how easily and quickly it is put up or taken down by those accustomed to its use. The ground being selected, the tepee is spread out upon it. Three poles are loosely tied together near the smaller ends, and thrust under the covering, passed through the orifice in the top, raised upright, and the lower ends spread out as far as possible. A rope or thong attached to the top of the covering is then thrown over the place of crossing of the poles. One woman pulls on the end of this rope (exactly as a sailor in setting a sail), while another widens the tripod of poles until the covering is stretched vertically and laterally. The other poles are then carried in one by one, the small end thrust through the top opening, is laid against the point of crossing of the first three, the large end being carried out as far as possible. When all the poles are in, they are arranged equidistant, in a symmetrical circle, stretching the covering as tightly a§ possible. A few wooden pins driven into the ground through slits in the bottom of the covering, on the outside, and the tepee is pitched.

When it is to be taken down all the loose poles are carried out, the rope holding the covering in place is loosened, the lower ends of the poles forming the tripod are brought near to each other, and the covering comes down of its own weight. Two quick-working women can put up a tepee in five minutes, and take it down in three.

All well-constructed tepees have an arrangement to prevent the wind from blowing directly down through the opening in the top. This varies with the tribe or inventive genius of the particular Indian. Sometimes it is a sort of winged cap, managed from below by a complicated system of strings. Ordinarily, it is simply a deer skin or piece of cloth fastened to, and between, two poles, which are laid against the tepee in such a way that the screen is partially above and on the windward side of the lodge. It is easily managed, and readily shifted with the wind.

The tepees of buffalo hide, now rare except among the northern Plains Indians, were frequently elaborately ornamented with paintings representing the remarkable achievements of the head of the lodge, or sometimes with representations of various kinds, supposed to be efficacious in keeping away evil spirits.

The fire is built in the centre, and the smoke is supposed to escape through an aperture in the top. The draught is, however, very defective, and, the tepee is usually, whenever a fire is built, too full of smoke to be bearable to any but an Indian.

The tepee is most admirably adapted to the wants and necessities of the Indians. Its shape secures it from being overturned by wind and storms, and it can be kept warm and comfortable, even in the coldest weather, by very little fuel, a most important desideratum on the treeless Plains.

The other kind of lodge is called a "wicky-up." It is a temporary hut, constructed of small, fresh-cut poles or wands, the large ends stuck in the ground, the small ends bent over and fastened together. This framework is scarcely ever more than three or four feet high, and it is covered with skins, blankets, or cloths. The tepee is the permanent residence of the Indian, the wicky-up the make-shift sleeping-place on hunts and marches. No matter how tired after the day's march; no matter what may be the pressing necessities of advance or retreat; no matter if intending to remain in camp but a few hours, the Plains Indian never, under any circumstances, sleeps in the open air. He must be protected from above, and if possessing but one blanket, he will make his framework, spread the blanket over it, and sleep on the bare ground, even in the coldest weather. Whether this is superstition or a habit derived from long experience I am unable to say, though I think it originated in a fear of evil spirits. When asked about it, they curtly reply that it is "not good to sleep out."

An Indian out alone will build for himself such a lodge, not larger than a dog-kennel—so small, indeed, that it seems impossible for a man to get into it. In cold weather he will build a true Indian tire in the centre of the small space, and curl himself contentedly around it. I have examined hundreds of these little wicky-ups, and always with increased wonder as to how the Indian managed to get into and sleep in it without knocking down the whole affair. Larger parties are equally economical of space, or labor, and I have often had my credulity tested by being assured by my Indian guide that ten, twelve, or more Indians slept in a wicky-up, which I could have declared would not hold scarcely half the number.

The Omaha Indians make a lodge by planting forked poles in the ground in a square or rectangle. Other poles are laid on these forks, and on these light wands, on which are fastened skins, cloths, blankets—anything that will keep out rain, (no easy matter, as they are too ignorant to give sufficient pitch to these roofs). The sides or walls are formed of mats made of peeled willow wands woven together with strings. When camp is moved, these mats are taken down, rolled into small compass, and packed on ponies.

The lodge of the Osages is almost exactly the shape of a wagon with its bows. Slender poles are set in the ground parallel to each other, at proper intervals, then bent over and tied together. Cross pieces sufficient to make the structure firm are then tied on. This frame, which is from twelve to twenty feet long by six to eight wide, is entirely covered with a cloth in one piece, like a wagon-cover, a flap being left for a door. When moving camp, they take only the cloth.

From the brush shelter of the Digger, the log and mud huts of the Navahos, to the elaborate and complicated piles of the Pueblos, almost every kind of lodge common to savage life can be found among the North American Indians.

The beds of the Plains Indians are piles of buffalo robes and blankets spread on the ground as close as possible to the outer circumference of the tepee. Of late years, the more wealthy make a bedstead by driving forks into the ground, and constructing on them a platform of poles a few inches high. This, however, takes up precious room, and is only found in tepees occupied by a few persons.

Nearly all the Plains Indians use pillows when at home in their tepees. They were formerly made almost universally of a rolled buffalo robe. Now they are made of skins of some of the smaller animals—a fox or badger—stuffed with grass, and some few have seen enough of the comforts of civilized life to cover them with cotton cloth. They use no sheets, saying they are cold and unhealthy. The beds, however arranged, serve the double purpose of sleeping-places by night and seats and lounges by day. They are not "made-up," though on fine days the bedding may be taken out, shaken, and spread in the sun. The one room, serving for cooking, eating, living and sleeping, for the reception of company and the lounging place for dogs, soon becomes inconceivably filthy.

Except the bedding, the "par-fleche" trunks containing the dried meat, extra clothing, finery, and valuables, an iron pot or two, a kettle, a water-pail, and a few tin cups, there is no furniture; nor is there any attempt at order in the arrangement of even these few articles.

There are no regular hours for meals, nor is there, as a rule, more than one meal a day. A pot or kettle full of meat is put on the fire. When sufficiently boiled it is placed in the centre of the floor, and the inmates of the tepee, crowding around, help themselves with knives or fingers. Some few of the more advanced now use tin or delf plates.

Until within a few years dried buffalo meat was used almost universally in lieu of bread, but the issues of flour, meal, and baking-powder by the Indian Department have civilized them so far that bread is almost an absolute necessity, and many of the squaws have learned to make quite good biscuits. They have not yet learned the art of making baker's bread, but they are very fond of it, begging or buying it whenever they come into a military post.

When the meal is finished, the pot is set aside, and when anyone gets hungry more than once a day, he goes without ceremony or formal preparation and helps himself.

They are hospitable to each other, always, if they have it, offering something to eat to visitors. If it is known that there is anything specially good to eat in any lodge, a lot of loafers will be sure to drop in, whenever more than ordinary smoke indicates that cooking is going on. These spongers always have the first chance at the pot, the occupants of the tepee contenting themselves with what is left.

Tea, coffee, and sugar are exceptions. These are carefully hoarded for the use of the family, and given only to distinguished visitors on grand occasions.

Strangers are always looked upon with suspicion. Except when the tribe is actually at war, a stranger, either white or Indian, may, by asking to see the chief, gain access to any Indian village. Once inside its limits, he is treated hospitably, and is safe; but there is nothing of the Arab about the "Noble Red Man," and his giving you a good meal to-day will not prevent his taking your scalp after you have left his camp to-morrow.

The wealth of the Indian is in his horses and mules. He has no taste or desire for the accumulation of more or other things than are necessary for the wants of his family for the time being.

Except in winter, the bands lead a nomadic life. Every few days everything has to be packed and unpacked, put on horses and taken off again, and the women who have to do all this work, are very sure gradually to abandon all those things which can well be spared.

All the clothing, finery, and smaller valuables, are packed in the "par-fleches," which are easily handled, but everything bulky and cumbersome, and not of absolute necessity, is thrown away.

Another cause of their poverty is the necessity of properly fitting out the dead for the journey to the Happy Hunting Grounds. They must have certain articles, even if the living go without, and this religious necessity keeps many families nearly impoverished in most articles of civilized manufacture.

Every tribe of Indians with which I am acquainted, understands perfectly the art of selecting a camping-place suited to its special necessities. To a novice this may seem easy, but it is really so difficult that I regard it as the final test of a Plainsman. To select the best camp-ground, even for a night on the Plains, requires a judgment, a "coup d'oeil," a knowledge of facts, and a consideration of possibilities possessed by comparatively few men. A thousand questions involving the comfort and safety of the party must be decided in a few moments, and as it were by instinct; and that the Indians so invariably select the camp best adapted to their wants, on that particular occasion, evidences a superior order of intellect, or instinct. Every party must not only take into consideration its own comfort, and that of its stock, but all the dangers to which they may be exposed, either from human enemies or from the elements. A hunting-party chooses other ground than would a war party, and each in making its selection, must combine its objects and intentions with all the surrounding possibilities.

The Apache, fearing man only, sacrifices everything to that fear, and locates his rancheria on the apparently inaccessible summit of some tall cliff, to which his women must bring the scant supply of water, by paths unknown to any but themselves.

I once followed a predatory" party of Comanches for more than thirty days, and the camp in which I finally surprised them was the only camp made by them in all that time that could have been approached without discovery.

Except in winter, the situation of a camp indicates something in reference to its occupants. Thus a camp near water, but away from all timber, will probably contain Sioux, who have a mortal dread of ambuscade; a camp on open prairie, but near timber, would be of Cheyennes or Arapahos; a camp prettily situated among open timber, Kiowas or Comanches; while a smoke issuing from the cover of a dense thicket, would indicate the camp of Osages, Omahas, or Shawnees.

In the" good old times," when the dog-soldiers ruled, the camps were arranged, not indeed with order, but with some regard to convenience and the properties. The council-lodge, the tepees of the chiefs and principal men, were pitched in a circle, enclosing a space greater or less, according to the number of lodges. This circle was the public square, from which were made by crier all announcements of orders and decisions of chiefs and council, notices of movements, everything of public interest or necessary to be known by all. This was the loafing and lounging place, the place for strutting and bragging, for gambling or trading horses, for war and ceremonial dances.

Irregularly straggling away from this general centre, and behind the tepee of each chief, were the lodges of his followers, some good, some bad, some mere "wicky ups" of brush. They were pitched with reference to the ground, without streets or order, some almost or quite touching, others some distance apart The women of each lodge selected the ground on which it was to stand, and not unfrequently the ownership of a specially good place was decided by a bout at hair pulling. The men never interfered with any of these feminine amusements, but sat apart, gravely discussing the affairs of the tribe, or the possibility of stealing some horses, or may be talking over the last camp scandal, until their wives had gotten through their quarrels, worry and turmoil, and had their lodges ready for them.

At the present time, each petty chief or head of a few lodges, selects his ground and has his tepee pitched, his followers pitching around him without order, and seemingly only bent on crowding him and each other. With unlimited expanse of beautiful ground on which to "locate," they almost invariably place their lodges so close together, that nothing can be said or done in one that is not known to all the occupants of the others.

We have a proverb that "no house is large enough for two families." The Indians have not only two or more families in the one room, but they so jam their lodges together, that all may be said to occupy one house. That all are not in one general and continuous row argues a condition of feminine temper much higher, or lower, than that accorded to civilization. As there are no yards, fences, or outhouses of any kind, an idea may be formed as to the privacy, decency, and cleanliness of Indian life.

The winter camp is regarded by the Indian himself as his true home. The excitement of war, of hunting, of constant movement, is over, and he is now to settle down to a period of almost complete inaction. Experienced warriors have been sent to all the streams, most loved by the tribe, and to make a thorough examination of all the country. When all have returned a council is held. The reports of the scouts are heard, and they are closely questioned as to shelter, wood, water, and grass or cotton-wood for the ponies. As each locality has its champions, the council sometimes debates the momentous question for days, once in a while, even sending other warriors to examine a favorite stream, about which, however, there is now a difference of opinion.

It is not now a question of room for a compact camp, but of the shelter furnished by the bluffs on each side of the stream, of the amount of timber and wooded thickets along its valley, of the sufficiency of grass or cotton-wood to keep the ponies alive.

When the stream has finally been selected, all go together. There is now no sort of attempt at order. The lodges of the followers of a chief may be scattered for miles, each taking advantage of the sheltered nooks, formed by thickets or bluffs. Here a single tepee is stuck away in a little corner, so hidden that one might pass within a few yards without seeing it; there two or three find room and shelter, there again bluffs, and thickets, and bend of stream all favoring, a dozen find comfortable lodgment. The great questions with each Indian are, shelter, convenience, and feed for the ponies, and these questions are paramount, though the desire to keep as near to each other as possible is apparent through all.

According therefore to the nature of the stream, its bluffs 'and thickets, and level valley, will a winter camp be compact or scattered. One winter a camp of one hundred and fifty lodges will occupy scarce a mile, another winter it may be extended four, five, or even six miles along the stream. Sometimes several friendly tribes occupy the same stream, making an immense camp.

On December 23, 1868, Custer attacked one end of a camp of Cheyennes, Arapahos, Kiowas, and Comanches, which extended for more than twenty miles along the Washita River. It contained not less than two thousand warriors, and he was exceedingly fortunate in not then meeting the fate which afterwards overtook him on the Little Big Horn.

The Washita Massacre resulted in the deaths of fifty Indians, mostly non-combatants, several hundred Indian ponies ordered shot by Custer, and fifty or more Indian wounded. Twenty-one soldiers were killed and thirteen wounded. Twenty of the KIA were under the command of Captain Joel Elliot, a friend of Captain Frederick Benteen, who was also at Washita. Benteen's letter to a friend criticizing the operation was published without his permission in a newspaper, making Custer, with whom Benteen never had a good relationship, furious. Benteen would later be credited by many of the Little Bighorn survivors as the chief engineer of their survival.—Ed. 2015

Some years after the Mexican war, about fifty American desperadoes, went to Chihuahua, and hired themselves to the governor of that Mexican state, to clear the country of the Apaches, who were devastating it. They organized themselves into a company under the leadership of John Glanton, one of the most notoriously cold-blooded ruffians that ever lived, and in a very short time became such a terror to the Indians, that they left the state entirely. As the company was paid "by the scalp," this state of things was not at all to its taste, and inquiries for Indians were pushed in all directions.

The captain finally discovered that an immense Apache winter camp was stretched along on the American side of the Grand Canon of the Rio Grande. He attacked one end of this camp at daylight one morning, and so scattered were the Indians and so difficult the ground, that his command took (it was said) over two hundred and fifty scalps, of men, women, and children, before the Indians could concentrate in sufficient force to make it prudent for him to retire.

To Indians at peace, and with food in plenty, the winter camp is the scene of constant enjoyment. After the varying excitements, the successes and vicissitudes, the constant labors of many months, the prospect of the winter's peace and rest, with its home life and home pleasures, comes like a soothing balm to all.

To those of the warriors who have passed the age of passionate excitements, (who have reached the "whist-age" of their English speaking contemporaries), this season brings the full enjoyment of those pleasures and excitements yet left to them in life. Their days are spent in gambling, their long winter evenings in endless repetitions of stories of their wonderful performances in days gone by, and their nights in the sound sweet sleep vouchsafed only to easy consciences.

The old women also have a good time.]No more taking down and putting up the tepee, no more packing and unpacking the ponies. To bring the wood and water, do the little cooking, to attend to the ponies, and possibly to dress a few skins, is all the labor devolved on them.

To the young of both sexes, whether married or single, this season brings unending excitement and pleasure. Now is the time for dances and feasts, for visits and frolics, and merry-makings of all kinds, and for this time, the "story-teller" has prepared and rehearsed his most marvellous recitals. Above all, it is the season for love-making "Love rules the camp," and now is woman's opportunity.

Without literature, without music or painting as arts, without further study of nature than is necessary for the safety or the needs of their daily life, with no knowledge or care for politics or finance, or the thousand questions of social or other science, that disturb and perplex the minds of civilized people, and with reasoning faculties little superior to instinct, there is among Indians no such thing as conversation as we understand it. There is plenty of talk but no interchange of ideas, no expression and comparison of views and beliefs, except on the most commonplace topics. Half a dozen old sages will be sitting around, quietly and gravely passing the pipe, and apparently engaged in important discussion. Nine times out of ten, their talk is the merest camp tattle, or about a stray horse, or sick colt, or where one killed a deer, or another saw a buffalo track. All serious questions are reserved for discussion in the council lodge, and the ordinary mental activity of the Indian may be estimated at zero.

During the pleasant months, he has constantly the healthy stimulus of active life; during the winter he is either in a state of lethargy, or of undue excitement. During the day, in the winter season, the men gamble or sleep, the women work or idle as suits each, but the moment it gets dark, everybody is on the "qui-vive," ready for any fun that presents itself. A few beats on a tom-tom bring all the inmates of the neighboring lodges, a dance or gambling bout is soon inaugurated, and oftentimes kept up until nearly morning.

The insufficiency and uncertainty of human happiness has been the theme of eloquent writers of all ages. I have a theory that every man's happiness is lodged in his own nature, and is, to a certain extent at least, independent of his external circumstances and surroundings. These primitive people demonstrate the general correctness of this theory, for they are habitually and universally the happiest people I ever saw. They thoroughly enjoy the present, make no worry over the possibilities of the future, and "never cry over spilt milk." It may be argued that their apparent happiness is only insensibility, the happiness of the mere animal, whose animal desires are satisfied. It may be so. I simply state facts, others may draw conclusions. The Indian is proud, sensitive, quick-tempered, easily wounded, easily excited, but though utterly unforgiving, he never broods. This in my opinion, is the whole secret of his happiness.

In spite of that dreadful institution, polygamy, and the fact that the wives are mere property, the domestic life of the Indian will bear comparison with that of average civilized communities. The husband as a rule, is kind; ruling, but with no harshness. The wives are generally faithful, obedient, and industrious. The children are spoiled, and a nuisance to all red visitors. Fortunately, the white man, the "bug-a-boo" of their baby days, is yet such an object of terror as to keep them at a respectful distance. Among themselves, the members of the family are perfectly easy and unrestrained. It is extremely rare that there is any quarrelling among the wives.

There is no such thing as nervousness in either sex. Living in but the one room, they are from babyhood accustomed to what would be unbearable annoyance to whites. The head of the lodge comes back tired from a hunt, throws himself down on a bed, and goes fast to sleep, though his two or three wives chatter around and his children tumble all over him. Everybody in the lodge seems to do just as he or she pleases, and this seems no annoyance to anybody else.

Unlike her civilized sister, the Indian woman, "in her hour of greatest need," does not need anyone. She would be shocked at the idea of having a man doctor. Parturition is a matter of no concern or trouble with her. In pleasant weather, the expectant mother betakes herself to the seclusion of some thicket; in winter she goes to a tepee provided in each band for the women. In a few hours she returns with the baby in its cradle on her back, and goes about her usual duties as if nothing had happened.

They never wean their children, but continue to nurse as long as the child wishes, or until another comes.

OCCUPATIONS OF CAMP AND LODGE

FROM the account I have given of then home life some idea may be formed of the ordinary occupations of Indians in their natural condition.

Preparations for war or the chase occupy such hours of the winter encampment as the noble red man can spare from gambling, love-making and personal adornment.

Each Indian must make for himself everything which he cannot procure by barter, and the opportunities for barter of the more common necessities are very few, the Indians not having even yet conceived the idea of making any articles for sale among themselves.

The saddle requires much time and care in its construction. Some Indians can never learn to make one, consequently this is more an article of barter than anything commonly made by Indians.

No single article varies so much in make and value as the bridle. The bit is always purchased, and is of every pattern, from the plain snaffle to the complicated and cruel contrivance of the Mexicans. The bridle of one Indian may be a mere head-stall of raw-hide attached to the bit, but without frontlet or throat-latch, and with reins of the same material, the whole not worth a dollar; that of another may be so elaborated by patient labor, and so garnished with silver, as to be worth a hundred dollars.

The Southern Indians have learned from the Mexicans the art of plaiting horsehair, and much of their work is very artistic and beautiful, besides being wonderfully serviceable. A small smooth stick of one-fourth of an inch in diameter is the mould over which the hair is plaited. When finished, the stick is withdrawn. The hair used is previously dyed of different colors, and it is so woven as to present pretty patterns. This hair, not being very strong, is used for the head-stall; the reins, which require strength, are plaited solid, but in the same pattern, showing both skill, taste and fitness.

The name "lariat" (Spanish, riata,) is applied by all frontiersmen and Indians to the rope or cord used for picketing or fastening their horses while grazing, and also to the thong used for catching wild animals—the lasso. They are the same, with a very great difference. The lasso may be used for picketing a horse, but the rope with which a horse is ordinarily picketed would never be of use as a lasso.

A good riata ("lasso") requires a great deal of labor and patient care. It is sometimes made of plaited hair from the manes and tails of horses, but these are not common, except where wild horses are plenty, one such riata requiring the hair of not less than twenty horses. It is generally made of the raw hide of buffalo or domestic cattle, freed from hair, cut into narrow strips, and plaited with infinite patience and care, so as to be perfectly round and smooth. Such a "riata," though costing less money than that of hair, is infinitely superior. It is smooth, round, heavy, runs easily and quickly to noose, and is as strong as a cable. Those tribes, as the Utes, who are unable to procure beef or buffalo skins, make beautiful lariats of thin strips of buckskin plaited together; but as these are used only for securing their horses they are usually plaited flat.

To make these articles is all that the male Indian "finds to do" in his ordinary winter life. Without occupation, without literature, without thought, how he can persuade himself to continue to exist can be explained only on the hypothesis that he is a natural "club man," or a mere animal.

"From rosy morn to dewy eve" there is always work for the Indian woman. Fortunately for her, the "aboriginal inhabitants" have as yet discovered no means of making a light sufficient to work by at night. It is true, they beg or buy a few candles from military posts, or traders, but these are sacredly preserved for dances and grand occasions.

But slave as she is, I doubt if she could be forced to work after dark, even if she had light. Custom, which holds her in so many inexorable bonds, comes to her aid in this case. In every tribe, night is the woman's right, and no matter how urgent the work which occupies her during daylight, the moment that dark comes, she bedecks herself in her best finery, and stands at the door of the lodge, her ear strained for the first beat of the tom-tom, which summons her to where she is for the nonce queen and ruler.

There was formerly one exception to this immunity from night work, but it has gone with the buffalo. At the time of the "great fall hunt," there was no rest nor excuse for her. She must work at any and all hours. If the herds were moving, the success of the hunt might depend on the rapidity with which the women performed their work on a batch of dead buffalo. These animals spoil very quickly if not disemboweled, and though the hunters tried to regulate the daily kill by the ability of the squaws to "clean up" after them, they could not, in the nature of things, always do so.

When the buffalo was dead the man's work was done. It was woman's work to skin and cut up the dead animal; and oftentimes when the men were exceptionally fortunate, the women were obliged to work hard and fast, all night long before their task was finished.

The meat, cut as closely as possible from the bones, is tied up in the skin, and packed to camp on the ponies. The entrails, emptied of their contents, form the principal food of all during the hunt, not only being the most delicious morsel, but not requiring a waste of time in cooking.

The skins are spread, flesh-side upward, on a level piece of ground, small slits are cut in the edges of each skin, and it is tightly stretched and fastened down by wooden pegs driven through the slits into the ground. The meat is cut into thin flakes and placed on poles or scaffolds to dry in the sun.

All this work must be done, as it were, instantly, for if the skin is allowed to dry unstretched, it can never be made of use as a robe, and the meat spoils if not "jerked" within a few hours.

This lively work lasts but a few weeks, and is looked upon by the workers themselves pretty much in the same way as notable civilized housewives look upon the yearly housecleaning, very disagreeable, but very enjoyable. The real work begins when, the hunt being over, the band has gone into its winter quarters, for then must the women prepare and utilize "the crop."

Some of the thickest bull's hides are placed to soak in water, in which is mixed wood ashes, or some natural alkali. This takes the hair off. The skin is then cut into the required shape, and stretched on a form, on which it is allowed to dry, when it not only retains its shape, but becomes almost as hard as iron. These boxes are of various shapes and sizes, some made like huge pocket-books, others like trunks. All are called "*parfleche*," though why, I have never been able to get a satisfactory explanation.

As soon as these *parfleches* or trunks are ready for use, the now thoroughly dry meat is pounded to powder between two stones. About two inches of this powdered meat is placed in the bottom of a par-fleche, and melted tallow is poured over it. Then another layer of meat is served in the same way, and so until the trunk is full. It is kept hot until the whole mass is thoroughly saturated. When cold, the *parfleches* are closed and tightly tied up. The contents, so prepared, will keep in good condition for several years. Probably the best feature of the process is that nothing is lost, the flesh of old and tough animals being, after this treatment, so nearly as good as that of young that few persons can tell the difference. I might reverse the statement and say that all meat is so utterly spoiled by the process that there is no longer room for comparatives, good or bad. This is the true Indian bread, and is used as bread when they have fresh meat. Boiled, it makes a soup not very palatable but nutritious. So long as the Indian has this dried meat he is entirely independent of all other food. Of late years, all the beef issued to the Indians on reservations, and not needed for immediate consumption, is treated in this way.

The dressing of skins is the next work. The thickest hides are put in soak of alkali, for materials for making shields, saddles, riatas, etc. Hides for making or repairing lodges are treated in the same way, but, after the hair has been removed, they are reduced in thickness, made pliable, and most frequently smoked.

Deer, antelope, and other thin skins are beautifully prepared for clothing, the hair being always removed. Some of these skins are so worked down that they are almost as thin and white as cotton cloth.

But the crowning process is the preparation of a buffalo robe. The skin of even the youngest and fattest cow is in its natural condition much too thick for use, being unwieldy and lacking pliability. This thickness must be reduced at least one-half, and the skin at the same time made soft and pliable. When the stretched skin has become dry and hard from the action of the sun, the woman goes to work upon it with a small implement, shaped somewhat like a carpenter's adze. It has a short handle of wood or elk-horn, tied on with rawhide, and is used with one hand. These tools are heirlooms in families, and greatly prized. It is exceedingly difficult to obtain one, especially one with an elk-horn handle, the Indians valuing them above price. With this tool the woman chips at the hardened skin, cutting off a thin shaving at every blow. The skill in the whole process consists in so directing and tempering the blows as to cut the skin, yet not cut too deep, and in finally obtaining a uniform thickness and perfectly smooth and even inner surface. To render the skin soft and pliable, the chipping is stopped every little while, and the chipped surface smeared with brains of buffalo, which are thoroughly rubbed in with a smooth stone.

When very great care and delicacy are required, the skin is stretched vertically on a frame of poles. It is claimed that the chipping process can be much more perfectly performed on a skin stretched in this way than on one stretched on the uneven and unyielding ground, but the latter is used for all common robes, because it is the easiest.

When the thinning and softening process is completed, the robe is taken out of its frame, trimmed, and sometimes smoked. It is now ready for use. It is a long and tedious process, and no one but an Indian would go through it.

Bat all this, though harder work, is the mere commencement of the long and patient labor which the loving wife bestows on the robe which the husband is to use on dress occasions. The whole inner surface is frequently covered with designs beautifully worked with porcupine quills, or grasses dyed in various colors. Sometimes the embellishments are paintings. I have seen many elegant robes that must have taken a year to finish.

Every animal brought into the camp brings work for the squaw. The buck comes in with a deer and drops it at the door. The squaw skins it, cuts up and preserves the meat, dresses the skin and fashions it into garments for some member of the family. Until within a very few years the needle was a piece of sharpened bone, the thread a fibre of sinew. These are yet used in the ornamentation of robes, but almost all the ordinary sewing is done with civilized appliances.

All Indians are excessively fond of bead-work, and not only the clothing, moccasins, gun-covers, quivers, knife-sheaths and tobacco pouches, but every little bag or ornament is covered with this work. Many of the designs are pretty and artistic. In stringing the beads for this work an ordinary needle is used, but in every case, except for articles made for sale, the thread used is sinew.

Only a few years ago the foregoing description of the ordinary employments of Indians was true to the letter, for almost every tribe west of the Missouri and east of the Rocky Mountains. It is yet true for most of them, but some few have taken, within these few years, long steps on the "white man's road," and the

A few years ago the Indian Bureau, with its usual sagacity, prohibited the sale of beads to the Indians by the traders at one or more of the agencies. The Indians were furious, claiming the right to spend their own money in bedecking themselves in their own way.

This apparently little point might have cost much money and many lives if the Bureau had not prudently "backed down." Occupations of both men and women of those tribes will not conform to my description.

The life in the winter encampment has scarcely been changed in any particular, but with the earliest spring come evidences of activity, a desire to get away, not attributable, as in the "good old time," to plans of forays for scalps and plunder, but to the desire of each head of a lodge or band to reach before anyone else does, the particular spot on which he has fixed for his location for the summer. No sooner has he reached it than all hands, men, women and children, fall to work as if the whole thing were a delightful frolic. Fences are made, ground broken up and seed planted; and all summer long many of the noble Red Men, with wives and children, may be found working in the fields nearly naked, sweaty, dirty, and unromantic.

The peerless warrior with "eye like the eagle," whose name a few short years ago was a terror, and whose swoop destruction, may be found patiently plodding between the handles of a plough. The tender maiden—wont in fiction to sacrifice herself to save her lover, or, reduced to despair, to fling herself from "tallest cliff into the raging flood beneath,"—may now be seen following the plough of the father, nimbly plying the sportive hoe, intent only on getting through with a square day's work, and thinking fondly of the square meal that is to follow it; or when the crop is laid by, challenging that father to a friendly contest in a wood-chopping match, in which, nine times out of ten, she beats him shamefully.

I consider myself a friend of the Indian, and as such, have some natural hesitation in divulging the secret of his present pursuits. Most of his civilized friends love him for his high crimes, his magnificent misdemeanors, his brilliant felonies. When they contrast the pictures drawn by Catlin, Cooper and others, of the daring and chivalrous warriors, beauteous and loving maidens—peers and counterparts of knights and mistresses whose deeds and loves gloss with romance all mediaeval literature—with these here presented; what he is, in their minds, with what he is in reality, I fear they will turn from him with loathing and disgust. With sentimentalists, brilliant crime always commands admiration, squalid labor deserves only contempt.

The last five years, more than any twenty preceding them, have convinced the wild Indians of the utter futility of their warfare against the United States Government. One and all, they are thoroughly whipped; and their contests in the future will be the acts of predatory parties (for which the Indians at large are no more responsible than is the Government of the United States for the acts of highwaymen in the Black Hills, or train-robbers in Missouri), or a deliberate determination of the bands and tribes to die fighting rather than by the slow torture of starvation to which the government condemns them.

The buffalo is gone, so also nearly all the other large game on which the Indians depended for food. They are confined to comparatively restricted reservations, and completely surrounded by whites. They are more perfectly aware of the stringency of their situation than any white man can possibly be, for they daily feel its pressure.

With no chance of success in war, with no possibility of providing food for themselves, with no adequate assistance from government, they thoroughly comprehend that their only hope for the future is in work, or as they express it, "in the white man's road."

They do not like it of course; it would be unnatural if they did. They accept it as the dire alternative against starvation.

Does anyone labor for the sake of labor? A man who spaded up a field simply to give himself labor would be considered a fit subject for the lunatic asylum.

Labor is the curse on Adam, and, however necessary and ennobling, is not an end but a means. We labor for money, for ambition, for health, for anything except for labor itself.

Basing arguments on the Indian contempt for work, many men in and out of Congress talk eloquent nonsense of the impossibility of ever bringing him to agricultural pursuits. The average Indian has no more hatred of labor, as such, than the average white man. Neither will labor unless an object is to be attained. Both will labor rather than starve. Heretofore the Indian could comfortably support himself in his usual and preferred life, without labor; and there being no other incentive, he would, in my opinion, have only proved himself an idiot, had he worked without an object.

TRADE AND BARTER

FROM the days when the Dutch ancestors of the nobility of Manhattan Island simplified their trade with the Indians by making the hand of each trader weigh one pound and his foot two pounds, to the present time, every scheme that ingenuity could devise has been used to prevent the Indians from gaining any definite idea of values.

Though every particle of the trade is really nothing but barter (the exchange of one commodity for another), the care of the trader is always to refer to money prices, and thus prevent the Indian from gaining an idea of the value of one article of barter as compared with the value of some other article of barter. All must be referred to money, and as, until quite recently, the Indian could not grasp the idea of a "circulating medium," he was always in a mystified condition—that is, in exactly the proper condition for the purpose of the trader. Thus the trader will say, "I will give you five, or ten, cents a pound for your dressed deer-skins;" "I will give you so much a piece for your wolf-skins," etc., etc. The Indian accepts, sells out, and then asks the trader how much it all comes to. Immediately after, the Indian commences to buy. The trader says: "I will sell you this calico for twenty-five cents a yard." The offer is accepted, and purchases continued until the credit is exhausted. To us the logical sequence that one yard of calico is worth two and one-half or five pounds of dressed deerskins is perfectly clear, but no such high order of ratiocination ever culminated in the brain of a wild Indian.

But before utterly condemning the Indian for his lack of perspicacity we must reflect that all values to him are mere accidents of his surroundings. Aside from his intentional mystification, and the absence of any competing trader or other means of arriving at relative values, nothing can have a fixed price to the Indian, his estimate of the value of any article being exactly in proportion to his need of it.

Our boyhood's hero, Robinson Crusoe, would have given half his island for the few seeds of corn which he fortunately discovered; and the Count de Moncerf, immured in the prison of the bandits, paid, with however many protests, his hundred thousand francs for a breakfast.

These tales of fiction are true to nature.

"Who can estimate the value of a match to the freezing wanderer on the wintry Plains? or of a cup of water to the shipwrecked mariner alone on the wide expanse of ocean?

There can be no fixed prices when things are weighed against necessities. The white man has the things, the Indian the necessities.

It would scarcely be fair to attribute the Indian ignorance or carelessness of values entirely to the causes above enumerated. By nature he is a perfect child, and when he wants anything he wants it with all his heart and mind and soul, immediately, and without reference to anything else. Like the child, who would gladly exchange the ten-dollar bill given him as a Christmas present for a red apple or a toy drum, the Indian will give anything he possesses for the merest bauble to which he takes a fancy. A novelty has the greatest charm, and he will pay a hundred times its value for an article new to him.

In 1867 a Sioux Indian came to. Fort Sedgwick, while I commanded it, having in his possession a very fine and elaborately painted buffalo robe. Many efforts were made by the officers to purchase it; money, sugar, coffee, flour, etc., to the amount of twenty dollars, were offered and refused.

Sometime after a sergeant passed, who had in his hand a paper containing two or three pounds of loaf sugar, cut into cubic blocks (cut-loaf, then new to frontier people and to Indians). He gave the Indian a few lumps and passed on. In a few moments the Indian came running after him, took the robe from his shoulders, and offered it for the paper of sugar. The exchange being made, he sat down on the ground and deliberately ate up every lump.

Years ago, when matches were not so universally used as now, a Lipan Indian was visiting Fort Martin Scott in Texas. One day an officer to whom he was talking took from his pocket a box of what, to the Indian, were merely little sticks, and, scratching one on a stone, lit his pipe. The Lipan eagerly inquired into this mystery, and looked on with astonishment while several matches were lighted for his gratification. Going to his camp nearby, he soon came back, bringing half a dozen beautifully dressed wildcat skins, which he offered for the wonderful box. The exchange was accepted, and he went off greatly pleased. Sometime after he was found sitting by a large stone, on which he was gravely striking match after match, holding each in his fingers until forced to drop it, and then carefully inspecting the scorched finger, as if to assure himself that it was real fire. This he continued until every match was burned.

During the Ute campaign of this summer, 1880, I purchased from those Indians several Navaho blankets. They are not only admirable as blankets, but fanciful in design, and very bright in colors. On my return to the Indian Territory the Cheyennes soon found out that I had them. Almost every man, woman, and child, of all the camps about me has been at my house to see them, all expressing the most unbounded admiration. Every persuasion has been used and inducement held out to me to "swap," and were I of a "speculative turn of mind" I could easily get two ponies (fifty to sixty dollars) for each of them.

Up to within a very few years the trade of Indians in furs and skins (peltries) was estimated at not less than twelve millions of dollars yearly, and the trade in other products of various kinds added not a little to the amount. Since the destruction of the buffalo the former trade has greatly fallen off, but there has been some gain in the other products.

There is a law on our statute book (section 2137) prohibiting persons other than Indians from killing game except for subsistence, and from hunting and trapping in the Indian country. This law is and has always been a dead letter, the whole of that country having been constantly overrun by white men, who made their living by killing game and trapping the furbearing animals. These men, aided by Indians, built up the great fur trade of North America, founding some of the most colossal fortunes in the world.

When I first came to the "Far West," thirty-two years ago, trapping was still an institution. Generally alone, sometimes in couples, rarely in more numerous companies, trappers ranged the whole country wherever peltries were to be had, taking each year sufficient to make a trade so immense that great cities like St. Louis may be said to have been built upon it.

It is a common matter of wonder among persons ignorant of the ways of the Plains, how these men could have voluntarily adopted a means of livelihood apparently so full of danger; and how it was possible for so many of them to escape from their "environment of perils" and live to enjoy a "green old age." The explanation is simple. The trappers generally started in a company from St. Louis, St. Jo., or someone of the outfitting towns. They were well provided not only with arms, traps, and other necessities to their business, but with a goodly assortment of so-called "Indian goods," articles likely to be most acceptable to the tribes among which they expected to domicile themselves.

Taking advantage of the intervals of peace between the tribes, and steering clear of those tribes supposed to be specially hostile to whites, they arrived in the country they proposed to trap over and immediately separated into small parties, many going off entirely alone. Each making his way to the village of Indians most convenient to the territory in which he wished to trap, proceeded to interview the chief whose friendship and protection were gained by generous presents. After a short sojourn, other presents purchased one or more squaws and a tepee. He thus became a member of the tribe, went where he pleased within the limits of its territory, and set his traps as suited his pleasure. His squaws did all the work, made and mended his clothing, cooked his food, skinned the animals caught, and properly cared for the pelts.

Within the limits of the territory of the tribe with which he was affiliated, he was as safe from harm as any other member of it, and the "hair-breadth 'scapes" of which we have read so much were those which he had in common with the Indians with whom he lived.

Besides the pelts taken by his own hand, he added to his store by purchases from the Indians, thus encouraging and stimulating them to extra activity in the pursuit of game, and greatly adding to his own profits. Each year his pelts were taken to the nearest trading-post of the Hudson Bay, or American Fur Company, where, after purchasing the supplies necessary for the ensuing year, he squandered the remainder at the gaming-table or in a furious orgie.

These were the "traders" with whom the majority of Indians first came in contact.

The profits of this business were so enormous that the government attempted to take control of it, and in 1834 passed a law (Sec. 2129, Revised Statutes) prohibiting any person from trading with Indians, except such as should have permits from certain United States officials. The only effect of this law was to divert these profits into certain channels. The condition of the Indian was in no way improved; he was still at the mercy of plunderers.

In 1866 a really good law was enacted (Sec. 2128, Rev. Stat.), evidently with the design of giving the Indian some of the advantages of competition, but this law has been utterly disregarded by the authorities, and the Indian ring still holds its felonious grip on the Indian throat.

Within a comparatively few years, almost all the wild Indian tribes have been subjugated and placed on reservations; an effort, ludicrous, were it not so sad, being still made to reconcile the absurdity of treating as sovereign nations people whom we actually hold as prisoners of war.

So long as the Indian had the buffalo he was enabled to subsist in comfort, even on these comparatively restricted areas, and his trade was of sufficient importance to excite competition between those' authorized by the Indian Bureau to trade with him.

At the present time Indian trade with whites is very simple. An individual is given the sole right to trade on a reservation, or with a certain tribe or tribes. He is the only person from whom the Indians can buy such articles as they need. He is the only person to whom they can sell such articles as they have to dispose of. The monopoly is complete, and under the illegal ruling of the Indian department there can be no competition.

The barefaced swindling of the unfortunate Indian that goes on under this condition of affairs can scarcely be conceived. Articles of civilized manufacture, now daily becoming more and more necessary to the Indian, are sold to him at hundreds per cent, profit.

Of course he need not buy if he does not wish to do so; but he wants the article, and is prevented from buying from anyone else; so he must either be swindled or go without it.

So also with his sales. He brings the trader a lot of peltries, and is offered in trade, five or ten per cent, of their value. He need not sell, of course. It is all a square and open business transaction with the trader. There is no force, nor even persuasion about it. If the Indian does not choose to accept the trader's price, he can take his peltries back with him to his camp.

The poor devil, hemmed in on all sides, accepts the situation exactly as he would an unavoidable death at the stake, and whatever he may think on the subject, makes no protest, but accepts any price offered, or gives any asked, without murmur or question.

The destruction of the buffalo has forced the Indians to adopt a great many expedients for raising money to buy those articles of civilized manufacture that have now become common necessaries among them. Of these expedients the most remarkable and unlooked for is work. Formerly only women worked. In Indian estimation, a man degraded himself by doing anything that had the appearance of labor. Now it is not unusual to see gangs of men and women cutting and piling cordwood, or raking and loading hay, as busy and noisy as civilized laborers.

Many of the contracts for the supply of fuel and hay to military posts are filled, partially at least, by the labor of Indian men and women.

In many instances the contractors are Indian traders, for their personal acquaintance with and influence among the Indians, and their ability to pay for work done in goods, give them a signal advantage over other bidders. In other cases, the contractor makes some agreement with the trader and pays his Indian laborers with orders on the latter. In either case, the result is the same swindling of the Indian.

A short time ago I was told by an Indian that he had cut twenty cords of wood for a contractor, for which he was to receive one dollar and twenty-five cents per cord. The wood was delivered, and he received an order on an Indian trader some sixty miles away for payment of the amount. In due time he presented the order, and was paid one pint cup of brown sugar for each cord of wood cut.

Paul's Valley, in the Chickasaw Nation, is one of the garden spots of earth. Thousands of bushels of corn are raised by the Indians in and near this valley. They can sell only to the Indian trader. I have been informed that the average price paid the Indians is fifteen cents per bushel in goods (three to five cents cash). This corn is really worth there over one dollar a bushel in cash.

From every article sold to and everything bought of an Indian the trader receives his hundreds of per cent, of profit. He has thorough control of the financial affairs of the tribe; not a transaction can be effected without paying him his enormous toll.

At present the trade is very much like that of the country merchant at the East, except that the trader fixes the price for both buying and selling. An Indian comes to the store when he has anything to sell, and taking out the entire proceeds in trade, returns to his home exactly like a farmer in the East.

The Indian barter among themselves is conducted as might be expected from what has been said. He is sharp in a horse trade, and generally correct in his estimate of the value of one article of daily use as compared to another. In these estimates, however, time is not considered. He has not yet arrived at that stage of progress when a "day's work" has a definite value. When considering the value of any article his first thought is, "Can I make it myself?" and if so, the number of days it will take him to do it is a matter of no consequence. A man will work a month to complete a bow and quiver of arrows and then sell them for five dollars. A woman will spend five dollars on beads, and work faithfully for three months making and ornamenting with them a cradle or some other article, and then sell it for ten dollars.

The inter-tribal trade varies very greatly in importance. Among the Plains tribes it is extremely limited. A trade is, however, springing up.

The Utes have a very considerable trade with the .Navahos, and these again with the Arizona tribes, even to the Gulf of California. I bought from a Ute Indian a beautiful necklace of sea-shells, which had been passed from hand to hand in trade all the way from the Pacific, coast.

INDIAN COOKS AND COOKING

UNLESS able to rival powers of Dr. Tanner, among Indians the fasting vegetarian would have little chance of 'survival.' In their natural condition the sole diet of the Plains Indians for at least nine months in the year is the flesh of animals, and are though they prefer it cooked, by no means averse to it raw.

In camp the duty of cooking is usually devolved on the oldest or least favorite squaw. There is no variety of style, no French methods, no necessity for titillating appetites already over-keen. A pot full of meat and water is put on the fire and boiled, but there is no definite point in the cooking process when the food is "done." If an Indian is especially hungry, he may commence on the contents of the pot by the time they are fairly warm. Generally, however, it is allowed to boil until the head of the lodge intimates that he is hungry, when the pot is set off the fire; and each, crowding around, helps him or herself with knives or fingers, sometimes with a huge stick, cut in the shape of a ladle. Among the more advanced tribes tin plates are now frequently used, and, sitting around on the beds or ground, the diners are helped successively by the old squaw who does the cooking. This is considered the civilized, the "ton-ish" way, but is not much liked, the helping squaw being always suspected of favoritism. There is no fault-finding about the cooking, and whether "half raw," or "done to rags," no objection is made, provided the meat be of good quality, and sufficient in quantity.

This is the habitual and formal style of cooking and eating in the permanent camp, and also on hunting and pleasure parties, when squaws are taken to cook for them; but on warlike or thieving expeditions, when no women are along, each buck cooks for himself, broiling his meat on the coals, or roasting it on a stick over the fire.

There is no doubt that good meat cooked in this way is far more palatable than that boiled, nor that the Indian greatly prefers his out-door style of cooking; but boiling is less trouble, and, therefore, preferred by the women. That he at home puts up with boiled meat every day of his life, when he prefers it broiled or roasted, is pretty good evidence that, however complete and vigorous his sway, however absolute his power over his family under certain circumstances, he is yet subject in his domestic circle to the same control, or influence, that falls to the lot of civilized man.

The Indian is a great epicure; knows the choicest titbits of every animal, and just how to cook it to suit his taste. The great fall hunt yields him the fullest enjoyment of his appetite, for then he not only has choice of the more savory parts, but, the women being employed in other work, it is not derogatory to his dignity to cook for himself.

His days are spent in all the delights and excitements of the chase, and almost the whole of his nights in feasting and revelry. This is the time for" marrow guts," for "hump ribs," and for "marrow bones." The first can, to the Indian, scarcely be improved by cooking, but the greatest epicures will wrap eight or ten feet around a stick, sprinkle it plentifully with salt, and hold it in a bright blaze until the melted fat streams down. The whole mass is swallowed almost red-hot, and is the choicest bonne bouche with which an Indian palate can be tickled.

In butchering, the women cut the meat as closely as possible from the bones, but leaving on and between the ribs many a glorious mouthful. Broad slabs of these ribs are placed before a fire of hot coals, turned, basted, and roasted *secundem artem*. The large bones of the hind legs are thrown upon the glowing coals, or hidden under the hot embers, then cracked the bones—nothing cracked between two stones, and the rich, delicious marrow sucked in quantities sufficient to ruin a white stomach forever.

Marrow-fat is believed by the Indians to be especially good for the hair, and during the feast the greasy hands are constantly wiped upon and passed through his long tails.

The Indian is an enormous feeder. But that corroborative evidence is so easily obtained, I should hesitate to give details of his wonderful capacity of stomach. In the course of a night of feasting, dancing, and story-telling, an average Indian will consume from ten to fifteen pounds of meat; and if he has abundance of food, and can make selection of the parts to be eaten, he will swallow, without indigestion or other inconvenience, not less than twenty pounds.

I was once on a hunt with an escort—the Sioux being very bad—of twenty infantry soldiers and seven Pawnee Indians. On the second day we killed a magnificent buck elk, one of the finest I ever saw, and weighing gross not less than seven hundred pounds. Cutting the carcass in two, behind the ribs, I reserved the hind-quarters to take back to camp, and taking a few pounds for the use of our mess, I gave the soldiers one fore-quarter, and the Indians the other. To these latter I also gave the entrails, which were eaten on the spot, raw.

The Indians danced and feasted all night, and came to me next morning for more meat. Seven Indians had had fifteen or twenty pounds more meat than twenty soldiers; yet next morning the soldiers had enough to last two whole days, the Indians had nothing. With fullest allowance for bone, they had averaged in the night's feast at least fifteen pounds apiece, but in the morning, like "Oliver Twist," they wanted "more."

An old Indian employed as guide at a military post was much liked and petted by the officers of the garrison, and was always invited to sit down to table if he happened in an officer's quarters at meal time. He soon found out that they breakfasted at different hours, and before a great while it was discovered that about twice a week the old fellow commenced with the earliest and wound up with the latest, so well timing himself as to secure four hearty breakfasts on one and the same morning. By a little management he might have secured a breakfast from someone of the officers every day in the week, but he preferred to have a good square meal, a regular surfeit, twice a week, and took this method of getting it, being ashamed to eat so much as he wanted at anyone house.

Some years ago an exploring party found itself in a country so barren of game that the efforts of its best hunters had been able to secure only one huge turkey gobbler, so old and tough that though parboiled, and boiled, and roasted, no one had been able to masticate him. Unwilling to lose so much meat, he was then cut up, put in a camp-kettle, and stewed for near twenty-four hours. Even this failing to soften him, he was about to be thrown out for the wolves, when a party of Indians made its appearance, with the inevitable demand for "chuck." The officer in command, having little else, bethought him of the turkey, and ordered it to be set before the Indians. The old chief carefully examined the contents of the kettle, then gravely informed his followers that it was "guacalote" (turkey), that to eat it would make them cowardly, that he was old, had not long to live, was not ambitious of further distinction, and would therefore risk it. After this exhortation he deliberately turned to the kettle, and in less than an hour emptied it completely, storing away, the officer declares, not less than two gallons, or sixteen pounds of solid and liquid food.

Even in their wildest state, all the Indians I have ever known use salt with their food when they can get it. This mineral is so generally distributed throughout the western country that it is easily obtained, though I have known it purchased at high prices.

The advanced tribes take greatly to condiments, using considerable quantities of both red and black pepper. Curious as it may appear, this last article is used frequently in tea and coffee. This is done by old men, who believe it invigorates them.

Among white hunters, the rule of parties hunting together is, that while the meat must be divided equally among all, the hide and horns belong to the man who shot the animal. Among Indians, the general rule is the same, but the special perquisite of the successful shot, and that on which he sets most store, is the entrails. As soon as the game is killed it is opened, and the lucky hunter seating himself beside the carcass, betakes himself to what is to him a most perfect repast. The smaller entrails go first, but he is not satisfied until bowels, stomach, liver, and not unfrequently, heart and lungs have all disappeared before his astounding appetite.

The liver of a very fat buffalo or elk will not unfrequently become granulated and broken up by overheating in a long chase. This, with the contents of the gall-bladder sprinkled over it, is one of the most delicious of all morsels that can titillate an Indian palate. A Pawnee chief, a great friend of mine, once brought and presented me with several pounds of this stuff tied up in a handkerchief. He was greatly astonished when I told him I could not eat it, but his mortification did not prevent his burying his face in the handkerchief, from which he scarcely lifted it until every particle of the horrid mess had disappeared.

The smaller entrails of even the largest animals are eaten raw.

Dog-flesh is regarded by the Sioux as almost a sacred dish, being reserved only for feasts on occasions of ceremony, or when desiring to do special honor to a distinguished guest. When very fat, wolf is considered nearly, if not quite, as good as dog.

The Cheyennes and Arapahos are very fond of fat puppy, but only eat dog when forced to it by hunger.

The Comanches are extremely fond of horse-flesh, preferring it to beef or even buffalo. The most delicate and delicious dish that a Comanche can set before his most distinguished guest is the foetus of a mare boiled in its own liquid.

Even when buffalo and other large game was most plentiful, skunk was most highly esteemed as an article of diet, and was considered specially beneficial to women in an interesting condition. The odor of the animal is no protection against the Indian, who seizes it by the tail and beats it against the ground until dead, regardless alike of the fetid discharge which would sicken a white man, or of the danger of 18 its bite, which in some portions of the country is almost certainly followed by that most horrible of all maladies, hydrophobia.

In their rambles about camp, heretofore spoken of, the boys kill with their arrows a good many birds, rabbits, and other small game. The larger portion of these is eaten by the boys themselves, but many are taken to camp, where they are eagerly pounced upon by the mothers, whose special prerogative they seem to be. A hole is raked in the ashes, the bird or animal is placed in it and covered over with ashes and coals. After half an hour, or less, it is taken out, beaten a few times against the ground to get rid of the ashes, the feathers pulled off (bringing the skin with them), and devoured, entrails and all.

This process of cooking is by no means appetizing to witness, but I can aver, from personal experience, that it is really the very best way to cook a small and delicately flavored bird, all its juices being retained.

Some few animals and birds were protected by superstition—though this was not strong enough to amount to absolute prohibition. They could not be eaten by the Indian under ordinary circumstances, but this did not prevent his eating them when the circumstances were extraordinary. Our favorite Christmas bird, the turkey, was tabooed to the Indian, who would not eat it, except when on the verge of starvation. He believed it would make him cowardly, and run from his enemies, as the turkey runs from his pursuers.

But all this is gone. Religion, superstition, public opinion, even self-respect, all give way before the cravings of an empty stomach.

Except in the item of a general uncleanliness, which was common then as now, the whole matter of the Indian food supply has undergone, within a few years, a complete change in most of the Indian tribes. Even as late as 1872, the food question was the least concern of Indian life; now it is the paramount, and with many of the tribes, I may say, the only question. Government has made prisoners of the Indians, confining them on reservations, has allowed white men to kill off the game supposed to be protected to them by laws, and now starves them with insufficient appropriations.

What was mere uncleanliness in the Indian's day of plenty, has degenerated into squalor. The Indian who only ten years ago contented himself with nothing but the very choicest portions of animal food, now, pinched by hunger, eats any and everything. Dogs, wolves, reptiles, half-decomposed horse-flesh, even carrion birds, all go to appease the gnawings of his famished stomach.

Last summer an Indian pony mired down in the quicksands of the river, a few miles below my post, and was drowned. The carcass was not discovered for some days. The Indians eagerly flocked around, and speedily stripped the putrid flesh from the bones, carrying it in triumph to their lodges.

Early in the fall of 1879, Stone Calf, a Cheyenne chief of standing, and a man of ability and character, came to my office and asked me to furnish rations to himself and his people. I explained to him that it was impossible, the orders of the War Department prohibiting Post Commanders from issuing rations to Indians, except by special direction of the Secretary of War.

He thought for some moments in silence, then said—

"Colonel, I want permission to go with my people to the 'Staked Plains,! to hunt."

I had no authority to give him such permission, but I might have been able to obtain it for him had I considered it safe and proper. To arrive at the "Staked Plains" he would be obliged to cross the "Panhandle" of Texas. That country is full of cattle, the Indians were nearly starving. If they crossed they were almost sure to kill some cattle, which would bring on a collision between them and the Texans. I therefore said—"No, I cannot give you the permission."

At this his face fell, and he looked very grave. Straightening himself up in his chair to the full height of his rather small figure, and looking squarely at me, "more in sorrow than in anger," he said—

"The agent will give me nothing to eat. You will give me nothing, and you will not let me go where I can get something for myself. I cannot stand it much longer. I tell you, Colonel, I had rather die fighting than die of starvation."

For the first time in my life I felt like taking an Indian to my heart. He was right, he was manly, and had justice on his side.

My official position required me to conceal my own sentiments, and try to soften the temper of his mind, but I have a great respect and admiration for Stone Calf. Were I an Indian, I fear that, with their provocations, I should be a bad Indian.

Every military post in the Indian country is besieged by these starving people. The slop-barrels and dump-piles are carefully scrutinized, and stuff that a cur would disdain is carried off in triumph. The offal about the butcher shop is quarrelled over, and devoured raw and on the spot. The warm blood of the slaughtered beeves is sucked up by numerous mouths before it has time to sink into the ground. Every horse that dies of disease or by accident, is at once converted into meat, and at Fort Reno, under the aegis of the Interior Department, and where hunger is supposed by people generally to be impossible, a dead horse or mule is no sooner dragged away from the vicinity of the post, than it is pounced upon, cut up, and carried off by the starved Indians. They ask no questions, and meat is meat, even though it was killed for farcy or glanders. Nothing is too disgustingly filthy to come amiss to the starving Indian.

Some tribes cultivate small patches of corn, vegetables, pumpkins, melons, etc. They are, however, generally eaten before they are ripe.

Some of the so-called wild tribes of the Indian Territory, as the Cheyennes and Arapahos, raise fairly good crops of corn, but it is generally hypothecated to, or soon finds its way for a mere song into the, hands of the monster devised by the government to keep the Indian in abject penury, the Indian trader.

THE BUFFALO AND ITS DESTRUCTION

IT is almost impossible for a civilized being to realize the value to the Plains Indian of the buffalo. It furnished him with home, food, clothing, bedding, horse equipment, almost everything. With it he was rich and happy, without it he is poor as poverty itself, and constantly on the verge of starvation.

Fifty years ago the buffalo ranged from the Plains of Texas to far north beyond the British line; from the Missouri and Upper Mississippi to the eastern slope of the Rocky Mountains. Every portion of this immense area, called the Plains, was either the permanent home of this animal, or might be expected to have each year one or more visits from migratory thousands.

These migrations were exceedingly erratic, depending somewhat on climate, but principally on the supply of grass.

From 1869 to 1873 I was stationed at various posts along the Arkansas River. Early in spring, as soon as the dry and apparently desert prairie had begun to change its coat of dingy brown to one of palest green, the horizon would begin to be dotted with buffalo, single, or in groups of two or three, forerunners of the coming herd. Thicker and thicker, and in larger, groups they come, until by the time the grass is well up, the whole vast landscape appears a mass of buffalo, some individuals feeding, others standing, others lying down, but the herd moving slowly, moving constantly to the northward. Of their number it was impossible to form even a conjecture.

At this season they are thin in flesh, and not at all wild, and a man on foot or horseback may approach quite close, or even ride into the herds, without causing more than a slight deviation from their course.

Determined as they are to pursue their journey northward, they are yet exceedingly cautious and timid about it, and on any alarm rush to the southward with all speed, until that alarm is dissipated. Especially is this the case when any unusual object appears in their rear, and so utterly regardless are they of consequences, that an old

Plainsman will not risk a wagon train in such a herd, where a rising ground will permit those in front to get a good view of their rear.

In May, 1871, I drove in a buggy from old Fort Zara to Fort Larned, on the Arkansas River. The distance is thirty-four miles. At least twenty-five miles of that distance was through an immense herd. The whole country appeared one mass of buffalo, moving slowly to the northward, and it was only when actually among them that it could be ascertained that the apparently solid mass was an agglomeration of countless small herds of from fifty to two hundred animals, separated from the surrounding herds by greater or less space, hut still separated.

The road ran along the broad valley of the Arkansas. Some miles from Zara a low line of hills rises from the plain on the right, gradually increasing in height, and approaching road and river, until they culminate in Pawnee Pock, when they again recede.

So long as I was in the broad level valley, the herds sullenly got out of my way, and turning, stared stupidly at me, some within thirty or forty yards. When, however, I had reached a point where the hills were no more than a mile from the road, the buffalo on the crests seeing an unusual object in their rear, turned, stared an instant, then started at full speed towards me (South), stampeding and bringing with them the numberless herds through which they passed, and pouring down upon me, no longer separated, but compacted into one immense mass of plunging animals, mad with fright, irresistible as an avalanche.

The situation was by no means pleasant. There was but one hope of escape. My horse was fortunately a quiet old beast that had rushed with me into many a herd, and been in at the death of many a buffalo. Penning him up, I waited until the front of this mass was within fifty yards, then, with a few well-directed shots, dropped some of the leaders, split the herd and sent it off in two streams to my right and left. When all had passed me they stopped, apparently perfectly satisfied, though thousands were yet within reach of my rifle, and many within less than a hundred yards. After my servant had cut out the tongues of the fallen, I proceeded on my journey, only to have a similar experience within a mile or two, and this occurred so often that I reached Fort Larned with twenty-six tongues in my wagon, representing the greatest number of buffalo that I can blame myself with having murdered in anyone day.

Some years, as in 1871, the buffalo appeared to move northward in one immense column, oftentimes from twenty to fifty miles in width, and of unknown depth from front to rear. Other years the northward journey was made in several parallel columns, moving at the same rate and with their numerous flankers covering a width of a hundred or more miles.

The line of march of this great spring migration was not always the same, though it was confined within certain limits. I am informed by old frontiersmen, that it has not, within twenty-five years, crossed the Arkansas Fiver, east of Great Bend, nor west of Big Sand Creek. The most favored routes crossed the Arkansas at the mouth of Walnut Creek, Pawnee Fork, Mulberry Creek, the Cimarron Crossing, and Big Sand Creek.

As the great herd proceeds northward it is constantly depleted, numbers wandering off to the right and left, until finally it is scattered in small herds far and wide over the vast feeding-grounds, where they pass the summer.

When the food in one locality fails, they go to another, and towards fall, when the grass of the high prairie becomes parched up by heat and drought, they gradually work their way back to the South, concentrating on the rich pastures of Texas and the Indian Territory, whence, the same instinct acting on all, they are ready to start together on the northward march, as soon as spring starts the grass.

It is but fair to say that this view is in direct conflict with the ideas of most "old Plainsmen," and of the Indians, who positively aver that the buffalo never returned south, and that each year's herd was composed of animals which had never made the journey before, and would never make it again. All admit the northern migration, that being too pronounced for any doubt or dispute, but refuse to admit the southern or return migration. Thousands of young calves were caught or killed every spring, proving that they were produced during this migration, and accompanied the herd northward, but because the buffalo did not return south in one vast body, as they went north, it was stoutly maintained that they did not go south at all. The white frontier advocates of the "no return" theory were easily confounded in argument, as they could give no reasonable hypothesis on which to account for the origin of the vast herd which yearly made its march northward. The Indian, however, was equal to the occasion. Every Plains Indian firmly believed that the buffalo were produced in countless numbers in a country under the ground; that every spring the surplus swarmed, like bees from a hive, out of great cave-like openings to this country, which were situated somewhere in the great "Llano Estacado," or Staked Plain of Texas. One Indian has gravely and solemnly assured me that he has been at those caverns, and with his own eyes saw the buffalo coming out in countless throngs. Others have told me that their fathers or uncles, or some other of the old men have been there. In 1879 Stone Calf assured me that he knew exactly where these caves were, though he had never seen them, that the Good God had provided this means for the constant supply of food for the Indian, and that however recklessly the white men might slaughter, they never could exterminate them. When last I saw him, the old man was beginning to waver in this belief, and feared that the Bad God had shut up the openings and that his people must starve.

During the spring and summer months the buffalo were but little disturbed by the Indians. Enough were killed to enable all to gorge themselves at will, but this was done quietly, by crawling or stalking. The greatest care was taken not to alarm and drive the herds away from the vicinity of the camp and villages.

Early in October, when the buffalo is at his fattest, preparations begin for the "great fall hunt," which was made for the purpose of killing sufficient animals, not only to furnish dried meat for the next winter's supply, but heavy skins for tepees, *parfleches*, saddles, etc., and lighter ones for clothing, bedding, and for trade. Runners were sent out to scour the country for long distances, and seek out the most eligible situation for the hunting-camp. It must be near water, of course; there must be plenty of timber, wherefrom to cut poles for the erection of the drying scaffolds; there must be level ground for stretching and drying the skin; and, above all, it must be in a region abounding in game.

The spot being selected, the whole band moved to it, lodges were pitched, scaffolds erected, and everything put in order for work. The dog-soldiers are masters now, and woe be to him who disobeys even the slightest of their democratic regulations. If the .game was not abundant, a few of the most sagacious hunters were sent out, who, taking advantage of winds or streams, set fire to the grass in such way as to denude the prairies, except within an area of fifteen or twenty miles contiguous to the camp. A prairie fire on the middle or northern Plains is not, as a rule, violent enough to be dangerous to animal life. The game does not stampede before it, as would appear from the pictures in the geographies, but gets out of the way, and collects on the unburned ground for the food supply, thus greatly diminishing the labor of the hunt. Other conditions being favorable, the camp is, whenever possible, pitched in a broken country, for the favorite and most successful mode of killing large numbers is by "the surround," and this is only practicable when hills and hollows, breaks and ravines render the approach to the herd easy, and prevent other herds from seeing or hearing the commotion and noise attendant upon its destruction.

All being ready the best hunters are out long before the dawn of day. If several herds of buffalo are discovered, that one is selected for slaughter whose position is -such that the preliminary manoeuvres of the surround and the shouts and shots of the conflict are least likely to disturb the others. A narrow valley, with many lateral ravines, is very favorable. If the herd is on a hill, or otherwise unfavorably situated, the hunters may wait for it to go to water, or by discreet appearances at intervals, drive it to the best spot. During all this time the whole masculine portion of the band capable of doing execution in the coming slaughter is congregated on horseback, in some adjacent ravine, out of sight of the buffalo, silent and trembling with suppressed excitement. The herd being in proper position, the leading hunters tell off the men, and send them under temporary captains to designated positions. Keeping carefully concealed, these parties pour down the valley to leeward, and spread gradually on each flank of the wind, until the herd is surrounded, except on the windward side. Seeing that every man is in his proper place, and all ready, the head hunter rapidly swings in a party to close the gap, gives the signal, and, with a yell that would almost wake the dead, the whole line dashes and closes on the game. The buffalo make desperate rushes, which are met in every direction by shouts and shots and circling horsemen, until, utterly bewildered, they almost stand still to await their fate. In a few moments the slaughter is complete. A few may have broken through the cordon and escaped. These are not pursued if other herds are in the vicinity.

The slaughter completed, the "soldiers" return to camp to swell and strut, and vaunt each his own individual exploits, while the women skin, cut up, and carry to camp almost every portion of the dead animals. As soon as those skins are stretched, that meat cut up in flakes and put to dry, or in other words, when the women's work is done, another surround is made with the like result, and this is continued until enough meat and skins are obtained, or until cold weather drives the Indians to their winter camp.

The weapon principally used in the surround was the revolving pistol, though some men used carbines, and others bows. When bows and arrows alone were used, each warrior, knowing his own arrows, had no difficulty in positively identifying the buffalo killed by him. These were his individual property entirely, except that he was assessed a certain proportion for the benefit of the widows or families which had no warrior to provide for them. If arrows of different men were found in the same dead buffalo, the ownership was decided by their position. If each warrior inflicted a mortal wound, the buffalo was divided, or not unfrequently given to some widow with a family. The head hunter decided all these questions, but an appeal could be taken from his decision to the general judgment of the dog-soldiers. Since the general use of firearms has rendered impossible the identification of the dead buffalo, the Indians have become more communistic in their ideas, and the whole of the meat and skins is divided after some rule of apportionment of their own invention. None but the lazy and the poor shots are satisfied with this arrangement, but it is the only solution of the problem left to them.

In those portions of the Plains where the depressions are too slight to favor "the surround," the arrangements are totally different. On discovering a herd the dog-soldiers were deployed in a wide semicircle, and approached the unsuspecting animals at a slow walk. When the near approach of this line alarmed the herd sufficiently to start it on the gallop, a signal was given and the whole line dashed in at once, pursuing and killing the frightened animals until every pony was completely pumped. In such case the camp was a migratory one, and pitched as near as possible to the scene of slaughter until the squaws "cleaned up," and the meat was cured; then broken up, and all proceeded in search of another herd.

In favorable localities the Sioux used to kill great numbers by first decoying a herd to the desired position, then suddenly appearing and driving the frightened animals over a precipice. The southern Plains Indians pursued the herds on horseback, killing with lances, which were the more effective from being noiseless.

The buffalo is the most stupid of any of the animal creation of which I have knowledge. If it sees or smells no enemy a herd will stand still until every individual is shot down. They will do this sometimes when the enemy is in plain view. Once needing fresh meat for my post I sat down on the ground on the level prairie, in plain view and within less than one hundred yards of a herd and shot down two cows and thirteen calves, the others not attempting to leave. We had actually to drive off the survivors by shouts and waving our hats, before we could butcher our game.

Probably from this very stupidity, it is at some times the most easily stampeded or panic-stricken of any of the Plains animals. A herd which during one hour may stand and be shot at, may the next hour rush headlong over the prairie in the wildest, blindest paroxysm of fear, oftentimes without any assignable cause. This peculiarity was the cause of an adventure which came near being my last.

I was changing posts in March, 1871, and had three or four wagons and a small escort. One night I camped on Big Coon Creek. It was too early for rain, and the weather was cold and blustering. My camp was, therefore, nearly in the bed of the creek, close under the shelter of the steep, almost bluff, banks, which border the stream. The nook in which I camped was small, and tents and wagons were unusually crowded together.

It was late at night and I was in bed. The camp, except one sentinel, was buried in sleep; the fires were out, darkness and silence reigned supreme. A faint and very distant roaring sound struck my ear. Thinking of water, I rushed out at once, and, running up the side of the bank, peered up the stream into the darkness to discover an approaching line of foam, precursor of the flood.

Just then the wind brought the sound more distinctly. It came from the prairie, not from the stream, and was approaching. I sent the sentinel to wake up the corporal and other two men of the guard, who soon made their appearance with their arms.

Explaining to the men in a few words the nature of the danger, I warned them to keep perfectly cool and to obey orders. By this time the black line of the moving mass of buffalo was distinctly visible. It was bearing directly down upon us with tremendous speed and irresistible force. We were in an excellent position for the protection of the camp, being directly between it and the buffalo, and about fifty yards from it. My only chance was to split the herd. If this could be done, we and the camp would be saved; if not, all would go to destruction together. Waiting until the advance line of buffalo was within thirty yards, the muskets were fired in rapid and continuous succession, and we in unison let out one of the most unearthly yells that ever split the throats of five badly-frightened men. A few of the leading animals fell dead, the others swerved from the fire and noise; the herd was split, and, tumbling in fright and confusion down the bank on each side of the camp, went thundering and roaring into the darkness.

The danger from Indians and the great distance from market had heretofore protected the buffalo from wholesale slaughter by whites, but by 1872 the buffalo region had been penetrated by no less than three great railroads, and the Indians had been forced from their vicinity. About this time too it was discovered that the tough, thick hide of the buffalo made admirable belting for machinery, and the dried skins readily commanded sale at three to four dollars each. The news spread like wild-fire, and soon the Union Pacific, Kansas Pacific, and Atchison Topeka and Santa Fe railroads, swarmed with hunters from all parts of the country, all excited with the prospect of having a buffalo hunt that would pay. By wagon, on horseback, and a-foot, the pot-hunters poured in, and soon the unfortunate buffalo was without a moment's peace or rest. Though hundreds of thousands of skins were sent to market, they scarcely indicated the slaughter. From want of skill in shooting, and want of knowledge in preserving the hides of those slain, one hide sent to market represented three, four, or even five dead buffalo.

The merchants of the small towns along the railroads were not slow to take advantage of this new opening. They furnished outfits, arms, ammunition, etc., to needy parties, and established great trades, by which many now ride in their carriages.

The buffalo melted away like snow before a summer's sun. Congress talked of interfering, but only talked. "Winter and summer, in season and out of season, the slaughter went on.

The fall of 1873 saw an immense accession of hunters, but by this time the local merchants, recognizing its importance, had got the trade pretty well into their own hands. Most of the hunting-parties were sent out by them, and were organized for even a greater destruction of buffalo, and with more care for the proper preservation .of the hides and meat. Central depots were established in localities where buffalo were plentiful. Parties were sent out from these which every few days brought back their spoil. Houses were built for smoking and coming the meat, and, though the waste was still incalculable, the results would be incredible but that the figures are taken from official statistics.

In 1871-2 there was apparently no limit to the numbers of buffalo.

In 1872 I was stationed at Fort Dodge, on the Arkansas, and was out on many hunting excursions. Except that one or two would be shot, as occasion required, for beef, no attention whatever was paid to buffalo (though our march lay through countless throngs), unless there were strangers with us. In the fall of that year three English gentlemen went out with me for a short hunt, and in their excitement bagged more buffalo than would have supplied a brigade. From within a few miles of the post our pleasure was actually marred by their numbers, as they interfered with our pursuit of other game.

In the fall of 1873 I went with some of the same gentlemen over the same ground. Where there were myriads of buffalo the year before, there were now myriads of carcasses. The air was foul with sickening stench, and the vast plain, which only a short twelvemonth before teemed with animal life, was a dead, solitary, putrid desert. We were obliged to travel southeast to the Cimarron, a distance of nearly ninety miles, before we found a respectable herd. Even there we found the inevitable hunter.

In October, 1874, I was on a short trip to the buffalo region south of Sidney barracks. A few buffalo were encountered, but there seemed to be more hunters than buffalo. The country south of the South Platte is without water for many miles, and the buffalo must satisfy their thirst at the river. Every approach of the herd to water was met by rifle bullets, and one or more buffalo bit the dust. Care was taken not to permit the others to drink, for then they would not return. Tortured with thirst the poor brutes approached again and again, always to be met by bullets, always to lose some of their number.

In places favorable to such action, as the south bank of the Platte, a herd of buffalo has, by shooting at it by day, and by lighting fires and firing guns at night, been kept from water for four days, or until it has been entirely destroyed. In many places the valley was offensive from the stench of putrefying carcasses.

During the three years 1872-73-74, at least five millions of buffalo were slaughtered for their hides.

This slaughter was all in violation of law, and in contravention of solemn treaties made with the Indians,* but it was the duty of no special person to put a stop to it. The Indian Bureau made a feeble effort to keep the white hunters out of the Indian Territory) but soon gave it up, and these parties spread all over the country, slaughtering the buffalo under the very noses of the Indians.

Some believe that it was an implicit policy of the government, knowing it would eventually impoverish the tribes and force them into agency life.

Ten years ago the Plains Indians had an ample supply of food, and could support life comfortably without the assistance of the government, ow everything is gone, and they are reduced to the condition of paupers, without food, shelter, clothing, or any of those necessaries of life which came from the buffalo; and without friends, except the harpies, who, under the guise of friendship, feed upon them.

CLOTHING, FINERY AND ADORNMENT

WHEN at home or alone with his own people, the ordinary summer dress of the male Indian is the breech-cloth, leggings and moccasins.

The breech-cloth is the simplest of all garments. A string is tied around the waist, one end of a piece of cloth, five to eight feet long by four inches wide, is drawn under the string in front, passed between the legs, and under the string behind. One loose end forms a flap in front reaching nearly to the knees, the other hangs behind like a tail, sometimes dragging the ground. This is all that the Indian thinks necessary for modesty or decency.

Dress is for display, not for use. I have already spoken of the "imitative faculty" of the Indian. It secures him frequent trouble. The very commonplace dress of the civilized whites is not at all to his taste. It gives no opportunity for display and is most confining and uncomfortable. Yet, with a heroism worthy the martyrs of old, he incases himself in this Pandora's box of ills, whenever he expects to come in contact with a white man of any position.

I one day drove up to a field where some Indians were at work ploughing, etc. They were dressed in breech-cloth and moccasins. As I came near, an Indian ran off from the party towards a wagon on the other side of the field. When I had talked a little while with the workmen, I drove off, and it was only afterwards that I discovered that I had given almost mortal offence to the chief man. Recognizing me, he ran off to his wagon, encased himself in what Josh Billings would call a "biled" shirt, pants, coat, hat, and even boots, only to find me gone on his return.

This sensitiveness is not common. I one day went on business to the camp of Little Raven, Oh-nas-tie, the head chief of the Arapahos; in his youth a skilful and renowned warrior, in his old age a natural gentleman. He was at work in the field, but being sent for, soon made his appearance. His dress consisted only of a shirt and a pair of moccasins. He was streaming with perspiration and covered with dirt, but he met me with his usual courtesy, and without the slightest apology for his dress or condition.

The male Indian has now three styles of dress. In his own home, or among themselves, it is simply breech-cloth and moccasins, except that when visiting he now wears a wide cotton mantle, not unlike a sheet, enveloping his whole person, frequently even his head, leaving only the face exposed. It is only among the extremely poor that we may look for the primitive fashions *en rigueur*, and even in his most natural and poverty-stricken condition he is so excessively fond of finery, that he always has something extra for grand occasions; a few feathers tied in the hair, a ring or two of brass wire for the ears, or wrists and ankles—anything to make a show.

The second style is that which he adopts when visiting or receiving visits from white men, and some article of white men's clothing is indispensable. There is no idea of incongruity or unfitness. Whatever the white man wears, the Indian will wear if he can get it. He sees the letters on the cap of a soldier, and being ignorant of their meaning, assumes that they are worn for ornament. He picks up a dilapidated old hat from the dump pile of a military post, covers it all over with broken crossed sabres, bent bugles, fragments of letters; and putting it on his head, struts around with quiet complaisance, perfectly assured that he is making a great sensation, and gratified at every notice taken of him.

I was present at probably the most important council of late years, between whites and Indians. Turkey Leg, a Cheyenne chief of considerable prominence, came into the council lodge, a buffalo robe tightly folded around him, though it was warm weather. Over his head and face he wore an ordinary green veil. Over that, perched on the very top of his head, and at least two sizes too small for him, was a tall straight-bodied stove-pipe hat. When he rose to speak, he retained the hat and veil, but dropped his buffalo robe, disclosing his other apparel, which consisted of a calico shirt and pair of moccasins.

It is scarcely possible to conceive of any absurdity or ridiculousness that is not constantly perpetrated by Indians in their desire to show themselves off in white men's clothing. I have never yet seen an Indian of what I call the wild tribes with a complete dress; even when they have the means and opportunity, they seem to prefer to take this innovation by instalments.

Last year I met Little Chief, and the other Northern Cheyennes, on their return from Washington. They were riding through southern Kansas, en route to their agency, and everywhere they created a sensation. A brawny buck with white shirt, elaborate necktie and felt hat, had buckskin leggings, and moccasins, and held over his head a lady's parasol. Another, buttoned to the chin in a thick coat, had his nether extremities covered in the same way, was without a hat, but fanned himself incessantly with a huge gaudily painted Chinese fan. Not one had a full suit of civilized clothing, and if each had studied his "get up," for a month, he could not have fitted himself out more ridiculously.

It is the same with all wild Indians. Though each thinks some article of civilized attire indispensable to his proper appearance before white men, he is perfectly content with one. One will surmount his Indian dress by a hat ornamented with feathers. Another will have a gaudy necktie, but no shirt, another a vest buttoned to the chin, supplemented by breech-cloth and moccasins. No more motley, ridiculous, overdressed, half-dressed, and undressed crowd can be found in the world, than a party of Indians "fixed up" to receive white company.

Boots and pantaloons are the bugbears of Indian life, and it is extremely rare even at the present day, that an Indian can be induced to wear either. When a man receives a pair of trowsers as his share of the issues of clothing by the Indian Bureau, he turns them over to a wife, who cuts out the whole seat and front, leaving the legs from half-way above the knee attached to the waistband by a piece of cloth two inches wide passing up the other side of the thigh and hip, thus making for her lord a serviceable pair of leggings, and having enough cloth left over for a pair for herself.

If the Indian is so unlucky as to draw a pair of boots or shoes, he as a rule immediately sells them for whatever he can get.

In the fall of 1879, I was near an Agency at the time of issue of the merchandise by the Agent. I was not present at the issue, but some hours after it was over, I was asked by my servant to come out and see an Indian who wanted to sell a coat. I complied and found an Indian on horseback, with a thick warm coat across the pommel of his saddle, which he had that morning received as his share of the merchandise. He held it up at once and proposed "swap."

Willing to ascertain the value from the Indian standpoint of this justice or benevolence of the Indian Department, I asked "how much?"

"Fifty cents" he replied.

"What will you do with the fifty cents?" I asked.

"Get chuck, heap hungry," he answered, laying his hands on his stomach and making a frightful grimace.

Chuck is a word in almost universal use among the Plains Indians of all tribes and languages. It means food.

The coat was worth at least six dollars. I tried to impress upon him its value as an article of wearing apparel, and to explain that he would need it in winter. His only answer was a look of infinite disgust. While we were talking another Indian rode up. After a few moments' conversation in their own language, the new-comer pulled out half-a-dollar, the coat was handed over, and each rode off apparently satisfied.

The Indian's third dress is that reserved for grand occasions of ceremony among themselves. On it he has expended a lifetime of thought, and all his ingenuity, and to its elaboration have been brought all the skill and patience of his wives. Considering the materials with which the Indians have to work, many of these dresses are very beautiful. Buckskin is the groundwork of all, but the garments themselves vary infinitely, according to the taste and means of the owner. Some are made of skin so fine, thin, and white, as almost to look like satin; others ornamented with equal elaboration, are of smoked skins, thick and dark-colored.

The upper garment of this gala dress generally takes the form of a tunic, but varies in cut and make from the wide pajama of the Orient, to the close-fitting hunting-shirt of our white borderers. It is painted, beaded, worked with porcupine quills and colored grasses; the seams marked with delicate fringes of deer or antelope skin, not unfrequently over a foot in length. Occasionally some successful warrior, who has a plethora of scalps, cuts one or more into narrow strips, and fringes his coat with the hair of his enemies. The leggings are generally of much the same shape and cut, but vary in their ornamentation quite as much as the tunic. The moccasins of each tribe differ in shape. Those for show are often so overloaded with ornamentation and bead-work, as to be utterly useless for service. The buffalo-robe cloak is a marvel of elaborate and painstaking labor. Porcupine quills, dyed, of various colors, are stitched to the flesh side by sinews, in patterns of different designs, often quite striking if not artistic in effect. Sometimes the inside of the robe will be covered with elaborate paintings, illustrative of the combats 'and memorable actions of the owner. At other times, the illustrations are mythological or purely fanciful, other times again they are of such a nature as cannot be described or depicted. The Indian idea, whether of man or woman, is essentially obscene, and it is to be regretted that many of their most successful artistic efforts have been on such subjects as will not bear repetition. The needlework ornamentation is always done by the women, the paintings, sometimes by the women, but generally by the man himself, especially when picturing his own exploits.

It is extremely rare to see an Indian, even though following the plough in his breech-cloth and moccasins, who has not bestowed some thought and pains on the dressing of his hair. Indian men of all the wild tribes allow their hair to grow, and as almost all Indian hair is exactly alike in color and texture, their special pride is in its length. The central and northern Plains tribes part their hair in the middle, and confine it in two long tails, one over, or just behind, each ear. These, pieced out with buffalo or horsehair to make them longer, are wrapped with a long and narrow piece of cloth, or beaver skin, cut in strips, the folds of which furnish receptacles of which the Indian makes great use. I have often been surprised to see an Indian pull out from his hair a letter, or a bundle of matches, or a stick for cleaning his pipe; anything that can be carried in a narrow compass is sure to go in his tails.

The Comanches and Kiowas comb the hair back from the face and plait it, with additions, in a single long tail, ornamented with silver or plated buckles, and often reaching nearly to the ground. These tails are untied scarce oftener than once a year, the combing and brushing being habitually confined to that portion of hair immediately on the head. This, however, receives great attention, and the warrior's hair is usually quite sleek and shiny from grease and frequent brushing.

They make a brush for themselves from the leaves of the soap-weed, or, far south, of the Spanish bayonet.

There is no article of dress or adornment so highly prized as the eagles' quills, and the killing of an eagle by an Indian is an event for as much congratulation and rejoicing among his family and friends, as an inheritance of a fortune by a white man. Every feather is utilized. The wing-quills go to the Indian's personal adornment, or are sold, bringing sometimes as much as two dollars each. The tail is cut off, pressed into fan shape, worth at least a pony, being a favorite ornament for the totem, and of use as a fan at the same time.

The head is cut off, skinned and stuffed, and is so much prized as an ornament by warriors, that a shrewd white man, who some years ago conceived the idea of sending to the states for some glass eagles'-eyes, reaped ample reward for his wit, getting a pony for each pair of eyes. They are more common now, and the price reasonable.

No warrior, who aspires to distinction, ever thinks himself fitted out until he has some article of head-gear ornamented with eagles' quills. A poor fellow may have but one, but it is his warrant of respectability. The happy few of each tribe who have war-bonnet, shield, lance and gun-cover, all ornamented with these quills, value them as a millionaire his estate, and they serve exactly the same purpose, often pushing forward a man who has no other claim to distinction.

None of the finery of the Indian can be washed, or otherwise cleaned, and as one suit frequently has to last a lifetime, its condition, in the later years of its usefulness, may be imagined.

Catlin describes among the Indians with whom he came in contact, a character which it has never been my lot to encounter—an Indian dandy, vain, effeminate, and devoting his life and energy solely to the adornment of his person.

All Indians are given to great elaboration of dress on occasions of display, and this is regulated solely by the taste and wealth of the wearer. Some dress much more than others, but I have doubts if any such character as Catlin's dandy could have place or standing among the Plains tribes, where manhood is the first requisite to a man.

At the age when every man, civilized or savage, is naturally something of a dandy, the Indian is poor, waiting, watching, and hoping for an opportunity to increase his store, by stealing the horses of somebody else. Whatever his disposition, he has not the means to be Catlin's dandy.

Among the Plains tribes there is a species of dandy, but he is entirely different from the idle, effeminate animal described by Catlin. He is generally the son of a rich and indulgent father, lives with the "old man," and is talked of as one having great expectations. He is a great catch, therefore unmarried; he dresses a great deal, is consequently a "lady-killer," but he must back up all this effeminacy by a first-class reputation for courage and endurance, and be as ready to fight as to flirt. Nothing less than an Indian "Claude Melnotte" can be a dandy on the Plains.

In the wilder tribes, the ordinary dress of the women of the present day is a skirt of buckskin, more or less ornamented, reaching from the waist to half way below the knee. The upper dress is a short jacket of the same material, but this is being rapidly replaced by more civilized covering, the women of those tribes in contact with Mexicans, soon learning to cover the head and body with a scarf or reboza, and those who sometimes see a white woman, taking naturally to the shawl. The women of nearly all the Plains tribes, now wear a calico dress (made by themselves, and not cut by a fashionable dressmaker), reaching from the neck to the ankles, and very like the camisal of the New Orleans French women. They wear leggings and moccasins, but no stockings. The shawl is worn universally over the head, after the style of the reboza, and the greatest effort at display made by the women is in this article, each trying to outdo her friend in variety and brilliancy of its coloring. When not actually at household work, the shawl is always worn. The woman, even in her own lodge, never stops to talk to a visitor, until she has first put on her brightest shawl. It is worn everywhere outside the lodge, riding, walking, visiting each other, or going to the Agency or a military post; even in the dance it is indispensable, and never removed. The natural inference to be drawn from this close and constant envelopment by the shawl is that the other clothing will not bear inspection. It is, however, only a fashion or custom handed down from the days when clothing was scanty. When out visiting, the women of the Cheyennes and Arapahos dress quite as well as the poorer class of whites. Under the shawl is a nice calico dress, a cape of the same material falling over the shoulders. Around the waist is a broad leather girdle, very similar to that so fashionable among white ladies a year or two ago, but ornamented with a close continuation of round pieces of silver or tin. From one side depends a long strap of leather, similarly ornamented, like the fan-holder of our ladies. Their ears are pierced with one, two, three or more holes, in the outer cartilage, in each of which is an ear-ring, generally of twenty-five-cent jewelry, but for which the trader may have received a horse. Around the neck is an elaborate, and sometimes handsome, necklace of beads. They are dressed well, though unlike civilized ladies, they hide it all.

In some of the far western tribes, especially those along the Colorado River, the only dress of the women consists of a short kirtle of fringe. Innumerable fringes of bark are attached to a band twenty or thirty feet long. This is wound around and around the waist, the loose fringes making a thick mat reaching nearly to the knees.

I was told by an old settler of Yuma that when he went there years before, though the men wore the breech-cloth and moccasins, the women were in *"puris naturalibus,"* their unadorned beauty being "set off" only by some patches of paint, and a few rings of brass wire on fingers, arms and legs. He stated further that a party of Mormons had been attacked by the Indians, and all killed except one woman. She was kept in captivity, and every article of her clothing taken to adorn the persons of her male captors. Her feminine instincts revolting against this, she made such kirtles as I have described, but was obliged to teach the Indian women to wear them before being herself permitted to benefit by her own modest ingenuity.

Until within about ten years the women of the Wichita Indians wore in summer no covering whatever on the body above the waist. Even on the most full-dress occasion a string of beads or wampum was all that fashion or modesty required.

At home the clothing of the children is "nothing to speak of," but all have a gala-dress, for visiting and grand occasions, on which the mothers have expended all their taste and skill. Some are elaborately ornamented, and quite valuable. One of the most so is a scarf of ordinary Indian cloth, ornamented with elk's-teeth. As these animals are now extremely rare on the Southern Plains, this scarf could scarcely be bought for less than two ponies (fifty to sixty dollars).

Among the wild tribes every man, woman and child is more or less painted. From the miserable Digger, who thinks himself perfectly dressed when his naked body is smeared with colored earth, to the wealthy chief, whose contact with whites enables him to give himself all the colors of the rainbow, no Indian, whatever may be his actual apparel, considers himself in full dress, unless he is painted. This rule has some exceptions among the better class of the Indians of the Territory, and some of the prominent chiefs of the wild tribes, as "Spotted Tail," "Ouray," and others, who follow the "white man's road," and have ceased entirely to wear paint.

All Indians are very fond of jewelry, and wear it in great profusion. All wear finger-rings of brass or silver, sometimes, on occasions of ceremony, in such profusion as seriously to interfere with the use of the hands. Both sexes wear bracelets, or hoops of brass on their arms, sometimes eight or ten on one arm, and generally above the elbow. Ear-rings are worn almost universally. The holes for insertion are made with a knife, and usually in the upper cartilage, and it is not at all unusual to see two, three, or more holes in each ear. I have seen an Indian with several huge brass rings in each ear, each supporting by connections of bead-work, shells, stones, pieces of bone, etc., until each pendant was a foot long, the whole weighing not less than half a pound. Of course the ears are dragged out of all shape, enlarged to twice their natural size, and much torn, occasionally almost entirely torn off.

Indians have remarkably good teeth, and rarely lose one except by accident. From army surgeons I have heard of a case or two of toothache, but I have never known an Indian to have a tooth extracted.

Not very long ago an officer of the army (who, having lost his upper teeth, wore a false set) was engaged in serious conversation with some Indians. His plate troubling him, he took it out and wiped it with his handkerchief. The Indians watched the process with unfeigned astonishment, and when the captain, putting the plate in his mouth, went on with the conversation, they sprung to their feet, and left the room and post in all haste, and with every symptom of extreme terror.

Buffalo, a bright, intelligent Cheyenne, now employed under my command as a scout, has but one eye. A few years ago an army surgeon, who took a fancy to him, inserted a glass eye in the vacant orbit. For a long time it was a constant amusement ,to him, and a dread to his companions, he insisting that he could see as well with that eye as with the other, and they putting him to all sorts of tests, which he was quick enough to foil. It was a long time before the Cheyennes got used to Buffalo's eye, and even now they regard it with suspicion as doubtful medicine.

THE STRUGGLE FOR EXISTENCE

LIKE most people who live much in the fresh air, the Indians are a healthy race, but their condition of health seems to be in a great degree dependent on their remaining in the country to which they are accustomed. The ill effect of change does not appear to be due to climatic influences, for those removed from malarial and unhealthy regions to more salubrious districts suffer more or less, though not of course so much as when the conditions are reversed. I believe that homesickness is the foundation of this ill effect, and that the extraordinary and unnatural diminution in the numbers of certain tribes is due to nostalgia more than any other cause.

Almost every year witnesses the enforced change of locations of some of the Indians. A tribe is ousted from the country in which were born all its living, and which contains the graves of all its dead. Those old enough to appreciate the misfortune, disheartened, despairing, in no mood to maintain the struggle for existence, are ready to fall, almost willing victims, to the first malady that assails them. The young grow up, and learn to love the country of their adoption, only in time to be themselves removed, and go through with the wretched experience of their fathers.

I have not the data for a careful comparison of the vital statistics of tribes, but my personal observation convinces me that those tribes which have been most frequently forced to move have suffered the greatest diminution in numbers, and this, too, without regard to the healthfulness or insalubrity of the country to which the move was made.

Witness the Pawnees, who, scarce fifty years ago, were numerically one of the most powerful tribes in the territory of the United States, but who, by the aggressions of equally warlike tribes, or by the power of the government, have been repeatedly forced to change their country, until now the bare remnant, a population of scarce a thousand souls, occupies a little corner of the Indian Territory twenty miles square. It is true that the Pawnees are an exceedingly warlike race, but their losses at the hands of their human enemies are entirely disproportioned to their loss by various maladies, whose foundation in my belief is simply nostalgia.

Of the removal of the Cherokees from North Carolina, the *Missionary Herald* said: "From the time they were gathered into camps by the United States troops, in May and June, 1838, till the time the last detachment reached the Arkansas country, which was about ten months, a careful estimate shows that not less than four thousand, or forty-five hundred were removed by death, being on an average from thirteen to fifteen deaths a day for the whole period, out of a population of sixteen thousand, or one fourth of the whole number. It does not appear that this mortality was owing to neglect or bad treatment while on the journey."

In ten months, more than one-fourth of a whole population is carried off by death, in a healthy country, without epidemic, without "war, pestilence or famine," and it never seems to have occurred to anyone to look for, much less assign a reason for it.

The Indian is naturally light-hearted and thoughtless, disposed to take the world as it comes and make the best of it. This is the philosophy he derives from his patience and endurance.

The possibility of starvation to which he is constantly exposed by the cc policy" now in vogue, engenders a feeling of aggressive desperation .rather than of hopeless despair. He becomes excessively indignant and dangerous, but, the crisis past, returns at once to his normal temper "laissez-faire."

His removal from his accustomed haunts is the only single misfortune over which I have ever known an Indian to brood.

The laws of the United States do not recognize banishment as penalty for any crime, yet the government habitually exercises the right to exile from their native homes a people with whom it holds treaty relations, and who, in the absence of any penal code, can commit no crime against the laws or people of the United States. This unjust and arbitrary exercise of power is a special and refined cruelty to the Indian, for white men are so constituted, and have so many resources, that not one in a hundred would feel such a misfortune as keenly as does the Indian.

Aside from its inhumanity, the policy of removal is more than questionable. A tribe, as the Modocs, or Nez Perces, which for generations has lived in the most amicable relations with white men, is, for a single outbreak, forced on it by injustice, greed and aggression, exiled to a strange land. Despairing and desperate, men who have been our life-long friends are converted into unforgiving enemies. Hoping, almost praying, for an excuse for outbreak, willing to risk death for even the slightest chance of regaining their loved homes, these fragments of bands are a constant source of anxiety to States containing over two millions of inhabitants, and require a force of troops to watch and control them, at an expense ten times greater than would feed, clothe, house, and make them valuable citizens in the countries for which they yearn.

It is time that the government began to understand that homesickness with Indians is a disease, a most dangerous malady, resulting in death to them, in loss of life and money to us.

Indians have plenty of courage and extraordinary endurance, but little of that rather indefinable quality called "pluck." The man who cheerfully and voluntarily submits himself to all the tortures of the Hôch-é-a-yum, will, on a bed of sickness, be as impatient and as fretful as a child. Hurts and wounds are matters of ocular demonstration easily understood; sickness is different. To be burning with fever, shaken with chills, or racked with rheumatism, is so foreign to their experience of what is common and natural to animal life, that it can be attributed only to the malevolent influence of the Bad God. No idea of a diagnosis has occurred to them, nor have they even advanced sufficiently to comprehend that there are different kinds of ordinary disease. Sickness is sickness, a direct manifestation of the evil power and will of the Bad God; that is all they know or think about it.

In a previous chapter I have given a detailed description of the exorcisms, chantings, and other religious ceremonies used by the medicine men in their conflicts with the Evil One. These are used in sickness only. The cure of a wound would never be attempted by such means, though the medicine men make pow-wows over the wounded man to prevent the Evil One from taking advantage of his situation. A wound is tangible, and though it results from the power of the Bad God, this does not prevent its being treated directly and oftentimes very success-fully.

Other than by the power of religion, there is but one single mode by which the alleviation and cure of diseases is attempted. This is the "sweat house," which, though differing somewhat with different tribes, is sufficiently the same for a general description. A small structure, six feet long by four or five feet broad, with a low arched roof, like a bake-oven, is built of rough stones and mud, close on the bank of a stream, the one opening on the side overlooking as nearly as possible a deep pool. A fire is built within, and when a proper degree of heat has been attained, the fire and ashes are raked out, the patient, stripped naked, crawls in, and the opening is closed with a blanket. When almost baked, and the perspiration streaming from every pore, he is taken out and plunged into the pool below. In most instances, and with the diseases most common to Indians—intermittent fever and rheumatism—this treatment is wonderfully efficacious. In other cases, and especially with small-pox, the Indian enters the water and the" happy hunting grounds" at the same instant. This result, however, will not prevent a repetition of the treatment with the next patient, and to this persistence is due much of the mortality incident to Indian disease.

From the day of his entrance into this world until maturity, the life of an Indian is truly a "struggle for existence." The women are generally healthy, and produce healthy children. The life of the weakly child is a short span, not necessarily because the parents kill it, as is generally believed, but because of the poor fare, hard life, and constant drudgery of the mother, and the exposure to which the child is subjected. Among civilized people, the sickly child has the best medical attendance, the most careful nursing; every assistance known to art is given to nature. Among Indians, nature has no assistance, and unless naturally strong enough to withstand the strain, the child dies. The greatest mortality is confined to very young children, and after passing its third or fourth year, the chance of the Indian child's death by disease is very much less than that of the white child. But through all the "clambering" age, and until entirely able to take care of itself, the Indian child's life is not only beset by the innumerable accidents and chances incident to its mode of living, but many, such as the breaking of limbs, bites from, snakes, which would be but temporary pain and inconvenience to the white, result in death to the Indian, from lack of proper treatment.

Contact with civilization, which presumably might have increased, has really lessened the chances of life of the young Indian, bringing measles, mumps, whooping-cough, and scarlet fever, maladies so common to civilization, that they are looked upon as a necessary experience in the life of every white child, but which are entirely unknown to the Indian in his natural state.

I shall never be able to believe that the actual Indian population of the United States fifty years ago, was more than a mere fraction of that given on paper by writers, who were either agents, interested in having as many on their papers as possible, or enthusiasts like Catlin, who evidently believed any boast the Indians chose to make as to their numbers. It is, however, a fact established beyond all possibility of doubt, that the actual diminution has been enormously great.

The principal cause of this diminution was smallpox, which fifty years ago, was probably the greatest scourge of all nations and people. Some few small tribes, living closely together for protection against powerful neighbors, as the Mandans, were almost completely annihilated, and some bands of the larger tribes lost half their numbers. The control of this terrible disease now possessed by science has led to its almost entire disappearance among whites, and as Indians get it only by contact with whites, or from infected clothing (said to have been sometimes purposely sent to them), it has now almost entirely disappeared from among them.

Another dreadful scourge, cholera, has periodically attacked them, and though not nearly so fatal to Indian life as small-pox, it has well done its work in the diminution of their numbers. I have heard of no case of small-pox among Indians for twenty years (except the very recent outbreak among the Utes, which, under the circumstances, appears very like design on the part of somebody), but whenever this country has been afflicted by cholera, the Indians have suffered more in proportion to numbers than whites.

They soon learn from the squaw men when the cholera has visited our shores, and take every precaution against it, breaking into small bands, and removing into the most secluded wilds, far from railroads, steamboats, or settlements.

In spite of this, and the most rigid quarantine, a band is occasionally attacked. How it reaches them is a mystery, no more to be accounted for than the spread of the horse disease of a few years ago, commonly called the epizootic, and which passed at a regular rate of speed, without contact or apparent cause, from the Atlantic to the Pacific, sparing no herd of horses, however isolated, either of Indian or white man.

The Indians regard all these diseases as simply the manifestation of the diabolic power and disposition of the Bad God, who, having in their encounter so worsted the Good God, as to render him temporarily powerless, seizes the opportunity to wreak his rage upon the defenceless people.

To describe the superstitious terror, the abject fear of these unfortunate savages, at such times, is beyond the power of words. When the epidemic is sufficiently pronounced for sure recognition, a wail of utter despair ascends to heaven. Camps and lodges are abandoned, the dead and dying left unburied and uncared for, and those yet unafflicted, breaking up into families, fly in every direction from the scene of suffering. They hope by the secrecy and celerity of their movements to baffle the pursuit of the Bad God. An unfortunate seized with the disease en route is forced to leave the party, to live or die solitary and alone in the wilderness. Husbands abandon their wives, children their aged parents, mothers their nursing infants, and this terrible race for life continues until the disease has worn itself out, either from want of contact, or lack of victims.

The places at which these terrible visitations have overtaken the Indians are forever regarded with superstitious terror, and no persuasion or bribe could induce an Indian, knowingly, to visit them.

Many years ago, with a small force, I was scouting in the Guadalupe Mountains in Texas, then a favorite hunting ground of the Indians. In going from one mountain pass to another, an old Indian trail was discovered. It was deep and wide, showed plain evidence of much and frequent usage, but no sign of recent travel. It evidently led to some spot which had been a favorite place of resort, but which, for some reason, had for several years been abandoned. Curious to know more I followed the trail. After winding along ridges for three or four miles, it led by a long and steep descent to a most charming valley, nestled and hidden in the very bosom of the mountains. This valley was about twelve miles long by an average of three-fourths of a mile in width. A beautiful stream wound in graceful curves from mountain to mountain as if seeking to leave no spot of the valley untouched by its invigorating influence. Tall, shapely trees clustered along the margins of the stream; smooth lawns of the greenest grass, dotted with clumps of shrubbery, and covered with lovely flowers of every hue, made a picture as fair as the eye of man could wish it.

Descending the stream for some two miles, we came, in one of the loveliest of the many lovely nooks, upon the remains of an Indian camp. Many of the old lodge poles were still standing, though the lodges themselves had long since gone to decay. Scattered about, rusted and rotten, were cooking utensils, arms, saddles, all the paraphernalia that go to make Indian wealth and Indian comfort. In the midst of these, and in every direction in and around the camp, were innumerable bones—the dislocated skeletons of the Indian inhabitants; some, almost entire, lying where the breath had left the bodies; others scattered and broken as they had been dragged, and gnawed, and left by the wolves. To all appearance not a thing had been touched by man; not a living soul had entered that camp since the day of its awful visitation by the Bad God.

Mental and nervous diseases are rare, though a "Crazy Woman" has given name to several streams in widely separated portions of the Plains. Idiotic children are occasionally found, and I have heard of one case of paralysis.

Rabies is not a Plains malady, and personally I have never known a single case on the Plains except in white men bitten by the skunk.

The Indians, however, say they are not unfrequently troubled with mad wolves. On the middle Plains they make their appearance in February and March. Having entered an Indian village the wolf will make no attempt to leave it, but rushing furiously from lodge to lodge, attacks everything that comes in its way, until killed or disabled. In every instance, death by hydrophobia is to the Indian the sure result of even the slightest scratch from the teeth of the rabid animal. They make no attempt at treatment, but philosophically commence preparations for the death sure to come in a few days.

After giving away all his property he quietly awaits the first paroxysms, then goes off alone, far away from camp, meets his fate calmly, or anticipates it by suicide.

The bite of a skunk, so extremely fatal to white men within certain limits of the Plains, seems to have no injurious effect whatever on the Indian, beyond the mere pain of the wound.

Suicide, generally, among whites, the result of over-sensitiveness or morbid selfishness, is to the Indian a religious *dernier ressort*, a mode, when all hope is gone, of escaping the persecution of the Bad God. In all my experience among Indians I have known but one single case of suicide for a frivolous cause. A Sioux boy of seventeen or eighteen years of age, who had all his life been greatly indulged and spoiled by his father, fell desperately in love with a young girl of the same tribe. The youth had no property, and the girl's parents demanded more for her than his father was disposed to pay. For several days he persistently, but vainly, pleaded with his father to pay the price demanded; and one morning, after a more than usually peremptory refusal, he walked in a fret out of the lodge, drew his pistol, placed it against his stomach, and fired, inflicting a mortal wound. He was carried into the lodge, and after lingering a day or two in great agony, died extremely penitent (when too late).

The father was thoroughly angry and disgusted, and after the act of self-destruction never spoke to the son, except to load him with reproaches, and abuse him as an utter fool, and after his death buried him without ceremony or honor.

Though Indians not unfrequently commit suicide to escape the power of the Bad God, as manifested in hydrophobia, paralysis, or similar terrible and hopeless afflictions, I have never heard of one committing the act to escape torture. In conflict with Indians, a white man will habitually save his last shot for himself, for he knows the terrible result of capture. An Indian sends his last shot at his enemy, and when captured takes pride in showing how bravely he can bear the worst that his enemy can do.

A few years ago, a citizen, living on the Chugwater Creek in Nebraska, told me a singular and dramatic story. In 1867-8, a small band of some half-dozen lodges, encamped near his house, was attacked with cholera. A young buck, being seized with the premonitory symptoms, saddled his horse, loaded himself with arms, saying, "The white men have brought this bad medicine into our country; I am going to die, but not by cholera. I mean to ride up the creek through the white settlements, and kill every white I meet until I am killed." The other men of the band, being peaceably disposed, and just then greatly needing the assistance of the whites, did all in their power to dissuade him from his purpose. Finding their entreaties of no avail, they waited until he had mounted his horse, and turned to start on his desperate raid, then shot him dead.

Catlin gives a most pitiable description of an old Ponca chief, who had been "exposed," that is, abandoned by his people, to die alone on the prairie. It is the only well-authenticated case I have ever heard of, and is so foreign to the ordinary conduct of Indians, that I think it must have been done on the order of the man left; possibly some sickly, religious idea of his old and feeble brain. All Indians, with whose customs I am at all conversant, take their old and sick with them in all removals of camp. They are carried on travois, or if very old or childish, in the wickerwork baskets commonly used for children.

The death-bed scene is as various as the character and condition of the person dying. Unlike civilized doctors, the medicine-men never "give up" a patient, but will continue to howl, chant, and beat the tomtom, until life is extinct. When, however, a chief or man of dignity and importance has made up his mind that his end is near, he sends off the howling women and ceremonious medicine-men, and calls in all his family and friends. Having made his verbal will, distributed his property, and made his last speeches to each, his final effort seems to be to make his exit with as good grace as possible. Sometimes he has himself dressed in his best clothing (that in which he will be buried), and seated in the centre of a silent group of relatives and friends, will breathe his last calmly and quietly. Sometimes lying flat on his back he will chant his death-song, even with his last breath. Sometimes, after making his will, he will go off alone to some thicket, from which his lifeless body is presently brought by his friends.

Death has no terrors to the Indian, nor has he any disquiet as to his future, consequently there are no horrible death-bed scenes.

Women and children die naturally, without fear, and without ostentation. Slaves, or persons of little moment, or those supposed to be affected with infectious or loathsome diseases, are frequently taken outside the lodge to die, not from inhumanity, but because, when a death occurs in a lodge, it must be taken down and its position changed.

Some years ago the lodge in which a death occurred was utterly destroyed, but the Indians are now too poor to give such vent to their affection or superstition.

GAMES OF SKILL AND CHANCE

THE summer life of the Indian is active. He seems to care nothing for heat, and in his natural state, most of his waking hours in pleasant weather are spent on horseback, hunting, or gadding about from camp to camp, from mere curiosity or love of company. He cannot, however, stand cold. Winter confines him to his lodge, and his life at this season would be miserable enough but for the excitement of gambling, dancing, and love-making.

Probably from having little else to do for a third, or half the year, the passion of gambling is excessively developed among all Indians. A blanket will be spread upon the ground, around which the Indians will group until the lodge is packed. The most common games played are as follows. Three or four of the men best known as dexterous manipulators, will be seated close on each side of the blanket facing each other. The betting is not confined to the players, almost every looker-on, man or woman, choosing sides, and backing his opinion with whatever he feels like risking. All the articles wagered are laid out on one side of the blanket, and a most heterogeneous agglomeration is sometimes presented.

A fine silver-mounted Mexican saddle is wagered against a war-bonnet of eagles' feathers, a shield against a bow and quiver full of arrows, a pair of moccasins against an old hat, or a dollar against a white shirt. The women bet their necklaces, leg ornaments, bead-work of every kind. Nothing is too costly or too worthless to minister to this appetite.

All the bets being up, the game commences. One of the players will hold up in his fingers a piece of bone, well-polished by frequent use, two to three inches long, by one-quarter inch in diameter. It is then enclosed between the two hands, and shifted from one to the other, with inconceivable dexterity and rapidity. His skill consists not only in completely mystifying his opponents, but by permitting occasional glimpses of the bone when the hands are together, to make it appear, that it is in one hand while it is really in the other.

The opponents watch carefully and patiently. At last one feels sufficiently sure to warrant a selection, and points quickly to one hand, which must instantly be stretched out and opened. If the bone is in that hand, the opponents of the manipulator count a point; if it is not, then his side counts a point. A man on the other side then takes the bone, and the process is exactly repeated.

Twenty-one points is game. When it is decided each winner takes possession of his stake, and the property staked against it, and another game is started.

As every Indian wants to bet, and as each has a shrewd eye to the main chance, and tries to match his wager against something a little more valuable, it will readily be perceived that "making the game," is by far the most important part of it, taking much time and a vast deal of noise, wrangling, bantering, chaffing and blowing. I have never seen any quarrelling, however, and they win or lose "like gentlemen" with unvarying good humor.

The Utes use two bones as exactly alike as possible, but around the middle of one is wound a small string. After a certain amount of manipulation, one is retained in each hand, and the hands then stretched out. The opponent selects a hand, which is opened, and if the wrapped bone is in it, he wins, if in the other hand, he loses. It is a mere game of guess.

This and other old games, though holding a strong place in the affections of the Indians, because they permit an unlimited number of players, are generally discarded by the more ardent gamblers, who, like the whist-playing lady, regret the loss of time "taken in dealing," or getting ready.

All the tribes are sufficiently civilized to possess and understand cards. Those who come in contact with Mexicans, are well versed in all the mysteries of "monte," while the reservation Indians acquire a knowledge of "poker," and "seven up," sufficient for all purposes of gambling, in a quarter the time it would take them to learn the alphabet. The wilder tribes invent games for themselves.

Cheating is a recognized part of all games among all Indians. Luck in holding, and skill in playing are both made subservient to skill in manipulation. The man who can deal himself the best hand is recognized as the best player, provided he is not caught at it. If detected he loses, and this being the only penalty, the game goes on.

In winter, the men play from morning till night, and not unfrequently from night till morning again. The stakes are high for a poor people. I have personally looked on at a game between two Arapahoe chiefs, where one hundred and twenty dollars depended on a single hand.

Indians are possessed of true gambling passion, and will, if in bad luck, lose blankets, robes, lodge, arms, ponies, wives, and even children (although this is extremely rare). Twenty-five years ago I knew of such a case among the Comanches. The unlucky gambler having lost wives, children and property, yielded all to the winner and started alone for Mexico to recuperate his fallen fortunes by stealing. This was not in those days so very unusual an occurrence.

An Indian does scarcely anything in secret. Having no such idea as is embodied in our English word "vice," he is entirely open and above-board, in everything except those few things to which custom attaches punishment. There is therefore no secrecy about the gambling. Notice is sent out betimes, and everybody invited. The sound of the "tom-tom" notifies all that the game is about to begin. During its progress the music is kept up. During the manipulations or pauses of the game, all join in song. Sometimes two noted players will get up a game "between themselves. Spectators crowd around, and if a man is losing heavily, the whole camp soon knows it. In such cases, the wives of the loser put in an appearance before matters have proceeded to extremities, and break up the game.

The Comanches have a game somewhat like" hide the slipper," in which an almost unlimited number may take part. Two individuals will choose sides, by alternate selection among those who wish to play, men or women. All then seat themselves in the parallel lines about eight feet apart, facing each other. The articles wagered are piled between the lines. All being ready, the leader of one side rising to his knees holds up the gambling bone, so that all may see it. He then closes it in the two hands, manipulating it so dexterously that it is impossible to see in which hand it is.

After a minute or more of rapid motion he suddenly thrusts one or generally both hands, into the outstretched hands of the person on the right and left. This marks the real commencement of the game, no guess of the other watching-side being permitted until after this movement. He may pass the bone to one or the other, or he may retain it himself. In either case, he continues his motions as if he had it, and each of those two, closing the hands, go through with the manipulations as if he had received it; passing or pretending to pass it on and on to the right and left, until every arm is waving, every hand apparently passing the bone and every player in a whirl of excitement. All this while, the other line is watching with craned necks and strained eyes for the slightest bungle in the manipulation, which will indicate where the bone is. Finally someone believes he sees it and suddenly points to a hand, which must be instantly thrust out and opened palm up. If the bone is in it the watching party wins one point, if not it loses. The other side then takes the bone and goes through the same performance. If during the manipulations the bone should be accidentally dropped, the other side takes a point and the bone. The game is usually twenty-one points, though the players may determine on any number.

This is the most exciting game I have ever seen played by Indians, and apparently the most fascinating to them.

Besides taking part in the round games of the men, the women have games of their own which I have never seen played by men. The most common is called the "plum-stone game," and is played by the women and children of nearly all the Plains tribes. The stone of the wild plum is polished and the flatter sides cut or scraped off, making them more flat. Some of these faces are then marked with different hieroglyphics, varying with the tribe, and some left blank. The game is played with eight such pieces, which are shaken together in a little bowl, or tin cup, and then thrown on a blanket. It is really nothing but our game of dice, complicated, however, by a system of counting so curious and arbitrary that it is almost impossible for a white man to learn it. Every possible combination of the hieroglyphics and blanks on the eight stones give a different count. This varies with the tribe. Among the Cheyennes the highest possible throw is two hundred, the lowest zero. The game is usually two thousand, though this greatly varies. Each player having the gambler's superstition as to what is her lucky number, tries to fix the game at that number. If the stakes are valuable the number fixed for the game is generally a compromise. In some tribes a certain combination of the stones wins and another combination loses the game, even though it be made on the first throw.

The Cheyenne women have another game of which they are passionately fond.

Small white beads are strung on a sinew, twelve or fourteen inches long; at one end, are fastened in a bunch, six loops, about an inch in diameter, of smaller beads similarly strung. Four polished bones of the bear's foot are then strung on this beaded string, the smaller ends toward the loops. Each of these bones #s perforated with sixteen holes in rows of four, and .at each end are two or three very small loops of red beads. The other end of the sinew is now fastened to a sharpened piece of wire, six to seven inches long, and the gambling instrument is complete.

The game is played by any number of players, each in turn. The needle is held horizontally between the thumb and fingers. The bones hanging down are steadied for an instant, then thrown forward and upward, and as they come opposite the point of the needle a rapid thrust is made. If the player be skilful the point of the needle will catch in some of the loops or perforations of the bones. For each loop at the lower extremity of the instrument caught by the needle, the player counts one hundred. Being put together in a bunch, it is rare that more than two or three are caught, though all six may be. One of the bones caught lengthwise on the needle counts twenty-five; two, fifty. Each little loop and perforation penetrated by the needle counts five. Though the complications are numerous, the count is simple. Thus suppose the needle passed through a little loop on third bone (five), then through the bone (twenty-five), then through a little loop at the other end of the bone (five), then through a loop on fourth bone (five), and finally through three of the terminal loops (three hundred), the count for the throw is the sum of all (three hundred and forty). I have never seen over five hundred made at a throw, though it is of course possible to make over six hundred. If the needle misses or fails to perforate loop or orifice, there is no count. The game is usually two thousand.

It will be noticed that in the women's games, the element of chance greatly preponderates, the variation in the possibilities of a single throw, from nothing to more than six hundred, being so great that skill would seem to have nothing to do with success. The Cheyenne woman is, however, hard to beat at this her favorite game. I have a few times been victorious by persistently aiming at the large lower loops, which, though so difficult to hit that five out of six throws were blanks, yet counted up handsomely when the throw was successful.

These two games are the common amusement and occupation of the Indian woman, when there is no special work to do, and as they are invariably played for stakes, she, on a small scale, is quite as much of a gambler as her husband or father.

The boys bet on everything, horse-races, foot-races, shooting at marks with arrows, etc., and are the most rascally little scoundrels in the world. One of the favorite games is for one to shoot an arrow into the ground at any distance he pleases. The others then shoot at it. To each whose arrow strikes within a certain distance of his he pays an arrow; each who fails to come within that distance pays an arrow to him. In these innocent pastimes the large boys swindle the smaller most egregiously, and nothing so delights them as to get hold of a little fellow whose proud father has just given him a new set of arrows. I have watched their performances with the greatest amusement. They are very like civilized rascals, and the victim soon learns to revenge himself on his swindlers by swindling some boy smaller and more ignorant than himself.

The vice of all others most unhappy in its consequences to the Indian is his love of strong drink. This passion for intoxication amounts almost to an insanity. Those who inhabit that portion of the continent where grows the Maguay plant, make from it an intoxicating beverage known as "mescal." Those of Arizona and California make from fermented corn a drink which they call "tizwin," as efficacious for a first-class "drunk" as anything that can be produced. The Plains Indian, behind all others in inventive faculty, is fain to fall back upon the white man for the means of indulging in his favorite passion.

To drink liquor as a beverage, for the gratification of taste, or for the sake of pleasurable conviviality, is something of which the Indian can form no conception. His idea of pleasure in the use of strong drink is to get drunk, and the quicker and more complete that effect, the better he likes it. He is very easily affected, a few tablespoonfuls setting him roaring, and half an ordinary tumbler putting him in his paradise for hours.

The Plains Indian will give anything in the way of ponies or peltries for whiskey, and having had one drink, will barter everything he possesses for another. There is no dirty act, from bearing false witness to prostituting his favorite wife, that an Indian will not commit when whiskey is held out as the incentive.

The laws of the United States are very stringent in their prohibition of the sale or gift of intoxicating liquors to Indians, as well as its introduction into the Indian Territory.

It is easy to make laws; it is not easy always to enforce them. When the laws were made, "Indian Territory" was the whole vast country west of the Mississippi; almost every portion of which was then occupied by Indians. Much of that territory is now formed into states, and the laws of these states protect its citizens in the sale of liquor if they take out a license.

Decision after decision has been made by learned judges and wise Indian Commissioners, in their efforts to reconcile the right to permit one man to sell liquor with the right to prohibit another man from getting drunk. The term "Indian Territory" has been gradually restricted in application, until at the present time, it means only the ground inside the limits of a declared Indian Reservation. A squatter who goes over that line to sell liquor subjects himself to fine and imprisonment, but he can put his cabin or wagon immediately on the state side of the line, and sell with impunity to all the Indians who come to him. Whether this is the intent of the law may be questioned, but that it is the actual working of the law is perfectly known to every frontiersman.

With the enormous profits derived from the business, it would take an army of constables and marshals to keep the frontier dealers from selling liquor to Indians, and it would go on all the same, even if the states prohibited it. The Indian is as eager for whiskey as the trader is for his profits, and the two together will outwit all the "myrmidons of the law" that can be sent after them.

The peculiarity of the Indian "drunk," is that if there be only liquor enough, it is quick and complete; consequently, he is not quarrelsome in his cups. There is no idea of conviviality. The beverage is far too precious to be shared, and the fortunate purchaser of a pint of whiskey will sneak off alone into a thicket, arrange a comfortable sleeping-place for himself, turn off the whole quantity at a draught, then lie down and get drunk and sober again without changing his position or disturbing anyone. For the number of drunkards, the very few murders or outrages committed while under the influence of drink is really remarkable. I have never yet seen a drunken Indian woman. They, however, look with amiable complacency on the bestiality of their husbands, and seem to regard it as a matter of course. On one occasion I witnessed the reverse. A Ute squaw was trying to take home her husband, who, not having quite enough whiskey, was only "obstinate" drunk. She was patient, he brutal. Finally he struck her. Seizing a good-sized rod, she fell upon and beat him unmercifully. When I approached to interfere, she threw down the stick and began to laugh, while the warrior husband sat upon the ground, blubbering like a whipped school-boy.

WONDERFUL FEATS AND MARVELLOUS EXPLOITS

NEXT to the dance, the most common and popular indoor amusement of the Indians, is story-telling, and a good story-teller is a man of importance. The bucks, squaws, and children, crowd to his lodge, or to any other where he may be, and spend the long winter evenings in listening to his recitals. These stories are as marvellous as the imagination of the inventor can create, jumbling gods and men, fabulous monsters and living animals, the possible and the impossible, in the most heterogeneous confusion. There is little point or wit in them, and scarcely any dramatic power, except the narrator be telling of some personal event, when he also acts the scene with all possible exaggeration.

The personal stories are generally very filthy, and the language of the plainest. They have no evasive ways of expressing things; a "spade is a spade," with a vengeance. The presence of women and children is not of the slightest consequence, and imposes no restraint, either in words or action.

One of the most curious spectacles is a story-teller and his audience, when the sign-language is used. Sitting or squatting in every position whence a good view can he had, silent and eager, all eyes are intently fixed on the story-teller, who, without a word of speech, is rapidly moving his hands, now one, now the other, now both together. Occasionally a grunt of satisfaction or approval runs around the circle. More and more eagerness of attention, writhings and twistings of body and limbs, show the increase of interest, and finally a burst of uproarious laughter and applause marks the point of the story.

The outdoor amusements of the Plains Indians are riding, shooting, racing, both on foot and horseback, wrestling, swimming, and, with the boys, a sort of game of "tag." In good weather nearly half a buck's waking hours are passed in the saddle. Hiding is second nature to him. Strapped astride of a horse when scarcely able to walk, he does not, when a man, remember a time when he could not ride.

Having never seen the riding of Arabs, Turcomans, Cossacks, and other world-renowned riders, I cannot say how the Indian compares with them, but I am satisfied that he is too nearly a Centaur to be surpassed by any.

The bit most commonly used among the southern Plains Indians is known as the "Mexican bit." It is a most cruel affair.

The saddle is a light frame of wood, the side-pieces shaped to fit a horse's back. The seat is not rounded, but almost perfectly straight, and forms very nearly right angles with the pommel and can tie. These are about eight inches high above the seat. The pommel ends with a rounded knob. The cantle, rather wide at top and bottom, is cut away in the middle to make a depression to fit the leg or heel of the rider, and forms his support when he wishes to throw himself on the side of his horse. The whole is covered with green hide, which in drying binds all the parts together, tight and strong almost as iron.

The girth is a broad band of plaited hair, terminating in iron rings, or bent wood, covered with raw-hide, if iron rings cannot be obtained. These rings are attached to the saddle on the principle of the "Mexican cinche," by which a man of ordinary strength can almost crush in a horse's ribs.

Great liberties of position are taken by an Indian on horseback, and it is of the utmost importance that the saddle be strong, and the girth fail not.

The stirrup is of thin wood, strengthened with raw-hide, by which material it is also fastened to the saddle. Some slight padding is put between the horse and a saddle, the skin of a wolf or buffalo calf, or in these later days, a piece of old blanket or grain sack. The stirrups are extremely short. They are of little use, except in mounting, or as rests to the foot when riding.

Civilized people mount on the left side of the horse, because the knights of old, from whom we get our ideas of horsemanship, wore their swords on that side, and could not, therefore, mount on the right without inconvenience from that weapon.

The Indian mounts always on the right side, and this is undoubtedly natural and most convenient, as it leaves the left hand free to hold the reins and manage the horse, while the right grasps the mane or pommel of the saddle.

In travelling, necessary stores are carried *en croupe*, or slung to the saddle on each side. One blanket or robe is around the rider's person, and he sits on another one if he has it. His gun is carried across his thighs, resting against the pommel, his bow and quiver are slung on the back by a strap passing from right to left, but which brings the quiver almost perpendicular with its opening over the right shoulder.

When travelling from place to place, under ordinary circumstances, a more unromantic or less dangerous-looking specimen could not be found than an Indian warrior. His seat and carriage are particularly ungraceful. The short stirrups force him to sit almost on the small of his back, and the back itself is rounded into an unseemly curve. His head is carried forward as far as the length of his neck will allow. His left hand holds the reins; his right is armed with a short stick, to which is attached a thong of the inevitable rawhide, and with a light blow of this he marks every step of his horse. He uses no spurs, but his heels are constantly drumming on the horse's ribs, with a nervous motion difficult to account for. He scarcely ever turns his head or moves his body, and, even when most watchful, appears to see nothing. He looks stiff, constrained and uncomfortable on horseback, and yet this uncouth object will perform feats of horsemanship actually incredible to one who has seen only civilized riding.

With his horse at full speed, he will pick up from the ground a small piece of coin. He will throw himself on the side of his horse, in such a position, that only a small portion of an arm and leg can be seen from the other side.

One method of racing is to start from a line, and rush full speed at a tree, the one who first touches it being winner. Another is to rush at a heavy pole placed horizontally about six feet from the ground, resting on forks firmly set. If the rider stops his horse an instant too soon he fails of touching the pole, if an instant too late, the horse passes under the pole, leaving the rider dangling to it, or thrown to the ground.

A third method is to fasten to the ground, two strips of buffalo-hide from six to ten feet apart. The starting-point is some two hundred yards from these strips, and the game is to run at full speed, jump the horse between the strips, turn him in his tracks, and return to the starting-point. The horse which fails to get beyond the first strip, with all four of his feet, or which gets a single foot beyond the second strip, is beaten, even though he makes the best time.

The training of the ponies has quite as much to do with the success of an Indian race as his speed or the address of the rider. Great pains are, therefore, taken in training, and a pony thoroughly up in his tricks is highly prized.

The Indian is an arrant jockey, and understands all the tricks of professional horse-racing as well as any veteran of Jerome Park. He rarely comes in competition with whites, because his passion being for trick races, as those described, he dislikes to come down to a square and fair race over a straight track. Besides this, it is really exceedingly difficult to hit on a fair distance between the Indian and American horse. The start being always from a halt, the small, quick pony is almost sure to win at from one hundred to three hundred yards, while the long stride of the American horse is equally sure of carrying him in winner from six hundred yards to two miles. A mile or two is then doubtful, after which it is safe to back the endurance of the pony.

A band of Comanches under Mu-la-que-top, once camped near Fort Chadbourne in Texas, and were frequent visitors and great nuisances as beggars at that post. Some of the officers were decidedly "horsey," several owning blooded horses, the relative speed of each being known, by repeated trials, almost to a foot. Mu-la-que-top was bantered for a race, and, after several days of manoeuvring, a race was made against the third best horse of the garrison, distance four hundred yards.

The Indians betted robes and plunder of various kinds, to the value of sixty or seventy dollars, against money, flour, sugar, &c., to a like amount. At the appointed time all the Indians and most of the garrison were assembled at the track. The Indians showed" a miserable sheep of a pony, with legs like churns; a three-inch coat of rough hair stuck out all over the body; and a general expression of neglect, helplessness, and patient suffering struck pity into the hearts of all beholders. The rider was a stalwart buck of one hundred and seventy pounds, looking big and strong enough to carry the poor beast on his shoulders. He was armed with a huge club, with which, after the word was given, he belabored the miserable animal from start to finish. To the astonishment of all the whites, the Indian won by a neck.

Another race was proposed by the officers, and, after much "dickering," accepted by the Indians, against the next best horse of the garrison. The bets were doubled 5 and in less than an hour the second race was run by the same pony, with the same apparent exertion and with exactly the same result.

The officers, thoroughly disgusted, proposed a third race, and brought to the ground a magnificent Kentucky mare, of the true Lexington blood, and known to beat the best of the others at least forty yards in four hundred. The Indians accepted the race, and not only doubled bets as before, but piled up everything they could raise, seemingly almost crazed with the excitement of their previous success. The riders mounted; the word was given. Throwing away his club, the Indian rider gave a whoop, at which the sheep-like pony pricked up his ears, and went away like the wind, almost two feet to the mare's one. The last fifty yards of the course was run by the pony with the rider sitting face to his tail, making hideous grimaces and beckoning to the rider of the mare to come on.

It afterwards transpired that the old sheep was a trick and straight race pony, celebrated among all the tribes of the south, and that Mu-la-que-top had only just returned from a visit to the Kickapoos, in the Indian nation, whom he had easily cleaned out of six hundred ponies.

In practising with bow and arrow, the Indian has a short loop of rawhide attached to the pommel of his saddle, which he passes over his head, and under his arm when he wishes to throw himself on the side of his horse. This, with the leg holding the can tie, gives him firm support, and leaves both arms free. He can, however, use only the right side of the horse. In pistol-practice, the loop is not necessary, and needing only one hand with the weapon, he can shelter himself on either side, holding on to the pommel with the left hand.

With all his power of endurance, his life in the open air, and his constant and violent exercise, the Indian is not physically a powerful man. He has not the slightest knowledge of the use of his fists, and the poorest member of the prize ring could carry off the belt from the whole red race. A short time ago a squaw man and Indian near this post, got into an altercation about the use of a horse. The white man finally struck the Indian with his fist. The latter, though apparently much the more powerful man, made no effort to return the blow, but went at once to the chief with a claim for damages. I have never heard of a fist-fight between Indians.

The boys wrestle a good deal, but without rule or science, a mere scuffle. An average white man will "get away" with the strongest and most active Indian, either in a wrestling-match, or in a foot-race for short distances. In a race for miles the Indian endurance will win against any ordinary white man, but no Indian, in his natural condition, could compete with one of our trained" go-as-you-please" racers. Having no idea of the effect of training on horses and men, the Indians cannot be made to believe that a man can get over five hundred and fifty miles in six days.

All Indians swim, as it were by instinct, and evince great courage and skill in the passage of the Plains rivers, dangerous from their swift currents, and terrible from their treacherous quicksands.

Among the middle Plains tribes there are no games of ball, nor any approach to the games of white children, except the game of "tag" mentioned; but among the Nez Perces and other western tribes the women are extremely fond of a game of ball similar to our "shinny" or "hockey," and play with great spirit.

The women ride astride, mount on the right side, use the same saddle, and are almost as much at home on it as the men, though, not having the same constant drill, they cannot perform the same marvellous feats.

Where no one can commit a moral wrong, there would appear to be no opportunity for what we call scandal, yet every act, incident, accident or condition is common talk for the whole band, to be discussed broadly, and without reservation, by old and young, male and female. The broad caricatures of the tattle of a New England village are merely faint conceptions of the capabilities in this direction of an Indian encampment. Each band being scarcely more than one large family, every individual in it is interested in everything to such an extent, that it is scarcely too much to say that there is absolutely nothing secret.

All persons who have been much among Indians are astounded at the wonderful speed and accuracy of Indian rumors. Something occurs to-day; it is known to-morrow at distances that appear incredible. In September, 1880, an outbreak occurred at Fort Reno, sixty miles from this post, (Cantonment, I. T.) The Indian scouts here knew and informed me of it before I heard of it by the telegraph line between the two posts. So, also, when Ouray was sick; his condition was known every day by us, though we were quite a hundred miles away, and the country between us exceedingly difficult.

In civilized communities, whether rightfully or not, old maids and widows have credit for the monopoly of the gossip and tattle. Among Indians it belongs to the old men; and from the appearance and qualities of the youngest colt, to the number and color of the stripes on every woman's shawl, these old fellows know and talk of everything.

I have said that an unmarried woman must never be found alone, and it would be the height of impropriety for her to go anywhere with any man except her father. They are exceedingly fond of gadding about, and easily overcome the difficulties thrown in their way by custom. Half a dozen girls and young married women will place themselves in charge of some old lady friend, under whose chaperonage they go when and where they please, and usually with perfect safety.

Some writers claim for Indian women such an excess of loyalty, as to assert that they hold in contempt one of their number who fails to do everything possible for her husband.

I have no experience of any such feeling. Each of the several wives of a man has her own peculiarities; one lazy, another active, one neat, another slovenly; but as a rule all seem to get along perfectly well together, and with the other women of the band.

One of the wives of my Cheyenne friend, Mr. Running Buffalo, is an exception, being so emphatic in her speech and action, that Buffalo is obliged to let her have an establishment of her own.

This, looked at rightly, may be regarded as a first step in civilization. No high order of civilization is possible without the advancement and independence of women; and in fact, the present progress of each nation and people from the utmost degradation to the highest enlightenment, can be fairly and accurately measured by the condition of its women.

I have heard frequent descriptions of the squaw-fights of the Indians on the Pacific coast, in which every woman of the band is engaged, each apparently on her own account, while the men stand around laughing, applauding, and encouraging. No such performances take place among the Plains Indians. Men, women, and children, all are less disposed to quarrel and wrangle than any people I have ever seen.

A rather amusing instance of personal collision occurred near this post in the spring of 1880. The Cheyenne wife of a Mexican half-breed, had, two years ago, left her husband for another man, taking with her, as is unusual, her child, a baby of a few months old. The band to which the Mexican belongs makes its summer camp near this post. Last April the runaway wife and new husband came here. The Mexican heard of it, went to them and demanded his child. The Indian husband told him to take it, but the wife, would not give it up. He went off and returned with the chief, who ordered the woman to give up the child. She again refused, when the two proceeded to take it by force. This was too much for the mother, who, throwing the child to her Indian husband, assaulted her two enemies so vigorously, that in two minutes both were soundly beaten and glad to escape. Before they could return with assistance, the child and its courageous mother were out of reach.

Ten years ago, that woman would have been hunted down by dog-soldiers and killed without remorse. Now the affair is only a matter of fun and laughter to every Indian, except the half-breed and the chief. The Indian progresses!

The little girls are very fond of dolls, and their mothers take great pains and show considerable skill in making them. Their dresses are frequently accurately copied, even to the minutest particulars, from the ceremonial dresses of the parents or friends.

The baby-houses are miniature tepees, and until large enough to be put to work, most of the waking hours of the girls are spent in this play.

POETRY AND SONGS

THE drum, or "tom-tom," is the universal, I may almost say, the only musical instrument of the Indians, for though there are others, no use whatever is made of them on public occasions by the middle and southern Plains Indians. The drum is the accompaniment to every religious ceremony, the necessity to every social gathering. Its beat signals the hour of rejoicing, the hour of mourning, and by its potent influence the Bad God is not unfrequently frustrated in his diabolic designs.

The primitive drum was a section cut from the trunk of a hollow tree, over one end of which was stretched and tightly fastened a thin raw skin. At present, an empty nail or pickle keg is often used, but the fashionable and preferred "tom-tom" of the Cheyenne Indians is made by stretching the raw skin over a common cheese-box.

There is usually no arrangement of drum-cords for tightening this head, and when it becomes loose and flabby from continued beating, it is restored to its original tone by holding it over a fire, sometimes a little water being first sprinkled on it. In any lengthened ceremony, or at the social dances, a fire is always kept up for tightening the drum-head.

In the fall of 1880, I was so fortunate as to be presented by a Cheyenne with a wonderful drum, the handiwork of some Indian of more than ordinary constructive skill. The body is the rough keg, in which was transported two large round cheeses. A raw skin is stretched over each end and connected by thongs of rawhide, laced after the manner of an ordinary kettle-drum. Another thong around the keg is looped about each two lacings, and forms an ingenious means of tightening the drum-heads.

This is the only Indian tom-tom I have ever seen with two heads. Its constructor evidently modelled it after the infantry drum.

The Sioux and some other of the northern Plains Indians, have another (to them) musical instrument—a rattle formed of a dried gourd in which are placed a number of small smooth stones.

Almost all the tribes have a reed instrument, a pipe or flute, ingeniously constructed. Two pieces of wood are fashioned and hollowed out, so that when joined together they have much the appearance of a flute. In one of these are made six holes for the fingers, and one nearer the mouth, after the manner of a whistle. After being smoothed and fitted with great patience and care, the two pieces are glued together with gum, and tightly bound with strings. A small tube at the upper end is the mouth-piece. They are very frequently elaborately ornamented. The tone is quite soft and harmonious.

Though there are more or less of these instruments in every band of Indians, they are never used on ceremonious or festive occasions, nor have I ever-heard an Indian attempt to play what even he might call a tune. The only music on them is the repetition again and again of a few chords, low, slow, and sometimes very sweet and weird. It is scarcely ever heard in the daytime, but after dark the love-sick youngster, placing himself beside the lodge of his inamorata, pours out the feelings of his heart in most doleful strains.

The Pawnees, Cheyennes, and Arapahos have yet another instrument. About an inch of the toe of a buffalo's hoof is cut off and dried. A small hole is made in the apex of this shell, through which is passed a buckskin string. A knot in one end of the string prevents the toe from slipping off. Twenty or thirty of these toes are tied to a stick, with a few inches' play to each, and the instrument is complete. It is held in the hand of the dancer and makes a dry rattling noise.

For music for all warlike and religious ceremonies, for gambling bouts, for dances, for all social gatherings and merry-makings, the Indian relies on his voice. Scarcely anything is done without this music, and similar and monotonous as it all appears to be to the uninstructed ear, each particular ceremony and dance has its own invariable music.

Probably from lack of education I can with difficulty tell a war song from any song of the Indian "German," yet the music of the one will put the Indian in a frenzy of military ardor, the music of the other throw him only into transports of passionate adoration of his partner in the dance.

Many of the songs have words, but by far the greater number are "songs without words,' but to which words may be adapted on special occasions. The words constantly vary, the music never.

The adaptation of words to a special song is frequently a matter of grave importance. A party of warriors returning from a successful foray, must embalm their exploits in song. They have decided on the music, but the work before them is to fit words to it which will be expressive and most highly eulogistic, not only of the performances of the party, but of each individual who has distinguished himself. Night after night is spent in this grand effort. One man will propose a line; all try the effect by singing it in chorus. If satisfactory, it is adopted; if not, rejected or amended. The song must be, and is, ready by the time they get home, and on the first occasion thereafter is sung to the pride and gratification of all.

So also in other songs. One man will adapt a set of words, whose appropriateness to some situation or personal peculiarity will make them popular for a little while, or until another set of words displaces them. Even the nursery songs of the mothers are a mere jumble, no two mothers using the same words, though singing the same song.

Occasionally a thought may be expressed with somewhat poetic metaphor, but the Plains Indians are utterly ignorant of rhyme, or metrical arrangement of verse, and seem incapable of following a thought beyond its first expression.

Indian songs are very curious, and though on all subjects, what may be termed the mechanism is the same in all. An isolated thought .is expressed in a few words, possibly in one compound word. This, followed by a number of meaningless sounds sufficient to fill out the music to the end of the beat, constitutes the first line or verse. The other lines are constructed in the same manner. Whatever is intended to be said is generally expressed in four lines or verses, though some of the songs have many lines.

The constant use of sounds without meaning, to fill up gaps in the lines, makes it easy for any Indian to be his or her own poet. It accounts also for the little weight that words give to Indian music, and the slight hold they take on the memory.

As a fair example of the songs with words, I give the love-song of a young Cheyenne warrior who courted a married woman. Ha yah, ha a yah, are not words, but represent sounds interjected to fill out the lines—

"O ta, ha ya, ha a yah, ha yah Ne e am e, ha a yah, ha yah Ne yuch te e how o to o, ha yah, ha Nas o.wi e, ha yah ha yah, ha."

"I am your lover, ha ya, ha a yah, ha yah,

I am not afraid to court you, ha a yah, ha yah Though you have a brave husband, ha yah, ha Will you elope with me? ha yah, ha yah ha."

Her answer is—

"Hame e nooeh e, hah ha ha ha vo o Ho oche ish it tah, ha ha ha ha yo Im e go o ha tom e to, ha ha yo e Im e am ah to o she, ha yo ha o."

"I will leave my husband, hah ha ha ha ha yo o But attend to what I say to you, ha ha ha ha yo You must be good to me, ha ha, yo e And not make love to other women, ha yo, ha o."

Below is a specimen of a song without words, but no spelling can do justice to the sounds produced:—

"Ha a e ha e yo, ha a e yo, a ha e yo Ha a e a e yah, ah ha e yah Ha a e a e yah ha how e yah How ow o how o how o o."

All Indians use the nose as a musical instrument, especially in the high notes. The lower tones are guttural, and the "ha yah," being as it were, beaten out of their bodies by the coming down of the feet in the dance, is more like a grunt than a musical sound. The songs without words contain a great variety of sounds, guttural, nasal, and natural, but generally all within one octave, though the sound designated in the music as f e" is habitually pitched far above.

I procured the services of Mr. Aschmann, the leader of the band of the 23d U. S. Infantry to reduce this music to score. The general similarity is so great that I give only a few illustrations. Mr. Aschmann says, "The rhythm of Indian music is, as a whole, very poor. Almost every song keeps within the limits of one octave, without change or effort for harmonious , melody. It is very seldom, however, that they bring in notes from different keys, or make other innovations sufficient to make the music discordant or unpleasant to listen to. Bagpipes or reed instruments are best adapted to reproduce the Indian music."

INDIAN DANCES—LUDICROUS EXPERIENCES.

PROBABLY from the fact that the music is always to the monotonous beat of the "tom-tom," the "step" of the Indian dance is always very nearly the same, however varied the figures. The feet are kept together, the whole weight of the body resting on the balls, the heels not touching the ground. The dancing effort consists in a little spring on both feet at the same time, so timed that the feet come down exactly on the beat of the "tom-tom." The best and most artistic dancers vary this by a little double spring, such as is often used by little white girls in "skipping the rope." The movement is accompanied by a corresponding rising and falling of the shoulders, and nervous jerking of the body, communicating a motion to almost every muscle of the system. The dancing is especially tiresome on the muscles in the calves of the legs, so much so, that a dance of half an hour would lay a white novice on his back for a week; yet the Indian will dance all night, and feel none the worse next day.

In exciting religious or other ceremonial dances, the "step" may be varied by bounds and springs into the air, but there is no effort at posturing.

In the ceremonial dances, in which warriors alone participate, the dancers generally form themselves into a circle facing inward, and sometimes join hands for a few moments, but any position or contact which tends to restraint is soon abandoned in the excitement to which they work themselves.

How such singing and such dancing can give the pleasure they undoubtedly do give is one of the problems of humanity, but for all purposes of excitement, indeed of frenzy, they are amply sufficient to the Indian.

I have already described the ceremonial of the "Hôch-é-a-yum," or "Medicine Dance" of the Cheyennes and Arapahos, which as nearly as possible is identical with the "Sun Dance" of the Dakotas. Almost all the wild tribes have a dance which is intended to represent the same idea, but the horrible tortures are omitted in all but the more warlike tribes, those who ennoble endurance as the loftiest of human virtues.

Indian dances are of three kinds; religious ceremonial, secular ceremonial, and social.

In some of the ceremonial dances, warriors only are permitted; in others women take a prominent part. All, men, women, and children, take part in the social dances, the greatest happiness of Indian life.

From the time when "David danced before the Lord," to the present day, primitive people have regarded some form of dance as a necessary adjunct to religious ceremony. Indeed, the remark is applicable to all peoples, whether primitive or enlightened, for there is no doubt that the changes of posture—sitting, standing, kneeling—of our Christian forms of worship, are merely a modification of the primitive idea; a recognition of the necessity of motion.

Indians are not polytheists, nor students of history, yet many of their religious dances and ceremonies might have been adopted bodily from Grecian ideas of three thousand years ago. Thus the great medicine dance" of the Florida Seminoles was celebrated at that season when the Indian corn was in its "roasting ear" state, and was therefore called by them the "green-corn dance."

The ceremonies commenced with processions and dances, and a feast of rejoicing, somewhat similar to the Cerelia of the ancient Romans, and wound up with a furious orgie devoted to Venus.

The Sioux also celebrate the "green-corn dance" at the proper season, but their final ceremonies, exactly the reverse of the Seminoles, might be in honor of Diana, being a religious and rigid test of the chastity of their women.

As a rule, one tribe has at least one purely religious dance each year. This much is insisted upon by the medicine men. Tribes which can afford the expense may have two or more.

All these religious dances embody the same idea, and are conducted upon much the same general principle as the great camp-meetings of some of our Christian denominations. The time and place are fixed by the medicine man, and ample notice given.

The "scalp dance," is next to the medicine dance in importance, and is the most common of all the ceremonial dances of the Indians.

The day after the return to the home encampment of a successful war party, by which scalps have been taken, a ceremony is performed by the warriors who took them, no other person whatever being permitted to be present.

I have been a spectator at a distance, but all to be seen was a number of Indians, sitting on the ground in a close circle. During this ceremony, the scalps are trimmed, cleared of all fleshy matter, and the skin cured by some process. Each scalp is then stretched by thongs inside of a hoop of wood a little larger than itself, and the hair carefully combed and greased. Each warrior then attaches his scalp or scalps, in their hoops, to a peeled willow wand, from eight to ten feet long.

This ceremony is called "counting the coups," and is "Big Medicine," that is, very important in a religious point of view. It is preparatory to the scalp dance.

When it has been satisfactorily completed, all the warriors march gravely one behind the other, back to camp, each bearing his wand with its burden of dangling scalps in his hand. The wands are planted in a circle in the centre of the camp.

By this time, the whole population of the village is crowded around this centre of interest. The warriors who took the scalps are now joined by those who had taken part in the fight, or who belonged to the party which did the fighting, and thus won for themselves the right to participate in the dance.

All assemble in a circle around and facing the circle of wands. At a signal, all the warriors join hands, and commence the monotonous song and dance, turning slowly about the scalps. As the dance progresses, the warriors soon loose hands, and varying the song by whoops and yells, and the dance by bounds, gestures and brandishing of weapons, work themselves up to a condition of excitement bordering on frenzy.

The eyes of the spectators are strained upon scalps and dancers as each slayer in turn springing from the circle, and bounding to his wand, vaunts in extravagant terms his own prowess, and acts over again the taking of the scalps.

When the fortunate takers of scalps have all exhausted themselves in self-laudation, others of the dancers spring by turns into the circle, each explains by what unfortunate interference of the" Bad God," he was prevented on this occasion from taking a scalp, and recounts in glowing language his successful prowess on some previous occasion, or what he proposes to do on the next opportunity. This is continued until each dancer has had full opportunity to show how brave and great a warrior he is. Dancers and spectators grow wild with excitement, and by the time the dance is over, the whole population is little short of insane.

This nervous intoxication is a special delight of the Indians, and when they feel like indulging in it, and there are no fresh scalps, they bring out some old ones, and go through with the same performance, the same scalps in "piping times of peace" being made to do duty over and over again.

I have been told that, wild as the dancers appear to be, each knows perfectly well what he is doing, having previously in some solitude gone over his speech and acted his part, time and again.

When a tribe has decided upon war, a ceremony or scene almost identical with that described is enacted. It is called "striking the post." The trunk of a tree from six inches to a foot in diameter is planted in the ground in the centre of the camp.

War parties are usually made up of volunteers. The chief who is to command the expedition sends criers through the camp, beating tom-toms and calling on every warrior to come to the post. The whole population of the village is soon assembled and the ceremonies commence. The warriors who have already decided to go form in a circle about the post, and, when worked up by song and dance to a proper state of excitement, each bounds in turn to the post, and striking it with his "coup-stick" gives a most glowing description of what he intends to do when he meets the enemy. Other warriors, excited by the recitals, join the dance and in turn strike the post, until a sufficient number have thus signified their intention of taking the field.

It is a ceremony of enlistment, and after "striking the post" nothing but sickness or other imperative cause will prevent an Indian from going with the expedition—it has become a matter of honor.

These are the war dances, and as every little predatory party must" strike the post," before it goes out and have its scalp dance (whether successful or not in taking them) when it gets back, the war spirit is kept at a fever heat. It is not too much to say that, in some of the wilder tribes and within a very few years of this writing, one or other of these frenzies was enacted at least once a week.

The Indians on reservations and in the vicinity of troops, have now almost abandoned them, as advertising either their purpose or its fulfilment. When, however, there is legitimate opportunity, these dances are still celebrated; and in every case where the United States has used Indian against Indian, those employed by the government have celebrated their going out and coming in, with all the old enthusiasm.

I was once spectator at a scalp dance which was a special and exceptional occasion, for not only had a goodly number of scalps been taken, but two prisoners—a woman of about forty, and boy of twelve years of age—were to grace the ceremony. The peeled wands bearing the hoops and stretched scalps had been planted in a circle in the ground. The prisoners were brought by the warriors who had captured them, from the lodge in which they were confined, and forced to take their places in the circle, their hands being held by the warriors on each side of them. The woman-prisoner accepted the situation, and in looks and actions appeared to take as enjoyable an interest in the dance as any of the proper performers. Not so the boy; with eyes downcast, without a voluntary motion of foot or body, he was dragged around the circle, taking only such walking-steps as were necessary to avoid being pulled down. All the turmoil and excitement failed to produce on him the slightest effect. Not once in the dance of more than an hour did he lift his eyes to the scalps, to which were directed all the eyes and attention of his captors. Not once did he evince the slightest interest in any of the proceedings, or make the slightest movement unless forced to it.

I could not but admire the proud determination of one so young to resist all the efforts of a crowd of enemies to force him into even a semblance of rejoicing over the scalps of his people, possibly of his own father.

Besides the above-described dances, which are common to, and much the same among all Indians, every tribe, almost every band, has one or more ceremonial dances. These have a general sameness, but differ according to the taste and inventive genius of the band. They are not intended to intoxicate with excitement, being purely spectacular, but are gotten up by the warriors for the purpose of display, and to render themselves pleasing in the eyes of their sweethearts.

The Indian is vainer than a peacock, and is never so happy as when tricked out in all the gaudy and tawdry finery that he can possibly heap upon himself.

The dancers in the "Hôch-é-a-yum," the "scalp dance," and "striking the post," generally go through' their performances in breech-cloth and moccasins alone. Those in the spectacular dances are overloaded with all the finery they possess or can borrow. These dances are, therefore, very grave and dignified, the performers not having freedom of movement to act out excitement, even did they feel it, and brusque movement might injure some of the finery.

The dancers form in a line, all facing the same way, but not joining hands, the | tom-tom" strikes up in slow time, all join in a monotonous song without words, and the movement commences. The dancing step is modified almost to a walk, and the figure is a lame attempt at imitating the evolutions of a company of infantry soldiers at drill.

It not unfrequently happens, that some of the warriors who have exceptionally beautiful ponies, horse-equipments, shields, etc., join this dance on horseback. They form on the flanks of the foot-dancers, follow their movements, and often elicit great admiration, not, as might be expected, for skilful horsemanship, but for their general style and perfection of ornamentation.

All Indians, men and women, are so at home on horseback, that gradations of horsemanship as recognized among civilized people are unknown.

These dances are great favorites with the women, who crowd around, applaud vociferously every change in the movement, and comment loudly on the beauties or faults of dress, and on the excellencies or deficiencies of the performers.

The women are allowed perfect freedom in these criticisms, which are yelled at the individual by name, who is required by Indian custom to keep a staid gravity of countenance and perfect temper, whether elevated to the seventh heaven of gratified vanity, by the laudations of some woman for whom he has a weakness, or exasperated almost beyond endurance by the ridicule of one whom he dislikes. The red coquettes take full advantage of their opportunity; and not a few love affairs, courtships, or changes of husband, date their commencement from the extravagant praises bestowed by some red beauty on a performer in this dance. The phenomenal peculiarity of Indian custom is, that a husband must listen unmoved, and without after action, to his wife's loudly expressed encomiums on another man.

One of the most curious of all Indian dances, is called the "begging dance." It is also least common, for it requires the active or passive participation of two tribes, which have become friendly after a period of hostility.

It is somewhat on the idea of a surprise-party. All the fighting men of one tribe, armed and dressed in their ordinary clothing, will suddenly and without previous notice rush upon the camp of the other, firing guns, sounding the war-whoop, and making every demonstration of a most furious attack.

The assaulted Indians pour out of their tepees, and recognizing the nature of the onslaught, put away their weapons, and form in a wide circle in the centre of the camp. The attacking party rush in as if about to destroy everything, but at a signal lay aside their arms, form inside the circle of spectators, and commence a ceremonial dance, a combination of dances, a war dance without its excitement and boastings, a spectacular dance without its dress and dignity.

It is emphatically a dance of reconciliation, and during its progress, the dancers, springing from their circle, and seizing each upon a warrior of the other tribe, hugs him with every demonstration of the warmest affection. But here ceases all resemblance to a civilized surprise-party, where the self-invited guests bring their own refreshments. Every unfortunate Indian embraced by a dancer is required by Indian custom to make him a present, and etiquette requires that he shall not be niggardly.

A "begging dance" is almost as grave a calamity to an Indian tribe as the raid of a hostile band. No one is killed or wounded, it is true, but the amount of plunder carried off is such as to incommode, if not impoverish, the unfortunates subject to it.

I have witnessed but one "begging dance." In his winter campaign of 1876-'77, against the Sioux, General Crook had about three hundred and fifty Indian allies. They were from five different tribes, almost all of which had until this time been bitterly hostile to each other. With rare tact he united these conflicting elements into one homogeneous and effective whole, effecting at least a nominal reconciliation between the Sioux and Pawnees, which tribes had been most bitter enemies for generations.

The aggressive campaign had terminated, and rumors of speedy return were rife in the camp.

One day I was sitting in my tent when I heard the terrible war-whoop, accompanied by a rattling succession of shots, and, rushing out, I saw a long line of Indians in skirmishing order, advancing at a run over a hill to the Pawnee camp. I could see that the Pawnees, though in commotion, did not appear to be alarmed, and as there was no excitement at headquarters, I presumed the demonstration to be a ceremony of some kind.

Getting my hat and overcoat, I made for the scene of action, but when I arrived the dance was already under full headway.

The Sioux, the most cunning of all the Plains tribes, taking advantage of the near approach of separation, had determined to add another to the terrible blows they had in late years dealt the Pawnees by giving them a "begging dance."

The Sioux were almost as numerous as the Pawnees, and the dance did not cease till every rascally dancer had hugged almost every individual Pawnee, and thus secured from him a liberal present.

The head chief of the Pawnees, a great friend of mine, known as Frank, but whose Indian name I never could master, literally stripped himself, giving to the Sioux chief a war-bonnet and dress, for which to my knowledge, he had refused one hundred dollars, and to other Indians, ponies, finery and clothing, to the value of over six hundred dollars. The unfortunate Pawnees were left almost in "*puris naturalibus.*"

The next day I met Frank, and remonstrated with him for his own and his people's foolishness in tamely submitting to be so swindled.

He admitted everything, said he knew the Sioux had done it purposely, and from hostile feeling, but that it was the "Indian road," and that he and his people would have been disgraced among all the Indians, had they not given as they did.

His only hope was that General Crook would delay his return march for a few days, in which case it was the intention of the Pawnees to give a return "begging dance" to the Sioux, in the hope of at least getting some of their things back. He did not expect to get all back, for he said, "The Sioux always were mean, stingy, cunning, and underhanded, while the Pawnees are well-known for their generosity and open-handedness."

Unfortunately for the good intentions of the Pawnees, the order for the return march was issued that very afternoon, and the poor Pawnees came back from the campaign poorer than ever, and without the hoped-for chance of getting even with their life-long enemies.

It may not be out of place here to remark, that a body of Indian warriors almost invariably uses the surprise-party" style of advance on a camp or village. A war party returning from a successful foray, will approach its own home-village with the greatest care and secrecy, bursting suddenly upon it with shots and whoops, and every appearance of a furious hostile attack. Small camps and villages whose occupants are unknown are approached in the same manner, and should the village be that of a hostile band, the demonstration is at once converted into a real attack. If the camp or village be large, the approach is very different.

The dances heretofore described, ministering as they do to the religious enthusiasm, the military ambition, or the personal vanity of the individuals, may be regarded as the pickles and sauces of Indian life, excellent as condiments, but not appetizing or healthy as constant diet.

Indians are very human. No people are so easily carried out of themselves by excitement, but fond as they are of this species of intoxication, they prefer for every-day life a milder pleasure. This they find in their social dances, which of all others yield them the most full, perfect, and unalloyed enjoyment.

I am safe in saying that when the weather permits, and this, on the high, dry Plains, is for full eight months of the year, every band of Indians secure from enemies, and untroubled by sickness, has at least five of these dances in every week.

Little preparation is necessary. Some frisky youngster will commence beating on his "tom-tom" at early nightfall, and in a very little while enough people of both sexes will have assembled for all purposes of enjoyment. Often these dances are held in the open air, but as light is necessary to their full enjoyment (as will be seen), they usually take place in a tepee, which is cleared of bedding and furniture in an incredibly short time.

If the assembly is expected to be large, and there be time enough beforehand, two tepees are pitched near together, the poles crossed and flaps lifted, so as to make one large room, which is scantily lighted by candles. There is no furniture whatever, and the guests sit on the ground.

Formal invitation is not considered necessary, the call of the" tom-tom" being notice to all who may wish to attend, Even when some warrior wishes to give an especially grand affair, he simply makes greater preparations. His proceedings are noted by numerous eyes, and the indications of preparation for supper will bring every man, woman, and child of the village.

There is no society among Indians, no difference in social grade, no social ostracism of women of any kind or for any cause. All meet at these dances on terms of the most absolute social equality.

The two tepees are pitched together, forming one large room, somewhat like two parlors, with open doors between. One of these rooms is occupied by the $ tom-tom" and the men, the other is for the women and dancing.

In one, half a dozen Indian men are squatted around the drum, each furnished with a stick three-fourths of an inch in diameter, and two feet long, one end of which is wound with a thick wad of cotton rags. These are the drum-sticks, and this is the whole orchestra. Each man has a place to beat on the drum-head, and taking the time from one of their number, all strike in unison. There is no attempt to flourish or roll, or flam, or perform any of the civilized tricks of drumming; it is simply the thump, thump, thump, of half a dozen sticks striking at the same time on one drum-head.

Soon after the first thump, the dancers begin to appear. Even at the grandest of these dances there is no ceremony. The host is probably at the drum, or, if an old man, smoking a pipe with his chums in a quiet corner. The hostess, and a few of their most intimate friends, and all the children, are squatted close under the wall of the tepee, so as to leave as large as possible a space for dancing. The visitors arrive, the men singly or together as it may happen; the women always several together, or accompanied by children.

Although there seems to be no particular sentiment against it, a man very rarely accompanies his wife to or from a dance. A married woman who would accept such attention from any man other than her husband, would commit the greatest breach of propriety. An unmarried girl doing so heinous a thing would become common property at once.

There are of course no dressing-rooms, nor are visitors met at the door by handshakings, or other evidences of welcome. The men find their way to the drum-room, and the women with much chattering, laughter, and frolic, squat around the dancing-room, leaving always ample space in the centre, even if they have to push up the wall of the tepee and sit outside.

It is a curious scene to one accustomed to civilized ideas and prejudices. A woman of standing and virtue is squatted beside, and in sprightly conversation with a female slave without virtue; the wife of a chief is being pulled and mauled by the children of the poorest and most worthless man of the band; two women who quarrelled this morning are now amicably discussing the dress of some mutual friend; but all now is light-hearted jollity and gladsome anticipation. Everybody is happy, even the woman with the newest and reddest shawl, for though she may be let severely alone, (the sex being the same everywhere), yet she too is happy, her feminine instinct assuring her that the others are only envious.

Enough dancers have assembled. The "tom-tom" beaters, who for the last ten minutes have been regaling themselves with a pipe, now (when it is duly smoked out) give the signal to begin by vigorous thumping on the drum. The women now rule, and calling out to the drummers, tell them what they wish to dance. The drummers commence their monotonous beat, almost every person present, both male and female, join in a song without words, in time with the beats of the "tom-tom."

After seeing and participating in both many times, I am quite prepared to aver that the dance most dear to the heart of American society-youth of both sexes, "the German," is stolen bodily from the Indians, except that our high civilization and sense of chivalrous propriety have changed the sex of the leaders.

Among Indians the leader of every social dance is always a woman. It is not to be understood that this leader is selected beforehand, and for the whole dance, as with us, but that after the music has fairly struck up, the woman who first gets up and comes dancing into the circle, is the leader for that figure. In some of the figures, two women or even three, will come out together.

In saying this much, I have already described the dance to all society people, but for the sake of those benighted whites who know not "the German," I will proceed with my description.

The step is always the same; that already described.

When the vigorous beats of the "tom-tom" and the sounding chorus of voices have so set her blood tingling that she is no longer restrained by her sense of modesty, a woman will get up, advance to the centre, and dance alone around, or partly around, the circle. She then advances to some man, (possibly one of the drum-beaters), seizes and leads him triumphantly to the centre, where they together dance around, sometimes arm in arm, but more frequently with their arms around each other, as in our round dances. After a circuit or two they separate, each taking up another partner of the opposite sex, and this is continued until there are as many couples on the floor as can dance comfortably. After from ten to twenty minutes, the music ceases, and the dancers separating, return alone each to his or her seat.

Sometimes, in violation of the well-known civilized rule, that "two is company, three a crowd," the figure will require two men to one woman, or the reverse, when the three, locked in mutual embrace, dance around together.

The "sign dance" is very pretty. A woman, after dancing around alone, will take up a man, lead him into the circle, place him opposite to her, both dancing. She will then say to him in the "sign language," "Here I am, ready to be made love to; what do you think of me?" He answers in the same language, as his wit or discretion prompts. This especial figure is one of the greatest favorites, the conversations being a collision of wits, every sally of which is received by the spectators with uproarious laughter and unbounded applause.

As may readily be inferred from what I have already said about Indians, these conversations are not characterized by the most perfect propriety, or even decency, but nothing that creates fun can be amiss to the Indian, and all must be taken with the most perfect good humor. It would be a monstrous breach of good manners to get angry at anything said or done in this figure.

Another figure creates great merriment. It is called the "kissing dance." The leading woman selects a partner as before. After dancing around together, they separate, and each selects another of opposite sex, and so on until the floor is filled. At a signal all go to their proper partners, that is, the leading woman goes back to the man she first selected, the two selected by him and her go together, those chosen by these go together, and so to the end. Then all seat themselves on the ground, couples facing-each other, when the man deliberately kisses the woman, the more modest couples drawing a shawl over their heads during this act.

The fun of this dance is, that while the leader can select the man she wishes to kiss, she and he can select those least likely to wish to kiss each other; she, taking up a young love-sick boy, and he a woman old enough to be his grandmother, or vice versa.

No end of fun is created by the complications that a few bright and mischievous couples can make.

In every case, the man is supposed to make some little present to the woman he kisses. If a woman in the dance offers to take out a man who does not wish to go, he can get off by paying a nickel, when somebody else is seized upon and taken out. This is a saving clause for those white witnesses of this dance whose taste rebels against the kisses of the red beauties, for no man, white or red, mere spectator or habitual dancer, can hope to escape without kissing, or buying himself off; and in this latter case he must have a pocket full of nickels, for every woman of the dance will "go for him," on that account alone. They like kisses, but they like nickels better.

One figure is called the "eating dance." The leader selects her partner and after a round or two, they go to where the refreshments are, and after helping themselves, bring something to eat, good or bad, great or small, which they each offer to another of the opposite sex, thus taking them out. These in turn go out and get something which they offer to others, and this is continued until the floor is full and all the dancers have something to eat in hand, when round and round they all go. No more ludicrous sight can be imagined than twenty or thirty couples hugging each other, dancing, singing, laughing, talking, eating, screaming, all at one and the same time.

The fun in this dance is in giving the person taken up something to eat which will create merriment. An old squaw, with her teeth worn to the gums, will be brought into the circle of dancers by a huge bone with no meat on it; a notoriously heavy feeder will be brought out by the smallest possible piece of cracker. Of course these all "get even," and a bountiful repast when they go out to get something to "take up" the next couple with, but the fun is that each has to keep in hand that which was given and to appear to enjoy it.

At the very last Cheyenne dance that I attended, I saw the only instance of anything like masquerade that I have ever seen among Indians, though I have heard it is not uncommon. One or other of three very pretty and bright little girls, of ten to twelve years old, had, with the forwardness of their age, gained the leadership in almost every figure. Two of them were well-known, but the other was for a long time supposed to be a stranger, creating no little wonderment. Finally, a young buck with whom she was dancing discovered that" she" was a boy dressed in his sister's clothing. The little rascal had played his part so well as to mystify the whole party for half the night, and with so pretty, sprightly, and natural an action, that half the bucks in the dance had made love to him. It was considered a wonderful feat, and made great sport.

I could enumerate many other figures, and there are yet many which I have not seen. Enough to say, that if not quite so infinite as the figures of "the German," it is only because the inventive faculty of the Indian is not so well developed as that of the white.

After a knowledge of the social dance, it is very easy to understand the wonderful hold it has upon the taste and affection of the Indian. Here are no chiefs, no commons, no master, no slave. All men are on an equality, all women are equal each to the other, and here, alone, in virtue of their leadership, a little superior to the men. There is no scandal, no ill-nature, for Indian etiquette requires that no one shall take offence. All is jollity and pleasure.

It is an informal social reunion, in which everyone may take part, where everybody is expected not only to be themselves in the very best possible humor, but to do everything in their power to promote the general pleasure.

The fun is broad, coarse, as might be expected of a savage race; but jollier, more light-hearted, better pleased people I have never seen at any social gathering, and the temper of the whole affair is perfect.

EXPERTNESS OF INDIAN SIGN-TALKERS

FOR as far back in the uncertain past as we can reasonably hope, through tradition and story, to reach any barely solid foundation of fact, the Indians of the Plains—that vast plateau between the Mississippi River and the Rocky Mountains—have been, of all Indians, the least disposed to content themselves within the boundaries of their own territories. This may have resulted from the peculiarly warlike character of these Indians, but most probably was the result of accident, or, more strictly speaking, was forced upon them by the all-important question of food.

All the Plains tribes depended almost entirely on the buffalo for everything. That animal, though regular in his migrations (going north in spring, and south in fall and winter), was exceedingly erratic, his visits to any particular section of country depending on his own food supply, the condition of the grass. One year, the country of a tribe of Indians might be overrun by herds whose numbers were simply incalculable; the next year, the same territory might be visited by scarcely a single animal.

If the buffalo did not come to the Indian, the Indian must go to the buffalo, at whatever hazard. Runners were sent out, the location of the buffalo discovered, and long journeys were made by tribes and bands into countries to which they had no claim.

The same necessity possibly actuating many bands and tribes, the country in the vicinity of the buffalo became dangerous ground. The tribe or band in whose territory they were, regarded the buffalo as their own property, an evidence of the favor of God. They resented the intrusion of other bands and hunting parties, not only as killing and driving off their property, but as interfering with their "medicine," the medicine chief taking care that all shall understand that his influence with God brought the buffalo. Each year, the country occupied by the buffalo became a vast battle-ground, the proper owners attacking the interlopers at every favorable opportunity.

But hunting parties met other hunting parties of tribes not hostile. To distinguish between the hostile and the friendly, and to communicate with, and possibly make common cause with the latter, some means of intercourse must be had. Not being able to speak or understand each other's language, communication was had by signs.

"We may suppose that at first only signs most natural and expressive were used. By-and-by other signs were introduced, always conventional, but becoming more and more arbitrary, until there resulted a means of communication almost as perfect as if each understood and spoke the oral language of the other. This means of communication is used in its completeness only by the Plains Indians, and is called by them the "sign language."

The use of signs to communicate ideas is common to all the world, not only to man, but to the brute creation, and from the simple pleasure evidenced by the wagging of a dog's tail, to abstruse problems in astronomy and metaphysics, every idea may be communicated by means of signs.

This method of intercourse was, like oral speech, natural and instinctive, and is in constant use to this day. It is an adjunct to oral speech, and must ever be one of the means by which humanity expresses or modifies its ideas. Not one of us, however civilized, or facile in the use of oral language, but every day of his life makes use of signs to express some wish or thought. What school-boy would dare to pretend to misunderstand the beckon of his teacher, or what urchin but has had his soul thrilled with inexpressible emotions at the simple pointing by his mother at the hole torn in his new trousers?

All people use more or less gestures or signs, but among the highly cultivated they are used only as adjectives, adverbs, interjections, to give emphasis and point to oral speech.

Speech is entirely arbitrary and conventional, but signs have their origin in feelings and emotions which are common to all mankind. Every spoken language requires another language to interpret it. The rudiments of the language of signs require on the one hand only so clear a conception of the idea or emotion as to make a sign expressive of its posture or effect, and on the other an equally clear conception, and a sufficient perceptive faculty.

Signs may be divided into two classes. First, those imitative or descriptive of some action, or expressive of some emotion or situation. These may be called natural signs, and are, with some modifications, common to all mankind—to the deaf and dumb pupil of civilization, and to the untamed savage of the Plains. Thus, pointing to the sun and indicating its course from east to west, is the natural and obvious sign expression for a day, and such is its meaning to all people who use sign language.

Second, those indicating names of tribes, persons, or things, or abstract ideas not sufficiently pronounced to admit of a natural sign picture. These signs are arbitrary, and vary in a very remarkable degree.

In a previous chapter I have spoken of the pride, self-conceit, or other cause which prevents an Indian of one tribe from speaking the language of another tribe.

Dr. Matthews, speaking of the Arickaree, Hidatsa, and Mandan Indians, says: "To the philologist it is an interesting fact, that this trio of savage clans, although now living in the same village, and having been next door neighbors to each other for more than a hundred years on terms of peace and intimacy, and to a great extent intermarried, speak, nevertheless, totally distinct languages which show no perceptible inclination to coalesce."

The same general statement is true of the Cheyennes and Arapahos. The parents reside year after year side by side in the same camps, the children play, fight, horse-race, gamble, and grow up together, yet one will never speak in the language of the other. The fact is a curious, almost incredible one, especially as the Indians themselves can or will give no explanation of it.

This peculiarity renders the use of a common language a matter of paramount importance to the Plains Indians.

When two people, whether civilized or savage, neither speaking nor understanding the oral language of the other, meet and wish to communicate, the first and most natural impulse is to attempt to gain or convey information by means of signs. Even at the very first attempt, some ideas will be interchanged, and after repeated efforts, they will have so far progressed as to be able to exchange ideas, with some certainty and satisfaction. The sign language undoubtedly sprung from this natural tendency, and has its foundation in those natural signs and gestures which are common to the races of mankind.

But while all Indians, as all white people, use signs, it by no means follows that they use the same signs or make or read them with the same facility and perfection. Oral speech is natural, and all men use the language to which they were brought up with a certain degree of ease and force. Beyond its simple forms, and outside a lodge of Plains Indians, the sign language is acquired, and different men use it skilfully or not, in accordance with the quickness of apprehension or skill as pantomimist of each.

Many of the Indian tribes are almost as little versed in the use of signs as ordinary white people. This is especially observable among the Utes, so much so that I one day asked Ouray to explain it. He told me that his people never used the sign language among themselves. Most of the warriors had picked up a little smattering of this language, and used it in their intercourse with the Plains Indians, or with the whites, just as most of them had acquired a slight knowledge of Spanish, by and for use in their trade with Mexicans and Apaches.

It is among the Plains Indians alone that gesture-speech has arrived at such perfection, that it may properly be called a language, and this, for the very sufficient reason that these tribes use it not only in intercourse with people whose oral language they neither speak or understand, but for every day intercourse among themselves. In their own camps and families, this language is used so constantly that it becomes a natural and instinctive habit; almost every man, even when using oral language, accompanying his words by sign-pictures conveying the same meaning. In this way wonderful facility and accuracy of expression by signs is attained.

That this excellence is acquired can readily be inferred from the marked difference in the ability to use it, not only in the tribes, but in the individuals of the same tribe. Almost all Plains Indians use it, some so exceptionally well, making their sign-pictures so clear, that they can readily be understood by anyone who has even a rudimentary knowledge of the art; yet I have met a few Plains Indians, who, though brought up with it, have never arrived at sufficient knowledge of the language to hold a conversation in it. Within a few days previous to this writing, an Arapahoe came to this post on business with a Cheyenne, and was obliged to obtain the services of the interpreter, being unable to use or understand signs.

"Within comparatively a few years, the attention of philologists has been particularly directed to the sign language. Some authorities assert that "all the tribes of North American Indians, have had and still use a common and identical sign language of ancient origin," "which serves as a medium of converse from Hudson Bay to the Gulf of Mexico." Others deny this.

Like most other broad statements, this, in my experience, is partly true and partly false. It is not "common" to all North American Indians. The Utes, the Pacific tribes who use "Chinook," the Indians of the Colorado River, the Apaches, Mohaves, Moquis, Pueblos, Navahos and others, use signs, as do all men, but they do not use or understand the sign language of the Plains. It is "common" to all Indians between the Mississippi River and the Rocky Mountains, and from the British line to the Gulf of Mexico; that is, to all the Plains Indians.

The Plains Indians themselves believe that the sign language was invented by the Kiowas, who, holding an intermediate position between the Comanches, Tonka-ways, Lipans, and other inhabitants of the vast plains of Texas, and the Pawnees, Sioux, Blackfeet, and other Northern tribes, were the general go-betweens; trading with all, or making peace or war, with, or for, any or all. It is certain that the Kiowas are at present more universally proficient in this language than any other Plains tribe. It is also certain that the tribes furthest away from them, and with whom they have least intercourse, use it with least facility.

The sign language is a true language, and like all other languages used by great numbers of, or widely scattered, people, it has its dialects and its provincialisms. It is not, strictly speaking, a "common or identical" language, but in all the vast area I have indicated, it varies less than the English language in its two small home islands, or the French language in the territory of France.

If the English language is "common and identical" in England, Ireland, Scotland, and Wales, then the sign language is "common and identical" to the Plains.

An American travelling in Scotland, Wales, Cornwall, or Yorkshire, is in endless trouble to understand the English spoken to him. An Englishman of no more intelligence or no better education will travel without this difficulty, for by contact and habit, he has gained some knowledge of the dialects and provincialisms. The Englishman will assert that the inhabitants of the British Islands speak a "common and identical" language; the American with equal positiveness will assert that the languages are different. This is all there is to the controversy on the sign language.

Taking into consideration the vastness of territory and the sparseness of population, the sign language is remarkably "identical." Considering further, the fact that the language is made up of signs representing not only all animated nature, but relationships, time, place, circumstances, thoughts, feelings, and abstract ideas of every kind, the uniformity is indeed marvellous. Put a pantomimist on the stage, and set a dozen expert scientists to record his action. It is certain that no two of them would use the same language, doubtful if any two of them would express the same idea.

So of the Indian tribes. One represents the deer by his horns, another by his fleetness, yet another by his broad white tail; but so apt are they at illustration and so quick of comprehension, that these dialects or provincialisms are mere momentary hindrances.

Many of them can express the same thing by several signs, and if the person with whom he is conversing fails to understand one, he will try another and another.

A curious peculiarity, illustrative of the imitative faculty of the Indian, is that he will catch and use the signs of the person with whom he is talking, though he may never have seen them before. An Indian is talking to a white man, slightly versed in the language, or other Indian with whose provincialisms he is not familiar. A sign is used which he does not understand. By close and careful watching, he will soon discover what the user means to represent by it, and if he then wishes to speak of that thing, he will use the sign of the other person, even though he knows it to be a wrong one.

In oral language, an idea may be expressed in an almost infinite variety of ways; the sign language, though not so flexible, yet gives ample facilities for varying the expression.

The oral languages of the Indian tribes with which I am acquainted, are crude and imperfect, consisting of nouns, verbs, adjectives, adverbs, lacking in case, number, tense, or mood, and run together in interminable strings, each of which presents, as it were, a word-picture, the whole giving a very definite idea of the facts sought to be communicated. This idiomatic mode of thought and expression offers peculiar facilities for the use of the sign language.

In translating into that language the thought or speech of a white man, the first necessity is to get rid of the particles, articles, conjunctions, prepositions, then to transpose and group the remainder, and to present each subordinate idea in such succession as finally to represent clearly and fully the whole idea. This is really the most difficult portion of the work of an interpreter, and requires a special faculty.

Besides the" dialects and provincialisms," there is another natural, but most serious difficulty in attempting to learn or to describe the sign language: so serious indeed that I doubt if any man ever arrived at even average excellence in the art unless habituated to its use from earliest childhood.

This difficulty results from the personality of each Indian, every man having his own style of expression, just as every white man has his own style of penmanship. This individuality of style may very properly be called the handwriting of the Indian; each, though making the same signs, makes them differently from all others, as the handwriting of each white man differs from that of all others.

Ask an Indian to give you the sign of anything, and he proceeds to make it formally, giving what may be regarded the sign in capital letters, differing from the sign he would make in rapid conversation, possibly quite as widely as the printed capital "B," differs from the small "b" of a rapidly written manuscript.

In addition to the difficulties already enumerated, there are yet others, in an almost infinite number and variety of abbreviations. For instance, to tell a man "to talk," the most common formal sign is made thus: hold the right hand in front of, the back near the mouth, ends of thumb and index finger joined into an O, the other fingers closed on the palm; throw the hand forward sharply by a quick motion of the wrist, and at the same time flip forward the index finger. This may be done once or several times.

The formal sign to "cease," or "stop doing" anything, is made by bringing the two hands, open and held vertically, in front of the body, one behind the other; then quickly pass one upward, the other downward, simulating somewhat the motion of the limbs of a pair of scissors, meaning "cut it off." This latter sign is made in conversation, in a variety of ways, but habitually with one hand only.

The formal sign for "stop talking," is first to make the formal sign for "talk," then the formal sign for "cut;" but this is commonly abbreviated by first making the formal sign "talk," with the right hand, and then immediately passing the same hand, open, fingers extended, downward, across and in front of the mouth, "talk cut."

But though the Plains Indian, if asked for the sign to "stop talking," will properly give the sign either in its extended or abbreviated form, as above, he in conversation abbreviates it so much further, that the sign loses almost all resemblance to its formal self. Whatever the position of the hand, a turn of the wrist, a flip of the forefinger, and a turn of the wrist back to its original position, is fully equivalent to the elaborate signs.

This, by the by, is one of the most significant and comprehensive of Indian signs. It may mean simple acquiescence, as we express by "very well," "all right;" or comprehension, "I understand;" impatience, "you have talked enough;" or downright anger, "shut up."

Examples of similar abbreviations could be given almost ad libitum.

That such liberties can be taken with it, and it yet so far preserve its original purity and completeness as to furnish a means of communication so perfect that individuals of tribes living a thousand miles apart, and who have never met before, can converse with ease and certainty, is the best evidence that it is a true language, founded on a solid basis of correct principles. To learn it sufficiently well for ordinary intercourse is no more difficult than to learn any foreign language; to master it, one must have been born in a lodge of Plains Indians, and have been accustomed to its daily and hourly use from his earliest to mature years.

Even among the Plains tribes, only the old, or at least middle-aged men, use it perfectly. I have never yet seen a woman, child, or young man, who was at all reliable in signs.

Every tribe of the Plains has not only its distinctive name, but also its sign, by which it is known and designated by all other Indians. In some cases, these signs indicate the character of the tribe; in others they appear to be purely arbitrary—at least, no Indian appears to be able to give any satisfactory explanation of their origin or meaning.

I give a few of these, to illustrate their peculiarities:—

Indian-generic. Left hand open, fingers extended and joined, palm down, is held in front of centre of body. The back of the hand is then gently rubbed with the fingers of the right hand.

Sioux. Pass the right hand open, palm down and horizontal, fingers extended from left to right across the throat, "Cut throat;" indicating their character and habit.

Cheyenne. The index finger of the left hand (or the whole hand) is held horizontally in front of the body. The index finger of the right hand is then passed across it several times, as if cutting, "Cut finger." Origin or reason for sign unknown. The Sioux indicate the Northern Cheyennes by making the cuts on the forearm, a little above the wrist.

Arapahoe. With index finger of right hand extended, rub right side of nose. Origin and meaning unknown.

Northern Arapahoe Join fingers and thumb of right hand, and strike the points on left breast several times.

Pawnees. Right hand, first two fingers extended and separated, is held behind the right ear, and then thrown forward; action repeated, "Wolf;" indicating character.

Comanche. Right hand extended to left and front of body, index finger extended, others closed. Draw the hand backward with a wriggling motion across the body, "Snake;" indicating character.

Kiowa. The open palm, held bowl-shaped, to right of and beside the face, is passed round and round in a circle. Supposed to indicate the peculiarity of these Indians in cutting the hair of the right side of the head.

Ute. Left hand held horizontally in front of the body, fingers extended, thumb closed on palm, edge of hand down. Then with extended fingers of right hand, rub gently towards the wrist, along the extended index finger of left hand; or make the sign for black and the generic sign for Indians. The Utes are very dark, and are called by the Plains tribes, "the black Indians."

Apache. Hold the left hand exactly as in sign for Ute. Then with extended fingers of right hand flip back and forth on the index of left hand, as a barber strops a razor. Origin and meaning unknown.

White Man. Right hand open, fingers extended and horizontal, carried to the left side of the head, then passed from left to right across the forehead, indicating the brim of a hat; "Hat wearers."

Mexican. The open palm, held bowl-shaped beneath the chin, is passed round and round in a circle; "Beard wearers."

Negro. Rub the extended fingers of the right hand on some dark object, and then make the sign for white man; "Black white man."

Able men are now engaged in classifying and arranging these signs into a vocabulary, with hope of such ultimate success as will place this among the languages open to the mastery of the student of books. I can, in these pages, give only the most superficial idea of the power and scope of this language, and to this end I add a few descriptions of signs.

Man. Index finger of right hand held erect before the face, back to front; push slightly outwards and upwards.

Woman. Right hand, fingers open but joined, back to front, is passed with a circular, sweeping motion to the right side of face and head, indicating flowing hair.

Marriage. Indices of right and left hands joined side by side, backs up, in front of body, thumbs and other fingers closed.

Husband. Sign for man, and marriage.

Wife. Sign for woman, and marriage.

Parentage. Right hand, bowl-shaped, turned towards right breast, as if grasping a pap.

Father. Sign for parentage, and man.

Mother. Sign for parentage, and woman.

Offspring. Right hand passed downwards in front of crotch, index extended, other fingers closed; sex indicated as before.

Brother. Index and middle finger of right hand placed in mouth, back of hand up, and sign for man.

Sister. Same, with sign for woman.

Cousin. Sign for brother and sister, as above; but if pressed for closer explanation, make sign for father (or mother), brother, and offspring, with additional sign for sex.

Brother-in-law. Hold left hand obliquely to the front, towards centre of body, forearm nearly horizontal, palm to the right, then pass the open right hand from the left shoulder downwards, with a circular sweep, around and outside the left hand.

Day. Hands open, fingers extended, palms upward, are carried from front and centre of body to each side, and held horizontal and motionless, backs down; indicating "all open."

Night. Hands open, fingers extended and joined, palms down, are carried to centre of body, and crossed, right hand above, but not touching, and held motionless; indicating "all closed."

Sun. Right hand and arm extended upwards, thumb and forefinger formed into a crescent, other fingers closed.

Moon. Sign for sun, and night.

Spring. Place right hand near the ground, back downward, the thumb and fingers extended upward (this is the sign for grass); then raise the hand a few inches once or twice, to represent the grass growing.

Summer. Both hands held high above and in front of the head, on each side, fingers extended and pointing obliquely downward; indicating the sun's rays.

Autumn, Left hand held well up in front and left of body, back to front, finger and thumb extended upward to represent the branches (this is the sign for tree); with right index touch a finger of left hand, and then carry right hand downward, as something falling slowly. Do this several times.

Winter. Both hands in front of body, fingers and thumbs closed, right hand above, are shaken backward and forward, with a shivering motion. This is also the sign for year and cold.

Time. Hands partially opened, backs to right and left thumbs and indices closed, as if holding a string between them, are held a few inches apart, in front of the body. This is the general sign, to ask the question.

Is it a Long or Short Time? The hands, held as above, are separated some inches, and then, brought near each other.

Long Time. The hands, held as above, are drawn apart by a series of jerking motions, the distance finally separated indicating the length of time.

Infinitely Long Time, Eternity. Make sign for "long time," for "not," and for "cut off."

Short Time. Hold the hands as above, some little distance apart, and then approach them to each other.

Counting; Question, How Many?. Hold the left hand in front of centre of body, palm up, fingers partially opened, but not joined; then with right index finger flip (towards body) rapidly and successively, two or three fingers of the left hand, commencing with the little finger.

One. Right hand closed, except index, back of hand to front, held in front of body; (almost identical with sign for man, that being distinguished by its upward motion).

Two. Same motion with index and little finger.

Three. Same with index, middle, and third fingers.

Four. Same with four fingers.

Five. All the fingers and thumb open, palm upright and to the front, with forward motion.

Six. Thumb of left hand held upright, fingers closed, is held in front of face, and in close juxtaposition to right hand, with all the digits extended. All are then advanced with a slight motion.

Seven. Same, with thumb and index of left hand.

Eight. Same, with thumb, index, and middle finger of left.

Nine. Same, with four fingers of left hand.

Ten. Both hands open, palms upright, fingers extended, with same forward motion.

Eleven. Make sign for ten, then bring the hands down and close them; then raise the right hand palm to front, all fingers closed except little finger, which is held upright.

Twelve. Same, little and third fingers held upright.

Thirteen. Same, little, third, and middle fingers held up.

Fourteen. Same, four fingers held up.

Fifteen. Right hand held up, all digits extended.

Sixteen. Same, right hand, and thumb of left, and so to nineteen.

Twenty. Sign made to a white man would be the repeated sign for ten, but in the "language," it is made by holding the right hand, all the fingers closed except the little and third fingers, to the right, but in front of the face, and then describe a circle to the left, in front of face. This motion multiplies by ten the number of fingers held up.

One Hundred. With both hands held upright before the face, fingers extended, palms to front, describe the semicircle to left.

One Thousand. Make sign for ten, and then the sign for hundred.

These may be all regarded as natural signs. I will give one example of what may be called a complex sign. To express liquid coffee, ready for the table, the Indian represents—

The Bean. Thumb pressed against forefinger of right hand, a short distance from the tip, other fingers closed; (a natural sign for any small object).

A Pot. Thumb and forefingers of both hands, open and crescent shaped, other fingers closed, palms inward, are held about a foot apart.

To Put on. Hands so held are moved downward towards ground, as if putting on a fire.

To Boil. Both hands held low in front of body, backs down, fingers, partially closed; then flip out thumbs and fingers, at same time making a slight upward motion of wrists.

To Drink. Right hand, held as if grasping a cup, is carried to the mouth, and turned up as in the act of drinking.

Coffee. The bean, that you put in a pot, and put on the fire, and boil, and then drink.

An expert sign-talker will make the five signs necessary to express coffee almost as quickly as that word can be uttered.

Seemingly impossible as it would appear from the foregoing description, two expert sign-talkers engaged in conversation will make every sign with one hand so distinctly as to be understood. Two Indians, each wrapped in a blanket tightly held with the left hand, will thrust the right from under its folds and engage in animated conversation. So also when on horseback, though the left hand is holding the reins, the conversation will not flag, nor be misunderstood.

INDIAN CHRONOLOGY

THE appliances of civilization, the comforts conferred on us by science, have become so much a matter of habit that we fail to realize them. When we wake up in the night, and strike a light on the instant, do we ever think how our grandfathers arrived at the same result by laborious effort with flint and steel, and vast expenditure of breath to fan the tiny spark into flame sufficient to light the attenuated tallow dip? So in everything we do and use.

But, had some evil genius the power and will to deprive us of one of the blessings conferred by science, he could strike a no more effective blow than to take away our system of computing time. Accustomed to the regularity, the simple perfection of the civilized method, we scarcely realize its value or the absolute chaos that would be the result of its loss.

In our calendar, every minute, every hour, day, month, and year, is absolutely fixed for us by stable points of reference. The whole life of a civilized being is regulated by time. He rises at a certain time in the morning; his meals, his business, his meeting with friends, his attendance at church or elsewhere, all are regulated by fixed times. He starts on a journey at a certain hour, and terminates it with equal regularity. Every duty, every pleasure, every movement of his life is regulated by time, and the watches of busy men are in demand for consultation at any and all times.

But it is not only in our daily duties and avocations that we realize the value of our system. Our years commencing on a certain day, and each having a number, we have a constant point of reference by which we are enabled to locate the occurrences of our past lives, or fix with some certainty our plans for the future.

These apparently trite remarks are intended to cause the reader to look into his own life, his memories of the past, movements of the present, and plans for the future, and see what would be the result to him could this element of certainty in time be eliminated. He will then be in a frame of mind better adapted to the contemplation of the condition of a people who have no time.

The Indians measure time solely by days, by sleeps, by moons, and by winters. There is no name for any subdivision of time less than a day. When it is desired to indicate any shorter period, he points to the heavens, and measuring off a space, says "it was as long as it would take the sun to go from there to there." "Day" is from daylight to darkness; "sleep," or night, from dark until daylight. There is no name for any day among the wild Indians, though those about agencies call Sunday "the day the white man does not work." There is no subdivision of time corresponding to our week.

A moon commences when the first faint streak of its crescent can be discovered in the west, and lasts until the next one appears, but the days of the moon are neither numbered nor named.

There is a difference among authorities as to whether or not the moons themselves are named. Brown gives names for nine moons corresponding to months. Maximillian gives the names of twelve moons; and Belden, who lived many years among the Sioux, asserts that" the Indians compute their time very much as white men do, only they use moons instead of months to designate the seasons, each answering to some month in our calendar." Then follows a list of twelve moons with Indian and English names. While I cannot contradict so positive and minute a statement of one so thoroughly in a position to know, I must assert with equal positiveness that I have never met any wild Indians, of the Sioux or other Plains tribes, who had a permanent, common, conventional name for any moon. The looseness of Belden's general statement, that "Indians compute time like white people," when his only particularization of similarity is between the months and moons, is in itself sufficient to render the whole statement questionable.

My experience is that the Indian, in attempting to fix on a particular moon, will designate it by some natural and well-known phenomenon which culminates during that moon. But two Indians of the same tribe may fix on different designations; and even the same Indian, on different occasions, may give different names to the same moon. Thus, an Indian of the middle Plains will to-day designate a spring moon as "the moon when corn is planted;" to-morrow, speaking of the same moon, he may call it "the moon when the buffalo comes." Moreover, though there are thirteen moons in our year, no observer has ever given an Indian name to the thirteenth. My opinion is, that if any of the wild tribes have given conventional names to twelve moons, it is not an indigenous idea, but borrowed from the whites.

There is no Indian word synonymous with our word year. "From winter to winter," is the nearest approach to it. The year commences at the first fall of snow. A man will tell you that he is so many winters old, which in the aggregate represents his years; but having no months or days, he never has a birthday. I have questioned many Indians of different tribes, and have never yet found one who could tell how many lunations (or moons) there are in a year; and this is unavoidable, for as the new year dates from the first snow, its commencement is uncertain, and its duration extremely indefinite.

"Stone," a very intelligent old Cheyenne, has been sitting with me in my quarters for the two hours immediately preceding the writing of this paragraph.

We talked of "snows" and "moons," until I fear the old man went off in a state of semi-idiocy. He is a Northern Cheyenne, and for the first twenty-five years of his life, his tribe occupied country contiguous to the Sioux. The tribes were friendly, and he learned a good deal about them and their customs. He has never heard a fixed name given to a moon by any Indians. At the question, "How many moons are there in a year?" he looked greatly puzzled, evidently never having thought of it before. Finally, however, brightening up, he answered—"Some years have more moons than others. One year may have only ten moons, but the next year may have fifteen."

The Indians who formerly inhabited the southern portion of Texas, where there is no snow fall, are said to have fixed the commencement of the year at the first "Norther," a furious and chilling wind that sweeps from the North, and of frequent occurrence during the winter months.

No year has any name or number, fixing a sequence or point of reference, but each band will designate a year by its most prominent occurrence; as a fight with hostiles, death of a chief, prevalence of disease, abundance or scarcity of food, or failing anything marvellous or striking, by the name of the stream on which was located the winter camp. But these are mere remembrances, and excellent as is the savage memory, they, after a few years fade into a jumble of disconnected facts without sequence or usefulness.

In 1874, a brother officer presented me with what purported to be a facsimile of a calendar of Sioux, together with its interpretation. The original was painted in colors, in Indian hieroglyphics on an elk skin, which was religiously preserved by the chief of the band, no addition being made without the grave consideration and sanction of the Council. Commencing with 1800, it gave the sign, or hieroglyph, designating the tribal name of each year in regular succession to 1870.

This was a wonderful step in advance of anything I had before known of Indian chronology, and I studied it with considerable assiduity.

In 1877, I heard that a pamphlet had been issued under the auspices of the Smithsonian, containing a Sioux calendar, and interpretations. I procured a copy for comparison with my calendar. To my annoyance, I found it the same thing. Sometime after I learned that an acting assistant surgeon, U. S. A., had been permitted by a chief, as a personal favor, to make a copy of a calendar in his possession. I wrote to the doctor, and he was kind enough to send me a copy. This time, I must admit, I was thoroughly disgusted to find only a second copy of my old chart. Several times since, I have heard of discoveries in this direction, but when I have run them to earth, it is only to find the same old thing.

I have, therefore, come to the conclusion that it is unique, that there is no other such calendar among Indians. It is possibly just as well that this is so, for I have never yet met an Indian of any tribe (and I have shown it to numbers) who could interpret any single one of the hieroglyphs; who had ever seen or heard of anything like it, or who could form any clear conception of its meaning and object, even when carefully explained to him.

To the few people who made this calendar and held it in charge, these pictures possibly have a definite meaning; to all others, they are merely senseless marks.

A careful examination of these hieroglyphs, even in the light of their interpretation, will demonstrate that it is scarcely a matter of surprise that they are understood by no Indians except those who invented them. I went over the whole series carefully with "Stone," who, though a Cheyenne, lived for many years near the Sioux. He recollects most of the principal events, though he did not understand, nor could he interpret, the symbols.

I asked him if an old woman had been found inside a buffalo cow. He assured me that it was true. He had heard of it at the time. The fact was authenticated by statements of the finders, sworn to in their most solemn and binding manner. It was believed by all the Sioux and Cheyennes, and he believed it.

Professor Brown gives a tradition of the Kootanie (Pacific coast) Indians, which is somewhat similar, but in this case involving a consequence most serious to the Indians, the origin of the Americans.

"Once on a time the Indians and the Pesioux (French Canadian voyageurs) lived together in such happiness that the Great Spirit above envied the happy condition of the Indian. So he came to the earth, and as he was riding on the prairies on the other side of the Rocky Mountains, he killed a buffalo, and out of the buffalo crawled a lank, lean figure, called a 'Boston man' (American), and from that day, to this, their troubles commenced, and there has never been peace for the Indian, and there never will be until they again go where their fathers are."

THEIR PICTURES AND INSCRIPTIONS

THERE is probably no single thing in which the tribes of United States Indians vary so widely as in their progress in the arts.

Although the Cherokees, Chickasaws, Choctaws, and other tribes or remnants, now occupying the Indian Territory, must be classed as in advance of all other Indians in their progress, it is simply because they can no longer properly be classed as Indians, except by race. For nearly fifty years they have been peculiarly the care of the government. They received large subsidies for the lands in the states formerly occupied by them, which, being invested for them in United States securities, have yielded sufficient income to place these tribes above actual want. Except during the rebellion (and then from no fault of theirs) there has been in all those years no outbreak or outrage by these Indians, proving that it is easy to manage Indians who are properly fed. Surrounded on almost all sides by whites, they have, in most things, become assimilated to whites. Schools have been established among them, and many of the more wealthy parents have sent their children of both sexes to the colleges and seminaries of the states, where they have received excellent education. In education, general intelligence and mode of life, the mass of these Indians are quite equal to the lower class of population of the south, either black or white.

Their civilization is not a natural growth, but is the result of their circumstances and surroundings. They are fully fitted to be, and should be citizens of the United States; that they are not so, is simply because it is to the pecuniary interest of some persons of influence to keep them as they are. Of their progress in the arts it is not necessary here to speak further than to say that it is nearly or quite on a par with that of the whites who surround them.

Of all those tribes whose progress may be said to be indigenous, the Pueblos, inheriting the semi-civilization of their reputed ancestors, the Aztecs, are far in advance. They have some knowledge of the rudiments of almost all the industrial and mechanic arts; building for themselves comfortable houses, constructing cisterns, tanks and dams for the storage of the spring rainfall of water;

digging long irrigating ditches; ploughing and hoeing the lands; planting trees; raising crops of grain, vegetables and fruits; breeding horses, sheep and goats; making pottery; spinning, weaving and tailoring, and providing themselves with ample means for a comfortable and happy existence. They have even some crude knowledge of working iron, though, so far as I have been able to discover, they have no idea where the metal comes from.

The labor is fairly divided among the sexes, the men caring for the stock, ploughing and planting the fields, gathering the crops, etc., the women, though also working in the fields during busy seasons, varying their labors with household duties, spinning, weaving, making clothing, blankets, baskets, and cooking for the family. Every able-bodied man or woman must work; and all seem to perform their parts carefully, diligently and cheerfully.

In the absence of any other well defined line of demarcation between semi-civilized and savage races, it would seem judicious to fix this line between those tribes where the men labor, and those where they do not. To have overcome the repugnance to work, natural to all savage people, is a long stride in advance. Accepting this as the line, the Pueblos are the only naturally semi-civilized race of United States Indians.

Next to these, but still savage, come the Navahos, who, though not descendants either of Aztecs or Toltecs, yet occupied an immense section of country adjoining the latter, and thus derived some benefit from their civilization. They live in rude huts of stone or logs, cemented with a stiff clay, commonly called adobe mud, from the fact that excellent sun-dried bricks, called "adobes" are made of it. They possess a few horses, large herds of sheep and goats; and their women till small patches of ground, raising corn, vegetables and melons. They spin and weave, and are justly celebrated for the beauty and excellence of their blankets. The men care for the flocks and herds, but perform no manual labor whatever.

It is difficult to decide which of the savage tribes comes next to the Navahos in its progress in the arts, and this for the reason that in each of the more advanced, art seems to take a direction special to that tribe. Thus, the Apaches, learning from their neighbors, the

Navahos, make beautiful baskets, jars, and pots, of grass, so closely woven as to hold water, and which also serve as cooking utensils; a thick coat of mud being smeared over the outside to prevent burning. But their inventive or ingenious faculty stops short at this. Their houses or *rancherias* are mere piles of branches and brush, scarcely more comfortable than the lair of a wild animal.

The Chippewas and other tribes of northern Indians build cabins of logs or poles and earth, which, covered with mats, skins or bark, are sufficient protection even in that rigorous climate. They also make excellent canoes of bark, and are great adepts at carving; their efforts in this direction being, however, confined almost exclusively to the ornamentation of pipes, totems, and war implements.

The Plains tribes proper have made little progress in any art not absolutely necessary to their mode of life, being dependent in their natural state almost entirely on the buffalo, the limit of their knowledge of the mechanic and industrial arts was the preparation and preservation of meat and skins, as explained in a previous chapter, and the fabrication of the arms and equipments necessary for war or the chase.

Carving may be regarded as the oldest of the ornamental arts, for to it we owe what very slight knowledge we have of pre-historic man. It is universal among North American Indians, the different tribes, however, varying in the degree of skill to which they have attained, from the rude efforts made by the Digger to carve his totem on the stick with which he digs his roots and kills his snakes and lizards, to the grotesque but well-executed designs of the tribes of Alaska. The Plains tribes have made little progress in this art, confining it almost exclusively to pipe manufacture. Like all other Indians they are extremely fond of ornament, but they express this fondness in bead-work, paint, feathers and fringes.

At a certain stage of its upward progress, every primitive people has sought to embalm its ideas, either by carvings or paintings. These representations are first purely idiomatic, or expressive of ideas, gradually become phonetic, or expressive of sounds, and thus lay the foundation for the alphabet.

The tribes of United States Indians have of themselves reached only the first stage, their representation expressing ideas only. Even in this they are so far from having any general and fixed system in such representation, that, beyond the most common symbols, the hieroglyphics of one Indian cannot be read or understood by another, even of the same tribe.

Much has been written of the wonderful genius of the Cherokee Indian, Sequoia or Guess, who, alone of all the American Aborigines, has made an alphabet suited to his language. While not disposed to detract from the merits of this remarkable achievement, I must nevertheless call attention to the fact that the conception was not original.

For some years Guess had had the advantage of the instruction of an excellent and learned missionary, Dr. Butrick, and in his alphabet, uses every one of our letters except X, though not in the same order, or with the same sound.

I have already given a description of the totem. Every Indian understands its significance, but, as in the case of the Sioux chronological chart, the effort of one to express abstract ideas by such symbols is so completely an individual act, as to be a "sealed book" to all others.

The Plains Indian delights in pictures, and you cannot please or entertain him better than by giving him a "picture book" to look at. He also delights in making pictures, especially of his own remarkable exploits and achievements, but I have never been able to discover that they use their slight knowledge of drawing to convey any but the most commonplace information.

In 1875, the Sioux Indians had, by force of arms and diplomacy, been separated into two classes, hostile and reservation Indians; the former in the field defiant; the latter supposed to be living quietly and peaceably at the expense of the United States. I was on an exploring expedition to the Black Hills; One day I crossed a fresh trail of Indians. On a hill a little distance off was planted a slight pole, ten or twelve feet high, to the top of which was fastened a streamer of white cotton cloth. Under a small cairn of stones at the foot of the pole was discovered a piece of skin carefully rolled and tied with a thong. On opening it I found a bundle of thirty-seven sticks tied together; a piece of cotton cloth on which were painted in colors some ten or twelve hieroglyphics; a small pouch containing tobacco, and another of corn. My interpreter, an old Mexican who had married and lived almost all his life among the Sioux, explained. The party which made the trail consisted of thirty-seven warriors; the hieroglyphics were the totems or signatures of the chiefs and most prominent men (all reservation Indians), and the totem of the band of hostile Sioux to which they were going; the tobacco indicated that they were going to "smoke," that is, join their fortunes with the hostiles; corn indicated that they had, or expected to have plenty to eat, (an unusual thing with reservation Indians); the white streamer invited their friends to follow them; while the pole marked the place of deposit of their communication.

If, as is generally believed, these Indians could have expressed all these ideas by painting, there would have been no need for so many other symbols.

A vast deal of research and wisdom have been devoted to the elucidation of Indian hieroglyphics. Inscriptions on rocks and trees have been photographed, or carefully and minutely copied, and sent to various learned bodies for interpretation. The lucubrations of these sages, are, as a rule, exactly on a par with those of the Pickwick club, over the stone sent by its learned founder from Cobh am.

In common with all "the rest of mankind," the Indian dearly loves to see his name in a conspicuous place. Wherever, near a camping-place of favorite resort, is found a large stone, or mass of rock, favorably situated, it will, almost invariably, be covered with drawings. In nearly every case, these are merely the signatures, the almost universal expression of vanity, of the warriors; or are designs and sketches made by the young men and boys in wantonness, and with no more hidden significance than those which the white schoolboy in his moments of laziness or mischief draws on his slate, or on the newly whitewashed fence of his neighbor.

"While this is literally true of most of the isolated figures drawn on rocks and trees by different hands, generally believed to be, and spoken of by learned writers as symbolic, it must yet be understood that the Plains Indians, more than most others, use pictures to express action and situation. There is a broad line of demarcation between symbolism and pictography. The Plains Indian uses the former but little, and then only as an adjunct to the latter, enabling him to show in his picture something which is impossible to his limited knowledge of drawing and perspective. Almost every warrior makes a picture of each prominent event of his life, and many of them keep a book in which their acts are thus recorded. But his pictures are not symbolic. The fight or other act is depicted as nearly as possible as the Indian wishes it to be seen; himself the prominent figure in the foreground, dealing death, or otherwise performing the act. Their pictures of fights in which numbers are engaged, are simply the representation of individuals who were prominent either for courage or from being killed or wounded. In such pictures symbolism is used to make up the deficiencies of the draughtsman; thus a great many marks of horses' feet indicate that great numbers were engaged; many arrows or bullets represented in the air show that the fight was hotly contested.

There is nothing in which white men differ more than in drawing. One draws exquisitely, another with equal opportunities, and equally as well educated in other respects, cannot draw at all. Not so with Indians 3 all draw, and though entirely without knowledge of perspective, all draw quite as well as the average of whites. If one wants Indian pictures, there is no need to hunt a special artist. All he has to do is to give some paper and a few colored pencils to any middle-aged warrior. I have many such pictures, drawn by men of different tribes, all so essentially alike in character and execution, that they might have been drawn by the same hand.

INDIAN WEAPONS—SKILL AND EXPERTNESS

THE bow is the natural weapon of the North American Indian. The first childish plaything of which he has recollection is the miniature bow and blunted arrows placed in his hands by his proud father, when he is scarcely four years old. Practising incessantly, he is, when nine or ten years of age, able to bring in from his daily rambles quite a store of larks, doves, thrushes, sparrows, rabbits, gophers, ground-squirrels, and other small deer for which he is greatly praised, particularly by his mother, to whose especial delectation they are presently devoted.

When sufficiently familiar and expert with his weapon as to warrant the experiment, he is furnished with arrows with iron points, an epoch in his life ranking with the day of possession by the white boy of his first gun. He now quits the companionship of the smaller boys, and in company with lads armed as himself, makes wide excursions after larger game, sometimes being gone from his lodge for several days.

In his earlier forays for scalps and plunder, he is armed with this weapon, for unless his father be exceptionally rich and generous, he can never hope to own a gun until he can procure the means to pay for it, or is so fortunate as to kill a man who has one.

As a rule, therefore, the Indian warrior does not arrive at firearms before about the average age of twenty-five; and though he sometimes becomes very expert with the new weapon, he is never as thoroughly at home with it as with his first love, the bow.

When I first came among Indians, only a very few possessed firearms, and those were of the most inferior kind. The bow was the universal weapon. Even those who possessed guns carried them more, I think, for the noise they made (what we would call moral effect), or because it was "the thing," than from any confidence in them; for though the gun was ostentatiously carried across the saddle, the bow and quiver of arrows was always slung on the back.

In my first fight with Indians I was greatly astonished to notice that those who ran away invariably took with them their bows and arrows, but abandoned their guns. My guide subsequently informed me that the Indians had little confidence in guns in a close fight. A whole quiver of arrows could be expended in the time it took to load and fire the gun once.

Almost all of the older warriors of tribes most closely in contact with whites have now guns and pistols, many of them the very best breech-loading arms in the market. This has very greatly diminished the use of the bow; but ammunition may be scarce, or the gun itself get out of order, and as no Indians have the proper tools, and very few the mechanical knowledge for its repair, the owner must take to his bow until he can get some white man to mend the gun for him. The young and the poor use the bow exclusively; those who possess firearms must use the bow occasionally; so that however rich and well-armed a band may be, the bow is yet an indispensable possession of every male Indian.

A good bow takes a long time and much care and labor in its construction. Those most highly prized among the Indians of central North America are ingeniously fabricated by carefully fitting together pieces of elk-horn, the whole glued together, and tightly wrapped with strips of the smaller intestines of deer, or slender threads of sinew, used wet, and which, when dry, tighten and unite all the parts into one compact and homogeneous whole, said to be stronger, tougher, more elastic, and more durable than a bow of any other materials. The great difficulty of its construction, the fact that it is liable to become useless in wet, or even in damp weather, and the more general use of firearms, have rendered obsolete this particular make of the weapon, and it can now scarcely be found, except in museums, or kept as heirlooms, handed down from father to son in some principal family.

The bow in common use among Indians is made of wood. The best is Osage Orange (the "*bois d'arc*" of the French trappers, now commonly called "bow dark" by white frontiersmen). This wood is indigenous to a comparatively limited area of country, and long journeys are sometimes made to obtain it, the venturous traveller bringing back whole pony-loads of the valuable commodity, and making a "good thing" by trading off his surplus. When this wood cannot be obtained, they use ash, elm, iron-wood, cedar, indeed almost any wood; for that most brittle, when cut into layers, fitted and glued together, and wound with sinew, will make a bow of requisite strength, though lacking in elasticity. I have been told that the traders sometimes sell to the Indians straight, well-grained pieces of oak, hickory, and even yew, but I have never seen an Indian bow of those woods.

Bows are short-distance weapons, for though a skilful Indian may throw an arrow nearly two hundred yards, it seems, after the first few yards, to lose its penetrative power and destructive force. Many stories are told of the ability of an Indian to throw an arrow through a buffalo, arid one author claims to have himself sent an arrow completely through an inch board. I can only say, that with considerable knowledge of many tribes, I have never seen any such feats. I have frequently seen an arrow imbedded in the body of the buffalo to the feather, but this only happens when no bone is touched. In my experience, the strongest Indian, with the best bow, cannot, even at a few feet, drive an arrow through a rib of the buffalo so as to inflict an immediately fatal wound.

The Comanches place the blade of the hunting-arrow in the same plane with the notch for the string, so that it may more surely pass between the ribs of the animal, which are up and down; for the same reason, the blade of the war-arrow is perpendicular to the notch, the ribs of the human enemy being horizontal.

The arrows require in the aggregate much more labor than the bow. Any hard, tough wood is used. It is scraped to proper size and taper, and must be perfectly round. The head is either of stone or iron—of late years, exclusively of iron, stone of the necessary hardness being difficult to work.

The shape of the iron arrow-head indicates the use to which it is expected to be put. Hunting-arrows have long, tapering blades, the rear shoulders sloping backward. The blade is firmly fastened to the shaft, and can easily be withdrawn from the wound. The war-arrow has a short, sharp blade, like a lancet; the rear shoulders slope forward, forming barbs; their attachment to the shaft is very slight, as it is intended that the head shall remain in the wound, and kill eventually, if not immediately.

However dangerous he may be to human and animal life with these weapons, the Indian is not a good shot with them at a target, especially if it be somewhat removed. Even at a little distance, he seems to lose confidence in himself. Put a five-cent piece in a split stick, at fifty or sixty yards, and by giving a dexterous twist he will make the arrow fly sideways, and knock down the money almost every time; but put an inch-square piece of paper on a board or tree, at the same distance, and he will hardly hit it once in a day's practice.

A party of Comanches came into a military fort where I was stationed, and after knocking down sticks holding money, and performing various feats with their bows, challenged any white man to shoot against them. The challenge was accepted by a young officer, who, though he had had no experience with bows and arrows since boyhood, easily beat them out of all they cared to lose, and sent them off thoroughly disgusted.

The wonderful thing about the Indian bow practice is the remarkable rapidity and force with which he can send his arrows. He will grasp five to ten arrows in his left hand, and discharge them so rapidly that the last will be on its flight before the first has touched the ground, and with such force that each would mortally wound a man at twenty or thirty yards. The blow of the string in this practice is so very severe on the left forearm, that when expecting to go into a fight this arm is always protected by a shield or gauntlet of stiff deerskin.

However apparently alike, the bows and arrows of each tribe differ so materially from those of other tribes, that an Indian, and even some frontiersmen, will, from a mere glance at either, say to what tribe it belongs.

I know of no tribe of Indians that now uses the war-club, so common and so elaborately ornamented in the days of Catlin. The tomahawk is still in use, but reduced from its former high estate as executioner of the direful will of its owner, to a mere ornament, carried as a lady carries her fan, or, still worse, devoted to the base purpose of chopping wood. Though there are yet many very elaborately ornamented tomahawks, they are regarded rather as an insignia of rank, to be carried on ceremonial occasions, but are scarcely thought of as weapons. Even as pipes, they are beginning to be voted a bore by the average Indian.

Knives are invaluable to all, not an Indian of any age or sex, except very small children, being without one. The scalping-knife is generally an ordinary butcher's knife, of English or American manufacture, the handle gaudily ornamented with brass round-headed trunk-tacks. In ordinary times of peace, it is a "servant of all work," but when scalps are expected, it is ground to one edge, and kept keen as a razor. It is carried in the belt, in a sheath, which, like all other Indian trappings, is plain or elaborately ornamented, according to the wealth or taste of the owner. The women's knives, used constantly for skinning game, are all ground to one edge, and are almost useless for other purposes.

Next to the bow, the great offensive weapon for all the horseback or Plains Indians, was, a few years ago, the lance. It consists of a shaft of from eight to twelve feet long, terminated by a head of stone or metal. Differing from the "knights of old," the Indians wanted no tough, stiff, ash poles, but selected light and rather pliable wands. The Comanches and Apaches not unfrequently use the long, dry stalks of the soap-plant (*phalangium pomaridranum*).

The favorite point was a long, straight sword blade, which they procured in great number from the Mexicans, and I have seen among them blades which, in beauty and temper, were—to use the words attributed to a gallant and well-known officer—"worthy of old Toledo himself."

Prior to the general introduction of repeating and breech-loading firearms, the lance was the most formidable weapon possessed by the Indians, and warfare with it was exceedingly destructive to life. To do injury at all, the bearer of the lance must come in actual contact with the enemy, and a battle of anything like equal numbers was a series of personal combats, in which one or the other "bit the dust."

Almost every Indian, even at the present day, possesses a shield. It is his only "weapon of defence." It is made of the hide of the neck of a buffalo or ox. This hide, almost a quarter of an inch in thickness, is deprived of hair, soaked, rubbed, pounded, cut into shape, and then dried. It is almost as impenetrable as iron, and when doubled, as is frequently the case, is almost a perfect protection against the very best rifle. No rifle-ball can penetrate unless it strikes squarely, and the shield being attached to the left arm by loops which allow it play, the impinging bullet is almost sure to be sent off in another direction.

As the eagle's-feather head-dress is the acme of all personal adornment, so the shield is the head and front, the topmost summit of warlike paraphernalia. On it he bestows infinite patience, care, and thought. Not only must it be perfect in shape, in fit, in make, but also in its "medicine." He thinks over it, he works over it, he prays over it; to its care and protection he commends his life; to its adornment he elaborates thought, and devotes his time and means; to it he appends his "medicine bag" and the scalps of his enemies; on its front is painted his totem; it occupies a conspicuous but safe place in his lodge, and is hung out every fair day in front of his door; it is his shield, his protector, his escutcheon, his medicine, almost his God.

Every male Indian who can buy, beg, borrow, or steal them, has now firearms of some kind. They are connoisseurs in these articles, and have the very best that their means or opportunities permit. Every man haying to procure his own arms when and how he can, there is no uniformity of make or calibre—a fortunate circumstance for his enemies, but extremely annoying to the Indian. The trade in arms is .entirely illicit. The trader slips into the Indian country, now here, now there, and not knowing beforehand the calibre of the ammunition required, takes that which is most commonly in use. Some guns of a band were almost always out of use on this account, but necessity, that great "mother of invention," has so stimulated the ordinarily uninventive brain of the Indian, that if he can only procure the moulds for a bullet that will fit his rifle, he manages the rest by an ingenious method of reloading his old shells peculiar to himself. He buys from the trader a box of the smallest percussion caps, and making an orifice in the centre of the base of the shell, forces the cap in until it is flush. Powder and lead can always be obtained from the traders 3 or, in default of these, cartridges of other calibre are broken up, and the materials used in reloading his shells. Indians say that the shells thus reloaded are nearly as good as the original cartridges, and that the shells are frequently reloaded forty or fifty times.

Many of the Indians possess revolving pistols of the very best kind, and have much less trouble on account of the ammunition, the calibre being more uniform.

The gun is generally carried across the saddle, in front of the rider. It is enveloped in a case of buckskin, sometimes elaborately fringed and beaded. The pistol is carried in a buckskin holster attached to the belt. This belt is of hide, or preferably of leather, fastened in front with a buckle. On the outside, a strip of buckskin is stitched in loops, each of the proper size to carry one cartridge. It is the ordinary "service-belt" of the army, somewhat roughly made. To this belt the Indian attaches almost all his "portable property." On the right side is the pistol, on the left the knife, the pouch for his pipe and tobacco, that for his tools and cleaning materials, his medicine bag; anything and everything finds its appropriate place on the belt.

A small party of Sioux once came into my camp, returning from an unsuccessful foray against the Pawnees. They were all well-armed, but the leader particularly attracted my attention. He was a stalwart, ruffianly-looking fellow of about twenty-five, handsomely dressed in buckskin. Across his saddle he carried a magnificent buffalo gun of the very best patent; on each side of his belt was a holster containing a beautiful, ivory-handled Colt's revolver, and slung across his shoulder was a most excellent field-glass. The rascal had been "in luck," killed some rich man on a hunt for pleasure, and secured his outfit.

SIGNAL FIRES AND SMOKES

THE elementary instruction of the youthful Indian cannot be called "drill" in the military, or indeed in any other sense of that term. He is not taught to ride, but being placed on a horse, at the most tender age, he learns to ride as he does to walk, by instinct and constant practise. Every Indian rides after a fashion of his own, not derived from teachers, but coming natural to him by constant practice, and his observation of his associates and elders. A father or old man may give a youngster a few words of advice regarding the management of a specially vicious horse, but as a rule each Indian, however young, is supposed to be entirely capable of managing any horse, and is therefore not overburdened with amiable and officious advisers.

An Indian boy of twelve or fifteen years of age is simply a miracle in his capacity for sticking to a horse. The older and stronger men are of course much more dexterous in the performance of all kinds of marvellous feats of horsemanship, but my experience is that the boy of fifteen is at his perfection, simply as a rider.

At six, seven, or eight years old, the boys begin to be made of use by the fathers, and in time of peace, when there is no danger of loss, except by straying, they are sent to herd the ponies; and it is not at all unusual for ten or fifteen of these little urchins to find themselves out for the whole day, and in sole charge of possibly several hundred ponies.

Each may start out in the morning and return in the evening mounted on the same staid old quadruped, but each has with him his "riata," and his bow and arrows, and when all get together they would not be human boys if they did not have a "good time." Every devilment that boys in their position could practise they are up to. The "riata" gives them the means of catching any horse at pleasure, and the speed of every horse of the entire herd is known to these little fellows better than to their fathers, for every horse is caught in turn, and every day witnesses a succession of horse-races.

One day when I had tired myself out in a long hunt, I sat down on a bluff overlooking a somewhat extensive valley. Half a mile from me, up the stream, I saw a herd of about twenty Indian ponies, which, though in herd, appeared to be in great commotion. Watching them intently through my glass, I found that the herder, a boy of ten or twelve, was successively "roping" every horse. Catching one with his lariat, he would mount him bareback, and take after another, sometimes making three, four, or half a dozen casts of his lasso before roping his victim. Mounting this, he went after another, and another. I watched him for more than half an hour, and when I finally started for my camp, he was yet heartily engaged in his fun. The boy was entirely alone, and unaware of any witness to his performance. He was simply amusing himself by this practice.

When the boys get tired of horse-racing, they take to their bows and practise at marks, either on foot or at speed on horseback. Every boy bets, of course, (he would not be his father's son if he did not gamble), arrows, knives, strings, nails, pieces of glass, and every boyish trumpery, and as his gains and losses are known, and commented upon by the family, he soon becomes an adept not only in his riding and shooting, but in the art of making bets.

A few years of such practice tells, and as I have before said, I consider the Indian boy, of from twelve to fifteen years old, the best rough rider and natural horseman in the world.

At about this age he begins to think himself a man, and to yearn for the position, fame, and honor of the warrior. He is given more liberty, younger brothers or sisters take his place on herd, while he, with others of the same age and aspirations, wanders about the country in search of the adventure which is to crown his ambition by making him a warrior. No military man can contemplate such a school for recruits without admiration, and one can readily sympathize with the enthusiastic cavalry officer who exclaimed," Give me the handling and discipline of such recruits as the Indian boys, and I can whip ail equal number of any cavalry in the world."

Until he is a warrior the Indian has never had a "drill," that is, he has had instruction in nothing. All he knows is self-taught. It is now the province of the chief so to instruct all this energy and capacity as to render it available for concentrated action. The actual force of a thousand men is exactly the same whether the men be disciplined or not. The effect of discipline and drill are simply to concentrate; to make the whole mass a machine which at the will of one, may exert this force in a certain direction or to a certain end. It is the actualization of the old fable of the bundle of sticks.

The Indian understands this perfectly, but the peculiarity of the tribal relation prevents any very decided enforcement of what we call discipline, and the lack of knowledge precludes the idea of anything like conventional drill.

The chief must do the best he can with the material he has, taking advantage of its wonderful individual skill, knowledge, and pliability, without trammelling it by any attempted adherence to rigid rules of tactics. There is, therefore, no fixed system of tactics, each chief instructing according to his own capacity and his idea of the capabilities of his materiel.

In time of peace there is very little drill or instruction of any kind by the chiefs or leading men, though sometimes when there are a good many Indians together, a chief may have a "show-drill," or grand parade of mounted men something in the nature of a review. There is no compulsion in the attendance of warriors. The claims of the stomach are always paramount, and those warriors who need meat for their families go to look for it, even on drill days.

In anticipation of war, the chief may call out his warriors for instruction every day, or at least several times each week.

There are no ranks, no organizations, no units of command, each sub-chief being surrounded by his followers in any order that they may happen to fall; but there are words or signals of command by which the same evolutions are repeatedly performed, more, it would appear, by the wonderful intuition of the individual Indian than by any instruction that could possibly have been given to him by a lifetime of drill.

Tactical manoeuvres of Indians always suppose an enemy, and previous to the drill the chief indicates to his command this supposed position, sometimes on open ground, at other times in hills and ravines. The chief now forms what may be designated his line of battle. This line consists of masses of Indians, more or less detached each from the other, each sub-chief being surrounded by his following, but all together forming a line of masses faced towards the supposed position of the enemy. To produce a moral effect on that enemy, the young and ardent, or those who have exceptionally good horses, are tearing over the ground, circling, at full speed, in front, rear, and flanks of the masses to which they belong, making a great show of force, and appearing to be numerically at least five times greater than they really are.

At a signal, the whole line will charge en masse and without order upon the supposed position of the enemy. At a word or signal it breaks or scatters like leaves before the storm. Another word or signal, a portion wheels, masses, and dashes on a flank, to scatter again at another signal. The plain is alive with flying, circling horsemen, now single, each lying flat on his horse, or hanging to his side to escape the shots of the pursuing enemy; now, joined together, they rush upon that enemy in a living mass of a charging, yelling terror.

The commands of the chief are sometimes communicated by the voice, but more generally, especially when there is any considerable force, by signals. These are devised after a system of the Indians' own invention, said to be a sort of offshoot of the sign language. This system of signals is most strong and sacred "medicine," the secret of which it would be dishonor and destruction to divulge. I have elsewhere spoken of the sacredness to an Indian of an oath, administered after their forms and "medicines." No earthly power could force him to disclose a secret learned under such an oath; and in answer to an effort at persuasion, he looks at you with wide-eyed astonishment, and says simply, "I have sworn."

Even the whites, intermarried and living with the Indians, are not admitted to this mystery. I have questioned many of these, and of Plains hunters, who, however, could only say that a system of signalling is in common use among Indians.

To the Indians themselves I have used both persuasion and bribes, always reaching the general admission of the use of such a system, but never arriving at even the slightest hint on which might be founded a practical system. I am inclined to believe that effective as it is in action, the system is a very crude and imperfect one, giving only the most general directions, very much indeed such an one as the sportsman uses in the management of his dogs in the field.

"Wonderful as the statement may appear, the signalling on a bright day, and when the sun is in the proper dircction, is done with a piece of looking-glass held in the hollow of the hand. The reflection of the sun's rays thrown on the command, communicates the orders of the chief. How this is done is the mystery which no one will divulge.

Once, standing on a little knoll overlooking the valley of the South Platte, I witnessed, almost at my feet, a drill of about a hundred warriors. Their commander, a Sioux chief, sat on his horse on a knoll a little way above me, and some two hundred yards from his command in the plain below. For more than half an hour he directed a drill which, for variety and promptness of action, could not be excelled (I doubt if equalled) by any cavalry in the world. There were no verbal commands, and all I could see was an occasional movement of the right arm. He afterwards told me that he had used a looking-glass.

Every writer on Indians, either of fact or fiction, has spoken of their use of smoke for communicating at long distances. These smokes are made singly or in groups, or to ascend into the air in different ways to each of which is attached a conventional meaning. Thus a single smoke ascending naturally means one thing; two smokes, another thing. A small fire is built on which is placed damp grass, creating a large volume of smoke. As it begins to ascend a blanket is held horizontally above it, and when the space beneath is quite full, the blanket is slipped off sideways and then quickly brought back to its place. Smoke managed in this way ascends in round puffs, miniature clouds, one meaning one thing, two another. When the signal is complete, the fire is extinguished.

With almost all Indians, a single smoke, ascending naturally, is a warning to all Indians within range of vision that there are strangers in the country; and such is their habitual caution that they make these signals even when in a state of profound peace. Every military command passing through an Indian country, will be preceded and flanked by these signal-smokes. To prevent its being mistaken for the smoke of a camp-fire, it is made on the side or top of a high hill, or on the plain, or a divide away from water. At night, fires are used as signals somewhat in the same way, not, however, so extensively, or with such effect, as smoke.

Besides these signals, which are used to convey information to persons beyond the sight of the maker, the Indians have other means equally remarkable for telegraphing to persons a long distance off, but who can be seen. Indian scouts are employed by the United States government at almost every post in the Indian country. Their services are invaluable, indeed indispensable to success against Indians. On the march, the leader or interpreter is kept with the commanding officer of the troops, while the scouts are sent far in advance or on the flank. Occasionally one shows himself, sometimes a mere speck on a distant ridge, and the interpreter will say at once what that scout desires to communicate. I learned some of these signals, which are all simple and entirely conventional. For instance, a scout rides to the top of a ridge or hill, pulls up his horse, stands motionless for two or three minutes, and then proceeds at a walk. He means, "All right, no signs of enemy or danger."

Another will dash at full speed to the top of the hill and ride rapidly round and round in a circle. He means, "Danger; get together as quickly as possible."

These and similar, are ordinary signals used by all Plains Indians. A party going off on a raid or thieving expedition, will often, before starting, settle on meanings for the signals different from those in common use. By this means they are able to communicate without disclosing their true meaning to any casual observer. The only really wonderful thing about this telegraphing is the very great distance it can be read by the Indians. While with an excellent field glass I could scarcely make out that the distant speck was a horseman, the Indian at my side would tell me what that speck wished to communicate.

Indian signalling and telegraphing are simply modifications and extensions of the sign language. All are offsprings of a necessity growing out of the number and variety of the Indian languages, and the constant wariness necessary and incidental to a life of peculiar danger.

I have already spoken of the religious belief which condemns every scalped warrior to annihilation, and of the heroism often displayed by the Indian in risking his own life to save unscalped the body of his chief or friend. This superstition is the primary cause of a drill peculiar to the Plains Indians. It is to stoop from the horse, when at full speed, and pick up objects from the ground. At first light objects are selected; these are gradually exchanged for heavier ones, until (it is said, for I have never seen it,) some few individuals attain such wonderful proficiency as to be able, alone and at full speed, to pick up from the ground and swing across his horse the body of the heaviest man.

This, however, is generally done by two Indians. Rushing neck and neck on either side of the prostrate form, each rider stoops at the same instant, seizes the part most convenient, and the combined strength and address of the two swing the body in front of one of the riders, who carries it away to a safe place.

In this drill the warriors take turns in picking and being picked up; for at any time during a fight each may have to act or be acted upon as foreshadowed in the drill. When drilling as wounded, the prostrate man will assist the others by extending arms and legs. When drilling as dead, not only is no help afforded, but the acting dead man assumes by turns every position, the most unnatural or even impossible that a really dead body might be supposed to fall into. This drill is practised in good weather most assiduously on all kinds of ground, until riders, ponies, and supposed dead and wounded are thoroughly proficient in their several parts.

To this drill is owing the fact that nearly every official report of a fight with Indians has a statement in effect as follows: "Indian loss unknown; several were seen to fall from their horses." On this drill are bestowed the hearty anathemas of every aspiring young officer, who, having marched, toiled, watched, and suffered for days and nights on the trail, and being finally rewarded by a good blow at the marauders, is obliged to return to his post empty-handed, with nothing to show, the Indians having carried off all their dead and wounded.

WARFARE—THRILLING ADVENTURES AND EXPERIENCES

THE description given of the early life of the Indian boy, of the necessities imposed on their mode of warfare 3 by their religious beliefs, and of their instructions and training for "the field," as warriors, foreshadow closely the peculiar characteristics of their fighting.

Courage is a quality common to both brutes and men, but there are numerous shades and lands of this common quality, some only of which characterize the mere animal, while these and others are developed among men in different degrees, according to their peculiarities as peoples. Estimates of this quality in the Indian vary exceedingly even among those whose capacity and position best qualify them to judge; and the Indian is forced by his historians to appear in turn in every character, from the ferocious hut cowardly beast, attacking only the most helpless, and ready to run at the first appearance of real danger, to the deadly fate, without fear as without mercy, whose very name is a terror.

An analysis of Indian courage will show that in this as in other things, he differs from other men only as might be expected from his surroundings. No man possesses more of that quality of brute courage which impels the smallest and most insignificant animal to fight to the death when cornered; and he possesses also in an eminent degree the courage which comes of confidence in his own arms and skill, and from constant familiarity with danger. No man can more gallantly dash into danger when his reward in honors, scalps, or plunder, appears sure and immediate. No man can take more chances when acting under the influence of superstition, in risking his life to carry off unscalped his dead and wounded comrades.

The Indian has no conception of the moral virtues, and as might naturally be expected, is without the moral or higher qualities of courage. He is especially lacking in intrepidity, that firmness of soul which enables a man to take his chances of wounds and death for the sake of principle, without expectation or even hope of reward, other than that which comes from a sense of duty performed.

As with all other people, the courage of the Indian is in keeping with his character and surroundings. The population being small, the life of each skilled warrior is of serious importance to the whole tribe. "To avoid unnecessary risks" and that "craft is superior to courage" are the grand fundamental principles of Indian education, impressed on the boys from their earliest years.

The Indian is patient and cunning; he relies on these qualities for the surprise of his enemy. He is excitable, nervous, easily stampeded, and, judging others by himself, he relies on the demoralization produced by a surprise "to deliver his enemy into his hand," without danger to himself. In this mode of warfare he has no superior, nor can he be excelled in the spirit with which he follows up a first successful effort; nor in the remorseless vigor and determination of his pursuit of a flying foe.

Their fights with each other are almost invariably surprises, in which the surprised party, almost equally invariably gets the worst of it, without reference to numbers. Should two hostile bands of nearly equal numbers meet on the Plains, a long contest is likely to ensue, in which the fighting is done at extreme long range, and consists principally in dashing about at the full speed of their ponies, making short feints of charges, yelling most vociferously, and once in a while firing a shot. Occasionally a young buck, anxious to signalize his bravery, will dash, well covered by his position on the side of his horse, up to within two or three hundred yards of the enemy, fire off his gun in mid career, and circle back to his own party. A youngster from the other side then shows his courage in the same way and with the same result. This goes on until one party shows signs of weakness or timidity, which so emboldens the other that it charges in real earnest, and the whipped band gets away as best it can. This is not usual, however. Generally the affair is kept up until the ponies of both sides are completely fagged out, when each party draws off to try to achieve by superior craft and cunning what it failed to do in open fight.

I have been told of a desperate battle in which not less than one hundred Indians were engaged four days; the warriors on each side displaying prodigies of valor, and in which one man was killed, by a mere accident.

If one party is greatly superior in numbers to the other, it dashes in at once, relying on the demoralization of the weaker side to prevent its doing damage. Then it is Indian against Indian, pony against pony, and unless the ground be particularly unfavorable, the beaten force breaking up, each man for himself, will get away with much less loss than would naturally be expected.

The first impulse of the Indian, on being surprised in his camp, is that natural to most animals under the impulse of fear, to scurry away as fast as his legs will carry him. He does not, however, forget his arms, nor lose his head to such an extent as to fail to take the shortest route to the nearest and best cover. While under this terror, or "stampede," as it is called on "the frontier," he is by no means to be feared, his shooting being wild in the extreme. Let him but come to bay in his cover, or receive a wound, and he at once recovers his presence of mind, and becomes again the really dangerous animal. When wounded he becomes especially dangerous: for, so long as he is unhurt, he will always sacrifice a chance to kill for a chance to escape. The moment he receives a disabling wound, he becomes utterly reckless, and seeming to devote his whole remaining energies to the one object of revenge, he fights with the fierceness of the wolf, but with coolness of aim and fixedness of purpose as long as his eye can distinguish an enemy or his finger pull a trigger.

Many a white man has been sent to his long home from carelessly going up to an Indian supposed to be dead. An officer of high rank in our service has suffered for many years from a wound inflicted under such circumstances. Stampeded and demoralized, an Indian was flying for his life without thought of using his arms. He was pursued, shot and fell, the horse of the pursuer literally jumping over him. At a short distance the horse was stopped, and the officer, in the act of turning about to go back to his victim, was struck under the shoulder-blade by an arrow sped with the last breath of the Indian.

A force of some twenty-five cavalry surprised a small party of Indians in a thick chaparral, through which, however, there were numerous glades and openings. The Indians scattered at once, and the soldiers scattered in pursuit. After some time, and when the cessation of firing indicated that the affair was over, the commander had the recall sounded. Soon one and then another came in, until the whole command was assembled, when, to the gratification of the officer, almost every man claimed to have killed an Indian. They went to collect the bodies. On reaching the first, it was found that nearly every soldier claimed to have killed him. A sergeant dismounted, and approached the body only barely to escape a vicious blow from a knife. When finally killed, it was discovered that the Indian had not less than twenty wounds. One, probably the first, had broken his hip, and thrown him from his horse. After that he had shot at every soldier that passed near him, attracting attention and being "killed" again and again, only to fight again when the next soldier came along. Instead of twenty, the soldiers got one Indian.

The tenacity of life of an Indian, the amount of lead he will carry off, indicates a nervous system so dull as to class him rather with brutes than with men. The shock or blow of a bullet will ordinarily paralyze so many nerves and muscles of a white man as to knock him down, even though not striking a vital part. The Indian gives no heed to such wounds, and to "drop him in his tracks," the bullet must reach the brain, the heart, or the spine. I have myself seen an Indian go off with two bullets through his body, within an inch or two of the spine, the only effect of which was to cause him to change his gait from a run to a dignified walk.

The fighting of Indians with each other is like that of wolves, cowardice until the enemy shows fear, or is known to be weak, and then the utmost ferocity. With their knowledge of the country, splendid horsemanship, physical endurance, apparent indifference to pain or privation, and wonderful tenacity of life, it is not at all remarkable that the battles and combats between warriors result in very little loss on either side. But when, by accident or superior craft and cunning, the warriors of one tribe succeed in surprising a camp of the other, of few warriors and many women and children, the slaughter is terrible, and the barbarities and atrocities worthy of fiends. Numerous instances are on record, but these horrors are unpleasant either to relate or read.

Another reason for the small loss of life in Indian contests with each other is, that they never fight to the best advantage except in their own territories. Unless in overwhelming force, a marauding party advances into the country of its enemy with fear and trembling, ready to fly to its own ground on the slightest appearance of danger. This peculiarity is the only serious difficulty in the way of the advantageous employment by the government of Indians against Indians. Unless under the command of a white leader in whom they have perfect confidence, and with "plenty of soldiers" to back them, these auxiliaries are not to be relied on.

The Utes and Southern Cheyennes illustrate the bitter hatred and mortal fear that many tribes have for each other, and which sometimes lead to ludicrous results. The Utes are a mountain tribe, the Southern Cheyennes a Plains tribe. Any single Indian of either tribe on his own ground counts himself equal to at least three of the other. Brave as they undoubtedly are, the Utes go upon the Plains with fear and trembling, while the Cheyennes will scarcely venture at all into any Ute country so broken as to prevent their operating to advantage on horseback. Though always at war with each other, it is rare that anybody is hurt, each being too wary to venture far into the territory of the other.

A mixed band of some fifteen hundred Sioux and Cheyennes hunting in 1874 went well up on the head waters of the Republican in search of buffalo. The Utes found them out, and a few warriors slipping into their camp during the night, stampeded their ponies at daylight, and in spite of the hot pursuit of the Sioux, reached the mountains with over two hundred head; and though there were in that band near four times as many warriors as are in the whole Ute tribe; and though they knew that the thieving party consisted of less than ten men, they preferred to lose their ponies to taking the risk of pursuit.

The Utes are the Switzers of America, and though the whole force of the mountain bands numbers but little over four hundred men, all the powerful Plains tribes, though holding them in utter contempt on the Plains, have absolute terror of them in the mountains.

An instance thoroughly illustrative of the Indian mode of warfare and the effect of surprise, came under my personal observation. In 1867, almost all the Plains tribes were on the war-path, making a last desperate effort to preserve to themselves the splendid buffalo country between the Platte and the Arkansas. A train of the Union Pacific Railroad had been thrown from the track, robbed, and burned by the Cheyennes. I was ordered to the protection of the railroad with a force of four companies of infantry, and a company, fifty strong, of Pawnee Indians under a white leader, Captain Murie. The troops were scattered along at the most exposed points, Captain Murie being stationed on the South Platte, opposite Plum Creek Station, on the overland stage road. At that time the Indians had a superstitious dread of the telegraph line, which they call the "talking wire." When passing under or near it on marauding expeditions they always cut and pull down a portion of it to prevent its telling on them. This superstition was, of course, a great advantage to us. One day I received telegrams from east and west informing me that the line was down at Plum Creek stage station. I at once telegraphed to Captain Murie, ordering him to send a party of his Indians across the river and find out what was the matter.

In an hour I received answer that there was a large force of hostile Indians in possession of the station. Ordering him to cross the river with his whole company, engage the enemy, and occupy him until I could reach him, I seized a locomotive and cars, put on every man I had, and went with all the speed of steam to the scene of action. Arriving at Plum Creek railroad station, while the men were being formed, I went on the top of the house, where there was a lookout, and through my glass saw the winding-up of one of the prettiest and most successful, fights that I have ever known among Indians.

As soon as he had crossed the river, Captain Murie discovered the position of the enemy, which was a most admirable one. Plum Creek is a deep bed, generally dry, some sixty feet wide, with high, almost perpendicular banks. The stage road crossed by a bridge. The Cheyenne line was drawn up about one hundred yards from the eastern end of this bridge, directly facing it. The right flank, which might be turned, was protected by eight or ten dismounted Indians posted in the loop-holed stable of the stage station. The Pawnees wore the uniform and used the tactics of the United States Army, and the Cheyenne leader evidently believed that the advancing force was United States cavalry. His plan was to permit them to partially cross the bridge, and then by a vigorous onslaught, accompanied by the usual yells and shaking of buffalo robes to frighten the restive and half-broken cavalry horses, render them unmanageable, and thus throw the whole force into confusion in a most difficult and dangerous position.

Noting that the Indian pickets retired rapidly, and without hostile demonstration, Captain Murie suspected some trap, and on closer examination of the Cheyenne position divined the stratagem of his enemy. Being greatly inferior in force (the Cheyennes numbering one hundred and fifty-four warriors), he resorted to a counter-stratagem. Dismounting his men under cover of the tall grass of the river bottom, he caused them to strip to Indian fighting costume (breech-cloth alone); then he made each put on his uniform hat, throw over his shoulders his uniform overcoat, buttoning only the top button. Then mounted and formed, he moved slowly to the attack, at the head of what to all appearance was a company of United States cavalry, too much encumbered with clothing to make a good fight.

The Pawnees advanced by the flank left in front. As soon as the leading files passed the bridge they inclined rapidly to the left, to enable those in rear to come up promptly into line. When nearly half the company had passed, the Cheyennes charged with furious yells. When they had arrived within probably fifty yards, the Pawnees threw off hats and overcoats, and with a true Indian yell dashed at their enemy. The latter, entirely surprised and utterly stampeded, wheeled their horses, and fled in confusion and dismay. The Pawnees took sixteen scalps, two prisoners, and a number of animals without a man or horse being even scratched. So little danger is there to fear from a "stampeded" Indian.

In fighting with white men a surprise is always made when possible; when this cannot be done, the Indians use other tactics modified to suit the circumstances of the case.

A pitched battle on anything like equal terms as regards numbers is almost impossible, first because the army is so small and so widely scattered over our vast territory, that it is everywhere greatly outnumbered; and second, because the Indians not being hampered with wagons, pack-mules, or other impediments, can always avoid battle. They are good soldiers and good generals, and voluntarily fight only when overwhelming numbers or some other marked advantage leads them to believe their success to be assured.

When such a battle is decided upon, and a considerable force is engaged, the different bands, each under its chief, are drawn up into an array—not a line, for Indian tactics permit no such restraint as lines necessitate. Those masses or groups are so disposed, however, as to form a general line of battle.

They may charge simultaneously, or individually. The Indians never receive a charge, and rarely meet one. When charged, the portion of the array immediately in front of the charging force breaks and melts away into individual Indians, while the bands on either side close in to attack and harass the flanks and rear of the charge. The dispersed Indians, wheeling in circles, form on the flanks to attack when practicable, or to break again when charged. Should the attacking force, carried away by excitement, become scattered in pursuit of the flying foe, its defeat and destruction is almost sure. The magnificent riding of the Indian, and his superb drill, in this his favorite style of fighting, give him an immense advantage. Avoiding by quick turns of the small and active ponies, the direct onslaught of their bulky foe, and circling like birds of prey, they collect together, fall upon his flanks and rear, overwhelm him, and disperse like magic, to repeat the process on another.

The Battle of the Rosebud [June 17, 1876] was a perfect illustration of Indian tactics. General Crook's right wing consisted of the allied Indians and two companies of infantry, his left entirely of cavalry. Slowly advancing on the enemy's position, the whole line was soon hotly engaged. The cavalry made a splendid charge on a position strongly held by the enemy, to find when it arrived on the spot, that enemy apparently ready to receive it, in another strong position in the rear. Another charge, and another with like result, until General Crook finding his wings completely disunited, the cavalry far in advance, and in danger of being overwhelmed, sent an aide to recall it. The cavalry had advanced almost without contest, but on its attempt to fall back it found itself completely surrounded. Indians poured from the hills and swarmed from every thicket and ravine; front, flank and rear, they were everywhere. Without a halt or break the steady troops moved on. One moment of fierce hand-to-hand conflict, the environing throngs were rent asunder, and the brave band regained its position in line of battle. Nothing but the courage and discipline of the command and the galling fire of the long-range rifles of the infantry saved it from complete destruction; and by every man who that day felt death's grip upon his throat, the little depression in which that terrible conflict took place is known as "The Valley of the Shadow of Death."

Indians thoroughly understand themselves and their white enemies. They have ample experience of the bulldog courage of our soldiers, and carefully avoiding its direct effect, rely for their success on the unruly, unbroken horses, and poor horsemanship of our cavalry. They know that repeated charges excite both horses and men, and expect to make their effective blow during the confusion and disintegration produced by that excitement.

In every plan of battle which they have had opportunity to arrange beforehand, provision is made for this hoped-for excitement. A huge trap had been arranged for Crook, which he only escaped by the recall of his cavalry.

So also in [General Nelson A.] Miles' last fight with "Crazy Horse," Indians who were there with "Crazy Horse" say that that chief had arranged an ambuscade on a grand scale, hoping and expecting to entrap Miles' whole force. He then sent a small body of about seventy-five young men with instructions to attack Miles, and after a sharp fight to retreat into the ambuscade. They made so good a fight that Miles did not feel disposed to follow up his victory, and thus escaped what "might have been" the fate of Custer.

Persons who remember the Indian fights of thirty years ago, and the easy work which Harney, Sumner, and other old officers of cavalry had in beating Indians, without regard to the numerical strength of the opposing forces, are very likely to draw inferences disparaging to the cavalry of the present day.

This is unjust. Our cavalry is as good to-day as it has ever been. The Indian has been metamorphosed. Before the Plains Indians obtained firearms, they were armed with bow and lance, and with these weapons were truly formidable, the fighting necessarily being almost hand-to-hand. But the Indian likes this close contest as little as anyone, and whenever he could procure a gun his more dangerous arms were discarded.

Thirty years ago, the rifle was little used by mounted Indians, as it could not be reloaded on horseback, but many of them were armed with guns of the most nondescript character, old Tower muskets, and smooth-bores of every antique pattern. Powder and lead were easily obtained from the traders. The former was carried in a horn, the latter was cut into pieces, which were roughly hammered into spherical form. These bullets were purposely made so much smaller than the bore of the gun as to run down when dropped into the muzzle. When going into a fight, the Indian filled his mouth with bullets. After firing he reloaded in full career, by turning up the powder-horn, pouring into his gun an unknown quantity of powder, and then spitting a bullet into the muzzle. There was very little danger to be apprehended from such weapons, so loaded, and the troops did not hesitate, even with the sabre alone, to rush on any odds of Indians.

Then came the revolver, which multiplied every soldier by six, and produced such an inspiring moral effect on the troops, and so entirely depressing an effect on the Indians, that the fights became simply chases, the soldiers attacking with perfect surety of success ten or twenty times their numbers.

After some years, the Indians began to obtain and use revolvers, and the fighting became more equal.

It remained, however, for the breech-loading rifle and metallic cartridges to transform the Plains Indian from an insignificant, scarcely dangerous adversary into as magnificent a soldier as the world can show. Already a perfect horseman, and accustomed all his life to the use of arms on horseback, all he needed was an accurate weapon, which could be easily and rapidly loaded while at full speed.

The Indian is inured from his cradle in all that goes to make a good soldier. In endurance of fatigue, hunger and pain, he has no superior; in patience and resource in difficulty or in danger he has scarcely an equal.

The United States cavalry soldier is enlisted for the short time of five years, and any able-bodied man is accepted, whether he has ever mounted a horse or not. His summers are spent in campaigning; his winters in getting his horse in condition for the next campaign. He has scarcely any mounted drill, for in summer he must save his horse for active work, and in winter the horse is unfit for it. He is building posts, stables, cantonments, driving a team or cutting fire-wood. He is "a hewer of wood and a drawer of water." That he can still contend with the Indian on anything like equal terms is his highest commendation, for the Indian is his superior in every soldier-like quality, except subordination to discipline, and indomitable courage.

The Indian and the old hunter or trapper of the Plains rarely came into collision. The latter was too cool and dangerous a customer to be attacked without due and careful preparation. Moreover, he was too poor to warrant the almost certain loss that must ensue to an attacking force. The Indians therefore contented themselves with watching his camp and stealing his hard-won peltries, his blankets and kettles, the first time he left them undefended.

The Indian's great delight is the attack of a wagon train. There is comparatively little risk, and his reward in ponies and plunder most ample. For days he will watch the slow-moving line, until he knows exactly the number and character of armed men that defend it. If their numbers or carelessness warrant a direct attack, he selects some place where the ground is unfavorable for corralling the wagons. Here he lies in wait, and at the proper time rushes out with terrifying yells, frightening the teams, which run away, overturning wagons, and throwing everything into confusion. Cool heads and steady hands are required at such moments, and if the whites fail in these their fate is soon decided.

If a direct attack involves too much risk, the Indian's next concern is to get possession of the horses and mules. He will follow the train for days, or even weeks, never seen, his presence never suspected. Lulled into false security, the white guardians become somewhat careless; the herd is permitted to wander too far from camp, or with a too slender guard. Like a thunderbolt from a clear sky the Indians rush into the herd with whoops and yells, scare it into stampede, and in a moment all disappear together.

One unaccustomed to Indian warfare would naturally suppose that cover, rocks, thickets, etc., would be the safest place for a small party attacked by an overwhelming force. Unless the thicket is large, no more fatal mistake can be made. In stealth, cunning and patience the Indian is the white man's superior. However closely the fugitive may hide himself, the Indians will find some means of getting at him without exposing themselves. His only hope is darkness, when the Indian's superstition renders him timid, and under its favorable cover he must put as many miles as possible between himself and that party of Indians.

A party of railroad surveyors at work on Lodge Pole Creek were suddenly attacked by a large force of Indians. One or two were killed, and the survivors took refuge in a dense thicket of sage brush, three or four feet high, and about one hundred and fifty yards in diameter. The thicket, though commanded by a bluff about two hundred yards off, was otherwise very favorably situated, the ground around it being smooth and bare, affording no cover. The whites had run in on the side nearest the bluff, and were congratulating themselves on their good position, when a pony carrying two warriors came at full speed across the open towards the farther side of the thicket. As he passed the edge the rearmost rider threw himself to the ground and crawled into the thicket. Another and another Indian was dropped in the same way, the whites firing at the flying horseman, but failing to hit, either from the speed, the distance, or from not daring to expose themselves sufficiently for a good shot. Several Indians, having got on the bluff, were harassing them with a hot fire, whilst these Indians who were dropped from the horses crawled into the thicket, and surrounded on three sides the wretched men. Scarcely moving a twig themselves, any movement of a bush by the whites was immediately followed by a shot. The protruded barrel of a rifle, or the exposure of the smallest portion of the person, was the target for a volley. When night came, three men, one wounded, stole out of the thicket and made their way to the nearest post, the only survivors of a party of eight or ten.

Another fatal mistake is to run away. It is a singular but well-established fact, that the mere act of running from an enemy has the tendency to demoralize the person running, and that even the bravest man under such circumstances is liable to "stampede" himself, or lose his head at the very time that all his coolness and judgment are most necessary. Riding furiously and without discretion, he will either throw his horse down by riding him into some ravine or hole, or tire him out so as to be easily overtaken. Fright has rendered the rider helpless, and he is killed without difficulty, or captured alive, to delight the women with his torture. I have known of one instance where a good plainsman, a citizen, who had been in several fights, a splendid rider and shot, became stampeded, and, when overtaken, stood quiet, pistol in hand, and allowed himself to be shot several times, and finally killed, without attempting the slightest defence.

A citizen, employed at Fort Dodge as herder, was one day out, fully armed, guarding the herd, when a small party of Indians dashed upon it. One attacked the herder, who turned his horse and rode direct for the garrison, but was overtaken and killed within two hundred yards of his quarters, without firing a shot.

The safest position for a small party is on a perfectly level plain without timber, rocks, holes, or other cover for an enemy, and large enough for the party to be well beyond fair shot from any ravine. If no such place can be got at, then take the nearest approach to it.

A good plainsman, when travelling with a small party on unknown ground, is always on the lookout for such favorable positions, and if "jumped" by Indians in bad ground be gets back to the last good place without loss of time, horse well in hand, going at a good round rate, but not running. These tactics are always adopted by the old trappers and hunters of the Plains, and by all plainsmen, old or new, who know Indians; and so well have the Indians come to understand it, that when they see two or three men take such a position, dismount, tie the legs of their horses, and sit down on the ground rifle in hand, they turn away and leave that party alone as "bad medicine." Of course, there are exceptions, when the Indians are very hostile, or the small party owns many and good horses; but these are only exceptions, and rare exceptions. The Indian does not want to be killed or wounded any more than a white man, and he thoroughly counts the cost of all risks. He knows how he himself fights when cornered; and his experience teaches him that the white will fight just as desperately and even more dangerously, and that an attack on a party so situated will probably cost more lives than the .scalps and horses of the party are worth. Besides, as I have elsewhere said, he lacks discipline and the courage that comes of discipline. He argues like a militiaman in presence of the enemy, who, being in line with a thousand other men, sees a hostile line a thousand strong advancing to the attack. "Heavens," thinks he, "what can I do against such a force?" and totally forgetting the thousand men in line with him, he incontinently takes to his heels, not from lack of courage but of discipline. The white soldier going into battle knows that many will be killed and wounded, but always expects that he himself will be lucky and escape unhurt. The disposition of the Indian is just the reverse; each thinks he is the one going to be hit, and every man of thirty or forty charging Indians will throw himself on the side of his horse on the presentation of a single rifle.

To the white defender such position is admirable, not only in affording no cover to the attack, but in bracing and steadying his own nerves. There is no chance of his stampeding himself; and a man is never so cool, nor fights so desperately, as when he has' made up his mind to live or die on one spot. Many a life has been saved by this simple proceeding, which would otherwise have been sacrificed. Sometimes the defenders get into a buffalo wallow. This is excellent, unless the ground be much broken by these depressions, in which case they can also be used, in the attack. If time be given the earth should be dug up with knives, and a rifle-pit be made. Even a very slight one is of immense advantage. I know of one successful defence against repeated and desperate charges of an overwhelming force, where the breastwork was the bodies of three live horses, thrown to the ground in a sort of triangle, and their legs firmly tied.

A frontier desperado, having committed a coldblooded murder at Hays City, was pursued by a party of whites and nearly overtaken. Stopping on a level prairie, he dismounted, drew his pistol, shot his horse dead, and, taking position under cover of the body, he killed and wounded three or four of his assailants, defended himself successfully until nightfall, and then escaped.

In 1867 I was with a party of officers elk-hunting on the Loup River. We had an escort of twelve or fifteen infantry soldiers, and six Pawnee Indians. We established our camp in a fine position, and each officer, taking one or more Indians, went hunting as it suited him. One day I was out with one Pawnee, and, not finding game, had ridden some twelve or fifteen miles from camp, when we were discovered by a band of between forty and fifty hostile Sioux, who immediately set upon us.

About four miles back I had noticed a splendid defensive position, one of the very best I have ever seen. Putting our horses at half speed we plunged into the *barrancas* of the "bad lands," and in half an hour emerged on the spot sought for. Here we dismounted and made our preparations for fight. The Pawnee positively refused to fight on foot, and when I was ready I found him ready also; not a rag of clothing on his body, and nothing but q, bridle on his horse. Prom some receptacle he had fished out a lot of narrow red, blue, and white ribbons, which he had tied in his hair, and in the mane and tail of his horse, and which, as he moved, streamed out for yards in the rear. Sitting perfectly naked, with unwonted ease and grace, on his barebacked horse, with fire in his eye, determination in his face, a Spencer carbine in one hand, the reins and a Colt's revolver in the other, he looked no mean ally in a fight for life. I had hardly time to admire his" get-up" when the whole plain in front seemed alive with yelling savages, charging directly down upon us. When they got within about two hundred and fifty yards I drew up my rifle; but before I could get an aim the whole band threw themselves on the sides of their horses and, swooping in circles like a flock of blackbirds, rushed back to the limit of the plain, about six hundred yards. Here they halted and held a consultation, and some of them, going off on the flanks, examined all the ground and approaches. Finding no line of attack except in front, they again essayed the charge, again to be sent to the rear by the mere raising of the rifle. This was again and again repeated with like result. Finally they withdrew beyond sight, and I wished to start; but the Pawnee said, "No, they will come again." They were absent for nearly an hour; I believe they were resting their horses. It was very hot, the whole affair was becoming very monotonous, and I was nodding, if not asleep, when the Pawnee said, "Here they come." I started up to And them within shot, and brought up my rifle; whereupon all ducked, wheeled, and went away as before, entirely out of sight. During all the charges the Pawnee had evinced the greatest eagerness for fight, and I had no little difficulty in keeping him by me whenever the enemy ran away after a charge. Answering yell for yell, he heaped upon them all the opprobrious epithets he could think of in English, Spanish, Sioux and Pawnee. When they wheeled and went off the last time, he turned to me with the most intense disgust and contempt, and said, emphatically, "Dam coward, Sioux! now go." So, after a four-hours' siege, we saddled our horses and returned to camp without molestation, but were followed the whole way; and from that time we had no sport or comfort in our hunt, the wretches preceding us by clay, driving away the game, and trying to burn us out every night; constantly making their unwelcome presence felt, and yet never giving us a chance for even a long shot at them.

In 1868, when crossing country with one cavalry orderly, I, on rising a little ridge, found myself within less than one hundred, yards of two Indians, who, going up the ravine at my feet, had just passed the position on which I was. Fortunately, it was a drizzly, disagreeable day, and they, having their heads covered up with their blankets, neither saw nor heard us. Waiting until they had got out of sight, I passed on a little distance, when I saw others and others, until I found that I was actually surrounded on three sides by parties of Indians, whose number I could not estimate. Several stopped and looked at us, then went on, evidently taking us for some of their own parties; and it was not until we had obtained a fair start for a high and level table-land which I knew of, about two miles off, that they discovered that we were whites. The alarm was given, and they came for us. My "orderly" being mounted on a mule, and the country being very rough and difficult, they had a great advantage in the race, and, on arriving at a good position on the plain, I had only time to loosen the girth, and tie my horse's head close down to his forefeet, when the whole yelling band appeared on the edge of the table-land. As soon as they saw my position they stopped, consulted, scattered, and, keeping well out of certain rifle range, went all around me looking for some ravine or other cover for a safe approach. Finding none, they returned to their first position, and had another consultation; after which they rode off in the direction they had come, and I saw no more of them. The whole affair, chase and siege, did not last over half an hour.

In 1871 I was changing stations from Fort Lyon to Fort Larned on the Arkansas, taking, of course, my servants and household property. I had several wagons and an ample infantry escort. About thirty miles west of Fort Dodge the wagon road crosses a portion of the high prairie called the "nine mile ridge." This high land is cut by several broad depressions, and towards the river broken by numberless little ravines—very favorable ground for antelope-hunting, and into these I, with my colored man-servant, was soon poking after game. It was a raw, foggy morning, and I had been hunting probably for two hours, when the fog lifted slightly, discovering two men on horseback about two hundred yards off, whom, as they had on overcoats, I took to be soldiers from Fort Dodge. As soon as they saw me, however, one of them rode the signal "danger," "collect together," and I began to think of my escort. Looking round I was greatly annoyed to find the spring wagon, in which was my colored cook, about six hundred yards from me, opposite the Indians, while the wagons and escort could not be seen. Making the best of the situation I galloped back to the spring wagon, had it driven well out into the plain, and the mules unhitched and well secured. The driver got out his rifle, and everything was satisfactory, except the presence of the cook. I not only feared she might be hit, but I knew the Indians would be more dangerous if a woman were likely to be a prize. Making her lie down in the bottom of the wagon, I packed around her lunch and other boxes, blankets, cushions, seats, everything that might stop a bullet, and gave her positive orders to remain perfectly quiet and concealed, no matter what took place. I then took position with my two men some paces on one side of the wagon, to spare it from shots. During all this time the Indians had been collecting, and, soon after I was ready, a line of about thirty moved slowly towards me. At about eight hundred yards they broke into a sharp canter. Expecting the charge to come in a moment, I went towards the wagon to be sure that the animals were tied safely, when, to my great indignation, I found Julia (the cook), revolver in hand, and her head thrust out of the front of the wagon. "Get back there," I angrily ordered; "do you want to be shot?" "Lord,

Colonel," she answered, "let me alone. I'll never have another chance to see an Indian fight." The earnestness of this, under the circumstances, most unexpected answer set all to laughing; and John, the husband, who a moment before was almost white with apprehension, regained, with good humor, his natural black. Every moment of delay being most important to us, I, when the Indians had got within about four hundred yards, stepped forward, made the Indian signal "Halt," and displayed a white handkerchief. To my great gratification they halted; and in a moment one came forward with what had once been a white flannel shirt, fastened to the pole of a lance. We met half way—I very friendly, he very gruff; I disposed to talk, he to be saucy. I asked the name of the tribe. He answered by demanding something to eat. I asked where they came from. He answered, "Powder, lead, sugar." We could not understand each other well, which I was rather thankful for, as it prolonged the talk. He wanted everything; and asked, not as a beggar, but demanded, as one having right. I am compelled to admit a certain amount of duplicity on this occasion, having, to gain time, promised things which I had no intention of performing.

The Indians had not seen the wagons, which were crossing one of the long depressions below the level of the Plain on which we were. They were sure of us, but preferred getting what we had without a fight if possible, especially as we had a good position. While we continued to talk I heard most welcome sounds, and, looking in that direction, saw the wagons coming at the full speed of the mules, while a line of "the boys in blue," rifle in hand, stretched at a run towards the spring wagon. I pointed them out to the Indian, and told him to go. He needed no second bidding, but rushed back to his party, which was in the greatest turmoil and confusion. I went back to the wagons, hitched up and started, the Indians holding a consultation.

As I regained the road the chief came to me with the flannel shirt flag. He was very much grieved. "I had deceived them. They could have killed us and taken everything we had before the troops came up. They did not kill us, because I promised to give them what they wanted; therefore I must give them all I promised. He wanted to go with his young men and sleep in my camp that night, that I might give them plenty to eat, and powder, lead, and other things I promised." I told him that he and his party were robbers and murderers; that he must go away; and that if he or any of them came near my march or my camp I would kill them. He left me and rode slowly back to his men, the most disgusted-looking Indian I ever saw. We went our way, leaving the band sitting in a circle on the ground, evidently discussing in no amiable frame of mind the outrage that had been perpetrated on them.

A very common mistake, and one especially easy to fall into when armed with a modern improved breech-loading rifle, is in firing too soon. In the "good old times" of muzzle-loading, the man who fired a shot without sure death to his enemy was very likely to "go under" himself. The Indian has great respect for a loaded, but none for an empty, rifle. He knows the value of nerve, and fully appreciates the dangerous character of the man who can refrain from firing until he has a sure shot. He is particularly susceptible to what is called "moral effect." Shots whistling harmlessly by his ears tend to encourage him, while the fall of a single man or horse will sometimes send a very determined band to the right-about.

A very curious custom of war among some of the Plains tribes is called "giving the coup."]o satisfactory explanation has been given as to how the custom originated, but I think it was probably introduced to prevent quarrels among warriors over the scalps of their fallen enemies, to an Indian the most valuable of all possessions. The name indicates that the custom obtained in the days of the old French trappers, predecessors of the Hudson Bay Company.

When a foe has fallen in a fight, the scalp belongs to that warrior who shall first strike the body with a weapon. Formerly it was required that it should be a deadly weapon, as a knife or tomahawk, but at the present day the blow is struck with a stick. This blow is the "coup," and the weapon is called the "coup-stick," and is an indispensable article in the outfit of a warrior going to battle.

These sticks are as varied as the taste and fancy of the owners. Some are merely slender wands, six to ten feet long; others are short and club-like, or shaped conveniently for throwing. All are ornamented with paint, feathers, porcupine-quills, beadwork, or furs.

Even among members of the same tribe, a blow with a "coup-stick" is an insult and disgrace only to be wiped out with blood.

In his celebrated winter campaign against the Sioux, General Crook had, as auxiliaries, about three hundred and fifty Indians of various tribes and bands, among them a considerable number of Sioux and four companies of Pawnees, these latter drilled and disciplined like soldiers. I have elsewhere spoken of the unrelenting hatred of these tribes each to the other. One day when the Pawnees were quietly marching along the road in formal ranks, and the Sioux were careering in individual freedom over the prairie, a young Sioux warrior rode up to the ranks, and to signalize at once his hatred to the tribe, and his contempt for Indians who would march in ranks, struck one of the Pawnees with his "coup-stick." In an instant, half-a-dozen revolvers were presented, and the Sioux would have paid for his temerity then and there but that the Pawnee discipline was so excellent that a word from the officer restrained them. That night, the Pawnee who had been struck went to Major North, the commander of all the Pawnees, told him with sobs of the disgrace that had been put upon him, and begged to be permitted to kill his assailant. This was of course refused, but Major North made such representation of the matter to General Crook, that the Sioux were thereafter effectually restrained from such little eccentricities.

The loss of his "coup-stick" in battle is to the Indian warrior a misfortune second only to the loss of his "medicine," and nothing short of a wound or the loss of his horse will save the loser from a certain amount of contempt.

In a fight, when an enemy falls, all those warriors in the vicinity rush for the body, each exerting every effort to be the first to strike it, those in rear hurling their "coup-sticks" at long distances in the hope of a fortunate strike. The instant a strike is made, the other warriors pick up their "coup-sticks," and go on with the fight, leaving the lucky striker to secure his scalp at his leisure.

If in a melee or running fight, a warrior kills an enemy, he must, to secure the proper recognition and reward, rush at once on the prostrate body, and strike his "coup" regardless of other enemies who may be at hand. This of course renders the Indian less formidable.

The enemy being in full flight, a brave and skilful warrior who would press on and on, adding victim after victim to his list, would return at last to find the scalps of all the enemies slain by his hands at the girdles of laggards in the race, to each of whom would be accorded all the honors due to one who had killed his man. While he who took all risks and did all the killing, and who in his eagerness to kill, may have passed even the last of his victims, has nothing whatever to show for his skill and gallantry, and is consequently without claim to honor or credit, the cowardly shirks, far in the rear, collect his scalps, and gain all the glory and applause. The consequence is, that when a foe falls, the slayer, even in the hottest race, and though other enemies are in his power, must, to obtain the proper recognition of his act, at once give up all thought of further killing, make his "coup," and take the scalp. It can readily be seen that this custom is entirely to the advantage of the fugitives, and accounts, in some measure, for so few Indians being killed in their fights among themselves.

A great deal of unnecessary sympathy has been wasted by the philanthropic world on the killing of squaws in battle. As a rule, no woman is hurt except by accident, or when fighting like a man. In the surprise and attack of an Indian village, when all is excitement, and bullets are flying in pursuit of every flying enemy, women and children are often killed and wounded. Women and children were killed at Gettysburg, and this is to be expected if combats take place where women and children are.

Even in the surprise of the most sudden attack, the squaws who cannot get away are prompt to make their sex known, holding up their hands and yelling "squaw," "squaw" and even in the excitement and thirst for blood engendered by battle, I have never heard of a woman being killed by any soldier of the regular army.

Many of the middle-aged and old women handle arms with great facility and address, and it is not at all uncommon for women to go on the "war-path" as warriors, armed and dressed as men.

Even when not so acting, the dress and mode of riding of men and women are so very similar, that in conflicts and pursuits on horseback, squaws are not unfrequently killed. This is and must remain unavoidable.

Among themselves Indians are not quarrelsome. Fisticuffs are unknown, and fights with weapons extremely rare. If an Indian has made up his mind to kill an enemy, he generally resorts to treachery, shoots him from an ambuscade, or assassinates him in any most convenient and safe way.

Personal conflicts are therefore almost always entirely unpremeditated. When a quarrel between two Indians has become so bitter that physical force is resorted to, each flies at the other, assailing him with whatever weapon he can first procure.

The formal duel is a peculiarly Christian institution, growing out of the supposed direct interference of God in behalf of the right. It was introduced into legal and religious trials, among Europeans, between the sixth and eighth centuries.

I have never found any account of the duel as an institution among any race or people except Christians. I was therefore greatly surprised to find on apparently excellent authority an account of a formal duel between two Sioux. I have made inquiries of numerous Indians of many tribes, especially Sioux, none of whom had ever known or ever heard of any such custom, nor even of a single case. I must therefore conclude either that these Sioux were "following the white man's road," that is, doing as they had seen white men do, or that Mr. Belden was drawing on his imagination.

ARMY LIFE ON THE PLAINS

THE history of the Army of the United States is a history of the territorial expanse of our country.

Bold and determined as were the bands of stalwart pioneers, who, reckless of personal danger, pushed far beyond the extremest limits of the called frontiers, they could have done e towards the advancement of that frontier, but for other bands, scarcely stronger numerically, but bound together by a bond stronger than iron, more impervious than the rock: discipline.

The history of the colonies is a record of conflict, and while the Republic was yet in its swaddling-clothes, those of its citizens most remote from the centres of wealth and power have been constantly confronted with a foe, acute, wily, and terrible, not only in his destructive force, hut in his vindictive energy of action.

Wild and free, burning for an opportunity for personal distinction, the Indian of each tribe came to look upon every man, not of that tribe, as his personal and tribal enemy. The settlement of strangers either white or red, upon lands claimed by that tribe was an invasion and an insult; and the interlopers were at once enemies, unless they had properly purchased the right to be there, either by presents, or by marriage with its women.

Men who had once tasted the sweets of solitude, freedom, or "elbow-room" as they called it, became so infatuated with it as to be impatient of crowding even by one of similar tastes and habits settled twenty miles away. This appears an exaggeration, but having witnessed its outcropping in most vindictive form on many occasions, and even within a year of this writing, I can personally vouch for the existence of the feeling among a class of frontiersmen.

Naturally the Indians felt this crowding even more than the pioneers, and they continually resented it. Isolated as were the whites they could have effected no permanent lodgment in the country of the savages, but for the small bodies of troops, which, locating themselves in advance, held the Indians in check, and became rallying-points in times of danger; nuclei of towns when that danger passed.

Since the establishment of our government, the army has been the bulwark of civilization; the rock on which the forces of barbarism were shattered and expended. Making amends for its deficiency in numbers by the most admirable discipline and indomitable courage, it has for a hundred years stood like a wall of adamant between the weak and scattered settlements and the savage foe; giving a continent to civilization and rendering possible an immigration unequalled in the history of the world.

Ever surrounded by overwhelming numbers of active and treacherous enemies; ever keeping a watchful eye on the safety of the settlements behind it; the army has ever been the real pioneer. At one time cheerfully undergoing hardships and privations; at another, manfully baring its breast to the shock of unequal battle; now by dint of pure manhood winning victories from overwhelming hordes of savages; now going down to deaths as heroic as those of the three hundred at Thermopylae.

About twelve P.M. of the night of the 26th November, 1868, Custer discovered on the banks of the Washita River, the camp of hostile Cheyennes under Black Kettle. Having no intention of attacking before daylight he had ample time to arrange his plan of action. He divided his command into four nearly equal parts. Retaining one, he sent the others to take positions on the other three sides of the enemy. Relying on the intelligent obedience to orders of the officers commanding the several columns, he, just in the gray of the morning, gave the concerted signal, and from four sides the troops dashed upon the startled enemy, completely surrounding the camp.

In a few moments the camp itself was in possession of the troops, but the undaunted savages, taking refuge behind trees and in ravines, maintained for several hours a desperate conflict.

Taking advantage of the cover of thick brush, some of the warriors mounted their ponies, and bursting through a weak part of the line of environing troops, escaped to the prairie. Major Elliott, who commanded one of the attacking columns, saw the act, and calling to some of his men dashed off in pursuit of the fugitives.

Neither he nor anyone of the nineteen men who accompanied him was ever again seen alive by any white man. The story of their fate was told by the position in which their bodies were found, and by the Indians themselves when the war was over.

Black Kettle's camp was the upper one of a series of camps of five different tribes of hostile savages, which extended for many miles along the river, and contained not less than three thousand fighting men.

The sounds of the attack on Black Kettle aroused the nearest camp; the alarm spread down the river with the speed of the swiftest ponies. While the old men and the women gathered up the ponies and the property, the fighting men poured out of the camps fully armed and equipped, and rushed to the assistance of Black Kettle.

Intent on his pursuit, and not suspecting the vicinity of other camps or Indians, Major Elliott suddenly found his little party entirely surrounded by an overwhelming horde of enemies who attacked him on all sides.

Dismounting, loosing their horses and forming in a circle, the little band of twenty brave men prepared to sell their lives as dearly as possible. Brave as they were, the contest was too unequal to be prolonged. In less than twenty minutes every man but one was dead.

Wounded in several places, his ammunition expended, Sergeant-Major Kennedy stood alone, sabre in hand, surrounded by the crowd of exulting savages. No shot was fired at him, no effort was made to kill him, but several of the Indians approached him with hands thrust out. "How?" "How?"

Too well he knew the meaning of this kindly demonstration! Merciful death had overtaken all his gallant comrades. He was to be reserved for all the horrors of the torture. In his prolonged agonies were his enemies to find consolation for the injuries the troops had inflicted upon them.

Realizing all, he saw that his only hope of escaping torture was in so exasperating the Indians that they would kill him at once. Seeming to surrender, he advanced towards the chief. They approached each other, hands extended. Quick as thought Kennedy's sword passed through the chief's body. One instant of terrified surprise on the part of the Indians; the next, twenty bullet-holes in Kennedy's body.

The merciful death had come to him.

The bodies of these brave men were subsequently found just where they died, in a circle of not over twenty yards in diameter.

I might multiply such instances of cool courage and undaunted heroism, until they would make a volume of themselves, but grateful as is the task of recording such noble deeds, I will leave it to other pens.

In a previous chapter I have noted the peculiarities of Indian fighting at different epochs, resulting from the difference in the weapons with which they were armed.

These prove that Indian does not differ from civilized warfare, in that, within certain limits, the shorter the effectiveness of the weapon, the more destructive it is to the life of the combatants. When soldiers were armed only with sword or pike, the shock of battle was a continuous succession of single combats, in which one of the combatants must of necessity be killed or disabled, or must run away. This accounts for the terrible destruction of life as set forth in the battles of the Bible, and in the profane histories of the earlier nations. When the Indian was armed with bow and lance, his fighting to be effective must be almost hand to hand, and the loss correspondingly great. Since they have procured arms effective at long distances, the destruction of life in battle is comparatively insignificant, and a "dead" Indian, an object most rare to see.

When fighting Indians, the officers of the army are exceptions to the comparative immunity from danger, consequent in civilized warfare, on the use of the long-range weapons. In "the good old times" of impetuous charges on horseback, the officer took his chance with the private soldier. Now, crouched behind rocks in almost inaccessible positions, the Indians (the very best skirmishers in the world) coolly pick off the officers of the attacking force. The reports of the battles and combats of the last ten years will show a loss of officers, in comparison to the loss of men, unprecedented in warfare.

As an example of the "old style" of Indian fighting I give a short sketch of the battle of White Stone Hill, between the United States forces, about one thousand strong, under General Sully, and a combination of Sioux and Blackfeet, numbering not less than twelve or fifteen hundred warriors.

In 1862-3, the Sioux Indians, taking advantage of the terrible intestine conflict in which the United States were engaged, and the consequent withdrawal of the troops from their country, had broken out with great violence, committing on the exposed and helpless settlers all the outrages and horrors known to savage warfare. When this could no longer be borne, two expeditions were sent against them, the first of which encountering the Indians, was easily beaten out of their country. The second, under General Sully, moved northward between the Missouri and James rivers, keeping strong detachments scouting in front and flank in the hope of discovering the main camp of Indians.

On the 3d of September, 1863, a battalion of the Sixth Iowa Cavalry, three hundred strong, under Major House, being some distance in advance, discovered a large camp of not less than four hundred lodges. A courier was sent in all haste to General Sully, Major House and his command watching the Indians.

General Sully reports, "Starting off with the Second Nebraska on the right, the Sixth Iowa on the left, one company of the Seventh Iowa and the battery in the centre, at a full gallop, we made the distance of over ten miles in much less than an hour."

On approaching the camp General Sully found the Indians leaving with such things as they could carry. The troops were sent to the right and left at full speed with orders to charge, surround and drive the Indians to their camp, in the hope of capturing all. In a few moments the whole force was furiously engaged, every man fighting "on his own hook." In every direction and far into the night the battle raged.

Fearing the most serious results from the scattering of his command, the general "ordered all the buglers to sound the 'rally,' and building large fires, remained under arms all night, collecting my men." At daylight next morning it was discovered that the Indians had decamped, leaving their dead and wounded, their camps and property of all kinds. "The camps of the Indians together with the country all around, was covered with their plunder."

This was the most severe blow that the Sioux had ever received. They lost about one hundred killed and wounded, one hundred and fifty-six prisoners, thirty-two men, and one hundred and twenty-four women and children, three hundred lodges, "four o: five hundred thousand pounds of dried buffalo meat," not less than a thousand ponies, and "a very large quantity of other property very valuable to the Indians." General Sully's loss was twenty killed and thirty-eight wounded.

This battle is, on a grand scale, a most admirable exemplification of the usual mode and general results of Indian fights in "the good old days" when the troops were armed with rifle and revolver, the Indians with bows or old smooth-bore muskets, down the barrel of which the bullets or slugs were spit from the mouth. Those days are over. An officer who would now attack even half his force of Indians with troops broken or scattered, and horses pumped by a ten-mile dash at full speed, would be very soon sent to the "Happy Hunting-grounds," with all his command.

ARMY EXPERIENCES ON THE FRONTIER

ON the 21st December, 1867, occurred near Fort Phil. Kearney the terrible battle commonly known as the "Phil. Kearney massacre," no white man being left to tell the tale of unsuccessful heroism. The whites were annihilated, but the Indian victory of overwhelming numbers was dearly bought by a loss in killed and wounded of more than four times the number of their gallant adversaries. The news of this terrible disaster sent a thrill of horror through the whole country. Active measures were at once taken by the War Department to wipe out this blot on its escutcheon by summary punishment of the enemy. Heavy reinforcements and ample supplies were immediately ordered to the beleaguered remnant of the garrison at Fort Phil. Kearney.

In this battle the Indians had not only the advantage of overwhelming numbers, but many of them were armed with Spencer and Winchester carbines. Our cavalry were armed with the Spencer carbines and revolvers, but the infantry had only the muzzle-loading rifled musket.—The original author is making the point that the Indians had repeating rifles and the army had single-shot carbines and muzzle-loaders. However, the Spencers would have had the advantage of better accuracy at range.—Ed. 2015

But just here came in the hitch absolutely unavoidable in a dual government.

The War Department wants peace, and thoroughly understanding the Indian character, knows that peace is impossible unless compelled by fear. The Indian Department wants peace, impelled thereto by a humanitarianism that pays best in times of peace. Having ready access to the ear and heart of every true philanthropist and Christian, who, knowing Indian wrongs, would gladly right them, it had power sufficient to suspend the warlike preparations and send out a commission to make peace with the enemy.

After great difficulty a treaty of peace was concluded on the basis of the abandonment of the posts on the Montana road, and great store of presents to the Indians.

As might naturally have been anticipated, the treaty thus concluded suspended hostilities only during the time it was in progress. The chiefs who had made the treaty were denounced by their followers in unmeasured terms.

Red Cloud, until this time a sub-chief of no special standing, seized the opportunity and declared war to the knife against the white man. The disaffected of all tribes and bands flocked to him; chiefs even of prominence being, in order to retain control of their bands, obliged to acknowledge his leadership.

Everywhere harassing trains and moving columns, he so interrupted communication, and was so uniformly successful in his attacks, that, emboldened by success, he determined on the utter destruction of the permanent garrisons. Fort Phil. Kearney, having already received so severe a blow, was selected for the first effort. Over this post he exercised the most watchful guardianship. Not a stick of wood or load of hay could be cut for the use of the garrison without the chance of a conflict.

By the end of July, 1867, he had collected a host of not less than three thousand fighting men, and with these advanced on the doomed Fort, so confident of victory that he was accompanied by great numbers of women to assist in carrying off the plunder.

But among the supplies which the post had received during the temporary suspension of hostilities, was a glorious weapon, never before in the hands of our infantry soldiers, the breech-loading rifle-musket, combining extreme long range and accuracy, with hitherto unknown rapidity of fire.

On the 31st day of July, 1867, in obedience to an order of the post commander, Captain and Brevet-Major James Powell, Twenty-seventh Infantry, with his company, consisting of himself, one lieutenant, and fifty-one enlisted men, proceeded to a place called Piney Island, about five miles from Fort Phil. Kearney, for the purpose of escorting and furnishing details to protect the laboring-parties engaged by Contractor J. P. Porter, in hauling fuel to the post. "Upon my arrival at the above-named place I found the train divided; one part encamped on a plateau, and with one exception, the position well selected for defence, and the best security that the country afforded for the stock; the other part was encamped about one mile distant in a south-westerly direction, on a commanding point across the Little Piney Creek, at the foot of the mountains. My details consisted in sending twelve men to protect the working parties of both trains, and thirteen men as escort to the trains when coming into the post."

The two encampments, while greatly facilitating the labor of the contractor, seriously complicated the problem of defence by so small a force. Major Powell wisely concluded to attempt the defence of but the one on the plateau.

Wagon-bodies of boiler-iron sufficiently thick to withstand a rifle-bullet had been furnished by the Quartermaster's Department to some of the most exposed frontier posts. I cannot assert positively that the sixteen wagon-bodies forming Major Powell's defensive work were of iron, but the disposition made of them by him, and the statement that they were loop-holed," is sufficient evidence that they were so. Indeed, the few casualties can be accounted for under no other hypothesis, the thin sides of an ordinary wooden wagon-bed offering to a bullet scarcely more resistance than paper.

Be that as it may, fourteen of these beds were lifted from the wheels and arranged as compactly as possible in a circle, the intervals between the ends of each two being filled with ox-bows, chains, logs, grain-sacks, clothing, anything that might stop a bullet. That side of this fortified corral most exposed to the assault of mounted men, was further strengthened by two such beds on the wheels, placed a little distance in front, which, while permitting the defenders to fire under them at an advancing foe, prevented an assailant from dashing in on horseback, and getting a plunging fire into the wagon-beds on the ground.

Major Powell had arms and ammunition not only for his company, but sufficient to supply all the citizen-workmen of the contractor, and all were laid out ready for instant use. This was the stronghold, the citadel. Here the guards maintained unceasing watch, and to this place of security every man, soldier or workman was ordered to fly in case of attack.

"About nine o'clock in the morning of August 2d, 1867, two hundred Indians attacked the herders in charge of the herd, driving them off; at the same time five hundred attacked the train at the foot of the mountain, driving off the men belonging there and burning it."

This attack coming suddenly, and as it were from between the two encampments, drove the guards and workmen up the side of the mountain, effectively separating them from Major Powell and the stronghold. These men and all the citizens working near the corral, except four, unable to comply with the orders to concentrate on Major Powell, took to their heels and made their way back to the fort, losing in this manoeuvre three soldiers and several citizens.

All the attention of the enemy was now concentrated upon the corral.

In the meantime Major Powell had completed his arrangements for the defence. The men were distributed all around the circle, lying down in the wagon-beds, and to confuse and disconcert the enemy, these beds were covered with blankets, thus entirely concealing the defenders.

"Some fifteen minutes afterwards," says Major Powell, "I was surrounded by about eight hundred mounted Indians, but, owing to the very effective fire of my small party, they were driven back with considerable loss."

But it is not in the words of a cold and almost unnaturally modest official report that the heroism of these thirty-two men can be described. Two officers, twenty-six private soldiers and four citizens, lay quiet in their improvised defences, awaiting the onslaught of unknown numbers of a brave and merciless foe, with perfect certainty that nothing but a merciful bullet, or their own cool heads, brave hearts, and steady nerves, stood between them and death by the most exquisite torture.

Elsewhere, I have stated that a man never fights so coolly and well as when he has made up his mind to live or die on one spot. Major Powell and his handful of noble men had made up their minds.

With a contempt of their adversaries begot of many victories, eight hundred magnificently mounted warriors dash fearlessly upon their apparently insignificant foe. Everywhere they are met with bullets; the leaders fall, others take their places, and though they ride directly on to the defences, they can get no sight of the defenders. Nothing is to be seen but the blanket-covered wagon-beds, but from these comes a blaze of accurate and continuous fire, before which the bravest and best go down until, utterly amazed and discomfited, the broken host whirls in confusion to the hills.

From the plateau on which the corral was located, the ground rises gradually in every direction, culminating, at from six hundred to a thousand yards, in low hills. During the conflict this magnificent amphitheatre was crowded with spectators, thousands of Indians swarming into view, watching the combat with the greatest interest.

Astounded and disconcerted by the unexpected and incomprehensible defeat of the attack, and realizing the absolute necessity of present success to the hoped-for final issue of the campaign, Red Cloud and his principal chiefs had a hurried consultation, and decided on an immediate attack with the whole force of Indians on foot.

Indian preparation for combat consisting in simply stripping himself of everything except his arms and ammunition, the arrangements were soon complete. Many of the warriors who were armed with Spencer or Winchester carbines, or muskets taken in the Phil. Kearney massacre, were sent in advance as skirmishers and sharpshooters. Crawling along ravines or covering themselves with shields of buffalo hide and bunches of grass, these men approached to within easy range and opened so terrible a concentric fire upon the corral, as must in a few moments have destroyed the defenders, except on the hypothesis that the wagon-beds were bullet proof.

Rut during this interval Major Powell had not been idle. His Lieutenant, Jenness, gallantly, and as he thought necessarily, exposing himself during the first attack, had been killed; one or two men had been killed or wounded, and the attack had developed certain weak points of his defences, which

All of this description which properly belongs to the Indian side, I obtained from a Sioux chief, who was severely wounded in the fight, and from other warriors, both Sioux and Cheyennes, who were in the battle were promptly strengthened with whatever was at hand. The firing was so rapid that the gun-barrels became overheated; spare guns were placed in each wagon-bed. Some of the men were poor shots and fired wildly; they were ordered not to fire, but to load and pass guns to the selected marksmen.

Before the crack of the first rifle of an Indian sharpshooter had signalled the grand attack, Powell was ready. From all sides these sharpshooters approached, slowly, covering themselves as best they could, and delivering a terrible and continuous fire. When they had arrived within easy range, the defenders of the corral opened a fire so searching and accurate that further advance was impossible.

But now from the hills swarmed a semicircle of warriors at least two thousand strong, under the leadership of the gallant young nephew of Red Cloud, anxious to signalize his valor, and to win the right to succeed his uncle as Head chief. When within about five hundred yards, the order to charge was given, and the whole line dashed on to the corral, to be, when they had almost touched it, hurled back in confusion and dismay. Again and again did the gallant line rally and charge, only to be again broken, discomfited and driven back; and it was only after "three continuous hours" of almost superhuman effort against this unseen, intangible foe, that the line became utterly demoralized, and fled in consternation to the hills.

Red Cloud and some of the older of his principal chiefs had watched the whole action. For a long time they thought the wonderfully continuous fire was clue to the fact that there were more men in the corral than it would appear to hold; but on the final repulse of the long succession of desperate charges, they concluded that the white man had made some "medicine guns" which would "fire all the time" without the aid of human hands, and that their best plan was to stop the conflict.

When the demoralized host had reached the safety of the hills, they were ordered not to fight anymore, but to recover the bodies of the killed and wounded. A cloud of skirmishers were sent out to cover this operation, with orders to keep up a continuous fire. All the killed and wounded nearest the hills were soon taken to the rear and cared for, but to recover those nearer to the corral was exceedingly difficult and dangerous. Taking one end of a long rope, formed by tying together many lariats, a warrior ran out into the open as far as he dared, then throwing himself on the ground and covering himself with a shield of thick buffalo hide, he crawled to the nearest dead or wounded man and fastened the rope around his ankles. The men in the woods at the other end of the rope then pulled on it, and dragged the man or body to a safe place. The rescuing warrior then crawled backward, protected by his shield.

While they were yet removing their dead and wounded, Major Smith arrived on the battle-field with reinforcements from the fort.

After the terrible reverses of the day, the Indians had no stomach for more fighting. They withdrew into the woods. Major Smith relieved the gallant garrison of the corral and took it with him back to the Fort. The Indians remained a day or two on the ground, caring for their wounded and burying their dead; then returned to their camp, dazed and overwhelmed. Having no knowledge of breech-loading muskets or iron wagon-beds, they attributed their failure to' the direct action of the Bad God. To this day this is the "Medicine fight" of the Sioux and Cheyennes. They refer to it in tones of awe and with "bated breath," as they speak of the occasional terrible visitations of cholera; a something incomprehensible; a horror without a name.

The loss of troops in the attack on the corral was one officer and two private soldiers killed and two private soldiers wounded. The Indian loss can never be positively known. Major Smith's relieving force numbered scarce a hundred men; and when he saw the overwhelming force of Indians, he readily comprehended, not only that it was suicidal to attack them, but that discretion and good soldiership required him to retire from so dangerous a neighborhood as promptly as possible, and before the Indians should recover from the first shock of their disaster. Gathering up the dead and wounded, the arms and ammunition, and taking the little band of heroic defenders, he left for the Fort. No time was taken to attempt to count the Indian dead. Roughly estimating the number of dead bodies lying immediately around the corral, Major Powell officially reported that he thought "there were not less than sixty killed and one hundred and twenty wounded." This was an excess of modesty, every other man in the fight estimating the number of

Indians killed at between three and four hundred. When it is remembered that from Major Powell's own statement between two and three thousand Indians charged, and continued "to charge us on foot for three continuous hours," that in these charges the Indians approached until they could almost touch the defences; that during all that time the loopholed wagon-beds were a blaze of continuous fire froth breech-loading rifles, even the last estimate seems too small.

The wounded Sioux chief who visited my post at North Platte, late in the fall of 1867, told me that the number of Indians in the fight was over three thousand, and that a prominent "medicine man" of the Sioux had told him that the total loss in killed and wounded of Indians of all tribes and bands in that fight was eleven hundred and thirty-seven. If this be true, the combatants were as one white to one hundred Indians; the losses, one white to two hundred and sixty-eight Indians.

It is like a story of the time of Cortez

One of the citizens who fought with Powell was a grizzled old trapper, who had spent his life on the frontier, and been in Indian fights without number. Some months after the battle, the Department Commander met and questioned him.

"How many Indians were in the attack," asked the General.

"Wall, Gin'r'l, I can't say for sartin, but I think thur wus nigh onto three thousand uv'em."

"How many were killed and wounded?"

"Wall, Gin'r'l, I can't say for sartin, but I think thur wur nigh onto a thousand ov'em hit."

"How many did you kill?"

"Wall, Gin'r'l, I can't say, but gi'-me a dead rest, I kin hit a dollar at fifty yards every time, and I fired with a dead rest at more'n fifty of them varmints inside of fifty yards."

"For Heaven's sake, how many times did you fire?" exclaimed the astonished General.

"Wall, Gin'r'l, I can't say, but I kept eight guns pretty well het up for mor'n three hours."

No such fight with Indians can ever again occur. Even before this time the Indians had breech-loaders, but they had had no experience of the terrible destructive power of these weapons, in the hands of cool and determined men protected by breastworks. At the present time nothing would induce even a hundred Indians to charge three or four whites, though protected only by a slight rifle-pit.

This may be called a "transition" fight. The Indian was just emerging from his scarcely dangerous days of bows and muzzle-loaders, and procuring an arm suited to his mode of fighting, becoming what he now is, the finest natural soldier in the world.

MACKENZIE'S FIGHT WITH THE CHEYENNES

SINCE this wonderful and most memorable battle of "Piney Island," or, as it is known to the army "Powell's fight," the conflicts between Indians and United States troops have presented a remarkable sameness. The strength of the Indian is in surprises or ambuscades, and I have heard of no single instance of his acceptance of battle in the open field, except as preliminary to some huge trap, or when relying on overwhelming preponderance of force. His tactics are always the same; never to receive a charge, but by constantly breaking, to separate the enemy into detached fragments; then suddenly concentrating to overwhelm these in detail. Having no trains or impediments of any kind, he is always able to avoid battle if the ground or opportunity does not suit him. The heavier slowly-moving troops, encumbered with trains of supplies, must attack when they can, and therefore almost always at disadvantage. Since the common use of breechloaders by both combatants, I know of no single instance where troops have gained any signal advantage over Indians in open fight, and this for the reason that the moment they gain even a slight advantage, the Indians disappear with a celerity that defies pursuit. On the other hand, if the Indians gain the advantage, they press it with a most masterful vigor, and there results a massacre, which, like that of Custer's command, for a moment appalls the country.

Fighting under these terrible disadvantages, the troops have learned to supplement courage with craft. The only really telling blow that can now be struck at Indians is a blow at their encampment; not that many are killed, but that to save their lives they are obliged to abandon their tepees and property. At present, therefore, a campaign against hostile Indians consists in warily marching into their territory and searching in every direction for their home encampment. If this can be surprised and destroyed, the Indians soon surrender, even though they may have lost few warriors killed and wounded.

To effect this "check-mate" it is absolutely necessary that the Indians should be entirely unaware of the near vicinity of the troops, and that all movements be made with the greatest care and circumspection; for even with their women and children, tepees and property, Indians can usually move faster than troops can follow. This entails upon the troops hardships and privations harassing in the extreme. Marches must be made at night; fires cannot be built in the day time for fear of the tell-tale smoke, and in the night only in the secluded depths of thickets and ravines, and then but for time sufficient to cook the scanty ration.

Since the inauguration, by General Crook, of the use of Indian allies in Indian warfare, these privations and hardships are materially lessened. Singly, or in bands of two, three, or more, these sleuth-hounds scatter far and wide, miles in advance and on the flanks of the troops. If a trail or other indication of hostiles is discovered, report is sent back to the commander, and the troops halted until the scouts can work up the position of the camp, when a night march is made, and the telling blow struck.

In a work of this kind, I am not expected even to give the names of the almost numberless, desperate and well-fought battles of the last ten years. I select for illustration, Mackenzie's battle with the Northern Cheyennes, not only as typical of the present state of Indian warfare, but because with little loss of life on either side, it crushed the bravest tribe of Indians on this continent.

When, in 1875, the Indian Bureau determined to remove all the so-called Powder-River Indians to Reservations, there was at once a furor of excitement among all the tribes and bands interested. Runners were sent from band to band, councils were held, and it was determined to brave the whole power of the United States rather than yield their independence or lose their beloved hunting-grounds.

In these councils the Cheyennes, though few in numbers, were conspicuous for their bitter hostility, and for their expressed determination to die on the field of battle rather than surrender a single foot of their lands. A coalition was formed between the Cheyennes and many bands of the great Dakotah or Sioux nation. Immense camps were formed for drill and mutual protection.

The traders of the Northern frontier were over-run with applications for the best arms and ammunition, and so determined were the Indians on the possession of these necessities to successful warfare, that in many instances a first-class, well-tanned buffalo robe was offered in barter for three metallic cartridges. At such prices, they, of course, very soon obtained a supply sufficiently ample to carry them through several campaigns.

The result of the grand Indian combination is well-known. Battles were fought whenever the Indians wished to fight. A few small bands were surprised and defeated, marches and counter-marches were made, great hardships endured by the ever patient and obedient little army, but though two arduous campaigns had been made, the balance of practical advantage was rather with the Indians.

The combination failed, not from the valor and sufferings of the troops, but through the genius, courage, and persistency of one man, who, having learned his lesson in the hard school of experience, dared, in spite of the wails of humanitarians, to adopt the Roman method, and fight fire with fire.

The Commander of the Department of the Platte enlisted large numbers of friendly Indians, and placed them under the command of white officers. These, acting in conjunction with the troops, so beleaguered the hostile savages, that their combination was soon broken up. Sitting Bull retired to the British possessions, the Cheyennes to their fastnesses in the foot-hills of the Elk Horn mountains. Crazy Horse alone maintained his ground in the heart of the Powder River country.

Late in the fall of 1876, General Crook marched from Fort Fetterman at the head of the most formidable force that has been sent against Indians for many years: eleven companies of cavalry under Mackenzie; four of artillery (armed and equipped as infantry) and eleven of infantry, under my command; and three hundred and fifty picked Indians, representing no less than five tribes, all under white officers. His objective was Crazy Horse, but on reaching the Crazy Woman's Fork of Powder River, it was learned through spies, that that astute chieftain had, either through prudence or sheer good luck, moved his camp to a position which might only be surprised by a long retrograde and round-about march.

The Cheyennes were known to be somewhere in the foot-hills, not far from Crook's position, and that General turned his attention to them. The Indian allies searched assiduously for their camp, and finally discovered it without being themselves discovered. On the 23d November Mackenzie, with seven hundred picked cavalry and the whole of the Indian allies, marched for the Cheyenne camp. On the 24th, being within striking distance, he halted to wait for cover of night. Marching again after dark over a country incredibly difficult and covered with snow, he before daylight reached a point from which could distinctly be heard the tom-toms and shouts of the Indians, who were indulging in a grand war-dance in honor of a recent successful attack on a small party of Crows. Here the command was halted to await the dawn.

Imagine the scene!

In the bottom of a dark and narrow gorge, whose rocky sides, scarcely distinguishable, rose sheer and straight a thousand feet above; underfoot the snow lay piled in rifts from two to four feet deep; the cold was intense; no fire could be built, and perfect silence must be preserved; the worn-out horses stood with heads bowed down, too tired to move; the stealthy change of position or quiet shuffle of the feet of the men, just enough to keep from freezing; and from the distance the steady beat of the tom-tom, and the shouts of triumph and yells of defiance of the unsuspecting enemy.

Gradually the noises of the Indian camp died out, and soon after faint gray streaks in the east heralded the approach of dawn. Silently the half-frozen troops lift their stiffened limbs into the saddle, and, obedient to the sign of their leader, move forward to the attack.

The Cheyenne camp was pitched in one of the characteristic cañon s of the foot-hills of the Big Horn Mountains. A narrow gorge, averaging not more than seventy-five yards wide at bottom, cleft -its tortuous way through overhanging cliffs and precipitous rocks, whose summits were more than a thousand feet above. The narrow bottom was scored by a ditch, which passed from side to side in endless convolutions, with banks everywhere precipitous, and only passable where the narrow Indian trail had worn a difficult pathway. The immediate banks of the stream supported a dense thicket of willows, but in the bends were narrow open spaces in every way just suited to Indian necessities. Into this principal cañon opened innumerable lateral cañon s, some longer, some shorter, with precipitous sides of height equal to that of the main gorge, but with bottoms bare of timber or brush, and clothed with the richest grasses. These served as great natural corrals for the herds of Indian ponies. For three miles along this main gorge, the narrow open spaces were occupied by the tepees of the Cheyennes.

When it was yet barely light enough to see the situation, the Indian allies in advance, with true Indian whoops and yells and rattling shots, fell upon one end of this long village, the heavier cavalry following at best speed to consummate the victory. At the first alarm, most of the Cheyennes, springing from their beds, and seizing their arms, had rushed to cover amid the (to white man) inaccessible rocks near the tops of the gorges. Some were killed as they ran, others met their fate in attempting to defend their lodges, in the sides of which they slashed great holes, and poured forth an incessant fire. Dull Knife, the principal chief, sprung to his arms, and calling to his followers to fight out the battle then and there, opened a rapid and effective fire. Nothing, however, could withstand the onset of the United States forces. When numbers of his men had fallen, and his youngest and favorite son had died fighting by his side, Dull Knife joined his flying band, and took refuge in the rocky sides of the cañon . In an incredibly short time the village from end to end was cleared of its inhabitants, and the whole camp fully in possession of the troops.

But now came the tug of war. Recovered from their first stampede, the Cheyennes occupied every vantage-ground. Every rock and overhanging height was held by determined warriors who poured an incessant fire upon the troops below. In vain were brilliant charges made; in vain the gallant McKinney dashed to his death; no power from below could dislodge such determined fighters from such a position; and it soon became apparent that the attacking force, ten hundred and fifty strong, was powerless against less than half its numbers of their gallant and well posted enemies.

Strenuous efforts were made to induce the Cheyennes to surrender, but every proposition was met by the most haughty and absolute defiance.

Recognizing the critical nature of the situation, Mackenzie gave orders for the destruction of the camp, and under a galling fire, tepees, bedding, clothing, buffalo robes, thousands of pounds of dried buffalo meat, cooking and other utensils, spare arms and ammunition, everything was given to the flames. Disposition was then made to protect as far as possible the troops from the fire which incessantly annoyed them, and thus the day wore away.

An Indian was dispatched to General Crook with a report and request for reinforcements. Having to follow down the cañon for many miles, this runner did not reach General Crook until about 10 A. M. the next day.

My command was immediately ordered to the rescue, and in an hour we were on the march, the men vying with each other in eagerness to succor their comrades. Though the ground was covered with snow, the foot-hills, twenty-six miles from our camp, were reached just at dark. For the next twelve or fifteen miles the scene was weird and wild in the extreme. Guided by the Indian, the command, generally in single rank, and following an old Indian trail almost obliterated by snow, wound its slow length up and down the sides of almost impassable ravines. The heavens were overclouded, the only light being from the snow. Now, with all his care, a man would slip and go plunging off into the darkness of a ravine, now half a company would slide together and land in one promiscuous mass in the snow-drifts below. Though some of the tumbles were nearly a hundred feet, no one was seriously hurt, and though the "Army in Flanders" was emulated, the command never flagged.

About 3 A. M. the guide lost the trail in the deep snows of a creek bottom. A halt was ordered, and in half an hour the whole command except the guard, each man wrapped in his blanket, was soundly sleeping on the snow. Just at dawn the trail was found, and the command, springing to arms, resumed its march. Soon after the sun had made its appearance we met some of Mackenzie's advance guards, and found that all our labor had been of no avail.

Unfortunately, the preceding night had been intensely cold, not less than twenty degrees below zero. Indians when in camp, and unsuspicious of danger, habitually sleep naked. The Cheyennes were so, and aroused as they were, had no time to clothe themselves; some few had seized a blanket or robe in their flight, but the large majority had no covering whatever. Human nature could not stand it, and notwithstanding their favorable tactical position, they were compelled to get back into the main cañon, and retreat to a position where they could build fires and procure food. Collecting their herds of ponies, they left during the night. Early next morning their departure was discovered, but Mackenzie's 'attempt at pursuit was frustrated in the first few miles, by a strong and determined rearguard posted as before in the rocks and summits of almost inaccessible cliffs.

Our loss in this battle was one officer and five soldiers killed, twenty-five soldiers and one enlisted Indian wounded. The Cheyenne loss in killed and wounded was probably about fifty.

Insignificant as it appears, this battle was a deathblow to the independence of a tribe of men as brave as ever trod the soil of Greece. The sufferings of these Indians during the three months succeeding the battle can never be known. Numbers perished, principally women and children. With no food but the flesh of their ponies, no covering but the green hides of the same faithful animals, the survivors with indomitable determination made their way across the bleak and snow-covered summits of the Big Horn Mountains, and after a long and most terrible march presented themselves to Crazy Horse, then encamped on Mizpah Creek.

At no time previous had the Cheyennes been otherwise than welcome visitors to the Sioux, but here was a band of near fifteen hundred people, absolutely impoverished, in want of tepees, clothing, food, everything. The warriors still possessed their gallant spirit, and burned for an opportunity for revenge upon their white enemies, but their arms were in poor condition, their ammunition expended. It was too great a tax on the Sioux chieftain, and he received the new comers so coldly and with so scant a charity that they soon left his inhospitable camp.

They had not been defeated, yet they had received a blow far worse than a bloody defeat, and from which it would take years to recover. Their women were suffering, their children dying, Crazy Horse, their last hope, had failed them. Struggle as they might their fate was too hard for them, and in 1877 they came in and surrendered.

One cannot but feel sympathy for any people, however savage, which, after displays of desperate courage in battle, of fortitude under untold hardship and misery, is forced at last to yield to the inevitable.

WINTER ON THE PLAINS

SUCH are the only really hurtful blows that the army can give to the Indian. Surprise is absolutely indispensable. During all the months of tolerable weather the warriors in search of game, or sent out as scouts, are scouring all the country for many miles about the camp; a force of troops can come, without being discovered, to within a night's forced march, only by the merest accident of good luck. It is exceedingly rare, therefore, that any important advantage is gained by a summer campaign against Indians.

In winter the Plains Indians, who are very susceptible to cold, remain in their tepees nearly all the time, going out only when forced to do so, and getting back as soon as possible to the pleasant warmth of their homes. Their ponies are wretchedly poor, and unable to bear their masters on any extended scout or hunt. They are in the very best possible condition to be surprised, and even to those who escape bullets, surprise is almost destruction from starvation and cold.

Discipline, Indian allies, surprise, and winter, are the powerful auxiliaries by the aid of which the scanty force of United States troops have for the last ten years been able to cope successfully with a greatly superior numerical force of an enemy, equally well-armed, and infinitely better in all those acquired traits that go to make a good partisan soldier.

But these winter campaigns, so terrible to the Indians, bring to the soldiers an amount of privation, hardships and suffering scarcely to be comprehended by persons unfamiliar with the peculiarities of the Plains themselves.

Extending over nineteen degrees of latitude, and varying in altitude from almost the sea-level to eight thousand feet above, the Plains present an almost infinite variation of climate; and besides the variations due to latitude and altitude, there are others resulting from the absence of those natural protectors of the earth's surface, trees, and from the aridity of the high Plains.

The summer's sun, beating down through the thin atmosphere, gives a temperature that would be destructive to life in more humid countries.

The winters are remarkable. For a week each day will be clear and bright as a mild October day in the East; then oftentimes without the slightest warning, a wind will come from the north, so piercing that an exposure to it for any length of time is certain death to any living thing. The thermometer may not indicate such excessive cold; the danger is from the sharp wind, which drives the cold like icy daggers through the body, and penetrating to every part, drags out the vital heat, leaving only a stiffened corpse of him who is so unfortunate as to be long exposed to it. But this danger can always be avoided if it be possible to get out of the wind. A day which would be death on the high Plains may scarcely be uncomfortably cold in a thicket at the bottom of a deep narrow cañon . Indians, plainsmen, and all indigenous animals understand this perfectly, and fly to shelter at the first puff.

When this "Norther" is accompanied by snow it is simply indescribable; worse than the "tourmente" of the Alps. The deepest cañon s and most secluded thickets often afford no protection; tents are blown down, horses stampeded, fires put out, and the wretched sufferers can only wrap their blankets about them and bury themselves in the snow. Such a storm overtook a party of fifteen men on Crooked Creek, twenty miles south of Fort Dodge, and though there were no resultant deaths, every man lost some portion of his body, ears, fingers, toes, hands or feet. The post surgeon, Dr. Tremaine, performed seventy capital amputations at Fort Dodge in the winter of 1872-3, one poor fellow losing both hands and both feet.

Fortunately for those of us who have to spend the greater part of our lives on the Plains, only a few such storms may be expected in one winter, and they generally last not longer than three days. The army suffers greatly from these, for however skilled in plains-craft the officers and men, there are occasions when movements must be made in the teeth of whatever difficulty and danger. A command may be overtaken by such a storm when rations and forage are nearly exhausted, and must brave the dangers of the elements to escape death from starvation; or the storm, coming as is usual without premonition, may overtake a command at a distance from friendly ravines.

When in command of Fort Sedgwick I was ordered to send a company of cavalry on important duty to the Republican River, in the worst month of winter, February. The country between that River and the Platte is as nearly a level as the plains ever are. The duty was performed and the company returned on time, but this was owing entirely to the pluck and will of the captain. After getting well on the march across the long divide between the rivers, the command was met by a most terrific gale and blinding snow-storm. The march was due north in the very teeth of the gale. The men were made to dismount and form in single file, each man leading his horse. The leading man with head bowed and his eyes fixed on a compass held in his hand, broke the way through the snow, as long as he could endure, then giving the compass to the next man, fell out to take his place in rear.

The cold was so intense, the toil so great, the suffering so intolerable, that some of the men refused to do more, and throwing themselves into the snow declared their determination to die there rather than make another effort. Orders, entreaties, even threats, accompanied by the presentation of a cocked revolver, proving alike unavailing, the captain finally put up his pistol, and falling upon them with the flat of his sabre, belabored them into the ranks, and brought all in safety to the post.

Nowhere have I seen suffering more cheerfully borne, than on General Crook's winter campaign in 1876. For two months the ground was constantly covered with snow from two or three to fifteen inches in depth. Often our only fuel was a scanty supply of green sage-brush; the cold was always intense, and several times the mercury was frozen in the bulbs of our thermometers.

We had ample experience of Arctic phenomena, magnificent Aurora Borealis, "sun-dogs," or the appearance of five suns, and the beautiful "bridal veil," every particle of moisture in the atmosphere being congealed in tiny particles, so that when the suns shone upon it, everything was seen as through a silver veil.

One day on the Belle Fourche, when on the return march, we were struck by a storm of unusual severity. General Crook hurried us into camp, under the bluffs and in the thickets of a small watercourse which was fortunately near, and under this cover we passed a good night. At daylight in the morning the wind had died out, but the thermometers were all frozen. After taking my breakfast, and while the men were getting ready for the march, I held my thermometer near the fire to thaw it out, hoping by exposing it afterwards to arrive at some approximate idea-of the cold. I kept it there until the mercury was above freezing, then hung it on a bush nearby and watched it. Though the sun was now just appearing the mercury froze again in less than five minutes. Many of our animals, among them the favorite horse of one of General Crook's staff-officers, froze to death that night.

Encumbered with all the wraps, extra clothing, hoods and masks that our "light marching" order permitted, we broke camp and marched merrily along, admiring the five suns, and the curiously broken features of the country as seen through the "veil." The morning was beautiful, the air perfectly calm. By nine A. M. my mask and hood became uncomfortable; the first was taken off, the other exchanged for a light felt hat. By ten my overcoat was tied behind my saddle. At eleven I stripped coat and thick gloves, and was yet too warm. Turning to the surgeon, who was riding beside me at the head of the column, I exclaimed against the weather:

"This is a terrible change, I fear it will affect the health of the men!"

Thrusting his hand into his breast-pocket the doctor drew out a thermometer, and rode for some distance dangling it by its ring on his bare finger, and occasionally looking at it. At last he said:

"Colonel, I don't think the heat will affect the health of the men. It is now eight degrees below zero."

A beautiful incident showing the esprit of our soldiers occurred on the same campaign. One morning on the northward march we broke camp on Wind River. The day was cold but clear, and many of the men had packed their overcoats on the wagons. When we had just gotten fairly out of reach of the wagons, there burst in our faces a terrible gale of wind and snow, so fierce as almost to stagger the column. With heads bowed down, the men trudged manfully along, the officers watching closely, and every few moments ordering some man to rub his cheek or nose with snow. In half an hour the gale subsided, and though the snow still fell, the cold was no longer dangerous. Just at this moment some glorious fellow in the ranks broke out in a sweet but manly voice with" Marching through Georgia." In an instant the strain was taken up, and the suffering of the previous half hour cast to the winds on the breath of five hundred lusty throats.

On December 26th, 1874, Captain Guy V. Henry [later seriously wounded at the Rosebud fight], in command of his Company "D" Third Cavalry, left its camp at Red Cloud Agency, pursuant to an order of the War Department to proceed to the Black Hills, and remove some miners reported to be there in violation of treaties. The Black Hills country was then almost entirely unknown. Warren had skirted it, Harney had passed near but to the southward of it, and Custer had dashed with his usual impetuosity directly through it, but to Captain Henry and his command, it was entirely unknown. On the second day he arrived at the Spotted Tail Agency, where he expected to secure the services of an Indian guide. The cold was so intense that the Indian refused to go, and a white man named Raymond was employed. He knew nothing of the country, but was an" old frontiersman," supposed to be entirely capable of going anywhere, and equal to every emergency. The march was made, no miners found, and the command had returned to within one day's journey of its post, having been out two weeks, and travelled over three hundred miles, without serious inconvenience, except from the intense cold, the thermometer ranging from 20° to 40° below zero.

About seven o'clock on the morning of this last day when the command had gotten well started on its march, it was struck by a most furious "Norther" "cutting like a razor." So intense was the cold that the men were dismounted to prevent freezing. The trail was soon obliterated, and wandering blindly through the drifting snow, holding with difficulty the almost frantic horses, the unhappy command struggled on. With hands and faces frozen, with noses and ears bleeding, with eyes absolutely sightless from the constant pelting of the frozen particles, the weaker men began to fall exhausted, willing to die rather than make further effort. These were strapped on their horses, and the command pushed on, not a hill or ravine or clump of trees to give even the most partial shelter.

Every moment but added to the helplessness of the party. Recognizing the certainty of the speedy destruction of the whole command, if the march were thus continued, Captain Henry in desperation gave the order to "mount," and when all had with difficulty dragged themselves into their saddles, "forward, gallop!"

"We all knew," said Captain Henry, "that this was a race for life; we were helpless; neither brain nor eye would longer serve us; the instinct of our horses could alone save those of us who could hold out."

Seeming to recognize the necessity of extra exertion and intelligence, the stiffened horses swept forward, even those whose powerless riders were strapped upon them keeping in or near the ranks. Succor came at last most unexpectedly. The leading horses dashed up to a little cabin in the wilderness, half buried in snow, and of the existence of which not one of the command had any previous knowledge. The white owner and his squaw wife received most hospitably their half-frozen visitors. The horses were turned into the corral, those running loose with powerless riders being soon caught and relieved of their inanimate burdens. The men were crowded into the little hovel, and every attention and care bestowed upon them.

When the storm abated an Indian was sent to the post, fifteen miles away, whence wagons and ambulances were sent to transport those who were unable to ride. There were no deaths, but not one of forty-five officers and men escaped without the loss of, or serious injuries to, some portion of his person. To this day many of those men are maimed and suffering from the effects of this "frontier experience."

But for the providential discovery of this little unknown .cabin of a" squaw man," the whole party must have perished miserably.

Not a winter passes, but scores its mark upon the army, in the shape of dead or maimed victims.

Ye, in power, who sit on cushioned chairs in comfortable offices, take these lessons to heart; think mercifully of the sufferings of those who are ordered to brave the dangers of a winter campaign on the Plains, and be always assured that there is, for such orders, an urgent necessity.

TAKING THE SCALP—THRILLING INCIDENTS

THE origin of the Indian custom of taking the scalps of their slain enemies seems to be lost in obscurity. Elsewhere I have spoken of the religious belief that the act of scalping annihilates the soul, but while the practice is common to all the tribes east of the Rocky Mountains, the belief seems to be confined to a comparatively few of the Plains tribes. Moreover, while the practice continues in full favor, the belief itself, like very many other of their ancient points of faith, is fast losing its hold over the minds of the red men.

I have been told by old men of the Cheyenne and Arapahoe tribes, that many years ago the belief in the annihilation of the soul by scalping the head was common to all the Indians between the Mississippi River and the Rocky Mountains, and that the custom originated in the desire of each warrior to lessen in this life, as much as possible, his chances of being annoyed by enemies in the future life.

The Indian beliefs and superstitions are so vague, so individual (each man while following the general creed, working in details to suit his own taste), and have moreover been so curiously confused by, and with, the teachings of missionaries, that I much doubt if it be possible at the present day to arrive with any certainty at any original Indian faith.

The practice most likely originated in the necessity of furnishing something as a proof of deeds of valor, and to prevent fraudulent or conflicting claims. At the present day among the Plains tribes, a scalp is of far more importance than merely to minister to the pride and vanity of the taker.

Scalps taken by an individual in fair single combat or by assassination are his personal property, but, of the scalps of enemies killed in battle, a certain portion is set aside. Of these a percentage goes to the chief, whether he was in the battle or not. Others are dedicated to the good God, and hung up in the "Medicine Lodge," sacred from the touch of any but the "medicine chief." Others are reserved, to be danced over, on the return of the war party to its village. After this ceremony they are returned to the warriors who took them.

A strong flavor of religious superstition attaches to a scalp, and many solemn contracts and binding obligations can only be made over or by means of a scalp.

It was a solemn day on Crazy Woman's fork of Powder River. On the preceding day Mackenzie had returned from his successful fight with the Northern Cheyennes, but bringing with him a train of travois, each bearing its burden of dead or wounded humanity. To-day the whole command had turned out to do honor to .the gallant dead, and perform for them our last duties. They had been laid away side by side in a little valley. No stone marked their resting-place, for that would insure desecration by our enemies as soon as we had left the vicinity.

I was sitting in my tent, musing in a somewhat softened mood over these violent deaths and lonely burials in this far-away wilderness, when the front of my tent was pulled aside, and the acting head chief of the Pawnees stalked in, gravely and without a word. We had long been friends, and had on several occasions been in tight places together.

He sat down on the side of my bed, looked at me for a moment kindly, but solemnly, and began in a low tone to mutter in his own language, half chant, half recitative. Knowing that he was making "medicine" of some kind, I looked on without comment. After some moments, he stood erect and stretched out his hand to me. I gave him my hand. He pulled me into a standing position, embraced me, passed his hands lightly over my head, face, arms, body, and legs to my feet, muttering all the while, embraced me again, then turned his back upon me and with his face turned towards Heaven, appeared to make adoration. He then turned to embrace and manipulate me again.

After some five minutes of this performance, he drew from his wallet a package, and unrolling it, disclosed the freshly taken scalp of an Indian. Touching me with this in various places and ways, he finally drew out his knife, divided the scalp carefully along the part of the hair, and handing me one half, embraced me again, kissing me on the forehead. "Now," said he in English, "you are my brother."

He subsequently informed me that this ceremony could not have been performed without the scalp.

The Indians of different tribes wear their hair in different styles, and scalps are therefore cut off in different ways. The warriors of the Eastern States wore their hair short, with the exception of a lock, some two or three inches in diameter, covering the centre of the head. This was allowed to grow, and was braided or tied up with feathers or porcupine quills to keep it upright, a standing defiance to their enemy.

The Pawnees used to clip the hair on each side of the head, leaving a roach or mane of some three inches in length, running from front to rear over the centre of the head. Just on the crown, the scalp-lock was cultivated to great length. This peculiar head-dress gave a most ferocious appearance, but was so marked that it was abandoned even before the Pawnees became "good Indians," their peculiar appearance at once fixing upon them any depredation.

All the Plains tribes wear the hair long. The Sioux, Crows, Winnebagos, part their hair in the middle, carrying the mass into two tails, one on each side of the head. The hair covering a space of about two inches in diameter just over the crown, is separated from these tails and plaited by the Sioux into one to three, by the Winnebagos, into six or seven, little independent tails which form the scalp-lock. In all these tribes, the scalp is removed by cutting only the skin on which the scalp-lock grows.

The Cheyennes and Arapahos part their hair in the middle, wearing it in two long tails one on each side of the head. The Kiowas also part the hair in the middle, but wear only one long tail, that on the left side of the head. The hair growing on the right side of the head is cut a little below the ear and worn loose. The Comanches comb the hair back from the forehead and plait it behind in one long tail. None of these Indians wear scalp-locks.

In scalping an Indian who wears no scalp-lock, a handful of hair is grasped on any part of the head and the knife passed beneath.

Only one scalp can be taken from the head of an Indian who wears a scalp-lock, for it must show the crown of the head, while an Indian who wears no scalp-lock may furnish enough tufts of hair-covered skin to enable each buck of a small party to furnish evidence that he has killed his man.

If time and opportunity be given, every Indian, in taking a scalp, will carefully remove every portion of the skin covered with hair in one piece, in many cases taking the ears with it.

Some special value or "medicine" virtue seems to be attached to hair-covered skin. The Indian has no hair on his face or person, and consequently scalps only the head of other Indians. The full-bearded white offers peculiar attractions to the scalper. Every portion of skin to which hair is attached, even to the small bit under the arms, is skinned off. I once saw, in an Indian camp, a scalp consisting of the entire skin of head, face, and body to the crotch, in one piece. It was thickly covered with hair, had been carefully cured, and peculiar value was set upon it as "big medicine."

It has been asserted by some writers that scalping is universal among Indians. This is an error. It is an eastern custom. West of the Rocky Mountain chain it is not habitually practised by the Indians. Occasionally a man may be scalped, but it appears to be an individual exception, a simple copying of what is known to be the custom among Eastern Indians; or what is more probable, it results from the imitative faculty of the Indian, who does that which he sees a white man do; for I regret to be obliged to admit that the majority of white men on the frontier are as prompt to take a scalp as any Indian.

Even by those tribes by which scalps are most highly prized, the scalp of a dead enemy is not always taken. The reason is wrapped in their superstitions. Even though an Indian may have so far progressed in religion as no longer to believe that the immortality of the soul depends on the final position of the scalp, he cannot so discard his early impressions as to be entirely careless of his action when a scalp is involved. Whether or not its removal annihilates the soul, he is yet sure that a scalp is strong "medicine," and equally sure that its taking by him will involve consequences to him, either very good or very bad, and he does not always know which. An Indian will never take the scalp of a colored soldier, nor does he give any reason for it; all to be got out of him by way of explanation is, "Buffalo soldier no good, heap bad medicine."

Many yet believe that, if not scalped, the soul of the dead enemy will bear in the future state all the mutilations and indignities inflicted on the body. When therefore so exasperated as to be willing to exchange the gratification of vanity for a surfeit of vengeance, the Indian leaves, the scalp on the head, but mutilates the body, as he wishes the soul mutilated to all eternity. Suicide, though not common among Indians, is "big medicine",' a high religious act. Through it the man rises superior to his gods. Whatever the special religious opinion of each Indian in regard to the taking of the scalps of slain enemies, I have never yet known a single case where the scalp of a suicide was stripped off, and in many cases the superstition is so strong as to prevent the Indians even from touching the body. If an unscalped body is found with many terrible wounds, gashed and mutilated, it was the deliberate purpose of the Indians to torment the soul; if it be found unmutilated with but one mortal wound, it is a case of suicide.

Though the bodies of all of Major Elliott's little party were subjected to the usual horrible mutilations and barbarities, only four or five of the least noted were scalped. So also iii every Indian massacre, mutilations of the body are almost the rule, but many of the bodies will be found unscalped.

It is said that Custer's body was found unscalped and unmutilated. If so, my knowledge of Indians convinces me that he died by his own hand.

There are a number of theories as to why Custer's corpse was not mutilated, as nearly all of the other dead at the Little Bighorn were. No powder burns were reported on his head wound so it is unlikely he committed suicide and it would not fit the personality of the man. One Cheyenne tradition states that Monasita, the Cheyenne woman that

Custer had taken as a concubine at Washita, was at Little Bighorn and recognized his body. She told a brave not to mutilate him.—Ed. 2015

In October, 1855, the post of Fort Davis, Texas, was established by the Head Quarters and six companies of the Eighth United States Infantry. I was the adjutant, but the quarter-master being absent, his duties devolved upon me. The site chosen being four or five thousand feet above the level of the sea, the winter weather was expected to be severe, and we immediately busied ourselves with preparations for such shelter as short time and scant materials would allow us to build.

I was ordered by the commanding officer to take the guide, Sam Cherry, and an escort of one non-commissioned officer and three privates, and, starting immediately after guard-mounting each morning, to scour the country, as far as I could go and return the same day, in search of timber suitable for saw-logs.

From about the 10th to the 30th of October I had thus been out, taking a different route each day. Signs of Indians had occasionally been seen, but not in large parties. These made us more careful, but caused no uneasiness.

After I had reported to the commanding officer after dark on the 30th, I asked:—

"Colonel, shall I go out to-morrow, as usual?"

"Why not?" he replied.

"It is muster-day, and I thought you might need me."

"Of course, I will. I had forgotten about muster. Detail a good sergeant to take your party to-morrow, and instruct him where you propose to go."

The detail was made, Sergeant Love of Company G taking my place. That night the party did not return. Next morning early the wagon-master of a train came in to the post greatly excited, and reported that the dead body of a man and horse had been found in the road about six miles from the post. A company of infantry was immediately ordered out, and proceeding to the spot found the body of Sam Cherry, pinned fast to the ground by the dead body of his horse. The search was continued, and in a lateral cañon were found the bodies of Sergeant Love and the three privates riddled with bullets, mutilated and disfigured, but giving every evidence of having sold their lives as brave men should. The trails were examined and the whole story worked out. The party had travelled along the road nearly to the entrance of the cañon of the Limpia, known as the "Wild Rose Pass," when suddenly about thirty mounted Indians dashed from the bushes along the stream, cutting it off from retreat towards the Fort, and driving it up the lateral cañon . Suspecting a trap, Sam Cherry suddenly turned, dashed through the line of Indians, regained the road, and ran for life, away from the Fort, followed by a number of yelling savages. He was evidently doing well, when his horse stumbled and fell, breaking his neck, and pinning Sam's leg to the ground. In an instant he was surrounded by the exultant Indians.

Raising himself slightly, Sam fired five shots at his enemies, then turning the muzzle against his own temple, he escaped the tortures of their vindictive rage by his "last shot." The baffled and terrified Indians went away as fast as their ponies could carry them, not touching the body, not even taking the arms.

PRISONERS AMONG INDIANS

THE Plains Indians never make captives of men. I have never known of a single instance, and if I have ever heard of one, I do not recollect it. Wounded and disarmed men are frequently taken prisoners, but they are held only for torture. Their doom is certain, and, but for the horrible sufferings they are yet to undergo, they may be regarded as already dead.

This is an unusual phase of barbarism, except among cannibals. Even the most primitive man, of whom we have account, found a better use for his enemy than to kill him, and the history of mankind shows that the murder of prisoners is the exception and not the rule. It also shows that these wholesale murders are usually done in the name of religion. The primitive Hebrew, following his faith, murdered without regard to age, sex, or condition. The Indian furnishes another link in the chain of evidence that he is a descendant of the "Lost Tribes," by doing the same thing.

The Indian does not, however, claim to do murder in the name of his religion. He does it because he likes it; because his savage instincts and vindictive temper impel him to it. His wives are his slaves; he needs no others, and the only satisfactory use to which he can put the male enemy that falls into his hands, is the gratification of that temper by witnessing the agonies of his enemy while undergoing the torture.

A ceremonial torture by fire is very unusual. Though so common among the tribes east of the Mississippi I doubt if it were ever practised (as a ceremony) by tribes west of that stream.

It is not at all unusual for a war party to "vent its spleen" by building a fire on the breast of a prisoner "staked out" on the ground, but in all my long service on the frontier, and experience among Indians, I have never known or heard of any case where a prisoner was formally tied to a stake and burned as a ceremony.

In the last chapter I gave an account of the fate of Sergeant Love and party. One of that party was a little drummer-boy of about twelve years of age. He had been sick, and was yet reported "in hospital," but, being nearly well and thinking he would not be missed, he slipped away from the hospital, borrowed a pony from one of the herders, and joined Sergeant Love's party, for a day's boyish frolic.

When the party was overwhelmed this boy was captured and taken to the Indian camp, and, speaking Spanish with tolerable fluency, was questioned at length by the captors, the interpreter being a Mexican boy captured some years before, and from whom I afterwards learned the following particulars. The boy's answers to them proving to the Indians that their scheme of attacking the post was sure to lead to disaster to them, they became very angry and turned him over to the squaws. These 'fiends in human shape stripped and tied him to a tree, and for some hours tormented him in every way their ingenuity could devise without endangering life. Becoming tired of this, they procured some "fat" pine knots, and splitting them into small splinters, stuck them into the skin until the unfortunate boy bristled like a porcupine. They then set fire to the splinters, and danced and yelled with delight when the poor boy cried and screamed with anguish. When the fire burned out they left him tied to the tree, exposed naked to the cold of that elevated region. Next morning he was tied, nearly dead, on a horse, and carried with the party, but after going about ten miles was found to be dead. He was then scalped, and his body flung among some rocks, where it was afterwards found by troops sent in pursuit.

The Indian is thoroughly skilled in all methods of torture, and well knows that that by fire is the most exquisite if it can only be prolonged. He therefore frequently resorts to it when time and opportunities serve. The victim is "staked out," pleasantly talked to. It is all the best kind of joke. Then a small fire is built near one of his feet. When that is so cooked as to have little sensation, another fire is built near the other foot; then the legs and arms and body, until the whole person has been crisped. Finally, a small fire is built on the naked breast, and kept up until life is extinct.

This extreme refinement of cruelty only occurs when the Indians are in specially good humor, and there is plenty of time and no danger. The temper of the Indian is so ungoverned that he can only be perfectly cruel when not angry, and if the victim knows enough of his character and language to taunt him into anger, he will probably be promptly dispatched. The nature and extent of all tortures depend upon the time, the materials at hand, and the temper in which the Indian happens to be.

In 1888 an attack was made by a party of Indians on a station of the Kansas Pacific Railroad. The men who were on herd were made prisoners almost without resistance. The other two or three successfully defended their position, to the great exasperation of the redskins, who, after losing several men, drew off.

Just at nightfall they took their prisoners to a position in plain view, but beyond rifle range of the station, stripped them of their clothing, "staked" them to the ground, built a fire on the breast of each, and while some sat near warming themselves with great apparent satisfaction, the others indulged in a dance of rejoicing. The cries and groans of the unfortunate men could be plainly heard by their friends, but nothing could be done, and it was not until far in the night that the cessation of complaint proved that life was extinct. Next morning the Indians were gone, but the blackened and half-burned bodies were found still fastened to the ground, not only scalped, but terribly mutilated, and one, being an unusually hairy man, almost skinned.

The fate of the wounded man who falls into the hands of the Indians depends very much on circumstances. In a close contest, or if the Indians have cause to be exceptionally angry, the wounded man is promptly dispatched. If there be plenty of time and no danger apprehended, the unfortunate prisoner will have full experience of the ingenuity in torture of these fiends. I have been told by Indians that none of the soldiers slain in either the Fort Phil Kearney or the Custer massacre were tortured. "The Indians were too mad" and killed them as soon as possible.

Cooper, and some other novelists, knew nothing of Indian character and customs when they placed their heroines prisoners in their hands. I believe I am perfectly safe in the assertion that there is not a single wild tribe of Indians in all the wide territory of the United States which does not regard the person of the female captive as the inherent right of the captor; and I venture to assert further that, with the single exception of the lady captured by the Nez Perces, under Joseph, in Yellowstone Park, no woman has, in the last thirty years, been taken prisoner by any wild Indians who did not, as soon after as practicable, become a victim to the brutality of every one of the party of her captors.

When a woman is captured by a party, she belongs equally to each and all, so long as the party is out. When it returns to the home encampment, she may be abandoned for a few days to the brutality of the men, and delight of the women, who torment her in every conceivable way; after which she becomes the exclusive property of the individual who captured her. In some instances he takes her to wife, and she has protection, as such; but in the very large majority of cases she is held by him as a slave, for the vilest purposes, being sold by her owner to anyone who wants her. In nearly all the tribes there are more or less of these slaves.

The life of such a woman is miserable beyond expression, the squaws forcing her to constant labor, and beating her on any, or without, provocation. She, however, fares and lodges exactly as the other members of the family of her owner, attends the dances, and is in no way socially ostracized. She brings her owner more or less revenue, dependent on her beauty; and, as property, is worth quite as much as an equally good-looking girl of virtue. She is a favorite stake at the gambling-board, and may change masters half a dozen times a day, as varies the for-tune of the game; passing from hand to hand; one day the property of the chief, the next day, of a common warrior. No discredit attaches to the ownership or farming out of these unhappy slaves.

Indians always prefer to capture rather than to kill women, they being merchantable property. White women are unusually valuable, one moderately good-looking being worth as many ponies as would buy from their fathers three or four Indian girls.

White women are especially valuable when the tribe gets tired of fighting and wants to make peace. A runner is sent to the agency, with an intimation of a desire for peace, and a willingness to bring in white captives. The Indians take great credit to themselves for bringing in these women, invariably demanding a large price, which the government equally invariably pays.

This is right, of course, no amount of money being too great to weigh against the delivery of a woman from the horror of such a situation. If after redeeming the captives, the government would properly punish the Indians, these horrors might be stopped; but so long as we strive to convince them by our actions and words, that we believe them to be thoroughly good fellows in giving up the prisoners, just so long will they strive to deserve our commendation by capturing and delivering up others.

One cause of our constant Indian wars is that the Indian knows he can make peace whenever he wishes. The government is mawkishly anxious for peace, and no matter what has been done by the Indian, he has but to intimate that he does not want to fight, and the conflict is over, the Indian unpunished.

I was once present when three white women, one a bright, sprightly, intelligent, married lady, were returned after a captivity of several months among the savages. This lady detailed to the wife of my intimate friend (from whom I received it) a story of horrors for which the life of every Indian of the tribe would scarcely atone, yet though the Indians who killed the men and carried off and outraged the women, were known by name to the authorities, no one was ever punished; nor does it seem to have entered into the minds of anyone in authority that punishment was deserved. There is absolutely no remedy for this state of things, so long as we regard the petty Indian Tribes as independent nations, with whom our intercourse must be regulated by treaty. We cannot make laws for other independent nations, and in the absence of law, punishment is mere vengeance.

I have before spoken of the very great fondness of Indians for children, in their raids on each other and on the whites, those children who are large enough to help themselves a little, and yet not old enough to be likely to have strong affection or memory, are carried off to the tribe, and adopted into it. These are sometimes adopted by men who have lost children, otherwise they are brought up in the families of their captors. In either case they are treated exactly as are the other children.

When arrived at maturity, the males sometimes return their own tribes. The females are sold in marriage by their adopted parents. They never, however, have quite the status of native-born women, and on the slightest indiscretion are likely to fall into the condition of slavery already described.

THE CAPTIVE'S FATE—INDIAN CRUELTY

CRUELTY is a trait natural and common to humanity. The savage dances with delight at the groans wrung from his enemy by physical torture; the enlightened gentleman plunges a dagger courteous words into the heart of his friend, and smiles blandly at his mental torture. I know kindly disposed and estimable savages, who would tie their enemy to the ground, and pleasantly warm themselves by the fire built on his naked breast. I know accomplished gentlemen standing high in the estimation of society, who never use an angry tone, yet whose wives have cause to envy the victim of the savage.

Journalist John Finerty of the Chicago Times was with Crook on the 1876 campaign and at the Rosebud fight. He detailed that physical savagery was not confined to Native-Americans during the Indian Wars. (See Finerty's classic account in War Path and Bivouac*) Sand Creek, Washita, and other fights included desecration of the dead by whites.—Ed. 2015*

Barbarism torments the body; civilization torments the soul. The savage remorselessly takes your scalp, your civilized friend as remorselessly swindles you out of your property. The progress of enlightenment of a people would seem to be measurable by their less or greater abhorrence of physical torture and the ingenuity and politeness with which mental torture may be inflicted. The actual cruelty is possibly about the same in either case, but it is the case of the savage that comes up for judgment.

The cruelty of the Indian is born in and bred with him, and clings to him through life. It is the very lowest type or development of cruelty, its manifestation being purely physical. As a boy, his especial delight is the torture of every bird or animal that falls into his hands. As a man, the torture of a human being gives him more pleasure than any other act of his life; and on no occasion is his laughter so joyous and heartfelt as when some especial ingenuity forces a cry of agony from the victim of his cruelty.

The torture of a human being is an active, exquisite pleasure. Cruelty to animals is equally marked, though simply a matter of indifference. An Indian will ride a horse, from whose back the skin and flesh have been torn by an ill-fitting saddle. He will ride him at speed until he drops, then force him to his feet and ride him again. A Plains saying is that "a white man will abandon a horse as broken down, and utterly unable to go further; a Mexican will then mount, ride him fifty miles and abandon him; an Indian will then mount and ride him for a week."

In extravagance of delight in the anticipation of a scene of torture, for hellish ingenuity in devising, and remorseless cruelty in inflicting pain, the Indian woman far exceeds her husband and son, and they can give her no keener enjoyment, when returning from a foray, than by bringing a prisoner on which this ingenuity can be practised; and as 'a rule, when a dead body is found specially mutilated, the head beaten, battered, and crushed out of shape by stones, it is squaw work.

Of all Indians, the Apaches have deservedly the credit of being the most ingeniously and relentlessly cruel. "While yet a dependency of Spain, the present Mexican state of Chihuahua was well peopled. Thriving settlements and prosperous ranches occupied every stream and spring, and the whole country was covered with cattle. While the Spanish power was dominant, the Apaches appear to have given little trouble, but taking advantage of the disturbances consequent to the revolution of 1824, they commenced upon the unfortunate state a series of depredations, so disastrous that in population and wealth it is now scarce "the shadow of its former self."

They destroyed property, killed cattle, carried off the women, killed and tortured the men from pure love of deviltry. One of their favorite tortures was to strip their unfortunate captive and bind him tightly to a huge cactus (*Peraskea Gigantea*) of the country.

To this day they are regarded as a fate to which everything is referable, and a common saying in regard to a bright boy is, "He will make a fine man if the Apaches do not tie him to a cactus." "Issue day" is a great day at the agencies. The women attend to draw their rations, the bucks to have a quasi-buffalo hunt. The beeves are delivered to the Indians "on the hoof" alive. At the appointed time every warrior is on his horse, ready and "eager for the fray." The boys surround the corral in which the cattle are confined, and practise with their arrows on the poor animals, until they are well-nigh frantic. The gate is then opened, and the herd rushes out, scattering widely over the plain, each animal followed by half a dozen yelling Indians. In ten to twenty minutes all are down, riddled with bullets and arrows. It is an exciting scene, but should be witnessed at a safe distance, as the Indians in their excitement throw their bullets in every direction. Ho sooner are the cattle down, than the squaws are at them. An officer told me that he had seen the tongue cut out of a beef while it was yet alive. This system of issue is a good school for cruelty.

Cruelty is both an amusement and a study. So much pleasure is derived from it, that an Indian is constantly thinking out new devices of torture, and how to prolong to the utmost those already known. His anatomical knowledge of the most sensitive portions of the human frame is most accurate, and the amount of whipping, cutting, flaying, and burning that he will make a human body undergo, without seriously affecting the vital power, is astonishing.

"When there is time for the indulgence of the pastime, no wounded man falls into his power but becomes at once the subject of experiment.

Of all the horrible stories which I have heard of Indian cruelty, one told me by old Espinosa is most vivid in its ghastly horror.

"When he was about twenty-four years old, a party of Comanches, from the same camp in which he lived, while on a raid into Mexico, attacked a large ranche. The inhabitants, being poorly armed, made little resistance, except a few men, who, getting into a courtyard, vigorously defended themselves with such weapons as came to their hands. All were soon dispatched, except one man, almost a giant in stature and strength, who, although armed only with an axe, killed one or two of his assailants and kept the others at bay. At last an Indian, getting on the wall, threw a lasso over his head, and, jerked off his feet, he was soon bound hand and foot. After the ruthless violation and murder of all the women, the children were fastened in a room, the ranche pillaged and set on fire in a dozen places. Taking with them as prisoner the one man who had signalized himself in the defence of the ranche, the Indians departed for their own country. On the long march the prisoner, though closely watched and guarded by day, and securely bound at night, was treated with extreme kindness. They complimented his courage in the highest terms; told him they intended taking him to their camp, adopting him into the tribe, and making a great chief of him. The trail followed, after leaving the head of the Nueces River, crossed the southern end of the high table-land known to whites as the "Staked Plains." At a water-hole on this table-land the party halted for several days. Telling the prisoner that they wanted it for some religious ceremony, they set him to digging a hole in the ground. Working with knife and hands, he, in a day or two, completed a pit about three feet in diameter and over five feet deep. Early next morning a rope was tightly tied about the ankles of the captive and wrapped spirally round his legs and body to the neck, binding his arms tightly to his sides. Rigid and immovable, the man was then planted upright like a post in the hole, the dirt filled in and tightly rammed down around him. When all was completed nothing but his head was visible. They then scalped his head, cut off his lips, eyelids, nose, and ears; danced around, mocked, taunted, and left him.

On their arrival at the camp the party described in detail their punishment of the Mexican, and in all the tribe it was regarded as an exquisite piece of pleasantry. The man would live, they said, for at least eight days, revived at night by the cold of the high Plains, to be driven mad next day by the hot sun beating on his scalped head and defenceless eyeballs, while myriads of flies would fill his wounds with maggots. This "joke" gained great celebrity among the southern Plains tribes, and the warrior who proposed it was regarded as an inventive genius of the first order.

The bodies of all men killed by Indians are almost always terribly mutilated, but it is not difficult to tell from the nature of this mutilation whether the bodies fell into their hands before or after death. If it be pierced with many bullet-holes or stuck full of arrows, or cut and slashed with deep and careless gashes, the spirit had passed before the Indian got possession; but artistic dissections, partial flayings, dislocations, breaking and splitting of fingers and toes, indicate that the poor fellow went to his long home with all the accompaniments of pain and horror that these devils can devise.

A few years ago, a gallant officer of cavalry surprised a village of Apaches. Among the prisoners was a sprightly girl of fourteen, who, taking the fancy of the officer's wife, was adopted into the family as a servant of all work. Nicely clothed, well fed, and kindly treated, she had every reason to be happy and contented.

Unfortunately she had been recently married, and her heart yearned for her lover-husband in the mountains. One morning she was gone. Alone, on foot, without food, she had started on a journey of more than a hundred miles to search for the scattered remnants of her band, secreted in the most secluded fastnesses. None but an Indian woman would have undertaken such a journey, none but an Indian would have succeeded. She was given up as hopelessly lost, when one morning she suddenly made her appearance. She had left, plump, clean, and well dressed; she returned naked, filthy, and emaciated.

On her arrival at the Apache camp, she found that her husband had been killed in the fight. Having now no protector, she was set upon by the other squaws and stripped of all her nice clothing. Starved and maltreated in every way, she finally made her escape from her red relatives and friends, to take refuge with her white enemies. Since then she has hated Indians with the most bitter, unrelenting hatred. She calls herself a white woman, and one cannot insult her more than by asking in her presence if she is an Indian.

Another officer, hunting Apaches in Arizona, one day surprised and captured three women, who were gathering the maguey plant. Two were left under a guard in camp, the other forced to conduct the troops to the Indian "rancheria." Just at daylight next morning, the two girls under guard began a most animated conversation, laughing heartily, and sometimes positively screaming with delight. They were talking over the attack of their own camp; and fancying how their fathers, mothers and lovers, terrified almost out of their wits, were scuttling away from the bullets, could find nothing but fun in the contemplation of the probable scenes. This is an excess of heartlessness not usual even among Indians.

I was once on a hunt with an Indian, whom, as he now wants to have a farm, take "the white man's road," and be a respectable citizen, I will call "Yellow Legs" (that not being his name). He is a good fellow, a splendid hunter, a man of more than average intelligence, quiet in his manner, but very blunt in his speech.

We had had a good day's hunt, and after supper were sitting smoking and chatting by the camp-fire, when this subject came up. After some conversation, I asked:—

"But how can you Indians be so heartlessly cruel?"

"Cruel," he repeated, "what do you call cruel?"

"Torturing your enemies; killing women and helpless children," I answered.

"Oome, oome," groaned Yellow Legs, sucking desperately at a cigar I had given him.

After a few moments he asked with an air of great care and circumspection:—

"Who made you?"

"God," I answered.

"And who is God?"

"The maker of all things.'

"I have heard of the white man's God. He makes everything, knows everything, does everything. Is he good?"

"Yes," I answered.

"Have you any other God?"

"No, there is but one God."

"Oome, oome, oome," groaned Yellow Legs. "If there is but one God, and he is good, how can you say that anything he does is bad? Does he not torture people with all sorts of diseases? Does he not kill women and children whenever he wants to. You are a fool, and talk like a preacher."

Civilization alone can translate savage cruelty.

DARING AND SKILL

IN Indian estimation, the skilful thief stands very nearly on a par with the daring fighter.

Success in war tends to ferocity among savages, indeed I am disposed to believe that success in single combat tends to brutalize every man. The admiration for a successful warrior is likely to be tempered with some fear of him, while admiration for the successful thief is only enhanced by envy of his skill and consequent wealth.

Indians are very like other people. Rich men have standing and consideration irrespective of their personal qualities, and without reference to how the riches were obtained. Besides this, Indians have peculiar ideas as to the rights of property. An act is not praiseworthy or criminal in itself, but from the standpoint from which it is viewed. It is the old fable, as to whose ox is gored.

An Indian steals the horses of an Indian of another tribe. In his own estimation and that of his tribe the act is admirable and worthy of all praise, while in the estimation of the loser and his tribe, the act is a most villainous theft, and the perpetrator deserving instant death.

To steal from a member of his own band is the greatest crime an Indian can commit; to steal from anyone else, and not be caught at it, is an act worthy the highest commendation. The man that steals an Indian's horse is a far greater enemy and criminal than he who steals his wife. No penalty except the payment of her marketable value attaches to the latter, while the doom of the captured horse-thief is certain death.

When not at war, Indians are not very careful of their horses, leaving the herd habitually in charge of the boys. The opportunities for stealing are so many and excellent that the temptation is often too strong to be resisted. A few reckless warriors will dash into a herd belonging to a neighboring and friendly tribe, and get away with as many as possible. To avoid identification (which would insure the return of the ponies and the punishment of the thieves, or involve the tribe in war), they will previously have disguised themselves in white men's clothing, or take care to drop arrows or moccasins of some far-away and usually hostile tribe.

This, however, is of late years a very uncommon occurrence. When the whole vast country was free to the Indian, the thieves could drive their stolen stock far away, dispose of, or enjoy it as seemed best. Now the lines of reservations restrict their roamings, and the stolen property can neither be concealed nor disposed of without discovery.

Where all are such magnificent thieves, it is difficult to decide which of the Plains tribes deserves the palm for stealing. The Indians themselves give it to the Comanches, whose designation in the sign language is a backward wriggling motion of the index finger, signifying a snake, and indicating the silent stealth of that tribe. There is no doubt that these Indians are the best and most successful sneak-thieves among red-skins. For crawling into a camp, cutting hopples and lariat ropes, and getting off undiscovered with the animals, they are unsurpassed and unsurpassable. I have known a Comanche to crawl into a bivouac, where a dozen old Texans, men accustomed to the wiles of the Indians, were sleeping each with horse tied to his wrist, by the lariat, cut a rope within six feet of the sleeper's person, and get away with the horse without waking a soul.

The corral fence at Fort Lincoln, Texas, was made of thorny chaparral brush, tightly pressed between upright posts set by twos. It was impassable for white man or horse, yet scarcely a week passed of the first summer after the establishment of the post, that the Indians did not get over this fence, and cutting horses from the picket line, endeavor to stampede them so thoroughly, as to make them break down the fence. This failed, and one or more Indians having been wounded at different times by the sentinels, a new plan was tried. The gate of the corral was a heavy wooden frame,, to which were hung two strong doors opening outward from the centre. These doors were chained together at night, and locked by the officer of the day, who kept the key. The only means of entering the corral after dark was by a small postern two feet by three, cut in one of the doors.

One night I was on duty as officer of the day; it was after twelve o'clock, and I was quietly getting ready to visit the guard and sentinels, when my movements were greatly accelerated by a shot proceeding apparently from the sentinel in the corral. Running at full speed, I entered the corral, to find the sentinel greatly excited. He had not fired; had seen or heard nothing but the shot which came apparently from the outside of the corral. By this time the guard had arrived, and procuring a lantern, we went outside and almost instantly stumbled over a body, which on examination proved to be that of the blacksmith, a quiet and excellent soldier. He had been shot through the heart and killed instantly. Next morning at daylight, the prince of all trailers, old Espinosa, was on the track. An officer and some twenty men were ordered out, and ran the Indians for fifty miles, getting so close to them that they broke and scattered, hiding themselves in the rocks and thickets of the Guadeloupe Mountains.

Espinosa found from the "sign" that the Indian had crawled around the corral fence, on to the parade ground, and was probably at work on the gate when the blacksmith suddenly came upon him and was shot, simply to further his own escape.

The effect of this murder was that the Comanches ceased to trouble Fort Lincoln, probably fearing retaliation.

It is true of all Indians, but especially a trait of Comanches, that when on a stealing expedition, they will not jeopardize the loss of a horse by firing a shot, except to save their own lives.

I was once with twenty infantry men stationed near a ranche named Las Laxas, guarding some fords of the Rio Grande, much used by the Comanches and Lipans. As protection against the excessive heat, I had built over and around my tent what Mexicans and frontiersmen call a *"ramada."* Forked poles are planted in the ground, other poles are laid on the forks, and on this frame is thrown a thick covering of leafy boughs. For the sides, poles are tied to the forks, and willows or other straight bushes are wattled in. It makes a most comfortable residence in the dry hot climate of the Plains, the tent being used only as bedchamber.

My men, similarly protected by *ramadas*, were some fifty yards away. Between us walked at night our only sentinel, and directly on his beat my horse was tied.

Late one night I was sitting in my *ramada* parlor, doing the most disagreeable duty that falls to the lot of a young officer—making out Quartermaster's papers—when my dog, lying at my feet, made a furious rush to the door, his hair all turned the wrong way. Somewhat startled I got up, walked to the door, and peered into the darkness, but seeing nothing, called to the sentinel, and as he had not seen or heard anything, I scolded the dog for making a false alarm. Some hours after, long before daylight, I was awakened by Mexicans from the ranche, who told me that Indians had been through and stolen all their horses. When daylight came I set the trailer to work up the case. About eight Indians had visited us. All but one had gone for the stock at the ranche. That one had fixed upon my horse, and his trail indicated that he had crawled about the *ramadas* half a dozen times, watching, hoping that the sentinel might be careless. He had come directly to my door; and, deeply indented in the soft ground not six feet from where I stood in the doorway, were the prints of his moccasins, showing where he had bounded for concealment behind a little mesquite bush when the dog made his onslaught.

Of course, he could have killed me, but he knew that a shot would rouse the command, and destroy all chances of stealing any horses from the ranche. He let me off, and undoubtedly considered himself well repaid, as the party got away safely with about twenty ponies. I could give numerous other instances personal to myself, or other officers, of the stealth and cunning of the Comanches, but enough has been told to prove their pre-eminence in these qualities.

For dash and boldness in thieving, I think the southern Cheyennes first, though closely emulated by Kiowas, Sioux, and Apaches.

In 1871, four companies of the Sixth United States Infantry were encamped for the night at Bear Creek, in Kansas. The mules belonging to the wagon train were quietly grazing, surrounded by herders and guard, when two Cheyenne Indians suddenly emerged from a little ravine, and shaking buffalo robes and yelling like fiends, dashed into the herd. In an instant all were off under the full headway of a stampede. It took but an instant for the command to turn out, but, in spite of hundreds of shots, the daring thieves succeeded in getting away with every animal.

Nearly every horse of four companies of the old Rifle Regiment were once lost near Fort Davis, Texas, by a sudden and daring dash, in the face of a strong guard, of less than half a dozen Mescalero Apaches. The Sioux in the north, and the Kiowas in Texas, repeat the story year after year, and hundreds of instances could be given if necessary.

A very remarkable ruse, and one which I have never heard of before or since, was tried on Captain Tupper, Sixth Cavalry. The captain had been out on a hard scout after the Cheyennes, and had succeeded in doing them some damage, though they had scattered and avoided a direct fight. Finding he could do them no more injury, and being short of rations, he started on his return to his post, Fort Dodge, Kansas, followed, however, by Indians, singly or in twos and threes, who, easily avoiding any direct onslaught of the heavier troops, effectually prevented hunting or straggling, and continually made efforts to get some of his horses. On the night before arrival at Fort Dodge, he encamped on Mulberry Creek. Every precaution was taken, and at dusk the horses were brought in, and besides being tied to the picket-rope, were hoppled. It was known that the Indians were all around them, for after dark they had made sufficient disturbance by yelling and firing shots to keep both men and horses in a high state of excitement.

Mulberry Creek is a deep bed with almost perpendicular banks. It is a peculiarly Plains stream, having water when it pleases. For a mile or more the water is running and in deep pools, for the next mile or more there is not a drop. The camp was in a sharp bend of the creek, peculiarly adapted for protection of the animals, being covered by this ditch, here almost impassable from deep water and steep banks.

The horses had been tied to a picket-line, at each end of which a fire was kept burning, so that no one could approach it without being seen. The men were bivouacked across the elbow, some little distance from the horses, and well beyond the firelight. In advance of these, sentinels lay flat on the ground and watched.

The Indians had quieted, and the camp settled into repose, when suddenly a huge ball of flame came rushing into camp, accompanied by the most terrific yells that ever split the throats even of Indians. Through and among the horses it went, rendering them so frantic with fear that some few burst the strong fetters with which they were held, and disappeared in the darkness. In an instant, and without command, the steady and well-disciplined soldiers seized their arms, and lying flat on the ground gave the Indians such a fusillade as to stop any desire to charge, and almost at the same moment the mysterious fire disappeared. The horses were soon quieted, and the camp settled itself to rest, which was not again disturbed.

Next morning the dead body of a miserable pony was found in the mud where the mysterious ball of fire had disappeared. The outside skin and flesh were burned to a cinder. The Indians had bound light grass and every inflammable material at hand all over the poor animal, then led him in the darkness as near as they dared go to the line of sentinels, turned his head in the right direction, and then set fire to him.

PLAINSCRAFT

THE Indian travels by instinct. Under no other hypothesis can we understand the marvellous journeys prolonged to months, and even years, made by individual Indians; or the ease and certainty with which, when tired of wandering, they make their way over the "trackless wastes" of the broad continent to the spot which they recognize as home.

With no knowledge of astronomy, of geography, or of the compass, the Indian performs feats of travelling for which a white man requires all three. To him there is no north, no south. In all the wide circle of the horizon there is not a single definite point of reference. He speaks of "sunrise" to designate the broad half of the horizon on which the sun rises and of "sunset" for the other side, but he makes no use of either for purpose of direction in travelling. So also in night travel; and though all races of men, in their emergence from the primitive condition, seem to have first used the stars as guides for assuring their journeys in a given direction, this seems never to have occurred to the Indian.

I have never yet seen an Indian who had mounted the ladder of human progress sufficiently far to have observed that there is one star which never perceptibly changes its place. With him there seems to be no necessity for such knowledge. Instinct—that incomprehensible something, that takes the lark to its nest in the wide sameness of the prairie, or the bee to its home in the hollow tree hidden in a labyrinth of such trees—is so strong in him, that he finds no need for geography, or points of compass.

Though the merest children ramble off from camp, on foot or on horseback for miles, I have heard of but a single instance of an Indian having been "lost;" and this is somewhat doubtful. The man was absent from his camp and family for some weeks. On his return, he had an elaborate story of being lost, with many adventures. It is far more probable that he had been on a thieving expedition, and covered his failure with this statement.

Ask an Indian how to go to a point at a distance, one mile or a hundred miles, and he will simply point out the direction. Press him closely, and if he has been to that point, he will by his minute description disclose another of his remarkable traits, his wonderful memory of landmarks.

Similar and monotonous as they appear to the uneducated eye, each hill and valley, each rock and clump of bushes, has for him its distinguishing features, which, once seen, he knows forever after, and careless as he appears when travelling, not one of these distinguishing features escapes him.

I have said that he travels by instinct, and this is always true on long journeys into unknown countries, or on the short trips of days or weeks spent in hunting. But for raids and forays, and for comfortable easy journeying from one portion of country to another, he makes use of these landmarks. This is his habitual and preferred mode of travel, and if going on such a journey into a country unknown to him, he consults with some warrior who has visited it; and it is simply astonishing how clearly the one describes, and the other comprehends, all that is necessary to make the journey a success.

The old guide Espinosa, from whom I learned the rudiments of plains-craft, told me that when he was a boy-prisoner among the Comanches, and the youngsters wished to go on a raid into a country unknown to them, it was customary for the older men to assemble the boys for instruction a few days before the time fixed for starting.

All being seated in a circle, a bundle of sticks was produced, marked with notches to represent the days. Commencing with the stick with one notch, an old man drew on the ground with his finger, a rude map illustrating the journey of the first day. The rivers, streams, hills, valleys, ravines, hidden water-holes, were all indicated with reference to prominent and carefully described landmarks. "When this was thoroughly understood, the stick representing the next day's march was illustrated in the same way, and so to the end. He further stated that he had known one party of young men and boys, the eldest not over nineteen, none of whom had ever been in Mexico, to start from the main camp on Brady's Creek in Texas, and make a raid into Mexico as far as the city of Monterey, solely by memory of information represented and fixed in their minds by these sticks. However improbable this may appear, it is not more improbable than any other explanation that can be given of such a wonderful journey.

A sequence of landmarks is more easily established and remembered than would appear probable to the uninitiated. The general direction is always preserved as far as possible. The first stage of the journey is towards some marked feature of the landscape, on or near that general direction, as a rocky cliff, a prominent knoll, or a gap in a ridge. Arriving at that point, some other prominent feature is selected, as far ahead as possible, and in the same general direction. The person following the Indian's direction will, on arriving at one landmark, readily recognize the next, and so on in sequence.

Unlike a white man, the Indian never feels so safe as when entirely alone. The sense of insecurity, the fear of surprise which haunts a war-party in an enemy's country, is not entertained by the solitary wanderer. He has no fears for his rear, for he knows how tedious and difficult is the process of working out the trail of a single man or horse. In advancing, he relies on his own sagacity and caution, and the immense advantage he has over his enemies in expecting and watching for them, while they are not expecting or looking for him. He seldom makes a fire, never sleeps near one. If he sees "sign" of the enemy, he hides himself in some place from which he can watch. If the enemy get sight of him, he doubles and hides in rocks and thickets, forcing his pursuers to hunt him by the slow process of trailing. In this way he protracts the pursuit until dark, and under its friendly cover, places as much distance as possible between himself and the dangerous neighborhood.

Doctor [Washington] Matthews, in his *Ethnology of the Hidatsa Indians*, gives account of two journeys made by solitary warriors from the Hidatsa village, one going far down the Lower Missouri, being absent twenty lunar months, the other to the Arctic regions, returning after a journey of seventeen months.

Of all the Indians, the Delawares seem to be most addicted to these solitary wanderings, undertaken, in their case at least, from pure curiosity and love of adventure.

Thirty years ago, John Connor, the head chief of this tribe, was living with his band near Fort Martin Scott in Texas, at which post I was stationed. He was then a man of about fifty years, and was justly renowned as having a more minute and extensive personal knowledge of the North American Continent than any other man ever had or probably will have. He was fond of telling of his adventures, and boy-like, I was never tired of listening to them; so we soon became great friends.

He told me, that when a boy of eighteen or nineteen, he conceived the most intense desire to see the ocean. At that time his band was sojourning on the banks of the Mississippi, within the limits of the then recently admitted state of Illinois. There were too many white people towards the East, so he decided to go West. Travelling on foot, generally alone, but occasionally with white or red trappers, he made his way to the mouth of the Columbia River, then south along the Pacific coast for many miles, until he came to a country occupied by Mexicans.

Liking these people, he remained some time among them, wandering as far south as the city of Durango, and learning to speak the language with some ease and fluency. Tiring of the sameness of city life, he returned through Texas to his people, having been absent nearly three years.

This was the longest continuous journey he had ever made, but afterwards he visited the city of Mexico, and in repeated journeys crossed and recrossed, north, south, east, and west, the vast expanse of wilderness, until he seemed to know every stream and mountain of the whole great continent west of the Mississippi River. And he knew it so well as to be able, not only to travel himself with certainty, but to instruct others how to travel. His brain seemed to be a vast reservoir of landmarks, arranged in sequence, ready for use for journeys in any direction or for any distance.

Black Beaver, the friend and guide of General (then Captain) Marcy,* was almost equally renowned for his wonderful journeys.

*Randolph B. Marcy, author, Civil War veteran, and father-in-law to General George Brinton McClellan.

Though not displayed in so marked a way, the Indian woman possesses this travelling instinct, only in a less degree than the man. The older women have a vast amount of outdoor work, hunting up stray ponies, etc., particularly in winter, when it is too cold for her lord and master to be out, or when he is probably losing the stray animals at the gaming-table.

Nothing is easier than to get lost in the sameness of the sand-hills, which border most of the Plains streams, but no amount of turning and twisting over the hills and through the thickets, ever interferes with the instinct that takes her direct to her camp whenever she wants to go there.

Several writers on Indians have been at pains to show the military precision of Indian movements in their changes of camp, one going so far as to declare that when the chief's tepee fluttered in the breeze, all other tepees must flutter; when his fell, all must fall. There could be no greater nonsense. When camp is to be moved, notice is formally given by criers, who, going through the village, repeat again and again the orders of the chief or dog-soldiers, that the camp will break up in the morning, and move to such a place on such a stream. If the journey be in a country supposed to be dangerous, all the young men are in the saddle soon after daylight, and scattered far and wide, covering all the country in front or on the flanks of the advance. A guard, generally of the older men, is left with the camp, and these bring up the rear. If there be no apprehension of danger, all the men so disposed will move off as soon as their horses are saddled. In either case the women come on with the pack-animals. All the packing of household-goods, striking the tepees, and loading the animals, is done by the women. Each family moves off when it is ready, the quick-working women of one family being well on the march before some of their slower neighbors have got their tepees down. I have many times seen Indian camps broken, and encountered or joined them on the march, and except when in momentary and most imminent danger, the whole movement is the reverse of military, being as individual as any such move could be. I once witnessed the breaking up and movement of a Sioux village of over three hundred lodges, probably fifteen hundred souls, going on the annual buffalo hunt. I was with a small hunting party camped near the village, and knowing that they were to move, I got up soon after daylight to see it. Early as I was, the movement had commenced, the long slopes of prairie being dotted with Indian men, some near, some far away, while Indians were constantly coming out of the tepees, and mounting the horses that stood saddled at the doors. By an hour after sunrise most of the men had disappeared, but by this time the camp had begun its movement. The pack-animals being loaded, the women mounted their ponies, and each family struck out in its own direction, and marched by itself, the only apparent care being to prevent the loose pack-animals of different families from mixing together. When the front of this column had got probably two miles from me, it was quite a mile in width, and even yet in the camp, squaws were striking tepees, and packing ponies.

On unusually level ground, and also in very rough and difficult country, where the range of vision is restricted, the Indians set up small mounds of stones. On the level mesas overlooking the precipitous cañon s of Lower Kansas, on the Uncompagre, and other (so-called) valleys of Colorado; in Utah, in the broken ground of the Laramie Plains, and all over the vast and difficult country north and east of the North Platte River, wherever the sameness of the water-worn steppes presents no natural distinctive "mark, such cairns are to be found.

I have heard many ingenious and far-fetched surmises as to their object. It is simply to establish a sequence of landmarks indicating the best route, and this purpose they serve admirably, not only in summer, but in winter, when snow has obliterated every other distinguishing mark. They, of course, only serve their purpose in open ground, where they can be seen, one from the other.

In timbered countries, so far north, or so elevated, as to be subject to deep and long-continued snows, stones will be found placed in the forks and branches of the trees, on each side of the route or trail, which when buried in snow, could not be followed except by this simple device.

The Indian travels comparatively little at night, never from choice, as he is unable to see his landmarks. When advancing on an enemy whom he hopes to surprise, or when escaping from too vigorous a pursuit, he overcomes this repugnance, and trusting to his instinct, gets along just as well, though not so comfortably.

READING "SIGN"—THE CAREER OF PEDRO ESPINOSA

AMONG frontier whites, the term trail is loosely and widely applied to any definite mark left on the ground, other than a road. Thus a wagon train going across country really makes a road, but its track is habitually called a trail, until use has beaten it into a road. Indeed, a few of the most prominent roads of the frontier always retain this designation, and it is common to hear men speak of the "Old Santa Fe trail," "the California trail," "the Salt Lake trail," though the routes so designated have been for many years thoroughly-beaten and well-travelled roads. The most noted of these was the "California trail," reaching from Leavenworth, Kansas, to Sacramento, a distance of near two thousand miles, through a wilderness, almost every foot of which was infested with hostile Indians.

For twelve or fifteen years this trail was daily travelled by stages, and many of the most thrilling and tragic episodes of frontier life arose from the constant efforts of the savages to capture these stages.

The drivers were heroes; and though each stage carried a small guard of soldiers, passengers who had "no stomach for the fray" were out of place on the California trail.

Scarcely a week passed but a stage was attacked. Occasionally one was waylaid, the horses shot down, the guards and passengers killed in fight or captured and subjected to horrible tortures.

One of the most exciting of frontier scenes was a running fight between a stage-load of guards and passengers and a horde of mounted savages. In such contests the savages were generally beaten off.

In the wilder regions of country, where there are no roads, the term "trail" is applied by Indians and frontiersmen, alike to the old beaten paths worn by the feet of their ponies and the dragging lodge-poles, and to the track or spoor of any animal. These are, however, differently designated, the beaten track being habitually spoken of as an "old trail." When, therefore, an Indian or frontiersman speaks of a trail, he habitually means the marks left on the ground by the recent passage of an animal or party.

"Sign" in frontier language means any evidence that something has been on that ground. The ashes of a fire, fragments of clothing, an empty can, footprints of men or animals, all are "sign." A trail is a succession of these marks or signs. A "trail" is made up of sign, but sign is by no means a trail. Feeding deer or scratching turkeys make sign, but it may be impossible to trail them. There may be an abundance of sign in and about an abandoned camp, yet if those who made it are moving cautiously, it may take the keenest eye, the closest scrutiny, and the utmost limits of this knowledge to detect the trail by which they left it. The safety of a party may depend on the proper reading of a" sign;" the success of a pursuit depends almost entirely on the ability of the pursuer to work out-trail."

Trailing is the art of evolving trail from sign. The requisites of a good trailer are sharp eyes, perfect knowledge of the appearance and character of the sign made by whatever is being trailed; and, when trailing Indians, a thorough knowledge of the country and the habits of the Indians.

To all people who live on the frontier, or in a sparsely settled country, some knowledge of trailing is absolutely necessary. A pony strays, or a cow fails to come home. There are no neighbors of whom inquiries can be made, or who might take up the runaway. It must be hunted up, and this can only be done surely by its trail. There seems, however, to be a lack of capacity on the part of the white man to become really expert in trailing, and this is not necessarily due to lack of early training, for white men who have been captured when boys, and lived with the Indians until maturity, are? and always remain comparative bunglers.

Ignoring the savage talent at its command, the government keeps numbers of these white (so-called) guides and trailers in its employ. In over thirty-two years' experience I have never yet seen one who was better than a mere schoolboy, when compared with Indian trailers. "Were there any meaning in the common cry of "efficiency and economy" something might be done in this direction.

It is a curious fact that Mexicans, under favorable circumstances, develop this faculty in a degree so marvellous as to be wonderful even to the Indians themselves. As a rule they are not remarkable either for courage or for veracity, but as trailers, guides, packers, they are invaluable.

The best trailer I ever saw was a Mexican, and he was also remarkable as abounding in the simple manly virtues.

Pedro Espinosa was born about the year 1810 in a little ranche on the banks of the Rio Grande, near the village of Laredo. When he was about nine years old this ranche was captured by a raiding band of Comanches, all the inhabitants put to death with the usual Indian accompaniments of horror, except a number of children of both sexes, who were carried into captivity.

On reaching the home encampment of the tribe these children were adopted into it, but though generally treated as Indian children, were carefully watched. When about thirteen years of age, Espinosa was permitted to accompany a war party on a raid against the Tonkaways, and so distinguished himself that he was made a warrior. Within a few years he became a distinguished and prominent man.

But though apparently thoroughly a Comanche Indian; though having several wives and a numerous family; though fighting with the bravest, stealing with the most crafty, and committing outrages with the most cruel; though taking part in all their councils and ceremonies, and identified with all their interests, he had never forgotten his native land, nor forgiven the violation and murder of his mother. He hated the Indians and their ways with the most bitter, unrelenting hatred, and his heart yearned for return to his own country and people.

Whether, in spite of most careful dissimulation, he revealed something of this feeling, or from the craft and suspicion natural to the Indian character, no opportunity was ever given him to carry his designs into effect. Though a dozen or more raids were made yearly into Mexico, he was never permitted to be one of a party that went near the Rio Grande.

Among his other accomplishments Espinosa was a most successful bear-hunter. The Guadeloupe Mountains (now in Texas) were then as now, infested by great numbers of these animals; and when Espinosa had been with the Indians nineteen years, he was permitted to go with a party to those mountains on-a bear-hunt.

One night when the other Indians were asleep, he crawled among the horses, selected the best two, without regard to ownership, and by morning had put many miles between himself and his late companions.

After a long journey he arrived safely at Laredo, where, the memories of his boyhood being perfect, he soon made himself known to his relatives. In course of time he married and settled down, and when I knew him he was a useful and honored member of the community in which he lived.

Utterly ignorant of all civilized knowledge, he was full of wisdom in all that pertained to his own mode of life. Brought up a thief, he was honest and faithful. Though nineteen years of his life had been passed amid the crime, horror and licentiousness of savage life, he was a firm friend, a kind and loving husband and father, a gentle, affectionate, loveable man.

In 1849 I commenced my "Plains" life at Fort Lincoln, Texas, not on the Plains, but on a military line established to protect the southern settlements of Texas from the incursions of the Plains Indians. Covering the Bandera and other much-used passes of the Guadeloupe Mountains, Fort Lincoln was an important position; and it was extremely necessary that a thoroughly competent and reliable man, well posted in all the wiles of the Indians, should be selected as guide and trailer for the troops stationed there. The choice fell on Espinosa. For many years he served the government well and faithfully, and at last yielded up his life in fidelity to it.

In 1861, when the traitor Twiggs had planned and was consummating the surrender of all the troops and material of Avar in Texas, Espinosa was selected to carry dispatches from Union men in San Antonio, to Colonel Peeve, then on his way to the coast with a command, notifying him of the condition of affairs, and warning him to turn back, and try to reach the states by way of Santa Fe. While executing this office, Espinosa was captured by some of the forces sent to intercept Peeve, and the dispatches found on his person. After reading them, his captors drew their pistols and shot him to death.

Espinosa has yet a warm place in my affection. He guided me in my first Indian fight; he gave me my first lessons in plains-craft, and in hunting for large game.

As a trailer he was a marvel, even to the Indians themselves; and cautious and skilful as might be the pursued, it seemed impossible to hide a trail from the trained eyes of this remarkable man. One or two of his exploits will show, better than any description, to what skill a trailer may attain.

I was once sent in pursuit of a party of murdering Comanches, who had been pursued, scattered, and the trail abandoned by a company of so-called Texas rangers. On the eighth day after the scattering, Espinosa took the trail of a single shod horse. When we were fairly into the rough, rocky Guadeloupe Mountains, he stopped, dismounted, and picked up from the foot of a tree the four shoes of the horse ridden by the Indian. With a grim smile he handed them to me, and informed me that the Indian intended to hide his trail. For six days we journeyed over the roughest mountains, turning and twisting in apparently the most objectless way, not a man in the whole command being able to discover, sometimes for hours, a single mark by which Espinosa might direct himself. Sometimes I lost patience, and demanded that he show me what he was following *poco tiempo*, (in a short time), he would blandly answer, and in a longer or shorter time, show me the clear-cut footprints of the horse in the soft bank of some mountain stream, or point with his long wiping-stick to most unmistakable "sign" in the droppings of the horse. Following the devious windings of this trail for nearly a hundred and fifty miles, scarcely ever at a loss, and only once or twice dismounting, more closely to examine the ground, he finally brought me to where the Indians had reunited.

Again I was in pursuit of a party of Comanches, several hundred strong. On reaching the head springs of the Perdinalis River, I found that the Indians had made there a halt of several days; that the vicinity for one or two miles in every direction was marked with the footprints of grazing horses; that the Indians had evidently scattered in every direction on leaving, and set fire to the prairie behind them. In despair I went into camp, and set Espinosa to work out the problem. At night he returned, unsuccessful but confident, having labored patiently for six or seven hours. Before dawn he was out again. About eleven o'clock I rode out on his trail, easily followed in the black ashes, and found him just about to return to me. He had succeeded. We returned to camp. The command, all ready, marched in rear of Espinosa for twelve or fifteen miles, when we struck the trail of the united Indians.

That night he explained how he had managed. Going down the river from the camping-ground of the Indians, so far as to be sure he was beyond the range of feeding-horses, he made a circuit, the camp as centre, carefully examining the ground. He soon discovered" sign." Dismounting and going down on his hands and knees, he, with his breath, blew away the light ashes, until sufficient prints were found to show the direction of the trail. Mounting his horse, he continued his circuit, finding other "sign," and fixing in the same way the direction of the trails which diverged from each other like lines from the centre of a circle. A second circuit about four miles from camp, discovered the trails, still diverging. A third circuit, a mile and a half beyond the last, discovered them, as he anticipated, converging. Carefully taking the direction of three or four, and finding they all pointed to a common centre, he fixed the direction of that point in his mind; and so beautifully was the whole problem worked out, that if he had been one of the Indians, previously instructed where to go, he could not have gone to that point more directly.

Their mode of life and natural capacity for this kind of education, make all Indians wonderful trailers; and although even the poorest among them is superior to any white man, the tribes and individuals differ in their capabilities as trailers in a degree hardly to be expected. The northern and central Plains Indians are comparatively poor trailers, buffalo having, until within a few years, been their means of support, and its pursuit requiring little knowledge of trailing. Those tribes which depend for their daily food on small animals and game, become expert in this art.

Of all tribes which inhabit the Plains, the small remnant of the Delawares are probably the most generally expert, though they are closely emulated by the Comanches. Even they, however, must yield to some of the mountain tribes. I doubt if any Indian ever quite attained the perfection attributed to his heroes by Cooper, though some of the feats told of the Apaches are almost as marvellous.

An officer of the Twenty-third Infantry, having a small force of soldiers, and some Apache guides, was scouting after hostile Apaches in Arizona. To be successful, all movements of troops had to be made at night, though the scouts stealthily spread over the country by day, looking for trails. One afternoon, a scout came in and reported that he had found a fresh trail, which he believed led to a "rancheria," or village of hostiles. After dark the command moved.

In due time the trail was found and carefully followed, the Indian scouts working out the devious route of the hostiles, through rocks and thickets, by feeling the ground with their fingers.

There was a halt and consultation in front, and word was sent back to the officer in command that a new and fresher track had crossed the trail they were pursuing. He went to the front. The scouts informed him that there was the fresh print in the soft ground of a naked foot on, but across, the general direction of the trail. Blankets were procured, and held up around the spot as a screen. A match was struck, by the light of which it was discovered that the new footprint was that of a bear. Following the original trail, before daylight the "rancheria" was discovered and the officer was enabled to make a successful attack.

Trailing is a most important and necessary part of the education of every Indian. Without knowledge of it he could neither disguise his own trail, or follow with any certainty the trail of his enemies, and in some portions of the country he would most certainly starve if he could not read "sign." He is taught from childhood to note every mark on the ground, to tell what made it, its age, and everything about it of importance to himself. His daily life as a hunter makes him thoroughly conversant with the habits of game animals. These and a pair of eyes exquisitely sharpened by constant use, enable him confidently to take and keep a trail, where a white man, even with sharp eyes and some practice, would only see an occasional unmeaning mark.

In the previous chapter, I have stated that on ordinary journeys through a country but little known to him, the Indian travels by "landmarks." A knowledge of this peculiarity greatly facilitates the pursuit, and a good trailer, especially in a rough and broken country, will soon so locate the series of landmarks by which the pursued are travelling as to be able when entering a valley or basin, to tell almost the exact spot where the trail will leave it. When, therefore, the pursued resorts to ruses and doubles, the pursuer wastes no time in carefully tracking him through all his windings, but goes at once to where his knowledge tells him the trail will pass, there looks for it, and finding it, pushes on with renewed confidence. The pursued may spend several hours in making a devious trail, which the pursuer will get over in as many minutes.

Only imminent danger will force such an Indian away from his sequence of landmarks. When, however, he finds his pursuers gaining on him, he abandons it at once, strikes off in the most unexpected and erratic way, resorting to every possible ruse, keeping on rocky ground, or in the bed of a brook, to delay or baffle the pursuit. If these fail, the party agree upon a place of reunion, fifty, sixty, or a hundred miles away, and scatter in every direction, each by himself, satisfied that no trailer is expert enough to follow a single track as rapidly as it can be made.

The hard ground of the high prairie is peculiarly favorable to the pursued; and the ease with which a horseman can travel anywhere, and in any direction, renders the trailing of the Plains Indians a slow and difficult process. It is not at all remarkable that so many arduous pursuits are simply waste of labor and horse-flesh, for it may be laid down as' a rule that a party of raiding warriors cannot be overtaken except by surprise. The pursuit of a tribe or village is different. Encumbered with the women, children, baggage and extra stock, their progress is necessarily slow, and they cannot scatter.

The most extraordinary feat of travel and pursuit within my knowledge took place in September and October, 1878. A part of the Northern Cheyennes, about one hundred and twenty men, with all their women and children, left Fort Reno in the Indian Territory, fought their way through one line of environing troops, evaded and outran two other lines.

These Indians, encumbered as they were, travelled nearly, if not quite, three hundred miles in ten days. They marched in open order, covering a belt of from three to eight miles wide, and making a trail on the hard prairie so slight that even an expert trailer could only have followed it with difficulty.

After their last fight with the troops (in which Colonel Lewis was killed), they were followed by Major Manck and his cavalry with such remorseless vigor, that they were forced into the settlements of Kansas to obtain a remount. Even with this, however, they were barely able to gain the shelter of the sand-hills west of the head of the Loup, where they secreted themselves in a country devoid of water except a few ponds known only to themselves. Here they were found completely exhausted, by troops of the Fourth line, and captured.

As trailers, Major Manck had a number of white guides, and one invaluable Pawnee Indian. The white scouts spread out fan-like far in advance, watching, and following the trail on the ground. The Pawnee travelled on his knowledge of the sequence of landmarks, by which the Indians used formerly to travel through this country, and though the white guides were frequently temporarily at fault, the Indian never hesitated a moment.

The weakness of the Indian is his trail. Could he get rid of it, he would be unconquerable except by treachery. Fortunately for his enemies he knows this weakness, giving it probably too much value.. Cunning, crafty, secret, swift, and enduring, he has perfect confidence in himself and his powers, but he knows that it is by means of the trail that he gives his enemy the most effective blows, and he is continually uneasy lest that enemy should turn the tables, and strike him by the same means. This is why he is so bold when alone, so timid when with a party.

A raiding party of Indians, coming to a recent trail of troops, will stop, examine, hesitate, follow it probably for miles. Concluding finally that there is no serious cause for alarm, they may go on toward their original destination. If another recent trail of troops be struck within a few miles, the party will most probably abandon its schemes and go back. This is not that the Indian fears to be intercepted. He cares nothing for the strategical disadvantage of an enemy in his rear, but the frequent and recent trails show the presence and activity of the troops. These may cross his trail at any moment, and following it, strike him by surprise in his camp.

In going on or returning from a raid, he cares nothing for advance guards, but always when he has cause to believe there is danger, some of the most trusty warriors follow on the trail as rear guards, three or four miles behind the main body. Surprise is destruction, and surprise is most likely to come from the rear and by means of his trail.

ADVENTURES ON THE PLAINS—EXCITING SCENES

HIS stealth, cunning, endurance, and knowledge of the habits of animals, make the Indian the best hunter in the world, but as a rule he is not remarkably successful. Considering the advantages , that these qualities give him, he is not comparable, as a game-killer, to the white hunter of the frontier. This is due principally to the fact that he is a very poor shot, ammunition being far too scarce and valuable to be expended in practice, and partially to his nervous excitability in the presence of game.

An Indian will spend hours patiently and stealthily searching for game in its probable haunts. When found, he may, if it is not in a position favorable to his approach, spend other hours as patiently watching it. The animal finally getting into good position, he crawls silently towards it, but aware of his deficiencies as a shot, and the value of his ammunition, and wishing to make "assurance doubly sure," he always tries to get nearer, and yet nearer, frequently frightening away the game long after he is within point-blank range. Time is nothing to the Indian. Having a fair shot at a deer, within a hundred yards, he will spend an hour trying to reduce the distance to seventy-five yards, then another hour in bringing it down to fifty yards. Many excellent opportunities are thus lost.

Once, when out hunting, I fired at a splendid buck, about one hundred and twenty yards from me, across a little prairie. It fell dead, when apparently from under its very feet, up sprang an Indian. Pie was within thirty yards of it, and yet trying to get nearer. His disgust at the inopportuneness of my shot was only equalled by his astonishment at the distance.

The bow could not be relied on to kill at much over thirty yards, and until the introduction of the long-range rifle, the large mass of game killed by Indians was within twenty yards. Even now fifty or sixty yards is a long shot at any animal, except antelope.

The Indian is an avaricious hunter. Let him get within his own distance of a single animal, and he is almost sure to get it; but if several animals are together, he is always hoping that his "medicine" is good enough to secure him a "pot-shot," from which he will get several or all. Aiming now at one, now at another, again at a bunch, he will work himself into such a state of excitement, that the chances are two to one that he becomes incautious and frightens the game, or firing, misses all.

In the mere hunting (finding and approaching game) there is as little difference between Indians as in their riding; but in success in bagging it, individuals and tribes differ in a remarkable degree, those tribes which depended on the buffalo having indifferent success with smaller game.

The pursuit of the buffalo was, after war, the noblest excitement of the Plains Indian, but the slaughter of this animal was accomplished differently by different tribes.

Even when buffalo were plentiful, they were carefully protected by the Middle Plains Tribes, no individual warrior of Cheyennes or Arapahos being permitted to ride into or after a herd, or even to shoot an animal unless it was alone, or the herds were moving. All were required to keep away from herds which were stationary, and thousands of buffalo might thus remain in the close vicinity of an Indian camp for weeks, when half a dozen white men would have frightened them all away in a few days.

So far as I am able to ascertain, either from writers or by questioning Indians, the "surround" of buffalo was peculiar to the Cheyennes and Arapahos. The Dacotas, an exceptionally improvident people, take no care of the buffalo. Two or three youngsters, out on a hunt, find a herd, and dashing into it, take great credit to themselves for killing one or two each; an act which among the Cheyennes would have been rewarded with a whipping, such as they would remember with terror all their lives.

Even in the great fall hunt, the Sioux make no "surround," but rely for their meat and skins on a square chase of the herd. The Crows, and some other far-northern tribes, are said to be as improvident as the Sioux, and kill the buffalo in the same way.

The Pawnees were famous for making quasi "surrounds," driving the buffalo over precipices, and killing immense numbers, many of which spoiled before the women could perform their work upon them.

The Kiowas and Comanches almost invariably used the lance in their chases after buffalo, a weapon all the more deadly because it was silent.

Surrounds of elk were made in much the same way by the middle Plains Indians. One or two small fragments of tribes now living in the Indian Territory used formerly to be wonderfully successful in killing elk on horseback. Each hunter was armed with a long pole, light but strong, the smaller end of which was split and forced open for about a foot, forming a Y. About six inches from the open end was fastened a knife-blade, sharpened to the keenest edge, and set diagonally in the Y, the whole being secured and strengthened with raw-hide.

A herd being discovered, the hunters approach against the wind, and dash suddenly upon the frightened beasts, which, confused by the onslaught, and having no leader, crowd together. Punning up behind an elk the hunter sets the crotch of his pole against the hind leg just above the knee. A sharp push severed the hamstring. The other leg was quickly served in the same way, and the game secured.

The mountain Indians make a sort of surround of elk in winter which is said to be very successful. During the deep snows, .this animal collects in great herds on the high exposed slopes from which the wind has driven the snow. A herd being discovered in such position, the Indians creep around, and drive them into a deep snow-drift, where they are butchered at leisure.

The Utes are said to make "surrounds" of antelope, but I do not know how it is done.

But all this was in the "good old times." Except those far north between the Missouri River and the British line, which have been protected from the insatiable "pot-hunter" by an environment of savage tribes, the buffalo is practically extinct.

Civilization has laid its hand on many of the best hunting-grounds. The "Republican country" (all that between the Platte and Arkansas

Rivers), which, only eight short years ago was a veritable hunter's paradise, teeming with animal life, is now dotted with farms and villages.

In May, 1871, I drove in a light wagon along the Arkansas River, from Walnut Creek to Pawnee Fork, through one herd of buffalo, not less than twenty-five miles wide, and extending north and south as far as the eye could reach. On the very ground on which Larned City now stands, I one day in pure wantonness gave chase in my light wagon to a herd of buffalo, and bagged two.

All the large game is rapidly going with the buffalo. Civilization crowds them into restricted areas, where they are set upon by the "pot-hunter," and the carcasses whirled off to Eastern markets.

Until within a few years the Plains Indian hunted the smaller animals, deer and antelope, as the white sportsman hunts them, more for pleasure than from actual need of the proceeds. The hunting was done on horseback, and only when he felt like it. Now the Indian is forced into competition with professional white hunters, armed with the most improved weapons. To secure game now he must work. What he lacks in skill as a shot, he tries to make up by care and patience in the hunt itself. Creeping noiselessly as a snake through thickets and jungle, or with his head covered by a cap of weeds or grass, crawling on his belly across the bare prairie, he will spend the whole day in labor that no white man would stand. He is very susceptible to cold, and in winter hunts very little, only when forced to it by actual hunger.

Late in the fall, antelope collect in herds, hundreds, even thousands, running together like sheep. Of late years, that is, since he obtained the breech-loading rifle, such a herd is a true godsend to the Indian.

Riding slowly and carefully as near as possible to the herd without alarming it, he suddenly dashes in, and riding almost among the terrified animals, pumps his bullets into them until his ammunition is expended, or his horse tired out. The antelope crowd together in their fright and present a mark not easy to miss. Eight or ten antelope is not an unusual number for a good hunter to bag from a large herd, in one such chase.

I have never yet seen a trap, pitfall, springe, or other device for taking game which might be suspected of being native to the Indian. I may even go further and assert, that (except the common steel trap) I have never seen or personally known of any trap being used by any Indian of any tribe with which I have come in contact. I once thought this peculiar to the Plains tribes, and due to the fact that having an abundance of large game, easily killed with bow or lance, their inventive faculty was never stimulated by necessity.

Wider experience has convinced me that this lack of inventive faculty is not confined to the Plains Indians. Many of the aboriginal inhabitants of the furbearing regions in the north are now good trappers, but the art is not natural to them, having been acquired from long intercourse with the old French trappers. Some few of the occupants of the Plains, as the Delawares, are good trappers, but they are merely imitators, using civilized traps exclusively.

Most of the tribes of the Pacific coast and on the waters of the Columbia and other great western streams, and some of the northern tribes east of the Mississippi, have traps and baskets for catching fish. But the southern Plains tribes have no such appliances. A few fish are killed by lance or arrows, but until within a very few years, these Indians had no knowledge of angling with line and hook. They are not fish-eaters, preferring even offal.

When the Cantonment (Indian Territory) was first established, an Indian would gladly exchange a beautiful bass of three or four pounds, for a pound of bacon or sugar. They have learned better now, and though they will not eat the fish themselves, they ask a higher price for it.

The Cheyennes and Arapahos have a curious tradition, or rather a religious superstition, regarding the buffalo. They believe that these animals are created within the bowels of the earth; that every year, when the young grass appears, herds of thousands pour-out of two holes in the ground, and, under the direction of the Good God, depart on their long journeys to the countries of those tribes whom he desires especially to favor, or who have the most potent medicine men. They believe that these holes are on the "Staked Plains," south of the Canadian, and east of the Pecos; and there are now living, men of both these tribes, who will take oath after their most solemn forms, that they have been to the spot, and seen the buffalo coming out in countless throngs.

I have once or twice mentioned "Stone Calf," a chief of the Southern Cheyennes, intelligent and influential. He is not a good Indian from the "Ring" standpoint, as he submits to starvation and imposition with a very bad grace. Last spring (1880), when begging for food, and urging me to permit him to go to the "Staked Plains" for buffalo, he assured me most solemnly that he knew where these holes are, and would be able to get all the buffalo he wanted.

I attempted to rally him on the absurdity of his belief, but found myself in a very few moments in such position as if I had attempted to banter a High Churchman on his belief in the Trinity, or a Roman Catholic on the authenticity of a miracle.

He was in real, solid earnest, and as I never interfere in the religious beliefs of people, I backed down as gracefully as possible.

Wherever the buffalo are yet to be found, the old rules for hunting yet obtain. The Indians on reservations are not permitted to go off for these hunts, without the presence of an officer and small force of troops. In September, 1880, a party of Sioux from the Standing Rock Agency, went on a buffalo hunt, accompanied by Lieut. Ogle of the 17th Infantry, and a small force. I append a synopsis of his report, showing the power and absolute control of the dog-soldiers and the general ceremony attending this (to the Indian) most important of duties and exciting of pleasures.

"The Indians conducted their march as though invading a hostile country. A large number of young men were appointed soldiers to conduct the march and hunt, and for the policing and protection of the camp. These men had their faces blackened. Seventy-five to one hundred marched on either flank, from one-half to a mile from the main body and parallel to it. They were mounted on the best ponies and looked like a body of cavalry. About a dozen unmounted men walked with each party, and were known as 'the walking chiefs.' Another party of walking chiefs preceded the main column and conducted the march. By walking they were enabled to determine when the women and children were tired, and the marches were short and the halts frequent.

"About dusk the runners sent out the night before came in and were received with great ceremony, the Indians collecting in a circle around a fire, singing, howling, and beating on tin cans. About one hundred of the best mounted young men dashed out at full speed to meet them, circling around them, the scene representing the grand entree of a circus. The chief embraced the runners and assisted them to dismount. Then a smoke was taken all around, and after three times invoking them to tell the truth as to what they had seen, the runners spoke for the first time. The report of buffalo seen created a great excitement. The Indians were forbidden to shoot, and some unlucky ones who were tempted by deer and antelope had their guns taken from them, and were soundly beaten with heavy clubs, their ribs being broken in some cases. On the 26th of September, camp was formed and the hunt commenced. A herd of seventy buffalo was surrounded and everyone killed, the Indians claiming them all, though Lieut. Ogle's party joined in the hunt "The Indians were anything but pleasant companions, and very disagreeable masters; and they issued orders that were odious to the white men, but which they thought it expedient to obey; so it was determined to leave them and return home by Grand Liver. To this the Indians objected, and declared that if the white men went that way they should go naked and on foot. They preferred that Lieut. Ogle and party should return the way they came, but wished them to remain, which they did. When they struck a herd the next day the Indians claimed it for themselves, but suggested that an old bull or two off on the right would furnish excellent sport for the whites. Following these bulls, they were fortunate in finding a large herd. Fourteen were shot, but when a party were sent for the robes the next day, it was found that the Indians had been ahead of them. The next day, Sept. 29, Lieut. Ogle returned to his post by the most direct route. At this time the Indians had killed two hundred antelopes, one hundred and fifty to two hundred buffalo, and a number of deer, otter, and beaver.

During their first day's run many accidents occurred, eleven Indians being thrown, and one having his arm broken. Another was reported shot."

ANECDOTES AND INCIDENTS

THE possession of domestic animals may be regarded as an exponent of civilization, the number and variety possessed by a people being usually in direct proportion to its advancement. Domestic animals indicate stability, and he who possesses them in variety must have a home. Indians are no exception to this rule, those tribes most advanced being best off in this respect, and vice versa.

The semi-civilized tribes of the Indian Territory have horses, cattle, sheep, hogs, and every animal ordinarily domesticated by whites, and barnyard fowls in great variety and abundance. The Zuni and other Pueblo Indians own and breed horses, cattle, sheep, goats, dogs, cats and chickens.

The wilder Indians who possess domestic animals, may fairly be divided into "animal-breeding" and "animal-stealing" tribes. In the first-class, the Navahos stand pre-eminent, owning and breeding immense herds of horses, asses, sheep and goats. They have dogs, but no cattle, cats, or fowls. The mountain Utes aspire to emulate the Navahos, but as yet only a few individuals have met with success. Ouray greatly encouraged this business, and himself possessed large herds of horses, asses, cattle and sheep.

The Plains tribes possess and breed only horses and dogs, the mules in their possession being invariably stolen, or purchased from other tribes. Many of the tribes west of the Rocky Mountains, particularly those in Eastern Oregon and Washington Territory, breed great numbers of horses.

Though the Apaches habitually own and occasionally breed horses, they belong properly to the "animal-stealing" class. They live in a country so totally devoid of all the ordinary necessaries of life, that during winter almost every horse, colt and mule is killed for food. In spring the stock is replenished at the expense of their neighbors.

The large mass of the tribes between the Rocky and coast ranges of mountains, neither own nor breed horses. They are excellent at stealing these animals, but either from ignorance of his proper use or from constant craving for animal food they no sooner get possession of a horse than he is killed and eaten.

The name "Digger" is applied loosely to a number of tribes of miserable Indians who roam about the deserts of Utah, Nevada, and California, or live in brush huts on reservations. These appear to be nearly as low down in this scale of humanity as it is possible to be. Their food is principally grasshoppers, green or dried. They have no domestic animals, not even a dog.

To the nomads of the Plains, the horse is now so invaluable that it is difficult to realize how they managed to live before they got possession of him. The horses introduced by the Spaniards must have been inferior in size, or the race has greatly degenerated. Compared to the ordinary American horses the Indian ponies are very small. Before the Cherokees were removed from North Carolina, they had a race of ponies very diminutive, but so strong and so extremely docile, ';hat extravagant sums were paid for them by whites, for the use of invalids and children. The mustang, or wild horse, from which the Indian pony comes, is an exceedingly vicious brute, and his descendants do not much improve in temper. It would be curious to inquire into the origin of the much smaller and more docile pony of the Cherokees.

To the Plains Indian the pony is an inseparable companion and an indispensable servitor. If an Indian had no pony, and could get none cheaper, he would readily give his favorite wife for one. Indeed, cheap as ponies are on the Plains, the ordinary price for a maiden is only from one to four; and though a rich man may be assessed five or six ponies for taking a poor man's wife, this comes from a spirit of fairness and equity, and is without necessary relation to the market value of either women or ponies. The pony is a necessity, the wife a luxury.

Averaging scarcely fourteen hands in height, he is rather slight in build, though always having powerful forequarters, good legs, short strong back, and full barrel. He has not the slightest appearance of "blood," though his sharp nervous ears and bright vicious eyes indicate unusual intelligence and temper, but the amount of work he can do, and the distance he can make in a specified (long) time, put him fairly on a level with the Arabian or any other of animal creation.

I once tried to buy a pony that took my fancy, and offered the owner (an American) what I considered a good price, forty dollars. He looked at me a moment in surprise, and said his lowest price was six hundred dollars. I thought the man a braggadocio and said nothing more. I subsequently learned that the man was a professional express-rider, and for the six months previous had been employed by the government and individuals of Chihuahua to carry mail once a week between Chihuahua and El Paso, nearly three hundred miles, the road being closed to ordinary travel by the Apaches. Hiding that one pony, he had made the distance in three consecutive nights, hiding by day, and next week made the distance back in the same time, receiving one hundred dollars for each trip. Six months of this work had not diminished the fire or flesh of that wonderful pony.

Though of indispensable value to the Indian, the pony receives not a particle of care or attention. He is never stabled, washed, rubbed, curried, blanketed, shod, fed nor doctored. When not under the saddle his life is spent in the herd. When, in the home camp, he brings his master from a hard day's work, the attentive wife slips off saddle and bridle, and lets him go to the herd, or feed at pleasure. When in a temporary camp, he is picketed and must make the best meal he can by cropping the grass within the limits of his tether.

On a march, the condition of his pony's back does not seem to trouble the Indian at all. The ill-fitting Indian saddle almost always tears the horse's back, and the rider accepts it as a dispensation of Providence, the act of the Bad God, for which he is not in any way responsible. In summer he may take the trouble to tie a cloth over the sores to keep the flies out, or when a foot becomes very tender from bad ground or long travel, he may tie it up in a piece of buffalo robe; but this is the extent of consideration the pony ever receives from his master.

In the winter he is a most miserable object, an animated skeleton. Exposed to the terrible cold and piercing winds of the Plains, his scanty and innutritious food buried beneath the snow, he would undoubtedly starve, but that the squaws cut down acres upon acres of young cottonwood for him to browse upon. At this season, with coat long, shabby and rough, matted with dirt and burrs, hips extended in the air, belly puffed out with sticks and bark swallowed in the vain attempt to appease the hunger that consumes him, forlorn, downcast and miserable, he looks an uncouth monster rather than a horse.

But when spring has mellowed the earth and drawn from her pregnant bosom the tender grass, he sheds the rough coat, scours the protuberant belly, and with rounded, supple form, head erect, ears and eyes full of bright intelligence, he is again ready to bear his master in fight and foray, to be trusted even to death.

The highest and best quality of the pony is his endurance. No animal could serve the careless and brutal Indian as he does. Even though starting on a journey of hundreds of miles, the Indian never spares his pony, but all along the line of march is dashing at full speed, now here, now there, at one time chasing a herd of antelope, at another scurrying away to the top of a ridge miles away, in mere curiosity to see what is beyond.

When the Northern Cheyennes broke away from the Agency, and made their desperate effort to get back to their loved northern homes, each warrior started with from two to ten ponies for his own use, and an ample number for the women, children and packs.

Courageous and confident, easily beating off the attacks of the few cavalry companies that were available for its pursuit, this gallant band of but one hundred and twenty-five fighting men, encumbered by more than four times their number of women and children, moved through the Indian Territory and Southern Kansas as nonchalantly as though a victorious and overwhelming army. Moving by easy stages, their march was only a picnic from one luxuriant grass-plat to another; the pleasure of the jaunt just agreeably varied by slight encounters with troops, and mimic buffalo-hunts among the herds of fat cattle.

On Poison Creek in Southern Kansas they encountered herds of real buffalo, a temptation so strong as to prove irresistible, and here the march was suspended to enable them to kill and "jerk" sufficient meat to carry them to the Missouri River.

These pleasurable commissariat duties were rather suddenly brought to an end by the near approach of a larger force of troops than they had hitherto encountered. Constant victory had given them such confidence in their own powers and "medicine," that, though knowing that the troops outnumbered them more than two to one, they determined to set a trap, and give their pursuers such a lesson as would effectually send them to the rear and insure an unmolested journey to their destination.

This portion of the Plains is a formation of carboniferous sandstone covered by a thin layer of alluvial. The running streams meander through valleys cut entirely through the stone. The lateral slopes or depressions gradually deepen until the stone foundation is reached, and following this with more or less wear for some little distance, plunge precipitately into cañon s whose bottoms are alluvial deposits, but whose sides are perpendicular walls of rock, from the tops of which the plain rises smoothly, gradually, and without the slightest cover for an approaching enemy. These are, by plainsmen, called "box cañons," and even though but ten to twenty feet in depth, they afford positions and opportunities for defence almost equal to those of the best artificial defensive works. A "box cañon" of unusually excellent defensive facilities was selected by the astute Cheyennes. It was exceptionally rich in luxurious grasses suitable for the stock; it contained several springs of water; its windings formed natural bastions; and toward its upper end it was so deep and narrow as to afford perfect protection to the women and children. The edges and weak places were strengthened by low walls of loose stones, behind which, entirely covered and hidden, the little band crouched for its deadly spring.

The Indians evidently anticipated that in the eagerness of pursuit the troops would rush blindly into this pitfall. But Col. Lewis knew his enemy. Vigorous as was his pursuit his advance was always covered by scouts.

The principal valley from which the Indians had entered the "box cañon," had for a day or two been the grazing-ground for their stock, and was everywhere marked with numerous tracks. The scouts would probably have passed without notice the entrance to the "box cañon ," and thus led Lewis, in spite of his caution, into an ambuscade from which he must have suffered severely, but for the constitutional impatience and excitability of the Indians. Though they knew that the troops for whom the trap was laid were but a short distance off, they were utterly unable to refrain from firing at the few advanced scouts. These shots, by disclosing their presence and position, deprived the trap of its only really dangerous feature.

The scouts promptly returned to the command and informed Col. Lewis of the situation.

Two companies of cavalry were dismounted, and advanced deployed as skirmishers, occupying one whole side of the "box cañon." A company of infantry occupied the other side. The lines closed in and the battle soon raged entirely to the dis-advantage of the Indians. After scarcely an hour of this sharp work, the savages, finding themselves completely environed, were so convinced of their own defeat as to have made a flag of truce to open communications, when Col. Lewis, incautiously exposing himself, was struck down by a rifle-bullet and died in a few moments.

This so demoralized the troops that they fell back, and night coming on, they retired from the field, and went into camp. The Indians were not slow to take advantage of this opportunity, and under the friendly cover of darkness, they escaped from the cañon and continued their flight towards the north. Before the battle had fairly joined, Lewis had sent a few of the very best marksmen among the scouts, to lie, perdu, among the rocks about the mouth of the cañon , with orders to kill as many as possible of the Indian ponies. This order had been so admirably executed, that, in spite of the utmost care on the part of the Indians, not less than seventy of their ponies had been destroyed. What remained were sufficient for a few days' march, but not for such a race as they now realized they had to run; so, deviating from their most direct route, the Indians turned to the eastward and made a raid into the settlements to procure a remount.

The horrors of that raid are a part of the history of Kansas, but in spite of the great number of horses taken, the Indians were so closely pressed by Major Manck and his cavalry, that, to this day, they cannot be made to believe that Manck made his wonderful marches with one and the same set of animals.

Treated properly, the pony will wear out two American horses; but in the hands of the Indian he is so abused and neglected that an energetic cavalry-officer will wear him out.

After endurance, the best quality of the pony is sureness of foot. He will climb a steep rocky hill with the activity and assurance of the mule; he will plunge down an almost precipitous declivity with the ease and indifference of the buffalo. In swamps and quicksands he is only excelled by the elk, and he will go at speed through sand-hills, or ground undermined by gophers, where an American horse would labor to get along faster than a walk, and fall in the first fifty yards of a gallop.

The amount of work got out of him by an Indian is simply astonishing. No mercy is shown; indeed, he never seems to realize that his pony is tired. Tell an Indian to find out something, and he will probably go and return at speed, though the distance be twenty miles. If the pony flags, he gets more whipping; if he gives out, another is saddled to go through the same experience.

The variation of quality and power of the Indian pony is very little as compared with that of our horses, so little indeed that a "pony" is the standard of values. One may be faster or stronger than another, but these advantages are likely to be counterbalanced by some special viciousness, or other defect. Age seems not to be considered, the animal being a "pony" so long as he has sufficient vital energy to get fat in the spring. I have never seen an Indian examine a horse's mouth, and am satisfied that, knowing nothing of judging age by the marks on the teeth, they yield it as a point of no consequence.

The loss of an eye or injury to a foot or leg is so serious a defect as to render him no longer a standard pony. When an Indian buys a number of ponies from another, they are not selected, but "cut off" from the herd, as one buys a lot of sheep. Those cut off are then examined, singly, »and if full-grown and not defective, are accepted.

In all large herds there are a few special favorites, riding, war, or trick ponies, which are excepted in all general bargains. Even when a man has stolen another's wife, these are not taken to pay for her, unless there are not enough of others.

No care whatever is taken in breeding, and it is difficult to make the Indian comprehend that the stock might be improved.

The wealth of an Indian is expressed by the number of ponies he owns. We say a man is worth so many dollars; the Indians say he is worth so many ponies.

In fixing the status of the individual, wealth has even more weight among Indians than among whites. To be influential and powerful, a man must have ample means and be liberal with it. When the tribes were rich, almost every middle-aged man owned his herd, and even now some of the more powerful chiefs own several hundred ponies. Each pony of a large herd has its work assigned it. The poorest or least valuable are used as pack-animals, scarcely ever being mounted except by the boys, in mischief. Steady, reliable old fellows are selected to drag the lodge-poles, on which are fastened the wicker-work cages in which are transported the old and infirm, and the children of from one to four years of age. Each squaw has her own pony, and also each child, old enough to ride one. Then come the hacks, used for gadding about, for visiting neighboring villages, and for hunting deer. Next in importance in the old time, were the trained "buffalo ponies," for which there is now no use. Next in value are the race horses, those trained to tricks being second only to the Indian's only real love, his war pony. This last is the only animal on which he ever bestows the slightest care. No one, but the owner is ever permitted to ride him, and the owner himself would think it desecration to mount him for an ordinary ride. On war parties he is carefully "saved-up," the owner riding another animal and leading him by a lariat. He gets the best grass; in his tail is tied the bag of good medicine; for him are reserved all the dangers and excitement of battle; to his speed and intelligence the Indian entrusts his honor and his life.

TRAPPERS, SQUAW MEN, POSTS AND INDIAN AGENTS

WHAT is "The Frontier"? It is safe to say that the two words do not impress the same idea on any two people. Common as is their use, they convey to all, from President to lowest rustic, only a hazy impression of something "out west;" an undefined boundary between civilization and barbarism.

This being true, it is not at all remarkable that the term "frontiersman" should have an equally loose and indefinite meaning; the name being applied to men of the most varied habits and characteristics, living lives as dissimilar the one to the other, as if they occupied different quarters of the globe.

Some "frontiersmen" live wholly within savage territory, among savages, from whom they differ only by a shade; others live entirely within civilized territory, and have no thought in common with savage life; but the large mass live now on one side, now on the other, as may be consistent with their individual well-being and safety for the time.

The ordinary citizen, in the rut of the daily routine of his civilized life, can scarcely be made to realize, that thousands of his fellow-citizens, sometimes intelligent, and occasionally accomplished, men, gladly exchange all the comforts and advantages of civilization, for the privation, hardship, danger and freedom of barbaric life.

With the single exception of the far-away Moqui Pueblos, I doubt if there be a tribe of Indians in the Territory of the United States, whose characters, habits, and ideas have not derived some tinge or shading from contact with whites.

Trappers were the pioneer frontiersmen.

The earlier trappers would seem to have been actuated by the disposition to rove, quite as much as by anxiety to make money, for not a few of them passed carelessly by streams richly stocked with beaver and otter, and in fair proximity to the trading-posts; to go far beyond, to streams less rich, or from whence, if animals were plenty, the pelts could not be got to market.

The adventures of these men have furnished material for many thrilling stories, but though capable of being glossed with romance (as even the Indian himself, in the hands of a Cooper), these adventures are only those every day incident to savage life.. The tribes were not as a rule specially hostile to whites, and access to the chief was not difficult. A few presents, and the purchase of one or more squaws constituted the adventurer a member of the tribe, identified with its interests, taking part in its successes, and suffering from its disasters.

But the labors of the individual trapper did not always satisfy his ambition or his greed. Indian custom saddled upon him the support of a greater or less number of the relations of his wives. He utilized this material and put them to work, setting and watching traps, killing game, etc., etc. These Indians, heretofore entirely ignorant of traps and trapping, became in time excellent trappers. The Hudson Bay Company recognized this, and, realizing the advantage of trading directly with the comparatively ignorant Indians, took away from the trappers this source of profit, by taking all the trapping Indians into their direct employ. This was and is done by furnishing, in the fall, to each of these Indians an outfit, provisions, traps, etc., without requiring immediate payment. This is called a "debt." In the spring the Indian comes in, brings his pelts, and pays off his debt. The posts are so isolated that the Indian is almost always forced to go to the same one to outfit, so that the risk is little.

Great as were the profits, it was soon discovered that these could be greatly enhanced. Heretofore entirely ignorant of any intoxicating fluid, the Indian developed a passion for fire-water so intense as to be little short of an insanity. After paying his "debt," he would give all the remaining pelts for the means for one good "drunk" (half a pint of whiskey), and when he got sober would contract another "debt" for next year's outfit.

The enormous profits of this traffic soon attracted another class of frontiersmen. These were the Indian traders. Nowhere could be found a more utterly debased and worthless set of men. Too lazy to work, even to trap (the laziest of all work), they made their living by pandering to the worst passions of the Indian. With their only stock in trade, a keg or two 'of the cheapest and poorest whiskey loaded on a light cart, or slung across a pack-horse, a couple of these men would in the early spring penetrate to the streams occupied by the trappers, and return in a few weeks with skins worth five hundred, or a thousand times their cost to them. There was no danger, for though the trappers might have killed them and taken the whiskey, such action would have deterred others from coming next spring.

This trade was a sore annoyance to the Company, as the trapper oftentimes drank up all his crop of pelts, and could not pay his debt. Strenuous efforts were made to break it up, but with so little result that the trader is now, as he has been for two hundred years, a prominent man; an institution of the frontier.

He fits out the great caravans, the perambulating groggeries, which keep the Indian in the depths of poverty and debasement; he furnishes most of the fine breech-loading fire-arms and metallic cartridges, which enable the Indians so stoutly to resist the aggressions of the whites; he supplies the Indians with all those contraband articles of which the Government, with its usual wisdom, prohibits the sale by any person in whose hands the trade might be regulated and controlled. He is not unfrequently the henchman and partner of the Indian Agent, and under cover of his name and ill-fame, this excellent man perpetrates the most atrocious frauds upon the unfortunate beings consigned by a benignant Government to his care.

These men frequently become very wealthy, building great outfitting stores and depots in favorable locations, and gain great influence, not only with the Indians, but sufficient among the magnates at Washington to secure the passage of laws for the benefit of themselves and their half-breed children. Their red wives, being only property, are no impediment to their possession of white wives and families in the States. As they grow old, some retire from business, return to their families in the States, and not unfrequently take a prominent position in society and public affairs, and are looked up to as authority on all Indian questions. Others pass the winter of their days in their western homes, surrounded in patriarchal manner by a crowd of admiring wives, children and dependents.

Next in order of frontiersmen comes the "squaw man."

The custom of adoption by marriage has resulted to the Indian in unmixed evil. Living with every Indian tribe are numbers of men, Americans, Frenchmen, Germans, Mexicans, Negroes, who, having purchased wives, are regarded as belonging to the tribe. Some of these men are the veriest outcasts, refugees who dare not set foot in any State. Others are adventurers without capital, who hope to make a petty living by speculating on the improvidence of the Indian. Others again are cattle men, who by taking Indian wives, gain the right to hold their cattle on Indian reservations. Others by like right open farms, and stock ranches.

In nearly every treaty it has made with Indians, the Government has bound itself to prevent the encroachments of white men. In not one single instance has any effort been made to carry out this provision of the treaties. White men go through and over the Indian Territory, or remain in it, just as it pleases them. For a certain class of whites, an Indian reservation is a veritable house of refuge, for here are no laws, no writs, no sheriffs, no jails, no penitentiaries, no hangman. Here is the secure home of the forger, the horse-thief, the murderer; here

> "He shall take who has the power,
> And he shall keep who can."

Before the grand influx of whites into Indian country, and while the tribes were yet intact, uncontrolled, preserving all their ancient customs, and enacting all their martial ceremonies, the epithet "squaw man" was applied to those few individuals who flinched or failed in the tortures of the initiatory ordeal of warrior. It was expressive of the utmost contempt.

Within the last few years, and at the present time, the name is given to those persons other than Indians, who by purchase of wives have been adopted or tolerated in the tribe. It is yet used as an expression of contempt, applicable to the most shiftless of this class; for though trappers and traders habitually take squaws to wife, this name is not usually applied to them. They have a visible, or at least ostensible means of support, and being regarded as somewhat permanent members of the tribe, are not on the same plane with the others, even in the estimation of the Indian "Squaw men" represent every class of men, from the educated gentleman, wearied of the hollow conventionalities of civilized life, to the bloodthirsty ruffian, more debased and degraded than the Indian himself.

'The meanest and most contemptible of these squaw men" are to be found around the agencies, hangers-on and dependents; sending their squaws to draw rations for the family, and making a livelihood by buying and selling their rations, from and to the Indians; by clandestinely dealing in arms and liquors, and in any other underhand way that requires no manual labor, their abhorrence. These are the pliant tools of corrupt agents, making affidavits to cover any deficiency, and swearing to any story made up for them beforehand.

At his own best games, in lying, stealing, drinking, treachery, and debauchery, the "squaw man" of this class is so far superior to the Indian as to gain his unqualified admiration, and he becomes a power among them by the display of qualities similar, but superior, to those held in highest estimation by them.

These men come most closely and directly in contact with the Indian, and it is from them that he gets his ideas of the character, capacity, morality, and religion of white men. Being able to go among the white settlements at will, they are often accused of acting as spies for the Indians, informing them where a valuable lot of horses or mules may be had for the taking. A specially fine lot of horses (said to belong to a prominent Pennsylvania politician) were being wintered on the west of the Laramie plains. A small party of Sioux Indians, starting from their camp on Powder River, went direct to the herd, and carried off everyone. It was afterward stated and believed, that a white "squaw man," living with the Sioux, found out the location of this herd while on a visit to the settlements. On his return to the tribe, he made up a party, and guided it to the spot.

These "squaw men" are also accused of wreaking personal vengeance by inciting Indians to some act of atrocity on their enemy. There is scarcely a crime of which they are not accused, and it is doubtful if there be a crime of which some of them are not capable.

There are in the United States about one hundred Indian reservations and agencies, at each of which there is an average of not less than ten of this class of "squaw men." The effect on the Indian of a thousand such "missionaries" may be imagined.

Marriage among Indians was already a sufficiently slight bond. These men purchase and abandon women at pleasure, debasing and prostituting them, and lowering the tone of the tribes. But a few years ago the Cheyenne women were models of chastity. Even yet they are, in this respect, the highest type of Indian women; but the cupidity of their fathers and husbands, and the money and license of the" squaw men," will eventually place them socially and morally on a level with the lowest. Nor does the injury end here. Abandoning their women at pleasure, these men leave them and their children a tax on the tribe or band, and in the present habitual condition of semi-starvation, to which all are reduced, the unfortunate mother, to keep body and soul together, is ofttimes forced to sell not only herself, but her children.

The "squaw men" are a serious injury to the United States Government.

The Mexicans have a proverb that "a woman is the best dictionary." The "squaw men" prove its correctness by soon acquiring enough of the language of the tribe in which they are domiciled to set up as interpreters, and most of the intercourse between the Government and the Indians is filtered through these men.

Confident of a certain power with and over Indians, almost every "squaw man" becomes something of a politician. He invariably has some "axe to grind" of his own, and his interpretations are always colored, or at least shaded, to suit his own ends.

There was scarcely an Indian of the Sioux nation who was not willing in 1875 to sell the Black Hills to the United States at a fair price. But the rascally "squaw men" among them, believing that the

Government would pay any price, and constantly mindful of their own interests, so worked and lobbied among the chiefs and warriors, that the terms demanded were simply ridiculous. In this case they injured the Indians, plunged the Government into a costly war, and overreached themselves.

A serious complication arose in September, 1880, which the "ring" men charge to the perversions of the interpreters, though these latter stoutly maintain that they interpreted correctly what was told them by the Secretary.

A deputation of chiefs of the Cheyennes and Arapahos went to Washington to see the Secretary of the Interior, and get, if possible, a definite idea of the boundaries of their reservation. They came back elate and joyous, saying that the Secretary had informed them that their reservation was bounded on the east by the Arkansas River, on the north by the state line of Kansas, and on the west and south by the Cimarron River, and they were advised to move into it immediately.

Now, almost every foot of ground within the limits specified is what is called "Cherokee lands," and is at this moment occupied by hundreds of thousands of cattle, the owners of which pay to the Cherokees, by and with the knowledge and consent of the United States Government, a per capita tax for the privilege of grazing.

Had the Cheyennes gone into that country, a collision with the white herders of those cattle would have been inevitable, for each would have wanted the grass for their own stock; involving a costly war and the probable ultimate destruction of the tribe.

Major Randall, the military commander at Fort Reno, and the officer most directly in control of these Indians, seeing at once the danger of the situation, and the incongruity of the alleged statement of the Secretary with the actual facts, explained all to the Indians, assuring them that the Secretary would not possibly have given them any such boundaries. He advised them not to go into that country. His wise counsel prevailed, and what might have been a matter of most serious consequence to all concerned, was happily evaded.

There is a law of the Statute Book prohibiting whites from intruding on Indian reservations, but, like all other laws relating to Indian affairs, (except those which divert the money into certain channels) it is a dead letter, not worth the paper it is printed on. The Government cannot or will not act when the Indian only is aggrieved.

There being no hope of advancing the Indian in morals and civilization by getting rid of the "squaw men," the only remedy left is, that Congress shall pass laws for the regulation of whites in Indian Territories, making marriage with a squaw a civil contract, voidable only by death, or by divorce for cause, adultery a misdemeanor, and bigamy a felony; and appoint judges or officers to see to the execution of these laws.

As I have before said, "the first step in Indian civilization is to give him a rule and guide to his conduct," and this can only be done by judicious laws properly executed.

FRONTIERSMEN, TEXAS COWBOYS AND BORDER DESPERADOES

BESIDES the classes of frontiersmen heretofore described, and which, though claiming to be American citizens, are Indians by adoption, Indians in manners, customs, habits, interests, everything except color; there are other classes which though frequently living in or near Indian territory, have no affiliation with, and are usually extremely hostile to, the savage denizens of the land.

First came the miners.

The history of the earlier miners is a record of brutal crimes, not only against the Indian inhabitants, but against each other. The lazy and reckless often banded together, jumping the claims of the weak and timid, and shooting like a dog the man supposed to be brave.

But order was gradually evolved even from this chaos. The Government passed laws defining and fixing the rights of miners, and in the absence of proper officers to enforce these laws, the better class of miners banded together, and fixed them upon the minds of the disorderly by the terrible sentences of Judge Lynch.

Considering the heterogeneous elements of which miners' society is composed, the universal custom of carrying deadly weapons, the recklessness of men under the influence of the strongest of passions, unfettered by the restraints of law, and deprived of the softening influence of reputable women, the mining communities of the present day are remarkable for the absence of crime.

To the discovery of the precious metals, and the passion of those who search for them, we owe a knowledge and development of the Great Western wilderness which could not have been gained by a century of ordinary effort. These men have built up great states, and peopled a vast continent. Restless, pushing, bent only on gold and silver, they have had no time and less inclination to consider the rights of the original owners of the soil. Men who would demolish the house of a white friend, were gold discovered beneath it, are not likely to stickle at territorial limits, or regard the lines of Indian Reservations.

Next in order came the Great American Buffalo Destroyer, fearless as a Bayard, unsavory as a skunk, whom I have sufficiently described in Chapter XXII.

For every single buffalo that roamed the Plains in 1871, there are in 1881 not less than two, and more probably four or five, of the descendants of the long horned cattle of Texas. The destroyers of the buffalo are followed by the preservers of the cattle.

Years ago, while yet a cherished portion of Mexico, Texas was famous for its cattle. Individuals owned thousands, even tens of thousands, which roamed almost at will, over the vast and fertile plains. The care of these was left to a few men and a crowd of Mexican boys from eight to twenty years of age; for not much money could be paid in wages, when the finest cow or fattest ox was worth but two or three dollars.

After the annexation of Texas to the United States the earlier drives of great herds of cattle were accompanied by such numbers of these boys, that all the herders were commonly called "Texas Cowboys;" and though the cattle business has now spread over the greater portion of the great West; though the price of cattle has increased so enormously that the best wages are given; and though the Mexican boys are replaced by full-grown white men, the appellative "cowboy" is everywhere "out, west" commonly applied to all those who herd cattle.

The daily life of the cowboy is so replete with privation, hardship and danger, that it is a marvel how any sane man can voluntarily assume it, yet thousands of men not only do assume it, but actually like it to infatuation.

I doubt if there be in the whole world a class of men who lead lives so solitary, so exposed to constant hardship and danger, as this.

A large herd of cattle will be guarded by a number of men, who have a common place for eating and sleeping, but they are never there together. Day and night, in good weather and bad weather, some of them must be with the herd. The men are divided up into reliefs, each relief being on duty in the Saddle not less than eight hours of the twenty-four, and each individual having a specified beat sometimes eight or ten miles long. Each relief must go around the whole herd, see that all are quiet and unmolested. The outside limits are carefully watched, and if any animals have strayed beyond them, their trail must be followed up, and the fugitives driven back to their proper grazing ground. Under ordinary circumstances, and when the herd is simply being held on certain good grazing ground, with abundance of-water, these duties are comparatively easy; but when the grass is poor, and water scarce, the animals stray continually, and great watchfulness and labor are required for their care.

Especially is this the case in winter, when the grass is covered with snow. Cattle in large herds are easily stampeded, becoming panic-stricken on very slight, and frequently without, provocation. Nothing so starts them as a Plains "Norther," and they will fly before a severe storm of wind and snow sometimes for incredible distances. These are the trying times for the cowboys. When a stampede occurs from any cause, every man must be in the saddle, follow the fleeing animals day and night, get control of the herd and bring it back to its ground. The worse the weather, the worse the stampede, and the greater the necessity for the presence and activity of the cowboys.

A terrible Norther, during the winter of 1880, stampeded many herds in Southern Kansas and the Cherokee strip, some of which made fully ninety miles to the south before being got under control. With and among them were numbers of cowboys, with only the scantiest ration of bread and meat, with no shelter or bedding, with no protection from the terrible cold except the clothing they happened to have on when the stampede was announced.

For fidelity to duty, for promptness and vigor of action, for resources in difficulty, and unshaken courage in danger, the cowboy has no superior among men.

But there is something in this peculiar life which develops not only the highest virtues, but the most ignoble of vices. It is not solitude, for the shepherds of the Plains lead lives quite as solitary, and they are generally quiet, inoffensive persons. The cowboy, on the contrary, is usually the most reckless of all the reckless desperadoes developed on the frontier. Disregarding equally the rights and lives of others, and utterly reckless of his own life; always ready with his weapons and spoiling for a fight, he is the terror of all who come near him, his visits to the frontier towns of Kansas and Nebraska being regarded as a calamity second only to a western tornado. His idea of enjoyment is to fill himself full of bad whiskey, mount his mustang, tear through the streets, whooping, yelling, flourishing and firing his pistols until the streets are deserted and every house closed, then with a grim smile of happiness he dashes off to his comrades to excite their envy by graphic pictures of his own exploits and the terror of the timid townspeople.

Cattle-stealing is a mania not confined solely to our Scotch ancestors. The frontier has many "cowboys" out of employ, many impecunious gentlemen who long yearningly for a herd of cattle. The "waifs and strays" of large herds, or even a considerable herd, carelessly guarded, will suddenly disappear. Sometimes the herdsmen and the cattle disappear together, and should the owner be absent, are likely to disappear for him for all time.

In 1872 the owner of a considerable herd returned to his ranche in Southeastern Kansas after a short absence, to find his herd and herders gone. Taking the trail alone, he plodded west for more than one hundred miles, when he found about half his herd in the possession of a notorious desperado near where Larned City now stands. On inquiry he found they had recently been purchased of a man who had gone still further west with the other half. Following on, he found his herd in charge of its reputed owner on the Arkansas River near Fort Dodge. The thief was the most notoriously bloodthirsty ruffian on the frontier. After a terrible combat the thief was killed, and the owner, collecting his cattle, returned with them eastward. Arriving at the ranche of the robber who had his others, he went to him and said quietly, "I have taken the scalp of your partner and got half my cattle. I want to know if I'll have to take your scalp to get the other half." The terrified ruffian gave them up without a contest.

A few years ago the beef contractor at one of the military posts in the Indian Territory had an adventure which I will let him tell in his own idiom.

"Wall, boys, I was mighty nigh onto busted that time, an' I'll tell you about it. You see I'd worked hard an' roughed it, an' got a nice little lot of cattle. The contract for this post was to be let, I bid on it, an' got it. Wall, my cattle was none of the best, the grass was poor, an' afore long the commandin' officer says to me, says he, 'There's complaints agin your beef, you must do better, or I will order the commissary to buy good beef and charge it to yer.' Says I,' Commandin' officer, I know my beef is none of the best, but give me a little time, and I'll get yer the very best.' 'All right,' says he,f but do it.' So next mornin' I put some money in my belt and started for Texas. I bought a hundred and fifty head of first class beef, and hired a Mexican boy to help me drive 'em. He was only a little chap about twelve years old, but he was powerful bright and handy, and, sand! lots! I had a breech-loadin' rifle, and pistols, but the Injuns was bad, so I bought a double-barrelled shotgun for the boy. Everything went on all right till we'd got into the territory about one hundred miles from here. One mornin' we was movin' along, when a man rode up to me. He was a small-sized man, but the handsomest man I ever seed, an' dressed the handsomest. He had on high boots, big silver spurs, an' buckskin breeches, an' a buckskin huntin'-shirt all over fringes, an' open at the front. He had on a white biled shirt, an' a red silk necktie with long ends a flyin' behind. Around his waist was a red silk sash, an' he wore a regular Mexican sombrero, an' his bridle an' saddle was Mexican, an' covered with silver. He was on a splendid mustang that bucked an' shied all the time, but he rode him like his skin. I tell you, boys, it was a handsome outfit. 'Good mornin',' says he, a liftin' up his hat mighty polite. 'Good mornin',' says I, an' with that we chatted along pleasant like. He told me that he had a big herd of cattle about three miles to the east, an' he was afraid I'd give'em the fever, an' he wanted me to keep more to the left, off his range. Wall, I was agreeable, an' he kept with me for a mile an' more, showin' me where to go and then thankin' me polite, he said good-bye, an' rode off. Wall now, boys, I had kept on the course he told me for about two hours, when just beyant a little rise I drove right into my gentleman friend an' six other fellers. Ridin' right up to me, my friend says, says he, 'after thinkin' it over, I have concluded it would be a pity to lose such a extra fine lot of beef cattle as you have got, so I have concluded to take'em in.' Wall, boys, I saw right through the thing in a minit. I knowed it were no use to fight agin so many, so I begged. I told him how I was situate, that if I didn't get them cattle to the post I was ruinated. He listened for a few minutes pretty quiet, an' I thot I had got him, when all at once he drawed a pistol, an' all the other fellers drawed their pistols at the same time.

"'My friend,' says he, 'we don't take no advantage of cattle-men, but them cattle of yours is the same as Government property. They is going to feed soldiers. All such property is as much ours as anybody's, now you git'—and with that he stuck his cocked pistol in my face, an' all the other six stuck their cocked pistols at me. Wall, boys, me and that Mexican boy—we left.

"Them fellers rounded up my cattle, an' drove'em back ther own way. Boys, my heart was most broke. I knowed I was ruinated if I lost them cattle. Wall, we travelled along for a mile or more, when I made up my mind. 'Domingo,' says I to the little Mexican, 'are you afeared to stay and take care of the hosses, while I settle with them chaps?' 'No,' says he, 'an' I'll help you ef you want me.'

"The country was about half prairie, an' t'other half the thickest kind of black jack, and scrub-oak thickets. I hid that boy an' them hosses wher a hound couldn't ev found'em, and when it got towards evenin', I started on foot to hunt up my friends' cattle camp, an' as I knowed I had to get in my work in the dark an' at close range, I took the boy's double-barrel shot-gun, each barrel loaded with sixteen buckshot, an' big size at that.

"About midnight I found the herd. The cattle was held in a prairie with thickets all around it. I poked around, keepin' in the thickets. They had about a thousand head not countin' mine. I found ther 'dug out.' Ther was two men on herd. I poked around till I found wher my cattle was. They knowed me, an' didn't make no fuss when I went among'em. Thar I laid down in the grass. In about an hour one of the herders rode right close on to me, an' I let him have one barrel. In a minit the other herder hollered out, 'what the h—l is that,' an' gettin no answer he galloped right over ther, and I give him the other barrel. I got back to the thicket and went to my camp, an' to sleep. Next mornin' when the sun was way up, that boy he woke me, an' says, says he, 'ther havin a high time in that camp, you had better be looking after'em.' Wall, I got my breakfast an went to look after'em. They wus in a big commotion, all of'em together, huntin' everywhere for my trail. I had wored mocassins, an' I knowed none of'em fellows could follow my trail. I had another big advantage of'em. They couldn't go nowhere unless they wus on hossback, and the brush wus so thick they had to ride in the open prairie whar I could see'em. I poked round in the thicket wher they couldn't see me. Next night I tried it agin, but they wus all on herd and held the cattle out in the prairie so fur from the woods that I had no show. I changed my plan, an' went back to my camp. Next mornin' I was out early pokin' in the thickets and watchin'. A lot of cattle grazed up towards a pint of woods. I knowed they would stop that soon, so I hid in that pint. Pretty soon a feller came chargin' round on a full run after them cattle. He was a likely chap, an' I felt a little oneasy until I recognized him as having stuck a pistol in my face two days before. I got him.

"Wall, boys, thar's no use in stringin' this thing out. Them chaps wus scared from the start, and would have got out of thar, if they hadn't had to go through thickets. I knowed that, an' took it easy. In three days I had gradually got away with them. They wus so few that they couldn't herd ther cattle. On the mornin' of the fourth day I noticed a lot of cattle feedin' off. They wus nigh two miles from the dug-out—I laid with'em, but in the thicket. Towards afternoon a feller came dashin' in at full speed an' rounded up within twenty feet of me. When he fell he was so tied up in his lariat that he stopped the hoss. I caught an' tied that hoss in a thicket, so that the others at the dug-out wouldn't know this man was dead.

After the second day I had never seed my fine captain. He had made the others take chances, but he had stayed in the dug-out, an' run no risk himself. I thought if I could get him I'd be all right. So, afore day next mornin' I hid in a break about twenty yards from the door of the dug-out, an just at daybreak I covered that door with my shot-gun, an' fired off my pistol with the other hand. As I expected, he jumped out of the door with his gun in his hand, but he had no chance an' no time, I doubled him up right in the door. In a few minits a white rag was stuck out of the door on a stick. I called to the man to come out, and put up his hands, an' he did. I walked up an' said to him,' I ought to kill you, but I won't if you will do as I tell yer. Get your hoss, cut out my cattle, and drive'em over to that hill.' He said, says he, 'I never saw you before, an' I don't know your cattle; I am the cook of this outfit, an' I am the only man left.' So I made him get me a hoss, an' he an me cut out my cattle, an' drove'em over near my camp, an' me an' the boy took'em, and by hard drivin' got to the post in time. It were a tight fit, boys; an' now, what'll yer have to drink."

To the miners and the cowboys we owe most of our complications with Indians. The one class in search of the precious metals; the other in search of good grazing grounds; the one over-running the mountains, the other pre-empting the plains and valleys; all, careless of the rights, and impatient of the claims, of Indians; all, with a ferocity begot of greed, hating the Indian, hating a Government which, they believe, protects and perpetually pauperizes the Indian at their expense; all ready and willing to bring on any conflict between the Government and the Indian, which may lessen the numbers and diminish the Territory of the latter; they go anywhere and everywhere, constantly pushing the Indian to the wall, constantly forcing issues suited to their own ends; constantly showing the inadequacy of the laws and forces of a popular government to the enforcement of unpopular measures, and rendering futile and ridiculous all treaties made with Indians.

The miners opened and settled the Black Hills in spite of Indian and Government; the cowboys will open the Territory in spite of Indian and Government. It is simply a question of time, and not a long time.

Those humane persons who have the true interests of the Indians at heart will do well to recognize the fact that there is no power in this Government to maintain the status quo. The Indian must be invested with the rights and duties of a citizen, or he must go. The majority of the people of this country may be willing to maintain him in idleness, pauperism, and in the possession of territories sufficient to maintain a great nation of whites. The miners and cowboys are not willing—they are on the ground. The problem is for their solution.

THRILLING PERSONAL EXPERIENCES

IN the "good old times" there was a class of frontiersmen, behind the trapper, trader, and squaw-man, but though in many cases actual settlers, tillers of the soil, yet carefully keeping as far as possible in advance of the tide of actual settlement. These were fugitives from justice and escaped criminals. These men would go beyond the line of settlements as far as they dared, build cabins, send for their families, and under assumed names commence life anew. They were a peculiar people. Almost all were extremely inquisitive and suspicious, but many had humane, hospitable traits, while others were as savage and dangerous as their Indian neighbors. The latter as a rule moved forward as the frontier advanced; the former, in many instances, living down the haunting fear of the officers of the law, became respected members of the communities which grew up around them.

In my earlier military life on the frontier I met numbers of these people, almost always self-convicted and easily distinguishable from the bona fide settlers. Invariably they were hospitable and ready to give aid or information to white strangers, but an adventure I had with one, nearly thirty years ago, gave me something of a distaste for their intimate companionship.

I was on a scouting and exploring expedition in Northern Texas. After many days and weeks of tedious travel without sign of settlement, I came upon a little one-room one-story log house, the owner of which had something of a farm in cultivation, and a small surplus of corn in store. My horses were nearly "played out," and I gladly availed myself of this opportunity to rest and recuperate men and animals.

The "squatter" was a tall, handsome man, in the prime of life, very hospitable, and urgent that I should take "bed and board" with him. Declining this, I nevertheless camped near his house for convenience, determined to remain until I had exhausted his stores of forage or got my horses in good marching order.

During several days I was with him whenever my duties permitted. He was an admirable hunter, I a mere novice, delighted with the opportunity to gain instruction and information. We hunted together every day most successfully. One day I went out alone, and failing in my designs against deer and turkeys, strayed into the heavily timbered river "bottom," and for an hour or two greatly enjoyed myself shooting squirrels. Securing a good bag, I started for my camp, but had gone but a few hundred yards when I came plump upon my frontier friend.

He was seated on a log, concealed within a little thicket, nervously fumbling with the lock of his rifle; and when I came to look closely at him, he had the most diabolic expression of countenance I ever saw on a man.

"Hello, old fellow," said I, on recognizing him, "have you had any luck?"

He made no answer for some time, but continued to thumb the lock of his gun, looking at me in such a way that I began to think him insane.

After some moments he broke out in a loud voice:

"Why, I could have killed you just as easy as winkin'; you don't pay no sort of attention when you are in the woods."

"You might have killed me any time in the last four days," I answered; "I have not been looking for danger from you."

He looked at me wildly for a moment, then rising with an effort, shouldered his rifle and came out and joined me.

"Ho man," said he, "could ha' come on me that way. It was a powerful temptation. I am glad I didn't shoot yer, but I wouldn't advise yer to go pokin' about that way often."

We returned together amicably to his house, where he insisted on my taking supper. During the meal he so impressed me with anecdotes of his past life (by his showing he had killed several men), and encomiums upon himself for not killing me when he had so good a chance, that so long as I remained in that neighborhood I never hunted alone without keeping as close a watch on all my surroundings as if the country had been infested with hostile Indians.

I have hunted with many Indians of different tribes, and do not believe that such an opportunity would have offered a like temptation to any Indian professing friendship, and whose tribe was at peace. The incident only shows that white men, ostracized and reckless, become more savage than the savages themselves. Assassination becomes a monomania.

I have known a frontier ruffian to make a journey of two hundred miles to have a fight with another whose fame as a "dead shot" rivalled his own.

In 1871 a deputy United States Marshal, of Southern Kansas—a wonderful two-handed shot, that is, using a pistol equally well with either hand—was ordered to arrest a notorious bully. In the conflict which ensued both were shot through the body. Some hours after, the dying ruffian asked how the Marshal was, and being told that he could not live until morning, expressed himself satisfied and happy "I am perfectly willing to die," said he," when I know I take along with me the best pistol-shot on this frontier."

The Marshal recovered.

Slade, the most successful assassin on the frontier, who had murdered in cold blood over fifty men, sometimes tying them to a stake and practising at them with his pistol, as he did Jules, was the most arrant coward in existence. When his own time came, he begged on his knees, crying and whining like a whipped cur.

Under all the selfishness, the recklessness, the indifference to the rights of property, and disregard of human life, many of these frontiersmen carry warm, human hearts, full of hospitality, generosity, kindness, and charity.

One of the most abominable old ruffians I ever knew, who, under the influence of greed or whiskey was a perfect devil, was, when not possessed by either of these fiends, .an honest, honorable, humane, tenderhearted gentleman. A merchant of means and good standing in one of our large cities, he fell under the influence of drink. His wife sued for and obtained a divorce and alimony. When he had gotten sober enough to realize the calamity, he sold out his store, settled all he had in the world—nearly one hundred and ninety thousand dollars—on his wife and three sons, and taking only a change of clothing and a frontier outfit of arms and necessaries, he buried himself in the wilderness.

I knew him well—hanging around a frontier town a filthy, greasy, blear-eyed, dangerous brute; in the wilderness a courageous, courteous, intellectual, gentleman.

There are "dangerous classes" in all communities. Frontiersmen come from all grades of society, all classes of people. With the restraints of law and public opinion they would present the different characteristics of ordinary humanity. Without law or moral surroundings they develop peculiarities, which, however, are only the shells in which circumstances and surroundings encase the men.

AMOS CHAPMAN—FACING DEATH

IN its duplex capacity, explorer of the wilderness and guardian of the frontier, the army finds constant use for men experienced in plainscraft and in knowledge of Indian habits and languages. Some of these men are employed as guides; for though an average officer, trusting to his instruments and general knowledge of country, may take a command safely through an unknown wilderness, this in very mountainous regions, or in those portions of the Plains where water is scarce, can only be done at the expense of frequent delays and considerable suffering.

The navigator of a ship requires no aid in deep water, but when he nears the shore he wants a pilot to guide the vessel through intricacies, the secret of which can only come from local knowledge. The commanding officer of an exploring expedition on land may be likened to the commander of a vessel near the shore. Though he perfectly knows his position, his bearings and his course, he knows not what rocks of precipitous mountains, what reefs of impassable *barrancas*, what shoals of waterless plains, lie between him and his goal. He therefore procures, if possible, the aid of someone who has already been over the ground.

Of all frontiersmen the old trappers were and are the best guides. Learning their lessons from the Indians with whom they were so constantly and intimately associated, these men travel entirely by landmarks; mountains, plains, rocks and brakes, the bosky dell, the lone tree, the quality of the grass, even the nature of the soil, each and all give a definite idea to the old trapper and fix the location forever in his mind. But the trappers moved down one stream and up another, and though safe guides, they are generally extremely slow and roundabout in their movements. Ignorant of geography and almost entirely independent of the points of the compass, they will take you where you wish to go and bring you safely back again, but they must do this in their own way, and each by his own sequence of landmarks.

In this present day of activity, they have lost much of their prestige. They are yet necessary to point out obscure springs and water-holes of the prairie, or labyrinthine passes over mountain-ranges, but their knowledge is of the past. Even "old Bridger" was hopelessly lost, when coming on to a secluded valley, hidden as he supposed from all knowledge of white men, he found a railroad running through it. Every day adds to army knowledge; every day diminishes the importance of guides.

The necessities of the army in the olden time, and the then remarkable services of these men, have caused many of their names to be handed down in the history of our frontier, which is but the history of the development of our country. [Jim] Bridger, Kit Carson, and many others, are names which will not be forgotten. As trappers they gained the local knowledge which they afterward applied to the services of their country.

To his other accomplishments the really valuable scout must add a fair knowledge of trailing, and in this art the cowboy is quite as efficient as older plainsmen, for he has more constant necessity for it.

No people understand mountainous regions so well as miners, or are better able to judge "the lay of the land" by its general surface marks.

Every class of plainsmen furnishes some requisite faculty or knowledge valuable in a scout.

The success of every expedition against Indians depends to a degree on the skill, fidelity and intelligence of the men employed as scouts, for not only is the command habitually dependent on them for good routes and comfortable camps, but the officer in command must rely on them almost entirely for his knowledge of the position and movements of the enemy. These they learn by scouting far in advance or on the flanks of the column, and here the knowledge of trailing becomes of the utmost importance.

An officer is ordered on an expedition into the Indian country. He looks in every direction among all the frontiersmen available, to find the men suited to his purpose. It is presumed that all are brave, so he only examines the applicants as to the qualities for which he especially needs them.

It is a curious fact that, outside of courage, the qualities most valuable in a scout are those least likely to command admiration among the ordinary associates of their possessor. Bridger was rather looked down upon because he was sober and frugal; Kit Carson was often sneered at, because, though known to be the bravest of the brave when a fight became absolutely necessary, he would never fight if he could possibly avoid it even by running away in the night.

It is a remarkable fact that frontiersmen, so utterly reckless of life that they will shoot each other for mere pastime, are oftentimes the most arrant cowards when the antagonist is an Indian.

Julesburg was celebrated for its desperadoes. No twenty-four hours passed without its contribution to Boots Hill (the cemetery whose every occupant was buried in his boots), and homicide was performed in the most genial whole-souled way, the shooter and shootee smiling pleasantly in each other's faces.

One day a small party of Indians appeared in the sand-hills back of the town. The alarm spread like wild fire. An ex-officer of the war galloped about calling for volunteers. In an hour a hundred men were in saddle, every one of whom had probably killed his man. The Indians had decamped, taking a number of horses. The trail was broad and easily followed. On dashed the hundred for ten or twelve miles. Said the ex-volunteer commander afterwards, "We had them sure. At the head of Ash Hollow we commenced to pass the played-out stock. My men were badly strung out. I called to them, 'A half-hour more, boys, and they are ours—close up, don't spare the spur!' In less than half an hour I turned a bend of the hollow, and there were the Indians within five hundred yards. I gave a great yell and turned to urge on the men. I was alone. There was not a single man of that whole hundred in sight. Well, I just turned around and got out of that as quick as I could, and you don't catch me again volunteering to command men called brave, simply because they shoot each other."

Of ten men employed as scouts nine will prove to be utterly worthless. Of fifty so employed one may prove to be really valuable, but, though hundreds, even thousands, of men have been so employed by the Government since the war, the number of really remarkable men among them can be counted on the fingers.

The services which these men are called on to perform are so important and valuable that the officer who benefits by them is sure to give the fullest credit; and men so honored in official reports come to be great men on the frontier. Fremont's reports made Kit Carson a renowned man. Custer immortalized California Joe; Custer, Merritt, and Carr made Wild Bill and Buffalo Bill, Plains celebrities "until time shall be no more."

One of the best and bravest, the most sober, quiet and genial of all the scouts I have ever known is Amos Chapman. Although yet young, a volume would scarcely suffice to give all the desperate adventures and "hair-breadth 'scapes" of this remarkable man. For fifteen years he has been almost continually employed by the Government, and his services and sufferings put him in the front rank of valuable citizens.

In 1874 [General Nelson] Miles was operating against the combined wild Indian forces of the Territory. The hostiles had gotten in his rear and intercepted his trains. It was extremely important that his situation should be known at Department Headquarters. On the 10th of September, 1874, a party consisting of one Sergeant, three private soldiers and two scouts, in all six men, were directed to proceed to Camp Supply with despatches. What befell them in their efforts to obey the order is fittingly told in the following letter from General Miles to the Adjutant-General of the Army:—

Headquarters, Ind. Terr. Expedition.
Camp on Washita River, Texas, Sept. 24, 1874.

Adjutant General, U. S. A.:—
(Thro' Office Asst. Adj't. Genl. Hdqrs. Dept, and Mil. Div of the Mo and of the Army.)

General: I deem it but a duty to brave men and faithful soldiers, to bring to the notice of the highest military authority an instance of indomitable courage, skill, and true heroism on the part of a detachment from this command, with the request that the actors may be rewarded, and their faithfulness and bravery recognized, by pensions, medals of honor, or in such way as may be deemed most fitting.

On the night of the 10th inst., a party consisting of Sergt. L. T. Woodhall, Co. "I," Privates Peter Rath, Co. "A," John Harrington, Co. "H," and George W. Smith, Co. "M," Sixth Cavalry, Scouts Amos Chapman and William Dixon, were sent as bearers of despatches from the camp of this command on McClellan Creek to Camp Supply, I. T.

At 6 A. M. of the 12th, when approaching the Washita River, they were met and surrounded by a band of one hundred and twenty-five Kiowas and Comanches, who had recently left their agency; at the first attack all were struck, Private Smith mortally, and three others severely wounded. Although enclosed on all sides and by overwhelming numbers, one of them succeeded, while they were under a severe fire, at short range, and while the others, with their rifles, were keeping the Indians at bay, in digging with his knife and hands a slight cover; after this had been secured, they placed themselves within it, the wounded walking with brave and painful efforts, and Private Smith, though he had received a mortal wound, sitting upright within the trench, to conceal the crippled condition of their party from the Indians.

From early morning till dark, outnumbered twenty-five to one, under an almost constant fire, and at such short range that they sometimes used their pistols, retaining the last charge to prevent capture and torture, this little party of five defended their lives and the person of their dying comrade, without food, and their only drink the rain-water that collected in a pool mingled with their own blood. There is no doubt but that they killed more than double their number, besides those that were wounded. The Indians abandoned the attack on the 12th at dark.

The exposure and distance from the command which were necessary incidents of their duty, were such that for thirty-six hours from the first attack, their condition could not be known, and not till midnight of the 13th could they receive medical attendance and food, exposed during this time to an incessant cold storm.

Sergt. Woodhall, Private Harrington, and Scout Chapman were seriously wounded. Private Smith died of his wounds on the morning of the 13th. Private Rath and Scout Dixon were struck but not disabled.

The simple recital of their deeds, and the mention of the odds against which they fought, how the wounded defended the dying, and the dying aided the wounded by exposure to fresh wounds after the power of action was gone, these alone present a scene of cool courage, heroism and self-sacrifice, which duty, as well as inclination, prompts us to recognize, but which we cannot fitly honor.

Very respectfully your obedient servant,

Nelson A. Miles.
Col. and Bvt. Maj. Genl. U.S.A. Commanding.

Heroic as was the conduct of all, that of Chapman deserves most special honor, for he received his wound while performing a deed, than which the loftiest manhood can find nothing nobler. The first intimation of the presence of Indians was a volley which wounded every man of the party. In an instant the Indians appeared on all sides. Dismounting and abandoning their horses, the brave band moved together for a hundred yards to a "buffalo wallow," a shallow, 'natural depression in the prairie. Chapman and Dixon, being but slightly wounded, worked hard and fast to deepen this depression, and as soon as it was sufficiently deep to afford some cover it was occupied and the work continued from within. Smith had fallen from his horse at the first fire and was supposed to be dead. Now, when the excitement of prompt and vigorous action had somewhat abated, the supposed dead body was seen slightly to move. He was alive, though entirely disabled. To leave him there was to ensure his death, for the Indians were firing at him. But how could the little garrison of wounded men assist him? Turning to his comrades Chapman said:" Now, boys, keep those infernal red-skins off of me and I will run down and pick up Smith, and bring him back before they can get at me." Laying down his rifle, he sprang out of the buffalo wallow, ran with all speed to Smith, seized and attempted to shoulder him. "Did any of you ever try to shoulder a wounded man?" asked Chapman, when telling the story. "Smith was not a large man, one hundred and sixty or seventy pounds, but I declare to you that he seemed to weigh a ton. Finally I laid down and got his chest across my back, and his arms around my neck and then got up with him. It was as much as I could do to stagger under him, for he couldn't help himself a bit. By the time I had got twenty or thirty yards, about fifteen Indians came for me at full speed of their ponies. They all knew me, and yelled f Amos! Amos! we have got you now.' I pulled my pistol, but I couldn't hold Smith on my back with one hand, so I let him drop. The boys in the buffalo wallow opened on the Indians just at the right time, and I opened on them with my pistol. There was a tumbling of ponies, and a scattering of Indians, and in a minute they were gone. I got Smith up again and made the best possible time, but before I could reach the wallow another gang came for me. I had only one or two shots in my pistol, so I didn't stop to fight, but ran for it. When I was in about twenty yards of the wallow, a little old scoundrel that I had fed fifty times rode almost on to me and fired. I fell with Smith on top of me, but as I didn't feel pain, I thought I had stepped in a hole. The Indians couldn't stay around there a minute, the boys kept it red-hot, so I jumped up, picked up Smith, and got safe in the wallow. 'Amos,' said Dixon, 'you are badly hurt.' 'No, I am not,' said I. 'Why look at your leg,' and sure enough, the leg was shot off just above the ankle joint, and I had been walking on the bone dragging the foot behind me, and in the excitement I never knew it, nor have I ever had any pain in my leg to this day."

The surgeon at Camp Supply amputated Chapman's leg below the knee, more than two weeks after the receipt of the wound, and in a week thereafter had to take away his clothing to keep him in bed.

Chapman is still in the government employ, as useful and as ready for a fight as any two-legged scout.

"By the time I had got twenty-or thirty yards, about fifteen Indians came for me at full speed of their ponies. They all knew me, and yelled, 'Amos! Amos! we have got you now.'"

One of the most remarkable defences ever made against overwhelming forces was that of Major Geo. A. Forsyth, United States Army, in command of a force of one Lieutenant of Infantry, an Acting Assistant Surgeon, and forty-eight scouts—fifty-one men all told.

He was scouting against Indians, in their loved hunting-grounds, the Republican Country. On the night of the 16th September, 1868, he encamped on the Arickaree Fork of the Republican River. Fresh signs of Indians in great force had been seen, but the little party was not uneasy. It was hunting Indians; it wanted to find Indians; and it found Indians. Just at dawn of the morning of September 17th, 1868, the guard gave the alarm, "Indians!" Every man sprang to his feet, secured his arms and horse, then turned his attention to a little band of six Indians, which dashed upon the camp, shaking buffalo robes, firing guns, and yelling like fiends, in the hope of stampeding the animals. In this they were frustrated, though they succeeded in getting the pack-mules and some few horses.

Satisfied that this was but the prelude to a more serious attack, Forsyth ordered his men to saddle up. This had scarcely been accomplished when over the hills, in every direction, poured swarms upon swarms of Indians.

The Arickaree Fork, like most other Plains streams, is a river, or mere brooklet, depending on the season of the year. In September it is a wide sand-bed, through which meanders a thread of water some eight feet wide by two inches deep. Just in front of Forsyth's camp was an island a hundred yards long by twenty or thirty wide, on which was a small growth of bushes. Realizing at once the advantage of this cover, slight as it was, and the disadvantage to the Indians of having to charge over the sandy bed of the stream, Forsyth ordered his men to take position on the island. A few of the best marksmen were placed under cover of the banks of the stream, while the command fastened the horses to the bushes on the island. These preliminaries were hardly completed when the more advanced Indians, throwing themselves from their horses, crawled up to within easy range and opened a fire so terrific that by nine o'clock in the morning Forsyth had been twice severely wounded (the left leg being shattered), Dr. Movers and two men killed, a number of others wounded, and every horse had been shot down.

But the gallant whites had not been idle. Many a dead and wounded Indian had been carried to the rear under their accurate and continuous fire. Disabled as he was, Forsyth did not flinch from the command. Lying, propped on his elbow, he saw everything, superintended everything. Under his direction, while the best shots were keeping the Indians at bay, the other men were digging for life, making rifle-pits, using the bodies of the dead horses as parapet. By nine o'clock the little party was in as good posture for defence as it could hope to be.

The Indians had made a mistake in not charging at the first attack. They now realized it and made preparation for an assault. Under the command of the Chief Roman Nose, a gallant band of about three hundred warriors, superbly mounted, formed just beyond rifle-shot below the island. A heavy skirmish line pressed closer and closer, with a fire so searching and accurate that the beleaguered garrison could not expose a head or arm to return it. Realizing what was coming, Forsyth put everything in readiness. The guns of the dead and wounded were loaded and placed near the best shots on the threatened side.

When the fire of the Indian skirmishers had completely silenced the fire of the whites, the signal was given, and Roman Nose thundered on to the beleaguered island. But when his gallant command had gotten so near that the Indian footmen could no longer fire for fear of hitting their friends, the line of parapet bristled with steady defenders. "Now!" shouted Forsyth, and the abandoned parapet blazed with death. On dash the gallant Indians. Roman Nose goes down in the sand of the river; the Medicine Chief falls at the very foot of the entrenchments; but nothing can stand the cool and accurate fire of the whites. The Indians falter; a ringing cheer, and another well-directed volley from the whites; they break and scatter beyond range.

The victory is won, but at terrible cost. Of the whole force of fifty-one men, twenty-three are dead or wounded.

Disheartened, but not despairing, the Indians now determine to destroy by siege the little band of whites that they are unable to beat by assault.

Their skirmishers surround the entrenchments and keep up a continuous and well-directed fire. This is continued all day, but at night they draw off. This is Forsyth's golden opportunity. He seizes it, and in the darkness dispatches two trusty scouts to the nearest military post for assistance.

All the next day the same fighting with dismounted warriors. The next night two more men sent with despatches are driven back by the Indians. On the third day it was evident that the Indians had become sick of the contest. The main body withdrew, but left a sufficient number to beleaguer and harass the suffering garrison.

That night Forsyth sent off two more scouts, who, as they did not return, were supposed to have gotten through the Indian lines.

On the 20th the uninjured men of the command were so far relieved of the constant apprehension of attack as to be able to give attention to the wounded, for up to this time no wound had been dressed.

But now came a worse enemy than Indians. In its eagerness to "do something," the command had been out so long that though husbanding its rations with the greatest care it had on the morning of the attack scarcely a mouthful to eat. During the first few days of siege it had had abundance of horse and mule meat, but this had become now so putrefied that no stomach could stand it; and the "horse and mule meat lying around loose," as Forsyth expressed it when the food consideration was presented to him, became in the end, by its intolerable stench, one of the serious discomforts of this remarkable experience.

On the 25th, after nine days of fighting, suffering, starvation and stench, the most welcome reinforcements came, and this little party was relieved from a situation the horrors of which no man can realize.

Lieutenant Beecher, Dr. Movers, and six men were killed. Eight others were disabled for life, but the other wounded twelve completely recovered.

In this fight the Indians had nine hundred warriors, the whites fifty-one all told. The Indians admit a loss of seventy-five killed and wounded. The whites lost eight killed and twenty wounded.

THE PRESENT AND FUTURE

IN the foregoing pages I have endeavored to give a clear, detailed, and accurate account of the life, habits, and mode of thought of the Plains Indians of the present day.

In concluding, while I abstain from any discussion of the "Indian Question," as unsuitable to a work of this kind, I cannot satisfactorily complete my labors without giving a synopsis of the present political situation of the Indians, and a slight sketch of my idea of what should be done towards the amelioration of the condition of this unhappy race.

It is difficult to approach the subject dispassionately, for next to the crime of slavery the foulest blot on the escutcheon of the Government of the United States is its treatment of the so-called "Wards of the Nation."

Among the many thousands who, I hope, will read these pages, there are very few who wish anything but good to the Indian race. American people as a rule are brave, consequently their instincts are habitually on the side of honor and mercy. Almost everyone has manhood enough to urge him to assist the weak and helpless.

A terrible epidemic, or disastrous conflagration, scores a portion of our country, the cry of suffering opens the hearts and purses of those in more favored localities, and nothing is left undone that can be done to alleviate the distress. A report is spread that Ireland is on the point of starvation, and American contributions pour in with a munificence so lavish as to shame the government most interested. The starving of even far-away India and China find aid and comfort from our people, whose charitable instincts are wide as the earth itself. It is only at our own doors, and towards a race whose care should be our peculiar duty, that we suddenly become incomprehensibly deaf to the appeals of those slowly but surely dying of absolute starvation.

The struggles of any foreign peoples to free themselves from the chains of tyranny find in us a most hearty sympathy. Yet we permit a whole race, in our own country, to groan and suffer under an official tyranny as remorseless as any on earth.

Some of the most charitable men I have ever known were abominable spendthrifts, by no possibility ever paying a just debt Charity to them was an active passion, payment a disagreeable duty. It Would seem that this in an eminent degree is our characteristic as a nation. So long as charity and sympathy are voluntary they are sweet virtues to be practised; when they become obligatory they are disagreeable duties, to be avoided if possible.

The Indian has no literature, no means of access to the great heart of the American people. The persons in whose hands he finds himself are interested in having things remain exactly as they are, and will not permit his sufferings to be known.

The crimes against the negro were open to, and seen by, all the world. The crimes against the Indian are unknown because purposely hidden, and because of his isolation. He suffers in secret, and therefore without sympathy.

Many eloquent writers have depicted the wrongs and the sufferings of the Indian; but I know of no single one who has not, however unwittingly, written in the interests of the Indian King; for the most honest and conscientious among them have been unable to see for the Indian any future not bounded by the status quo.

There is no future for the Indian as Indian; but I can see for him long vistas of honor and usefulness when he shall have become a citizen of the United States. If we had said to the Irish or to the Germans, "You may live among us, but you shall never be citizens," would we have been as great a nation to-day?

Since the inception of our Government we have said this to the Indian; and yet we wonder why he cannot be a citizen. At this moment the Cherokees, Chickasaws, Choctaws, the remnants of the Six Nations in New York, the Pueblos of New Mexico and Arizona, are as fit for citizenship as the average of white emigrants to our soil. "We tell them flatly, "You are Indians—an inferior race. You have not sense or discretion enough to hold property or take care of yourselves. You are on a par with prisoners and lunatics, we will take care of you." And we do it; but, gracious Heaven! what caret

But a few years ago the Indian was wild, free and independent. Now he is a prisoner of war, restrained of his liberty and confined on circumscribed areas. But a few years ago he was rich in ponies and property; now he is so poor that "no man will do him reverence." But a few years ago the Plains furnished him ample supply of food; now he is constantly on the verge of starvation. But a few years ago war and the chase gave ample vent to all his ambition and energy; now he is expected to be content and satisfied with an empty stomach and nothing to do. But a few years ago tribal government was so strong as to deter them from the commission of outrages among themselves. We have broken down the tribal authority and substituted nothing in its place. The Indian is absolutely without law, either human or divine. The well-disposed are at the mercy of the evil-disposed; yet we wonder that the Indian does not progress.

By refusing to give him land and a home in severalty, we carefully prevent the development of any ambitious longings for individual wealth and independence; and by withholding any reward from labor we as carefully prevent the formation of any habits of industry; yet we wonder why the Indian is not ambitious and industrious.

Were it possible to induce the American people to act towards Indians as they do towards persons of other nationalities, I have said enough; but such action is not possible under the present management.

Before the war of the Rebellion, the "Indian trade"—by which must be understood the five to eight millions appropriated by Congress, and the purchase and sale of commodities between white and red men—was estimated by competent persons at not less than forty millions a year. Since the destruction of the buffalo, and the confinement of Indians on limited reservations, this gross amount has been reduced probably one-half.

I have detailed how this trade is conducted, and it will be readily seen that poor as the Indian now is, he yet affords good picking to those whose business it is to, coin him into money. These men are a "power in the land," not only by means of the money squeezed from the Indian, but, "clothing themselves with hypocrisy, as with a garment," and pretending to be the Indian's best friends, they gain the ears and the assistance of those true and pure humanitarians who, being ignorant of the facts, believe whatever these deceivers tell them.

The prolific source of all Indian ills is that most tragic of national farces called the "Treaty System." By it we have taken advantage of the greed or ignorance of chiefs, to swindle the Indians out of their lands. Every so-called treaty has been opposed, always by a minority, and sometimes by a great majority of the tribe interested, and these opponents are always dissatisfied and disposed to be hostile. Sometimes, as in several cases on record, the chiefs themselves have refused to be swindled. The Government has not hesitated, but deposing the refractory chiefs, has set up others, its own creatures, and concluded the melancholy farce, by entering into a solemn treaty, to which the United States were actually party of both parts.

We profess to regard the Indian tribes as "interior dependent nations." The "Treaty System" so far recognizes their independence as to make it impossible for us to enact laws for their control and benefit, or to give them any standard by which to regulate their conduct. By holding intercourse with them only as "bodies politic" we keep all on the same plane; there is no recognition of individual worth or advancement; no prospect of citizenship is ever held out, and there is no hope for any man ever to be more or better than the mere conventional Indian.

But the crowning feature of this "system" is that the Government at this moment has formal "treaty" arrangements with hundreds of petty tribes, all of which are now held on reservations, actually prisoners of war. The recognition of this fact is absolutely necessary; the very first step towards the improvement of the condition of the Indian. In violation of treaties, or by virtue of treaties procured by fraud, the Indian is confined to reservations. In violation of law, the game on which he depended for food has been destroyed by white men.

The United States having made prisoners of the Indians, and having by negligence permitted them to be deprived of the means of self-support, is in honor bound to see that they do not suffer. Is this obligation of honor fulfilled? Far from it! On the contrary, we leave our helpless prisoners to starve, and shoot without mercy the reckless few who, goaded to desperation by their sufferings, dare to cross the dead line of the reservation.

In this horrid crime every voter of the United States is either actively or passively implicated, for it has its root in the legislative branch of the Government. The appropriations for the support of the Indians are entirely inadequate, the most favored tribes receiving no more than about eight cents a day for the support of each individual.

All this is criminal. It is time that all persons responsible for the care and condition of the Indians should recognize that they are prisoners of war, and that justice and humanity alike require that they be supported until such time as they can learn to support themselves in their new mode of life.

To advance, the Indian like other men must have an object in life—an incentive to effort. Many of the so-called wild tribes are willing to labor, and do labor right manfully for the one crop, which is all they can rely on under the present management. Give each a farm of his own, and many of them will soon be independent of government support.

Through the fault of a system of government which pays little attention to the rights of those who have no votes, no representation, and no redress in the courts, the control and management of the Indians have been so far an utter failure—debasing, pauperizing, and exterminating them.

The Indian is in a state of progression common at some time in their history to all nations and peoples. The efforts made for his advance in civilization have so far failed of beneficial result, not from exceptional stupidity or barbarism, or other peculiarity of character or habit of the subject, but because men of power and influence find there is more money to be made of him by leaving him as he is.

These are a few, a very few, of the wrongs and iniquities practised upon the Indians by those who profess to be his friends; and which, if continued, will in a few years lead to his utter extermination.

There is but one hope for him. "Treaty systems" and tribal relations must be broken up, and the Indians individually absorbed in the great family of American citizens. This must necessarily be a gradual process, and in the meantime some plan must be adopted which, while protecting him from the harpies who now feed upon him, shall soonest fit him for the honors and responsibilities of an American citizen. I give the outline of the plan which I believe best suited to that end.

1. Turn the Indians over to the War Department.

2. Abolish the Indian Bureau as now constituted, with all the laws and parts of laws establishing it and controlling or directing its operations. Replace the Commissioner of Indian Affairs, the Superintendents, Inspectors, Agents, &e., by detailed army officers, and let the Indians be supplied by and through the Quartermasters and Commissary Departments of the army.

3. Abrogate all existing treaties.

4. Abolish all trade and intercourse laws now on the Statute Book. Give the Indians the same rights in trade as are enjoyed by citizens of the United States (arms and liquors excepted), until the Indians shall have become citizens.

5. Enact laws for the control and guidance of the Indians until they have as citizens come under the operation of the common law.

6. Make Commanding Officers of military posts in Indian territory or on reservations ex-officio Superintendents of Indian Affairs, and give them magisterial authority over the Indians so long as they live in unorganized territory.

7. Give the Indians farms in severalty, not, however, requiring each to live on his farm, but encouraging them to form permanent settlements and villages.

8. All the land of the reservations not allotted to Indians to be bought of them by the Government and thrown open to settlement by whites.

9. Give the Indian the ballot, and all the rights and duties of citizenship, as soon as the country in which he resides shall have been organized into a county.

10. Feed the wild Indian. See that he has sufficient food, even to the exclusion, if necessary, of all other supplies.

Whether or not the above propositions will effect the end designed will depend entirely on the mode of carrying out the first and second.

For some years there has been a great deal of flippant talk, both in and out of Congress, about the transfer of the Indian Bureau to the War Department, the enemies of the measure asserting positively that the passage of such a bill would be the utter destruction of the Indians; its friends with equal positiveness asserting that it would civilize the Indian, cause wars to cease, and redound in every way to the advantage of the country and the Indian.

The transfer to the War Department of the Indian Bureau as now constituted, would effect nothing except to saddle the War Department with the onus of its actions. The Indian Bureau is the means by and through which are perpetrated most of the wrongs and outrages I have described. Its defects and wrongs are inherent to itself—have" grown with its growth and strengthened with its strength." By means of its machinery a comparatively few men swindle, pauperize, and degrade the Indian, and keep the country plunged in endless war.

To be effective for good, the change in the system of management of the Indians must be radical; complete not only in machinery, but in men. With such a change, my plan is entirely feasible, and will, I believe, result in cessation of Indian wars, in economy to the country, and, above all, in converting two hundred and fifty thousand savages into good citizens—in converting an element of weakness and enormous expense into an element of pride and power.

The real friends of the Indian are injuring his cause by demanding too much. They insist that the treaties shall be regarded as binding for all time. There is no power in this Government which can much longer delay the settlement by whites of the Indian territory, and it is a mere question of time when all the reservations will be overrun. The Government tried faithfully to keep the whites out of the Black Hills, which was an Indian reservation. It failed signally.

The Indians now hold under treaty stipulations over forty-one millions of acres of land. It cannot be expected that a population which united would make a city less populous than Cincinnati, shall be for all time maintained in possession of lands sufficient for the support of the whole population, white and red, of the United States.

Against the resistless tide of immigration the Indian has absolutely no chance. His only hope is in setting with the tide, and this he can only do as an American citizen.

As a people we are disposed to place little value on human life, unless that life happens to be taken by Indians.

Let us take into consideration:

That the Indians are savages;

That while abolishing tribal authority we substitute nothing therefor, leaving the Indians absolutely without rule of life or conduct;

That they are now amenable to no law, civil, military, or divine, except the law of retaliation;

That they are prisoners of war, confined against their will on restricted areas;

That the civilized world makes it not only the right, but the duty of the prisoner of war to escape, if he can;

That in treating them, and with them, only as tribes, we ignore individual obligation; and by blaming all alike we take away from the well-disposed all incentive to good behavior;

That we endeavor to repress the ardor and aspirations of a naturally ambitious race by keeping them penned up on reservations, disarmed, and with nothing to do, when by giving them occupation we might divert this ambition into other and useful channels;

And last and most important:

That we keep them always hungry; sometimes on the verge of starvation;

And it must be conceded that the Indian behaves much better than we have any right to expect.

The actual number of murders and outrages committed by Indians on citizens is so small as would scarcely be thought of if perpetrated by whites. In the summer of 1867, white men in Julesburg robbed and murdered more citizens than all the Indians have robbed and murdered during anyone of ten years past. In 1873, Dodge City emulated the fame and shame of Julesburg; and at the present moment there is scarcely a busy town along the lines of railroad now pushing through Arizona, New Mexico, and Texas, that does not have its almost daily murder. I may even come nearer to civilization; for I believe the records will show that more outrages on life and property have been perpetrated during the last year by whites in the two States of Kentucky and Missouri than in the same time by all the Indians in all the length and breadth of our extended frontier.

I speak of outrages against citizens. The killing of soldiers in battle is not to be regarded as murder or outrage. It is simply the necessary adjunct to our pernicious system of Indian management.

The newspapers of the land are much to blame for the exaggerated feeling against Indians. The local paper of a frontier town will carefully avoid any mention of the daily or nightly killings by its inhabitants; but let a frontiersman be killed, or even scared by Indians, and column after column is devoted to the minutest, and most generally imaginary, details. This can readily be accounted for, each little frontier town desiring the presence of troops, not for protection, but for the money they spend.

That the Eastern papers should so readily take up this cry, giving a line to a murder by a Kentucky gentleman, a column to a murder by an Indian, can only be accounted for by the desire for sensation.

L'ENVOI

AS regards the Indian, the citizens of the United States may be divided into four classes. *First.*—Earnest, honorable, thinking men, humanitarians by instinct, education, and surroundings. *Second.*—Professional humanitarians, who feed upon and make a trade of the Indians. *Third.*—Exterminators. *Fourth.*—The great mass of the people, knowing little of, and caring less for, the Indian.

I am perfectly aware that in the foregoing pages I have affronted the first three classes.

Basing themselves on justice and honor, some of the very best and purest of our citizens fight for the Indian a Quixotic battle with the windmills. Misled by Cooper, Catlin, and other enthusiastic authors, and by the fictional colorings of professional humanitarians, they have set up an ideal Indian, clothed with graces and virtues, which a moment of calm and unprejudiced reflection must show to be impossible in a savage. Forgetting the fact that civilization claims by right of discovery or possession, all lands occupied by barbarians, they demand that our intercourse with Indians shall be regulated by treaties, and that these treaties shall be binding on all, and for all time. This is a generous instinct worthy of honorable men, but is just as impracticable as if those men should determine that there shall be no more poor among whites. Civilization must and will destroy the savage and possess his lands, unless that savage is given an exactly equal right of possession, and this can only be done by making him a citizen.

To the professional humanitarians I have nothing to say, except to assure them of my unalterable hostility, and determination to use every faculty with which I am endowed to wrench the Indian from their sordid grasp.

To the thinking men of the third class I would say, "Hold! consider that the Indian is a fellow-creature; that his savage condition is his misfortune, and greatly our fault: that as a citizen he can be made a valuable acquisition to the country. Look at the numbers of intellectual, cultivated Indians now in the Territory; and recollect that but for the indomitable courage, perseverance, and brains of Juarez, a full-blood Indian, our sister republic would now be groaning under the tyranny of a foreign Emperor."

Scarce a score of years have passed since even the most honorable, earnest philanthropists of the country were torn with doubts as to the effect of the sudden elevation of three millions of slaves to the rights and duties of citizenship.

Against the most obstinate prejudice; in spite of difficulties such as few peoples have had to encounter, the Negro race has demonstrated the justice of emancipation by a thirst for knowledge and a capacity for instruction, which put to shame the present lower class of southern whites.

Enlightened or savage human nature is much the same. Men rise to meet emergencies. That the poor and ignorant of almost every land and clime swell the number of our valuable citizens, should encourage us to extend the experiment of freedom and citizenship.

But a few years ago, "Abolitionist" was a term of bitter reproach. Now, every man in the country whose opinions are worth notice is an "Abolitionist."

"A little leaven leaveneth the whole lump."

The only hope for the Indian is in the interest and compassion of a few true men, who, like the handful of "Abolitionists" of thirty years ago, have pluck and strength to fight, against any odds, an apparently ever losing battle. These in turn must rely upon the great, brave, honest human heart of the American people. To that I and they must appeal! to the press; to the pulpit; to every voter in the land; to every lover of humanity. Arouse to this grand work. No slave now treads the soil of this noble land. Force your representatives to release the Indian from an official bondage more remorseless, more hideous than slavery itself. Deliver him from his pretended friends, and lift him into fellowship with the citizens of our loved and glorious country.

THE END

Discover more lost history from BIG BYTE BOOKS

Printed in Great Britain
by Amazon